Love is private, and in medieval literature especially is seen as demanding secrecy, yet to tell stories about it is to make it public. Looking, often accompanied by listening, is the means by which love is brought into the public realm and by which legal evidence of adulterous love can be obtained. Medieval romances contain many scenes in which secret watchers and listeners play leading roles, and in which the problematic relation of sight to truth is a central theme. The effect of such scenes is to place the poem's audience as secret watchers and listeners; and in later medieval narratives, as the role of the storyteller comes to be realized, the poet too sees himself in the undignified role of a voyeur.

A. C. Spearing's book explores these and related themes, first in relation to medieval and modern theories and instances of looking, and then through a series of readings of romances and first-person narratives, including works by Beroul, Chrétien, Marie de France, Gottfried von Strassburg, Chaucer, Lydgate, Douglas, Dunbar, and Skelton. Its focus on looking also leads to the recovery of some less well-known works such as *Partonope of Blois* and *The Squire of Low Degree*. The general approach is psychoanalytic, but the reading of specific medieval texts always has primacy, and this in turn makes possible a running critique of current conceptions of the gaze in relation to power and gender.

THE MEDIEVAL POET AS VOYEUR

THE MEDIEVAL POET AS VOYEUR

Looking and Listening in Medieval Love-Narratives

A. C. SPEARING

William R. Kenan Professor of English, University of Virginia
Fellow of Queens' College, Cambridge

CAMBRIDGE
UNIVERSITY PRESS

Published by the Press Syndicate of the University of Cambridge
The Pitt Building, Trumpington Street, Cambridge CB2 1RP
40 West 20th Street, New York, NY 10011–4211, USA
10 Stamford Road, Oakleigh, Victoria 3166, Australia

© Cambridge University Press 1993

First published 1993

Printed in Great Britain at the University Press, Cambridge

A catalogue record for this book is available from the British Library

Library of Congress cataloguing in publication data
Spearing, A. C.
The medieval poet as voyeur: looking and listening in medieval
love-narratives / A. C. Spearing.
p.   cm.
Includes bibliographical references and index.
ISBN 0–521–41094–0
1. Poetry, Medieval – History and criticism. 2. Love poetry –
History and criticism. 3. Voyeurism in literature.
4. Point-of-view (Literature) 1. Title.
PN691.S64   1993
808.1'354 –   dc20   92–8129 CIP

ISBN 0 521 41094 0 hardback

Contents

Preface

The conscious origin of this book (of its unconscious origins the less said the better) lies in a course of lectures given in the English Faculty at Cambridge. These were then summarized as a paper read at Harvard and at Pennsylvania State University in 1986 and published as 'The Medieval Poet as Voyeur', in *The Olde Daunce: Love, Friendship, Sex and Marriage in the Medieval World*, ed. Robert R. Edwards and Stephen Spector (Albany: State University of New York Press, 1991), pp. 57–86, © 1991 State University of New York, to whom I am grateful for permission to use most of the paper here in revised form. Subsequently the material, now vastly expanded, became the basis of two courses of graduate seminars given at the University of Virginia; I am greatly obliged to the participants in ENMD 961 (1989) and ENMD 983 (1990) for the enthusiasm and critical sharpness with which they helped me to think about many of the texts and issues discussed in the book.

In earlier versions parts of the book have been published as follows. Chapter 5 incorporates substantial parts of 'Marie de France and Her Middle English Adapters', *Studies in the Age of Chaucer* 12 (1990), 116–56; grateful acknowledgments to the publishers (the New Chaucer Society) and to the editor. Chapter 9 is based on 'Secrecy, Listening, and Telling in *The Squyr of Lowe Degre*', *Journal of Medieval and Renaissance Studies* 20 (1990), 273–92; grateful acknowledgments to the publishers (Duke University Press) and editors. Chapter 13 is a rewritten and expanded version of pages 215–23 of my *Medieval to Renaissance in English Poetry* (Cambridge: Cambridge University Press, 1985). All reused material has been carefully revised.

I have sometimes modified cited translations of non-English texts in the interest of greater literalness. Italics in quotations are mine unless otherwise noted.

The abbreviation *SE* stands for *The Standard Edition of the Complete Psychological Works of Sigmund Freud* (London: Hogarth, 1953–74).

In writing this book I have been unusually dependent on the help of friends and colleagues. Virtually all those to whom I mentioned the topic I was working on recommended primary or secondary reading that I ought to do, and this would be a better (and also much longer) book if I had managed to cover all the ground they suggested. I record some specific debts in the endnotes, but I want to express grateful thanks to the following for commenting, sometimes in great detail, on versions of these chapters: Chapter 5, Sarah Kay and Anne Rooney; Chapter 7, Pat Gill (to whom I am also grateful for more general reading suggestions); Chapters 7 and 8, Susan Crane; Chapter 9, Lee Patterson (as reader for *The Journal of Medieval and Renaissance Studies*); Chapters 10 and 13, Hoyt Duggan. My largest debts are to Lisa Samuels, who read earlier drafts in minute detail and gave such invaluable assistance in shaping the whole book that in many ways it is hers as much as mine, and to Barbara Nolan, who has read almost every chapter, sometimes in successive versions, and on whose encouragement and learned and tactful criticism I have greatly relied. Errors and follies are of course my own responsibility.

A. C. Spearing

Charlottesville
December 1991

CHAPTER I

Theories of looking

Love is a favourite theme of medieval narrative, yet in Western civilization love is a private experience, and one for which, in medieval texts especially, secrecy is often regarded as a prerequisite. How then can it be the theme of narrative, when to narrate, to tell, is to make public? This is the problem from which the present book begins; and it focuses on looking, and secondarily on listening, as the means by which private experience is brought into the public sphere. Within medieval love-narratives, secret observers, concealed from the lovers as the lovers are from society at large, are frequently represented as responsible for exposing private experience to the public gaze; as readers of or listeners to such narratives, we too can be made to feel that we are secret observers; and, in the later Middle Ages especially, the love-poet is often realized as one who looks and tells, himself a secret observer of experiences in which he does not participate.[1] The verse-narratives I shall discuss in Chapters 3 to 14 fall into two large categories: those in the third person, in the form of romances and associated narratives, and those in the first person, in the form of dream-poems and analogous narratives or *dits*. Poems of other types that deal with human love might have been included; but the book is long enough already, and it seemed better to trace two connected traditions than to aim at a comprehensiveness that could only be sketchy.

Looking has been a theme of special importance in psycho-analysis, film studies, and other modern bodies of theory concerning desire, gender and power. It would scarcely be possible to discuss this book's topic without regard to these theoretical approaches, and for me reading in these areas has been of real value in calling attention to what is happening in the texts I consider and in suggesting ways of thinking about how they work. This book is not, however, intended to offer a theory of looking; what led me to write it was a wish to understand some intriguing features of medieval love-narratives, and also to gain wider attention for poems (such as *Partonope of Blois* and *The Squyr of Lowe Degre*) that modern readers might otherwise be unlikely to encounter. Though my approach is generally psychoanalytic, I have found it helpful to this project not to commit myself to any single theory, but to retain freedom of manoeuvre in deploying the large categories in terms of which its field is defined: looking, listening, secrecy, desire, gender, and power. One cannot help observing that the competitive intellectual labour and the (often unacknowledged) emotional stress involved in theorizing about these matters tend to reduce texts to a merely exemplary status rather than to encourage an attitude of exploration and discovery. The 'grand theory' that has gained such high prestige in the 'human sciences'[2] frequently constitutes itself as a dominating and totalizing metaphysic of such a kind that no imaginable new observation, no pleasure given by any actual poem, could count as evidence against it or cause it to be modified. Consider, as an instance from within this book's field, a magisterial remark by Jacques Lacan in response to a question after one of his lectures 'Of the Gaze as *Objet Petit a*': 'it is in so far as all human desire is based on castration that the eye assumes its virulent, aggressive function, and not simply its luring function as in nature'.[3] My lack of confidence that this assertion (or indeed any of the theories that place the look among what Freud calls the 'psychical consequences of the anatomical distinction between the sexes')[4] is wholly true makes me prefer to keep my distance from such styles of theorizing – to engage with them, let us say, as a voyeur rather than on closer terms. Hence the way the book is organized, with a primary emphasis on texts rather than theories. In this first chapter I shall examine treatments of looking and secrecy in some modern and medieval thought; then I shall discuss the organization of the private and public spaces in which secrecy and looking occur in medieval narratives; and finally the meanings of secrecy and power within those spaces. In Chapter 2 I shall introduce some of the book's more specific themes and questions through analyses of relatively brief texts, not all from the medieval period. After that, each chapter will focus on a single text or small group of texts, beginning with romances and moving on to dream-poems and *dits*. The book's interest and value must stand or fall by its capacity to illuminate the individual poems it studies.

The word 'voyeur' has gained its currency from the discourse of psychoanalysis.[5] I often use it, as is nowadays common, in a more general sense than Freud gave it; but it may be useful to begin with a Freudian definition of voyeurism before passing on to some treatments of looking in medieval thought. Freud's fundamental statement occurs in *Three Essays on the Theory of Sexuality*, first published in 1905 and republished several times with substantial revisions. In the first essay, 'The Sexual Aberrations', Freud states his basic assumptions:

The normal sexual aim is regarded as being the union of the genitals in the act known as copulation ... But even in the most normal sexual process we may detect rudiments which, if they had developed, would have led to the deviations described as 'perversions'. For there are certain intermediate relations to the sexual object, such as touching and looking at it, which lie on the road towards copulation and are recognized as being preliminary sexual aims. On the one hand these activities are themselves accompanied by pleasure, and on the other they intensify the excitation, which should persist until the final sexual aim is attained ... Perversions are sexual activities which either (*a*) *extend*, in an anatomical sense, beyond the regions of the body that are designed for sexual union, or (*b*) *linger* over the intermediate relations to the sexual object which should normally be traversed rapidly on the path towards the final sexual aim. (pp. 149–50)[6]

Later Freud explains that any factor that hinders or postpones this final aim, 'such as impotence, the high price of the sexual object or the danger of the sexual act' (p. 155), will encourage lingering over the intermediate activities. To linger over touching 'can scarcely be counted a perversion' (p. 156) so long as it leads to the final goal. He goes on:

The same holds true of seeing ... Visual impressions remain the most frequent pathway along which libidinal excitation is aroused; indeed, natural selection counts upon the accessibility of this pathway ... when it encourages the development of beauty in the sexual object. The progressive concealment of the body which goes along with civilization keeps sexual curiosity awake. This curiosity seeks to complete the sexual object by revealing its hidden parts ... It is usual for most normal people to linger to some extent over the intermediate sexual aim of a looking that has a sexual tinge to it ... On the other hand, this pleasure in looking becomes a perversion (*a*) if it is restricted exclusively to the genitals, or (*b*) if it is connected with the overriding of disgust (as in the case of *voyeurs* or people who look on at excretory functions),[7] or (*c*), if, instead of being *preparatory* to the normal sexual aim, it supplants it ... The force which opposes scopophilia, but which may be overridden by it (in a manner parallel to what we have previously seen in the case of disgust), is *shame*. (pp. 156–7)

The concepts of normality and perversion in these passages differ from those assumed by the ecclesiastical thought of the Middle Ages in that the goal they define as normal is genital copulation, where ecclesiastical thought requires that this should be only intermediate to the further goal of reproduction. Freud also asserts, however, that 'It seems probable that the sexual instinct [*Sexualtrieb*] is in the first instance independent of its object' (p. 148), and this would leave the way open for a conception of sexual behaviour in which normality and abnormality would have a merely statistical sense, and a fixation of desire upon looking could not be regarded as perverse.[8] In the *Three Essays* 'sexual desire is characteristically unstable, both in object and in aim'.[9] In this respect there appears to be a gap or contradiction within the work's thought that Freud does not resolve and may not even have noticed.[10]

A recent study of medieval teaching on sexual matters offers the following summary statement:

Three major patterns of sexual doctrine underlie the diverse beliefs about sexual morality that have been current in Western Christendom since the patristic period. One pattern centered on the reproductive function of sex and established nature as the criterion of what was licit; the second focused on the notion that sex was impure, a source of shame and defilement; the third emphasized sexual relations as a source of intimacy, as a symbol and expression of conjugal love. Medieval writers placed greater emphasis upon the first two patterns.[11]

The main stream of 'official' medieval thought on the psychology and ethics of sexual love gives a marked importance to looking, but always as one stage in the movement towards physical possession; which means towards sin. The orthodox clerical thought, constantly repeated in moral and penitential treatises, is based on the principle that 'sexual intercourse was permitted only between a man and a woman who were legitimately married to one another, and then only if done for the sake of procreation'.[12] Reproduction is the only 'natural' goal of sexual desire, but the means to that goal are seen as being, since the Fall, irremediably corrupt. All human sexual activity is more or less sinful – even marital copulation with reproduction as its outcome is sinful, especially if engaged in for the sake of pleasure[13] – and looking is the first step on this path to sin. A modern historian of science observes that 'All early natural philosophers acknowledged that vision is man's most noble and dependable sense'.[14] The same is true of theologians – Aquinas remarks that 'the sense of sight has a special dignity; it is more spiritual and subtle than any other sense'[15] – and a medieval encyclopaedia explains that this is because it is associated with fire, the subtlest of the elements: 'Of þe wittes þe siȝt is most sotil for þe kinde þerof is fury'.[16] The 'subtlety' of sight has to do with its unique status among the senses as the only one that involves no material contact with its object (even hearing is based on the changes induced by sound-waves, as Chaucer's eagle explains in *The House of Fame*); and this means that it gives least satisfaction to bodily desire. This paradoxical nature of sight, as the subtlest and most reliable sense, yet the one that least satisfies the body's appetite for material possession of its object, is of crucial importance to voyeurism.

Sight's subtlety rendered it especially liable to corruption: Saint John Chrysostom had lamented that, 'for the sake of the brief pleasure of a glance, we sustain a kind of lengthened and continual torture ... The beauty of a woman is the greatest snare. Or rather, not the beauty of a woman, but unchastened gazing!'[17] A convenient vernacular illustration of the primacy of sight in the movement towards sin is found in Chaucer's *Parson's Tale*. This orthodox handbook on penance, translated largely from two thirteenth-century Latin *summae* by Raymund of Pennaforte and William Peraldus, shows little sign of expressing any personal opinions arrived at by the author of *Troilus and Criseyde* and *The Miller's Tale*. Its second part consists of a treatment of the seven deadly sins and their remedies. Marriage is mentioned only as a remedy against lechery, and Chaucer explains that even within marriage there can scarcely be 'flesshly assemblinge' without at least venial sin, 'for the corrupcion and for the delit' (x 941).[18] Under lechery itself, beginning with adultery, Chaucer writes of the Devil's five fingers, used for trapping people into his power. These are, in order, looking, touching, speech, kissing, and 'the stynkynge dede of Leccherie' (x 861). His complete description of the Devil's first finger is:

The firste fynger is the fool lookynge of the fool womman and of the fool man; that sleeth, right as the basilicok sleeth folk by the venym of his sighte, for the coveitise of eyen folweth the coveitise of the herte. (x 852)

This triply foolish looking is pleasurable, or it would be no temptation, but there is no suggestion that, as in voyeurism proper, it might
be a goal in itself.

The same is true, surprisingly enough, even of medieval uses of
the term 'lust of the eyes' (*concupiscentia oculorum*). This regularly
appears in religious thought among the 'three temptations' derived
from 1 John 2:15–16:

Love not the world, nor the things which are in the world. If any man love
the world, the charity of the Father is not in him.

For all that is in the world is the concupiscence of the flesh and the
concupiscence of the eyes and the pride of life, which is not of the Father
but is of the world.[19]

It might be expected that 'lust of the eyes' would correspond to
scopophilia, the focusing of desire in the act of looking, but this is not
so. The triad *concupiscentia carnis, concupiscentia oculorum, superbia vitae,*
is normally associated with another triad relating to the psychology
of sin: suggestion, delectation, consent. Lust of the eyes corresponds
to delectation in general, and is connected not with looking but with
curiosity or avarice. Thus in *Piers Plowman* the advice given to Wille
by the personification 'Coveitise of Eighes' is not to take pleasure in
looking but to 'Have no conscience how thow come to goode' (XI
53)[20] and to spend his wealth on buying prayer and pardons from
friars.

There are, however, occasional suggestions within the ecclesiastical tradition that looking might itself constitute a sexual goal.
One instance occurs in another English penitential handbook,
Robert Mannyng's *Handlyng Synne*, an early fourteenth-century
translation of an Anglo-Norman *Manuel des Pechiez*. In his discussion
of lechery, Mannyng explains that outward chastity is of no value if
accompanied by 'fylþes of þoght' (7566).[21] Such thoughts are grave
sins if one takes pleasure in them, and especially if one desires to put
them into action. He goes on:

> more synne hyt ys
> Whan þou sekest þy wyl of flessh
> To þe lust of lecherye,
> Yn handlyng or dremyng of folye,
> Þurgh þoghtes or syghtes þat þou ses
> And yn alle ouþre pryuytes.
> God hymself forbedeþ al þys:
> Þey gete no part of heuene blys.   (7577–84)

Mannyng's argument is not perfectly clear, but a possible rendering might be:

it is greater sin when you seek your fleshly will in lecherous desire in handling[22] or dreaming of folly, through thoughts or sights you see, and in all other secret matters. God himself forbids all this; such sinners shall not share in the bliss of heaven.

This implies the possibility that both sight and its recollection might become sources of sexual pleasure in themselves; particularly perhaps that fantasies involving sight – dreams, or daydreams like those in which Januarie indulges in *The Merchant's Tale* – could be intrinsically lecherous and thus sinful. If that is a correct interpretation, then Mannyng is referring to what Freud calls scopophilia or voyeurism.

The same psychology, accompanied by quite different ethical and emotional attitudes, is found in secular treatments of human love. Two ways of thought exist in tension within the literate culture of medieval Europe, neither reducible to the other, though the heavier intellectual artillery was certainly on the religious side. What the religious writers call lechery, the secular writers call love. When Chaucer's Wife of Bath exclaims, 'Allas, allas! That evere love was synne!' (*Canterbury Tales* III 614), she is alluding to the opposition between two complete value-systems. This can be illustrated, for example, from the *De amore* of Andreas Capellanus, probably written in the 1180s. The provenance and overall purpose of this treatise remain matters of controversy, but I use it as a convenient illustration of a virtually universal medieval psychology of love. Andreas begins the first section of his first book, under the title 'Quid sit amor', with the statement: 'Love is an inborn suffering which results from the sight of, and uncontrolled thinking about, the beauty of the other sex' [*Amor est passio quaedam innata procedens ex visione et immoderata cogitatione formae alterius sexus*] (pp. 32–3).[23] In explanation, he continues, 'A careful scrutiny of the truth shows that it arises not from any action, but solely from the thought formed by the mind as a result of the thing seen'; and again, 'So this emotion of love is inborn, arising from seeing and thinking' (p. 35). Seeing always comes first; and indeed Andreas even argues that 'Blindness is a hindrance to love because a blind man has not the faculty of sight to provide his mind with objects provoking uncontrolled thought' (p. 41). We might suppose that a blind person could fall in love under the influence of touch and hearing and deductions about character arrived at through all the other senses; but Andreas is so convinced that love must begin with sight that he thinks this simply impossible.

The notion that love has its origin in looking goes back to classical antiquity; but Andreas, no great classical scholar, may simply be reflecting what is found in the secular literature of his own milieu. Whether or not he wrote under the same patronage (that of Marie de Champagne), he probably knew the work of his contemporary, Chrétien de Troyes. I shall discuss later some of Chrétien's treatments of looking, but I anticipate that discussion here by quoting from a soliloquy in *Cligés* (about 1176), one of his earliest romances. It is spoken by Cligés's father Alixandre, the hero of the romance's first part, after falling in love with Soredamors. In the course of the soliloquy Alixandre develops what becomes a familiar topos: Love's arrow wounds the heart by passing through the eye. The soliloquy is represented as an internal dialogue:

> Ce qu'Amors m'aprant et ansaingne,
> Doi je garder et maintenir;
> Car tost m'an puet granz biens venir.
> Mes trop me bat, ice m'esmaie.
> – Ja n'i pert il ne cos ne plaie,
> Et si te plains? Don n'as tu tort?
> – Nenil; qu'il m'a navré si fort,
> Que jusqu'au cuer m'a son dart tret,
> N'ancor ne l'a a lui retret.
> – Comant le t'a donc tret el cors,
> Quant la plaie ne pert defors?
> Ce me diras, savoir le vuel!
> Par ou le t'a il tret?
>   – Par l'uel.
> – Par l'uel? Et si nel t'a crevé?
> – An l'uel ne m'a il rien grevé;
> Mes au cuer me grieve formant.
> – Or me di donc reison, comant
> Li darz est parmi l'uel passez,
> Qu'il n'an est bleciez ne quassez.
> Se li darz parmi l'uel i antre,
> Li cuers por quoi se diaut el vantre,
> Que li iauz aussi ne s'an diaut,
> Qui le premier cop an requiaut?
> – De ce sai je bien reison randre:
> Li iauz n'a soing de rien antandre

Ne rien n'i puet feire a nul fuer;
Mes c'est li mireors au cuer,
Et par cest mireor trespasse,
Si qu'il ne le blesce ne quasse,
Li feus, don li cuers est espris.   (686–715)

I should obey and observe the lesson Love teaches me, for I might soon
reap great benefit from it. But he frightens me by belabouring me so.
– You're complaining, when there's no trace of a blow or wound? Aren't
you mistaken, then?
– No, for he has gravely wounded me to the extent of shooting his arrow
right to my heart and hasn't yet pulled it out again.
– How, then, has he shot you with it in the body without the wound
showing on the outside? Tell me: I should like to know. Where has he shot
you?
– Through the eye.
– Through the eye? Without putting it out?
– He hasn't hurt me at all in the eye, but causes me such pain in the heart.
– Well, explain to me how the arrow has passed through the eye without its
being wounded or damaged. If the dart goes in through the eye, why is the
heart hurt in the breast, but not the eye as well, which has been struck first?
– I can readily explain that: the eye is not concerned with comprehending
anything and is totally incapable of doing so; but it is the mirror for the
heart, and through this mirror there passes, without damaging or breaking
it, the fire that sets the heart ablaze.[24]

To reach the heart and thus affect the victim's thought and
feeling, Cupid's arrow must first penetrate the eye. This way of
expressing the idea that love begins with a look was probably
borrowed by Chrétien from *Eneas*, an anonymous *roman d'antiquité* of
some twenty years earlier. There, in an episode without equivalent
in the Virgilian source, Lavine sees Eneas from her window and
instantly falls in love with him. She complains,

N'avra Amors de moi merci?
Il me navra an un esgart,
en l'oil me feri de son dart,
de celui d'or, qui fet amer;
tot lo me fist el cuer coler.   (8158–62)

Will love have no mercy on me? He has wounded me with a glance. He has
struck me in the eye with his dart, with the gold one which causes love: he
has struck me to the heart.[25]

It has been suggested that this trope may originate in the Arabic
erotic literature that was then becoming known in the West;[26]

whether or not this is so, it was constantly repeated in later medieval romances, lyrics, dream-poems, indeed in every kind of courtly composition. The implication is that the look is aggressive, but it is often accompanied by the paradox that the one who looks is wounded by what the eye receives, whether or not that is itself a look returned by its object. Behind the idea of the looker wounded by a look may lie scientific theories, going back to Plato's *Timaeus* and *Theaetetus*, that understood sight itself as taking place through a combined extramission and intromission of rays or streams of light. Equally, though, the idea may be only a reflection of a general truth about the double role of looking for animals as well as human beings; for, as a recent scientific study observes, 'Whenever organisms use vision, the eyes become signals as well as channels'.[27] In medieval texts the first looker is usually, but not always, male; Lavine is a striking example of a woman who takes the initiative in looking and thereby suffers a fatal wound. Chrétien's elaborate explanation in *Cligés* perhaps implies that the trope was not yet well know; ultimately it hardens into a cliché of courtly literature, but, as we shall see, even after becoming a commonplace it can still be used with powerful imaginative effect.

I turn now to another kind of connection between looking and sexuality. We have seen that Freud, briefly and without explanation, identifies shame as the force that opposes scopophilia. The feeling of shame (as opposed to the inward sense of guilt) is based on what we believe others to think of us: it is our response to an awareness that we are or may be the object of an unfavourable judgment from outside. Thus, given the primacy of sight as the medium of perception, shame is the product of the sense of being seen, or rather of the possibility of being seen; so that, paradoxically, what deters us from being watchers is the fear of being watched. This general truth has been convincingly affirmed by Jean-Paul Sartre. He writes, in a section of *Being and Nothingness* entitled 'The Look':

> Here I am bent over the keyhole; suddenly I hear a footstep. I shudder as a wave of shame sweeps over me. Somebody has seen me. I straighten up. My eyes run over the deserted corridor. It was a false alarm. I breathe a sigh of relief.

As this example shows, one need not be watched in order to experience shame; it is enough to be forced to recognize one's vulnerability to being watched, to being (in terms of Sartre's philosophy) an object in the eyes of some other subject. 'Pure shame', he explains later, generalizing the notion still further,

is not a feeling of being this or that guilty object but in general of being *an* object; that is, of *recognizing myself* in this degraded, fixed, and dependent being which I am for the Other. Shame is the feeling of an *original fall*, not because of the fact that I may have committed this or that particular fault but simply that I have "fallen" into the world in the midst of things and that I need the mediation of the Other in order to be what I am.

Modesty and in particular the fear of being surprised in a state of nakedness are only a symbolic specification of original shame; the body symbolizes here our defenseless state as objects.[28]

No doubt it is difficult to watch without being watched; the person peering through the bedroom keyhole is peculiarly vulnerable. But why should watching sexual activity be thought especially shameful, to such an extent that Freud can specify shame as the barrier to scopophilia? Two factors are perhaps involved. The first is that to watch implies an inability to perform; this is connected with the lack of bodily contact and satisfaction involved in sight, and I shall return to it later. The second is that human beings almost invariably choose, as far as possible, to conduct sexual relations in private and in secret, where they cannot be watched. Why this should be so remains to be asked. An important discussion of this question, which underlies much medieval thought about human sexuality, is found in Book XIV of St Augustine's *City of God*.[29] Augustine begins from the observable fact of sexual shame, which seems inexplicable on rational grounds. In Chapter 17 he notes the origin of bodily shame as recounted in Genesis. Before the Fall, Adam and Eve 'were both naked ... and were not ashamed' (Genesis 2:25). But once they had eaten the forbidden fruit, 'the eyes of them both were opened: and when they perceived themselves to be naked, they sewed together fig leaves, and made themselves aprons' (Genesis 3:7). It is to this moment that Sartre refers in the passage quoted above, where he reads the Genesis myth as an existentialist allegory. (The connection between shame and sight is, we shall find, recurrent.)[30] Here, Augustine argues, is the root and explanation of the sexual shame felt by all human beings ever since. He puts it with magisterial concision: 'Thus their shamefastness wisely covered that which lust disobediently incited as a memory of their disobedient wills justly herein punished [*Quod itaque adversus*

damnatam culpa inoboedientiae voluntatem libido inoboedienter movebat, verecundia pudenter tegebat]: and from hence all mankind, springing from one origin, have it naturally in them to keep their members covered . . .' (p. 48).[31]

In Chapter 18 Augustine traces the consequences of this crisis in the life of his own time. He writes:

But the act of lust, not only in punishable adulteries, but even in the use of harlots which the earthly city allows, is ashamed of the public view [*publicum . . . conspectum*], although the deed be liable unto no pain of law: and houses of ill fame themselves have their secret provisions for it, even because of natural shame . . . But now for copulation in marriage, which according to the laws of matrimony must be used for propagation's sake: does it not seek a corner [*cubile*, literally 'chamber'] for performance, though it be honest and lawful? Does not the bridegroom turn all the feast-masters, the attendants, the music, and all others out of his chamber, before he begins to embrace his bride? And whereas . . . all honest deeds . . . love to be known; this honest deed alone if it desires to be known yet blushes to be seen [*erubescat videri*]. For who knows not what the man must do to the woman to have a child begotten, seeing the wife is solemnly married for this end? But when this is done, the children themselves, if they have had any before, shall not know. For this act does desire the sight of the mind, yet so as it flies the view of the eye [*lucem . . . oculorum*]. Why, unless this lawful act of nature is (from our first parents) accompanied with our penal shame? (p. 49)

In the following chapter Augustine notes that the display of our other passions, such as wrath, is not accompanied by shame, and asks,

what is the reason except it is not the emotion but the consenting will that moves the other members, performing those acts of the emotions, because it rules as chief in their use? For he that being angry rails or strikes, could not do it unless the tongue and the hand are appointed to do so by the will, which moves them also when anger is absent; but in the members of generation, lust has so peculiarly made them its own property, that they cannot move, if it be away . . . This is the cause of shame and avoidance of beholders in this act: and the reason why a man being in unlawful anger with his neighbour, had rather have a thousand look upon him [*spectantium multitudinem*], than [the gaze of] one [*unius aspectum*] when he is in carnal copulation with his wife. (p. 50)

The sexual organs are not under the will's control, and this is why their actions are accompanied by shame.

In later chapters Augustine develops this thought further. Our shameful lack of control over our own bodies is an appropriate consequence of the Fall: man's sinful disobedience to God is punished by the disobedience of man's own body to his will. For 'man' Augustine generally writes *homo* (of masculine gender but meaning 'human being') rather than the specifically male *vir*; nevertheless, the use of a masculine term is surely a concealed part of his argument, given that the male body's disobedience to its owner's will in sexual matters is more apparent to the eye than that of the female body. Augustine does not claim that, but for the Fall, there would have been no carnal relations; on the contrary, marriage was made in paradise. But he argues that, if Adam had not fallen, reproduction would have occurred without lust, and the sexual organs would have been as obedient as our other organs: 'The seed of generation should have been sown in the vessel, as corn is now in the field' (p. 54).

At this point, Augustine turns to his readers and ingeniously exploits their likely reactions to his argument to illustrate its truth.

What I would say more in this kind, modesty bids me forbear a little, and first ask pardon of chaste ears. I need not do it, but might proceed in any discourse pertinent to this theme freely, and without any fear to be obscene, or imputation of impurity to the words, being as honestly spoken of these as others are of any other bodily members. Therefore he that reads this with unchaste suggestions, let him accuse his own guilt, not the nature of the question. (p. 54).

If we feel discomfort at talk of the sexual organs, it is because we too are fallen; we inherit the punishment that has made human sexuality shameful. Augustine proceeds to imagine how prelapsarian intercourse might have occurred, and once more makes use of the readers' likely embarrassment to strengthen his argument: 'This theme is immodest, and therefore let us conjecture as we can, how the first parents of man were, ere they were ashamed. Needs must *our* discourse hereupon rather yield to shamefacedness than trust to eloquence' (p. 57). Augustine and Freud have more in common than might be expected: both see their readers' resistance to their doctrine as evidence for its truth.

It is surely an observable truth that marital copulation, though legally and morally licit, aims to conceal itself from watching eyes: 'does it not seek a [chamber] for performance, though it be honest and lawful?' But, if we now return to medieval life, the question arises as to the availability even of a chamber as the setting for

marital, not to mention extramarital, relations. What provision
was made for privacy in medieval households? Freud regards the
witnessing of parental intercourse by children as an event of
special significance occurring only 'through some chance domestic
occurrence';[32] but his experience was restricted to the European
bourgeoisie of his time, among whom it could be taken for granted
that every married couple would possess a private bedroom. Even
Augustine, in the fifth century, evidently assumes a prosperous
patrician household where the bridal pair can exclude others from
their bedchamber once the ceremony is over. No such assumption
could ever have been made so far as the peasantry were concerned; for the majority of human beings private space has never
existed, and sexual activity must normally have occurred in the
presence of others. This book is concerned primarily with secular
written narratives from the Middle Ages, and that generally
means narratives deriving from milieux of exceptional prosperity
and leisure – those of the nobility and gentry, and perhaps, in the
later Middle Ages, of well-to-do merchants and professionals who
could aspire to quasi-aristocratic material standards. We need to
enquire into the availability of private space in these privileged
households.

Especially in the earlier Middle Ages it is extremely hard to
distinguish between reality and fiction, because so much of the
evidence about secular social life is fictional. Much of it comes from
romances themselves, which, with all their distortion and idealization, are sometimes all the social history we possess. Somewhat
more is known about the reality of life in religious orders, because
both their buildings and their written rules sometimes survive; and
social historians can make use of what is known of monasteries as a
clue to life in lay aristocratic households. For the later Middle Ages
more evidence has been preserved about secular upper-class life:
there are more surviving buildings and more written accounts (as in
wills, records of the domestic organization of royal and noble
families, courtesy books, books of advice about running households,
details mentioned in chronicles . . .), and we also have more pictorial
evidence as the visual arts come to give more detailed representations of material aspects of the secular world. It remains difficult
to separate reality from fiction: chronicles tend to follow the same
conventions as romances, and the very acts of writing or painting
involve selection and coding. For my purpose, though, these limits

need not matter too much, because my aim is precisely to learn to read medieval fictions.[33]

Much information about these matters, applying chiefly to France, is summarized in the first two chapters of Georges Duby's *Revelations of the Medieval World*, to which I am greatly indebted. Later we shall consider the domestic settings of some specific narratives, but here, guided by Duby and his collaborators, I venture some generalization about the broad structuring of the medieval household. The crucial distinction is between inside and outside: in the Middle Ages there is none of that attempt to make the house merge into its surroundings found in the modern 'garden city' or suburb. Outside is dangerous, wild, unorganized; and it must be remembered that a large proportion of the medieval landscape, especially in Northern Europe, was uncultivated forest. Thus both house and city need to be surrounded by barriers intended to keep danger out; not just walls as strong as possible, but also fences, ramparts and moats. To take a fictional example, when in *Sir Gawain and the Green Knight* Gawain comes upon a splendid castle in the wintry northern forest, it is enclosed many times over. It is set in a clearing, itself 'loken vnder' (765)[34] the boughs of huge trees – thus the forest itself is imagined as a kind of enclosure. Then there are ditches enclosing the clearing; inside them a spiked palisade that encloses a 'park' (768); next a 'depe double dich' (786) full of water; finally the high walls of 'harde hewen ston' (789) of the castle's outer courtyard. And Gawain, as he waits outside, can see, inside that outer wall, a lofty hall defended by towers, and many pinnacles and chimneys. Every effort has been made to separate the civilized domain of Sir Bertilak's household from the wilderness outside its multiple enclosures.

In one sense, whatever is inside the enclosure of a house or town can be thought of as private space; but in another and more important sense it cannot, because 'private' takes its full meaning from its opposition to 'public'. What is outside the enclosure of a castle such as Gawain sees is not public because it is not civilized at all, even if it should be the private preserve of a lord who keeps it for hunting. On the contrary, in romances the extra-mural forest is the place where knights ride off on solitary quests, or where hermits dwell in deliberately chosen solitude; it is also a place to which lovers sometimes flee, as Tristan and Iseult do, in order to be private.[35]

The real opposition between public and private space is within the castle walls; it is between the hall and the chamber.

Every residence of every great lord in the Middle Ages had two focal points, the lord's chamber, and the hall ... The hustle and bustle of the hall was never more than a minute or two from the seclusion of the chamber.[36]

The hall is, relatively speaking, an open space; it is where the household assemble, and in early medieval times where they live the whole indoor part of their lives – where they eat and sleep and keep warm and entertain themselves (for example by having heroic lays or romances recited to them). It is also where the lord exercises his public power, stating law, delivering judgment, and presiding over the communal meal. The chamber, on the other hand, is the lord's private sphere; it is where he and his wife sleep, where they withdraw when they want to be secret, where more intimate acts are performed. In the earlier Middle Ages, even a royal household might evidently have only one chamber: this is the situation in King Mark's household in Beroul's *Tristan*, and there, as in other romances, the royal chamber provides sleeping accommodation not just for the king and queen but also for attendants and specially favoured household members. Paradoxically, the possession of such a private space is an index of the power that is exercised outside rather than inside it. There is another paradox too. Those of the highest rank were the only earlier-medieval layfolk likely to possess the means to achieve indoor privacy; yet it is a marker of high rank to be constantly accompanied by an entourage of courtiers of vassals. A striking illustration occurs in Beroul, when Mark learns that Tristan and Iseult have been discovered sleeping together in the forest of Morrois. The king summons his most trusted knights into his chamber and forbids them to follow him, giving as his reason that a girl has asked him to visit her alone – presumably for an amorous encounter. His knights are horrified, not on grounds of safety or morality, but simply because a king ought never to be alone:

> Rois, est ce gas,
> A aler vos sous nule part?
> Ainz ne fu rois qui n'ait regart.   (1926–8)

King, is this a joke, that you are going somewhere alone? No king ever failed to take proper precautions.[37]

Those who possessed the means of achieving privacy were precisely those whose rank made it most difficult for them to enjoy it.

In the later Middle Ages, the notion of private life expanded in conjunction with the multiplication of private rooms. It is hard to say which comes first, the desire for privacy or the material arrangements that make it possible. However much you desire privacy, you cannot have a private room unless you can afford it – which is why so much love-making in medieval fiction takes place in the open air, and therefore not in winter. On the other hand, given the cultural pressures towards ostentation and largesse, a medieval lord able to afford privacy might still prefer to devote his resources to splendid robes, jewels, and feasts. The *Gawain*-poet's Sir Bertilak evidently has wealth enough to indulge both traditional and modern tastes, and in the up-to-date castle that Gawain sees in the forest, the multiplicity of chimneys indicates the multiplicity of chambers, each heated by its own fireplace.[38]

In the earlier Middle Ages, then, even the royal chamber may not be truly private in a modern sense, because people other than the king and his wife regularly sleep there; but to be allowed to frequent and sleep in the royal chamber is to be admitted to special intimacy with the king, as his servant, counsellor, or friend. This is a position of privilege but may also be one of danger. And this ambivalence of the chamber survives throughout the Middle Ages for another reason too. The hall, the public space, is essentially though not exclusively masculine, because in this patriarchal society only men in general possess public status. Women in general belong to the private sphere; and thus the chamber which the lord shares with his wife tends to be felt to be feminine as well as private. Romances habitually present women as either delightful or dangerous, and often as both at once. Women stand outside the open hierarchy of public, male life, a hierarchy theoretically based on physical strength, moral integrity, and rationality; women are volatile, unpredictable, seductive, mysterious, magical, everything that from the male viewpoint is Other. The central feature of the chamber is the bed, the place where male and female are joined. This is an enclosed private space at the heart of all the other enclosures; usually curtained, it is literally enclosed. Again I adduce that paradigmatic romance *Sir Gawain and the Green Knight*. Taken into Sir Bertilak's castle as a guest, Gawain ends by sleeping in a curtained bed in a private bedchamber, apparently as safe as a wandering knight could be, entirely protected from the perils of forest and winter. But there he is visited by his host's seductive wife, and thus led into a danger that is both moral and physical. The bed is often the most dangerous place in a romance as well as the safest.

We need to learn to read the meanings built into the spatial settings of romances. But what does this imply? Despite the widespread belief, sometimes encouraged by medievalists, that the key to an understanding of medieval civilization lies in learning certain esoteric codes by which it was governed and unified, this is not necessarily true of the semiotics of medieval space. Spaces are symbolic; but this is not to imply that they are metaphorical, in the sense of standing for other things or ideas to which they are linked by convention or resemblance. The symbolism of spaces is metonymic rather than metaphoric; halls are really halls, chambers are really chambers, beds are really beds, but they carry charges of associative meaning derived from their real functions in medieval households. The meanings of secular spaces are not the product of what is sometimes imagined to be a peculiarly medieval symbolic consciousness, as may be the case with medieval religious symbolism. Spaces in medieval narratives may of course be explicitly allegorized – as with the *Minnegrotte* in Gottfried von Strassburg's *Tristan*, or the temples of the gods in Chaucer's *Knight's Tale* – but in themselves medieval spaces are neither more nor less symbolic than those of modern narratives and modern life. We may find it more difficult to recognize and read the spatial symbolism of our own culture, because we are shaped and enclosed by it. But there are unquestionably systems of meaning and not merely practical functions involved in the spaces and spatial divisions of airports, hotels, apartment blocks, police headquarters, and the other favourite settings of modern narratives in the cinema, television, and writing.

Other material features besides those discussed may mark the difference between private and public. Lacking a private room, fictional characters can also use spaces only partially enclosed, such as niches and window embrasures, for private conversations and other encounters. The development of the bay window must have been valued not only as a means of providing light and a view, but also as a space for private life. Curtains too are important, as a way of creating temporary enclosures, and not just the curtains round a bed. Though *Troilus and Criseyde* is set in the elaborate domestic architecture of Chaucer's time, Pandarus needs to employ curtains or screens as well as rooms, secret passages and possibly privies and sewers (the meaning of the terms used is sometimes uncertain), to create a private space where the lovers can meet. Gardens and orchards too are places where privacy may be achieved. The garden or orchard often provides an escape, in good weather, from the obtrusive company of the hall. It too is an enclosed space, with a wall round it, but it can have an ambiguous status and meaning, because it is both inside and outside. It is a natural setting, open to the heavens, but tamed and structured by human artifice: the trees are in straight rows, the flowers in neat beds, water flows from a sculptured fountain. It is well known that the symbolism of gardens is particularly rich, because of the connections with Eden and paradise, blessedness and Fall.[39]

Given these varying distinctions and gradations between private and public, marked by physical spaces, the boundaries between the two spheres are likely to be particularly important. In epic narratives such as the *Chanson de Roland* or the alliterative *Morte Arthure*, virtually all action is public: it concerns men, with women playing only very subordinate roles, and it takes place largely in the hall or the unenclosed open air. But in the romances to be discussed below, interaction between public and private will often be of crucial importance. These poems are not simply narratives of love, confined to the private sphere; they concern the loves – sometimes adulterous – of those who have public status and public responsibilities. The love of Tristan and Iseult is of special interest precisely because it impinges on such public matters as Iseult's status as wife to Mark, Mark's status as king, and Tristan's status as Mark's nephew and vassal. The question then arises, how does the private *become* public? Here looking is of crucial importance: the private becomes public by being seen, and it can be seen because of the gaps in the boundaries between the two spheres. According to feudal law, the chief evidence for adultery, evidence sufficient to permit and require public action to be taken within the bounds of justice, was that of sight.[40] Circumstantial evidence is insufficient; the offending couple must be witnessed *in flagrante delicto* if they are to be legally punishable. So spies and spying are necessary; and windows become of special importance as one means by which lovers' privacy can be violated. Light and darkness are also important, not because of any symbolic system requiring that they represent, say, good and evil, but as functional parts of the material setting of narratives. We may need to remind ourselves how dark it was in the medieval world, and how expensive and inefficient candles were as a means of indoor lighting. There may be a window to see through, but if there is insufficient light to see by, no evidence and thus no material for narrative will be available.

One explanation for the emphasis on the secrecy of love in medieval courtly literature is of course that, if love is adulterous, it impinges on the public sphere, and must be kept secret if it is not to be prohibited and punished. But this explanation is not sufficiently general. It is true that some of the most famous medieval love-stories concern adultery: those of Tristan and Iseult and of Lancelot and Guenevere are the best known. In these stories the fact that the deceived husband is a king provides the opportunity for concealment in the form of a royal bedchamber; it makes the deception particularly wounding because of the association of that private space with the king's very being; and at the same time it makes the impingement of the private on the public of crucial importance. But many medieval love-stories do not involve adultery, or even explicit parental opposition, and yet they still emphasize secrecy: Chaucer's *Troilus and Criseyde* is a striking example. Explanations in terms of an alleged courtly 'code' or 'convention' explain nothing; they only drive us to ask why such a code existed, for the supposed code is no more than an extrapolation from the practices assumed by certain narratives. No doubt the shamefulness of the sexual act, as explained by Augustine, is a relevant factor; it might be thought to induce a wish to conceal the whole process culminating in that act, however idealistically the process may be imagined in courtly literature. On the other hand, the sinfulness of sexual love, so strongly emphasized in religious writings, is not a prominent and certainly not a controlling feature of many secular narratives. In Beroul's *Tristan* even the hermit Ogrin, to whom the lovers turn for advice, seems as much concerned with preserving Iseult's reputation and keeping Mark in ignorance as with condemning their love: 'Por honte oster et mal covrir / Doit on un poi par bel mentir' (2353–4) [In order to escape shame and conceal evil, you have to be able to tell a few lies].

More important, perhaps, is the value attached to secrecy itself in a world where privacy was difficult to achieve. Secrecy may be seen specifically as a means of heightening erotic pleasure: Andreas Capellanus, referring vaguely to authorities that must include Ovid, notes that

They say [love] can be increased in particular by making it an infrequent and difficult business for lovers to set eyes on each other, for the greater the difficulty of offering and receiving shared consolations, the greater become the desire for, and feeling of, love. (p. 229)[41]

The point is repeated by Criseida in Boccaccio's *Filostrato*,[42] though not by Chaucer's Criseyde. More fundamental still is the general claim made by D. A. Miller for secrecy as the guardian of private experience. Referring to the representation of subjectivity in the novel, he observes that 'secrecy would seem to be a mode whose ultimate meaning lies in the subject's formal insistence that he is radically inaccessible to the culture that would otherwise entirely determine him'. He adds:

In a world where the explicit exposure of the subject would manifest how thoroughly he has been inscribed within a socially given totality, secrecy would be the spiritual exercise by which the subject is allowed to conceive of himself as a resistance ... Secrecy would thus be the subjective practice in which the oppositions of private/public, inside/outside, subject/object are established and their first term kept inviolate.[43]

Setting aside questions of the differential modes of operation of power in the medieval and modern worlds, these sentences describe with uncanny accuracy a medieval situation that Miller presumably does not have in mind; they even hint at the analogy between personal religious devotion and the cult of human love, both of which apparently emerged in the twelfth century.

The private sphere includes not just outward events transacted in the private space of the chamber or the orchard; it also includes all that we mean by the inner life – the thoughts and feelings, perhaps betrayed only fleetingly and ambiguously by glances or lowered eyes, blushing or turning pale, that are otherwise the most secret realm of all – 'the chambir of my thought' as a late-medieval poet puts it.[44] There must be some connection, though its precise nature is hard to specify, between these two kinds of privacy – the existence of objectively private space and the cultivation of a subjective realm of individual being. What is clear is that the inner life begins to assume greater interest and importance in secular narratives from the twelfth century on; it is precisely what Chrétien explores in Alixandre's inner dialogue quoted above. And the sharing of a rich inner life between two individuals, each of whom is the source of its richness in the other, perhaps produces the greatest possible intensification of inner experience. There must be two, so as to stimulate the flow of feeling and thought, and the realization of a subjectivity that is first single and then shared; there may be confidential friends, one for each lover, to aid the articulation of the inner life; but there must not be more, or the preciousness that comes from shared secrecy itself will be destroyed. The inner life is intense precisely because it is narrowly channelled by barriers that keep others out. One might even guess that the external barriers to publicly acknowledged union in romances (not just husbands, but parents, political antagonisms, and other external factors) have to be imagined in order to make secrecy necessary and thus to make a specially intense kind of private experience possible.

One other topic must be taken up before I turn to the examples on which I rely to introduce and explicate the concerns of the following chapters. Watching is an activity of great importance in medieval love-narratives, and medieval thought, as we have seen, connects looking with sexual desire. Yet the above discussion of secrecy indicates that looking is also connected with power, the function of secrecy being to create a real or imagined refuge against the determining claims of the public sphere. This link is manifest in medieval representations of rulers. The scope of the prince's gaze marks his public dominion, as may be seen with Chaucer's Duke Theseus. In *The Knight's Tale*, as he rides in triumph to Athens from his victory over the Amazons, the story begins,

> Whan he was come almoost unto the toun
> In al his wele and in his mooste pride,
> He was war, *as he caste his eye aside*,
> Where that ther kneled in the heighe weye
> A compaignye of ladyes, tweye and tweye ...   (1 894–8)

And it ends when he sends for Palamon and Emelye to appear before his *parlement*, and

> Whan they were set, and hust was al the place,
> And Theseus abiden hadde a space
> Er any word cam fram his wise brest,
> *His eyen sette he ther as was his lest* ...   (1 2981–4)

In recent theory one influential way of thinking about looking has associated it at once with power and with gender. A passage from John Berger's pioneering *Ways of Seeing* conveys the gist of this approach:

men act and *women appear*. Men look at women. Women watch themselves being looked at. This determines not only most relations between men and women but also the relation of women to themselves. The surveyor of woman in herself is male: the surveyed female. Thus she turns herself into an object – and most particularly an object of vision: a sight.

Berger proceeds to discuss the association of shame with sight in the Genesis myth, and the way in which pictorial representations of Adam and Eve show them turning towards the spectator, as if it were our gaze that shamed them rather than that of each other or of God. He argues that this is especially true of the female nude in Western art, at least from the Renaissance onwards: the naked woman is represented as 'aware of being seen by a spectator', and that spectator is male. 'She is naked as the spectator sees her', Berger writes, and

Often – as with the favourite subject of Susannah and the Elders – this is the actual theme of the picture. We join the Elders to spy on Susannah taking her bath. She looks back at us looking at her.

The Elders are men, literal voyeurs spying on a naked woman; and the kind of look exemplified by the ratification of their voyeurism in the work of art is what has come to be known as 'the male gaze'. To quote Berger once more,

In the average European oil painting of the nude the principal protagonist is never painted. He is the spectator in front of the picture and he is presumed to be a man. Everything is addressed to him. Everything must appear to be the result of his being there. It is for him that the figures have assumed their nudity.[45]

The male gaze is a look which signifies the power of men over women, the power to define women as objects or commodities, passive recipients of male desire, put on display for male enjoyment.

This concept has been prominent in film theory, not only in connection with glamour photography and pornographic movies, but through an alleged identification of the camera's look with the objectifying male gaze, and thus an identification of the visual pleasure of cinema with phallocentrism. In a much-quoted article, Laura Mulvey has even argued that the connection between cinematic pleasure and voyeuristic male dominance is so close and intricate that the only remedy is the drastic one of destroying cinematic pleasure itself.[46] Whatever the general validity of this theoretical approach, it is plainly capable of bearing valuably on the

treatment of watching in medieval narratives; yet it seems to me that
the watcher's look in love-narratives cannot always be understood
in terms of 'male gaze' theory. Most, though not all, of the fictional
watchers are certainly male, one reason being that, within the patriarchal society of the Middle Ages, it is only from the male and therefore public side of the public/private boundary that the private can
be made public. And most medieval writers are male; thus, insofar
as their narratorial positions are realized as those of watchers, the
same pattern will be likely to apply. Yet the connection between
power and gender in the act of looking is not necessarily as direct as
the theory assumes. Not all looking, even by men, is of the same
kind; even Berger claims only that the male gaze determines '*most*
relations between men and women*'. Certainly, the gaze may often
be an assertion of power over a distance that makes for invulnerability on the gazer's part; but it may also be an expression of longing,
where the distance between the eye and its object marks an absence
of power and thus signifies frustration. This is already implied in the
scholastic conception, mentioned above, of sight as the only sense
not materially affected by its object. Its 'nobility' is thus guaranteed,
but looking can be a poor substitute for closer contact. In Chaucer's
Franklin's Tale, when the young squire Aurelius falls in love with
Dorigen in her husband's absence, he dares not reveal his love,

> Save that, paraventure, somtyme at daunces,
> Ther yonge folk kepen hir observaunces,
> It may wel be he looked on hir face
> In swich a wise as man that asketh grace;
> But nothyng wiste she of his entente.   (v 955–9)

Doubtless it would be possible to reinterpret such longing looks in
terms of the 'male gaze' paradigm, but to do so would be to elevate a
totalizing theory above the variety of literary and human experience. Again, in the 'heart-and-eye' topos illustrated above from
Cligés and *Eneas*, the male may be represented as passive before a
penetrating female glance. A ballade by Charles d'Orléans provides
a striking instance: the male speaker has been struck 'Thorughout
myn eye' with 'the dart of loue' and now his heart cowers naked and
helpless before his mistress's eyes, which are 'armed with pleasure':

> How may he him diffende, þe pouer hert,
> Ageyn two eyen when they vpon him light,
> Which nakid is, withouten cloth or shert,
> Where in plesere the eyen are armyd bright?[47]

The relations between power and desire, and the ways they are expressed in looking, are complex and often ambiguous, and will need to be analysed with some flexibility rather than reduced to a single pattern.[48]

Further, we shall find in medieval texts that what the watcher watches is often not simply a woman but a man and a woman together; and, whether or not this is so, it does not appear that the two sexes are always treated differently as the objects of watching. Moreover, we shall observe that in many medieval narratives the female watcher plays an important part. In the development of a love-affair the woman's glances are often as frequent as the man's, and also as active, in that they are not merely glances in response to · · glances received, the looks of one aware of being looked at. Again, one recurrent situation in romances is what has been named the 'chivalry topos'.[49] Here knights fighting in a battle or tournament are watched, and know themselves to be watched, by female spectators. The knights display their skill and courage the more intensely to impress the watching ladies; the ladies are moved to love by that male display. This topos occurs in many romances, and it puts men in an active and women in a passive role; but it does not define women as objects or even as commodities – at least, they are no more commodities than men are. Doubtless it would always be possible to theorize female looking in these (or any) circumstances in such a way as to make it a 'transvestite' or 'masochistic' identification with the preconceived male gaze; but the motivation for this theoretical move would lie in the desire for intellectual mastery (as in Lacan's 'all human desire is based on castration') rather than in response to the demands of specific medieval texts. The concept of the 'male gaze' and its accompanying body of thought provides a valuable stimulus for thinking about watching in medieval love-narratives; but it cannot be transferred without modification from modern semiotics, psychoanalysis and film-theory to the texts discussed in this book.

CHAPTER 2

Examples of looking

I have been sketching the framework of ideas within which my subject has taken shape. However, many of the issues involved in a consideration of looking and listening in medieval love-narratives are best introduced through an examination of individual cases. In this second introductory chapter I bring together a miscellany of short texts, some in the first person, some in the third. My discussion is intended to bring into preliminary focus some questions that will be raised by the romances and *dits* with which this book is chiefly concerned.

My first example is a German lyric by Walther von der Vogelweide (*c.* 1170–*c.* 1230). It is of a kind common in several medieval languages, though rarely expressed with such charm and felicity. The speaker is a peasant girl who describes her encounter with a knight, which involved love-making and was therefore secret. There were no human witnesses, only a nightingale, and the nonsense-word *tandaradei*, forming the refrain, represents the nightingale's song and reminds us of its presence; perhaps it also represents the act of love.

Under der linden	Under the lime-tree
an der heide,	in the meadow,
dâ unser zweier bette was,	where the two of us had our bed,
dâ mugt ir vinden	there you may find
schône beide	both beautiful
gebrochen bluomen unde gras.	broken flowers and grass.
vor dem walde in einem tal,	in the front of the flowers in a valley,
tandaradei	*tandaradei*,
schône sanc diu nahtegal.	the nightingale sang beautifully.
Ich kam gegangen	I came walking
zue der ouwe:	to the meadow:
dô was min friedel[1] comen ê.	my lover was there before me.
dâ wart ich enpfangen,	there I was received,
here frouwe,	noble lady,
daz ich bin saelic iemer mê.	in such a way that I am happy for ever.
kuster mich? wol tûsentstunt:	did he kiss me? at least a thousand times:
tandaradei,	*tandaradei*,
seht wie rôt mir ist der munt.	see how red my mouth is.

Dô het er gemachet	There he made
alsô rîche	a bed
von bluomen eine bettestat.	rich with flowers.
des wirt noh gelachet	if anyone should come
inneclîche,	by the same path and see it,
kumt ieman an daz selbe pfat.	he would have an amused smile.
bi den rôsen er wol mac,	among the roses he can certainly,
tandaradei,	*tandaradei*
merken wâ mirz houbet lac.	see where my head lay.
Daz er bî mir laege,	That he lay by me,
wessez iemen	if anyone knew it,
(nu enwelle got!) sô schamt ich mich	(God forbid!) then I would be ashamed.
was er mit mir pflaege,	what he did with me
niemer nieman	no-one ever
bevinde daz, wan er unt ich,	will find out, only he and I,
und ein kleinez vogellin:	and a little bird,
tandaradei,	*tandaradei*,
daz mac wol getriuwe sin.[2]	and he will not betray me.[3]

The love-encounter should be secret, and the girl would feel shame if anyone knew what had happened. Shame rather than guilt: the distinction, drawn above in connection with Sartre's characterization of the look, will recur. Guilt I take to be the feeling, usually associated with conscience, that accompanies the sense of having done wrong, regardless of others' knowledge. Shame is produced by a real or imagined sense of being observed; guilt is internalized, and is generally thought to accompany a fuller development of the inner life. The distinction, though not always clear in practice, will be important in principle. In the girl's circumstances, to feel oneself watched is to feel shame. As Sartre indicates, it may be equally shameful to be a secret watcher, if the watcher then learns or fears that he in turn is watched. Birds, though, are presumably unable to feel shame, and there is no indication that Walther's nightingale is ashamed: its *tandaradei* appears to be cheerful and untroubled.

Yet the girl has betrayed her secret by speaking the poem's words; its outdoor setting, transformed into a private 'bedroom' by the romantic interlude, is made public again in the act of narration. That the girl is speaking *to* someone, within the fiction, is made explicit from the beginning: 'there *you* may find' the broken flowers and grass that betray what has happened. 'Did he kiss me?' is a question asked of someone, and 'see how red my mouth is' is a command addressed to someone. 'If anyone should come by the same path' he would see the 'bed' and would laugh inwardly at what it revealed; so again at least a circumstantial witness is envisaged. And finally, 'if anyone knew it' – knew that the knight had lain with the speaker – she would be ashamed. The poem purports to exclude possible watchers, yet its secrecy has been penetrated not only by the nightingale but by these persons named as *ir* and *ieman*. Each stanza not only reveals what the poem claims to conceal, but calls attention to that revelation by its very words.

The nightingale is the poet's surrogate within the poem; and the word *vogel*, bird, occurs not only in the diminutive form *vogellin* applied to the nightingale, but also as part of the poet's surname, Vogelweide. Walther's contemporary Gottfried von Strassburg, in his *Tristan*, has a passage surveying his poetic predecessors and contemporaries, where he calls lyric poets who compose music as well as words 'nightingales'. He states that the leading nightingale among those living is 'her of Vogelweide'[4] – that is, the author of this very lyric. So it is not anachronistic to suppose that Walther could have been conscious of the parallel between his role and the nightingale's in this poem. Once we become hearers or readers of the poem's words, we are put imaginatively in his and the nightingale's position: we become secret onlookers at a sexual encounter in which we have no part: we become voyeurs.

The distance between eye and object is an essential feature of watching, and it is this that makes possible the mastery postulated of the 'male gaze' and also the frustrated longing, the very opposite of mastery, that I have suggested may equally be conveyed by a look. The physical distance traversed by sight has an analogy in the aesthetic distance involved in the act of reading: however strong the illusory presence of the fiction, as readers we can never literally participate in the narrated action; nor, on the other hand, are we vulnerable to the dangers in which it might involve us in reality.[5] That is not to say, however, that the reader's virtual voyeurism is necessarily accompanied by shame. In this case the poem is irresistibly cheerful: it is full of witty contradictions, between the naïve fictional speaker and the sophisticated poet, between the bird as poet and the poet as bird, and the overall effect is of lighthearted celebration. As a reader, I do not blush; I find myself easily able to enter into the unfallen innocence with which the nightingale views the act of love. The bird is the poet's surrogate, but it also lacks both desire and capacity to participate in what it sees, and in this sense it acts as a buffer between the reader and shame. All the same, the poem invites us to reflect on the ambiguities and dubieties of the poet's role and our own as witnesses and revealers of someone else's love-making.

Another poem by a Minnesinger, Heinrich von Morungen (d. 1222), will serve to illustrate further this medieval self-consciousness about the roles of poet and audience as spies. The first two stanzas of a five-stanza lyric will sufficiently make the point:

> Ich bin iemer eine und nicht eine
> der grôzen minne der ich nie wart frî.
> wêren nun die huoter algemeine
> toup unde blint, swenne ich wêre bî,
> sô môht ich mîn leit
> eteswenne mit gelâze ir künden
> und mich mit rede zuo ir gefründen,
> sô wurde ir wunders vil von mir geseit.
>
> Mîner ougen tougenlîchez spêen,
> daz ich ze boten an si senden muoz,
> daz neme durch got von mir für ein flêen,
> und ob si lache, daz sî mir ein gruoz.
> in weiz wer dâ sanc
> 'ein sitich unde ein star ân alle sinne
> wol gelernten daz si sprêchen Minne':
> wol sprechent siz und habent des niemer danc ...

I am always alone, and yet never alone from powerful *Minne*, from whom I have never been free. If only the spies were all deaf and blind whenever I am with her, then I would be able to make her know my pain, courteously, now and then; and by conversation I would make myself her friend. Then wonderful things would be said to her by me.

May she, for God's sake, take for a supplication the secretive searching of my eyes, the look I must send her as a messenger; and then if she would smile, let that be a greeting to me. I do not know who it was that sang there: 'A parrot or a starling without any intelligence would have learned to say "*Minne*"': they say it well but have no thought of what they say ...[6]

Here the poet speaks in his own part, as lover. He speaks about his lady because he is prevented from speaking to her by the constant presence of *huoter*, the spies who, as we shall see in romances discussed in subsequent chapters, are so often imagined as surrounding medieval lovers. He is always alone, yet never alone because his constant companion is *Minne*, the love within his heart that finds no physical expression, not even in conversation with the lady. If only he could be with her, and free from the spies, he could express his feelings in wonderful words and thus gain her pity and friendship. Since he cannot speak, all he can do is pray that she will read his secret looks, and respond to them with an equally secret smile. A talking bird may be able to say the word *Minne*, but the bird has no thought corresponding to the word's sound; the poet, presumably, is just the opposite – he dares not speak the word, but his heart is full of the thought.

All this implies silence and secrecy as the necessary mode of communication between lovers in the voyeuristic world of the court. Yet the paradox is obvious: Heinrich conveys this meaning in a lyric which betrays the secret to any listener, a lyric indeed designed to be sung aloud to a courtly audience, including presumably the spies. He says, or sings, 'I do not know who it was that sang *"ein sitich unde ein star ân alle sinne / wol gelernten daz si sprêchen Minne"*'; but it was Heinrich himself who composed those words and sang them to the same audience in another of his lyrics. The parallel between poet and bird reappears: the bird may be a spontaneous and innocent celebrant of love, like the nightingale, or it may be an uncomprehending (and therefore equally innocent) repeater of others' words, like the parrot.[7] Heinrich, as he implicitly contrasts himself with a parrot, is indeed behaving as a parrot, repeating words that already exist – only they are his own words in a previous poem. One way to resolve the paradoxes is that of Frederick Goldin, who proposes that the poem creates two audiences: the imagined audience of spies, the enemy, and the real audience who are lovers themselves and therefore understand the poet's poetry and the true nature of his love.[8] Though possible, this division of the audience seems somewhat arbitrary. As I understand it, the role the poem offers to its reader or listener is a double one as both lover and spy. To respond at all is to be induced to adopt the voyeur's position, watching for supposedly secret glances and smiles, reading between the lines for quotation and implication, imagining for oneself the wonders that might pass between the lovers if only they could be alone together. After all, to return to the problem from which I began, in a poem love can never be secret and lovers can never be alone, because the poet and the reader are always present too, as if concealed behind an arras, taking note and taking notes.

My next example is a Middle English narrative too long to be quoted here in full: *A Pistel of Susan*, a fourteenth-century adaptation in alliterative stanzas of the story of Susanna and the Elders. This story, a self-contained addition to the Old Testament Book of Daniel, subsequently relegated to the Apocrypha, was read in the Middle Ages as having Scriptural authority. It tells of two old judges who spy on Joakim's beautiful wife Susanna as she bathes in her orchard. They then reveal themselves, attempt to seduce her, and when she rebuffs them claim to have watched her committing adultery with a young man. She is condemned to death, but the boy Daniel traps them into contradiction about the species of tree under which the adultery they allegedly witnessed took place. The Elders are condemned to death and Susanna is freed. As John Berger notes, the story's scene of voyeurism is a 'favourite subject' of pictorial art from the Renaissance on; voyeurism is portrayed in a voyeuristic spirit, inviting the spectator to share the Elders' lustful gaze at Susanna, and often implicitly attributing to her something of the conscious self-display of a striptease performer.

The anonymous fourteenth-century poet responds intelligently and feelingly to Daniel 13, but he also sets it at a certain historical distance, reading its emphasis on justice and judgment as locating it in the age of the Old Law, the 'law of Moses', in which Susanna was instructed (verse 3) and according to which the Elders were punished (verse 62). For him as a medieval Christian, though the 'maundement of Moises' was a gift of 'þe Trinité' (19–21),[9] the New Law that it figured and that was to be fulfilled in Christ's teachings was available to him and his audience, but not yet to the poem's characters. It is for the poet to teach his readers a lesson in God's mercy not explicit in the Scriptural text:

> Hose leeueþ on þat Lord, þar him not lees,
> Þat þus his seruaunt saued þat schold ha be schent
> Vnsete. (358–60)

Within his story, the essential difference between good and evil is that between 'riȝtwys jugement' (60) and the 'wrongwys domes' (37) of the Elders, though Susanna rises above the Mosaic law to pray, 'Grete God of his grace þis gomes forgeue / Þat doþ me derfliche be ded' (241–2). The poet medievalizes and anglicizes the story's judicial framework,[10] providing 'justises on bench' (183) distinct from the Elders; thus, as often in medieval romances of adultery, the courtroom is where the private is made public and

where, in order to provide proof of the adulterous act, what has been
seen, whether really or allegedly, is told.

The public setting in *A Pistel of Susan* is the court of law, the *sale*
(196, 301) or hall, where first Susanna is arraigned and then the
Elders are interrogated 'be proces apert' (294) 'Tofore þe folk and þe
faunt' (329); finally it gives way to the larger public space of the city
streets, through which the Elders are dragged 'bi comuyn assent'
(357) before the eyes of all on their way to execution. The private
setting is Joakim's orchard, a *gardeyn* (42) enclosed by walls with
ʒates (122) and a 'priué posterne' (159), and set within the larger
enclosure of 'His innes and his orchardes', all surrounded by 'a dep
dich' (5). This is where he is accustomed to engage in private
enjoyment with his friends – 'Þer Jewes with Joachim priueliche gon
playe' (28) – and it is especially associated, like the chamber in the
medieval household generally, with the intimacy of marriage and
the feminine. Thus the orchard is described not just as Joakim's but
also as Susanna's, 'hire ʒerde, / Þat was hir hosbondes and hire'
(118–19), and its feminine associations are underlined; we are told
twice that it was where she went to enjoy herself with her two female
attendants:

> Wiþ two maidenes al on,
> Semelyche Suson,
> On dayes in þe merion
>   Of murþes wol here.   (49–52)

> In þe seson of somere with Sibell and Jane
> Heo greiþed hire til hire gardin þat growed so grene ...   (66–7)

A major addition of the poet's consists of four stanzas, beginning
with the lines just quoted, describing this place of female pleasure
(66–117). He composes a catalogue of trees, birds, fruit and herbs;
each category is given one stanza, and the 'bob-and-wheel' with
which each stanza concludes links it forward by anticipating the
next category (parrots and nightingales at the end of the trees, dates
and damsons at the end of the birds, spices at the end of the fruit).
The modern reader might be puzzled to know why the poet felt the
need to spend one seventh of his poem describing what Scripture
leaves undescribed. No doubt, within the encyclopaedic aesthetic of
later medieval poetry, such a display of intricate artistry might seem
to justify itelf. Moreover, the domestic order that the Elders are
about to violate is evoked by the neatly arranged plenitude of species

in the garden, 'With ruwe and rubarbe raunged ariht' (112). The modern editor is doubtless right, too, to point to evocations of Genesis (paradise with its serpent) and the Song of Songs (the garden enclosed that both is and contains the virgin Bride).[11] It might even be noted that, in terms of detective-story verisimilitude, the more the species of trees mentioned, the more plausible the Elders' confusion when interrogated by Daniel. But, above all, the orchard substitutes for Susanna herself: it takes the place of her fruitful and desirable body, which the poet – unlike the Renaissance painters who succeeded him – does not display unclothed to the reader's gaze. The enumerative account of the garden's contents is itself a sufficient violation of privacy, Susanna's and that of her husband, the rightful possessor both of the garden and of her body; and the 'irrelevant' amplification calls attention to what it conceals. The Elders frequent the orchard 'To fonge floures and fruit' (43), and the poet immediately adds,

> And whon þei seiȝ Susan, semelich of hewe,
> Þei weor so set vppon hire, miȝt þei not sese;
> Þei wolde enchaunte þat child hou schold heo eschewe,
> And þus þis cherles vnchaste in chaumbre hir chese
>   To fere.   (44–8)

The desire for flowers and fruit is scarcely distinguishable from the sexual appetite, stimulated through the eye, that makes the Elders fantasize the orchard as bedchamber.

    The substitution of the orchard for the female body might seem to weaken the story's voyeuristic potential, and indeed there is less stress on sight and looking in *A Pistel of Susan* than might be expected; but the effect remains more voyeuristic than that of its Scriptural source. Susanna's removal of her clothes is mentioned three times. First 'þe wyf werp of hir wedes vnwerde' (124), and then

> By a wynliche welle
> Susan caste of hir kelle;
> Bote feole ferlys hire bifelle
>   Bi midday or none.   (127–30)

The foreboding implied in *vnwerde* [unprotected] and more emphatically stated in lines 129–130 invites our complicity in the anticipated violation. The effect is familiar from horror movies: why are we watching this woman undressing if not in pleasurable expectation of 'feole ferlys' that will take advantage of her vulnerability? The third mention of her disrobing reminds us, surely gratuitously, that she is still *en déshabille* when she summons help after the Elders have propositioned her:

> Whon kene men of hir court comen til hir cri,
> Heo hedde cast of hir calle and hire keuercheue.   (157–8)

One is tempted to speak of a discreetly soft-focus eroticism, evoking nakedness rather than nudity,[12] but the point is rather that the garments mentioned as missing are symbolic: the head-coverings (*kelle* or *calle* and *keuercheue*) signify a married woman in the medieval sartorial code, and their absence under the gaze of the Elders, the 'men of hir court', and ourselves (indeed of any male but her husband) is a gross impropriety.

In the court scene Susanna is more directly subjected to the male gaze:

> Hire here was ȝolow as wyre,
> Of gold fyned wiþ fyre,
> Hire scholdres schaply and schire,
>   Þat bureliche was bare.   (192–5)

The gold-wire comparison for blonde hair was conventional and could scarcely be arousing, but, as before, we have to remember that the poet ought not to be in a position to offer it, because a married woman's hair should not be uncovered in public. An erotic charge will tend to accrue to the exposure of any bodily part normally covered by clothing, and for many centuries the hair of a woman, and especially of a married woman, could stand metonymically for her whole body. The Vulgate too enters into the sense of public display at this point, noting that 'Susanna was exceedingly delicate and beautiful to behold' (verse 31); but this lacks specificity, and the medieval poet's lingering over her shapely and beautifully bare shoulders goes considerably further towards inviting *us* to share in the gaze that turns her into a helplessly delectable object. This is the poem's most voyeuristic moment; but it preserves us from sharing fully the shame of the Elders' scopophilia, by being placed not in the furtive privacy of the orchard but in the public courtroom, where all are entitled to gaze.

Both Daniel 13 and the English poem can be read as concerned throughout with concealment from sight and exposure to sight. The poet and his readers are implicated, as we have seen, both in the

secret watching of the Elders and, more fully, in the public gaze of
the court room and the city. But above all, directing the action and
ensuring that the hidden truth will eventually be revealed by Daniel,
is God. He is situated outside all enclosures, outside even 'the sercle
of sees' (10) that surrounds the human action and that God drew
with his great compass at the moment of Creation. Within it He is
unseen; unlike earthly princes, God does not display His power to
public gaze as He extends and defines it with His own gaze. God is
more effectively concealed in heaven than the Elders, 'drawen in
derne' (131), who, as watchers and judges, are earthly travesties of
this heavenly watcher and judge. When they are spying on Susanna,

> For siht of here souerayn, soþli to say,
> Heore hor heuedes fro heuene þei hid apon one.   (57–8)

But such concealment is futile, for God's very inaccessibility to sight
means that all earthly things, even truths concealed in the human
heart, are visible to Him. Thus Susanna prays,

> Seþþe þou maiȝt not be sene
> Wiþ no fleschliche eyene,
> Þou wost wel I am clene.
>   Haue merci on me.   (270–3)

And the outcome is that under God's direction the Elders' 'synnes
be seene' (309), first by Daniel and then by the Israelites. The
piercing look of a hidden spy finally triumphs; and when we are
placed as sharers of God's watchful sight in a narrative sanctioned
by its Scriptural origin, our voyeurism may feel thoroughly acceptable. In considering looking in other narratives, especially those
where the framework is explicitly religious, we shall have to take
account of God's eye and its unseen panoptic gaze.

   In this story watchers are punished under the direction of a
heavenly watcher; and in many medieval narratives human watching is envisaged as a punishable offence. One mythic paradigm
frequently evoked by such narratives is that of Actaeon. The
best-known version was Ovid's, in Book III of the *Metamorphoses*,
where it occurs in a sequence of stories of forbidden sights: Cadmus
and the serpent's teeth, Semele, Narcissus. Young Actaeon,
returning with his men from a successful hunt, enters by chance a
secret valley where the chaste goddess Diana is bathing with her
nymphs after they too have been hunting. Seeing him, the nymphs

surround their naked mistress; she blushes, and throws water at
Actaeon's face, saying 'nunc tibi me posito visam velamine narres, /
si poteris narrare, licet!' (192–3) [Now you are free to tell that you
have seen me all unrobed – if you can tell].[13] He is transformed into
a stag, runs away, sees his new shape in a pool, and ' "Me miserum!"
dicturus erat: vox nulla secuta est!' (201) ['Oh, woe is me!' he tries to
say; but no words come]. His hunting hounds chase him; he longs to
tell them 'Actaeon ego sum' (230) [I am Actaeon], but is unable to
do so, and even as his companions call for him his hounds kill him.

Ovid insists that Actaeon was not responsible for what happened;
there was no guilty intention behind his accidental look, and in that
sense he was no voyeur. Nor does the narrative invite any serious
complicity in voyeurism on the reader's part; the removal of Diana's
robe and sandals and the binding up of her hair for the bath are
mentioned, but *we* never see her naked – she is concealed from us as
from Actaeon by her protective nymphs. There is not even as much
of a striptease effect as in the scene based on this in *The Faerie Queene*
where Venus discovers Diana and her nymphs bathing and Spenser
lingers somewhat over 'their daintie limbes' and 'her ... breasts
vnbraste', and has Diana's hair left seductively 'loose about her
shoulders' rather than pinned up in the businesslike manner of
Ovid's Diana.[14] Ovid frames his narrative between passages questioning the justice of Actaeon's punishment; he begins,

> at bene si quaeras, Fortunae crimen in illo,
> non scelus invenies; quod enim scelus error habebat?   (141–2)

But if you seek the truth, you will find the cause of this in fortune's fault and
not in any crime of his. For what crime had mere mischance?

and he ends,

> Rumor in ambiguo est; aliis violentior aequo
> visa dea est, alii laudant dignamque severa
> virginitate vocant: pars invenit utraque causas.   (253–5)

Common talk wavered this way and that: to some the goddess seemed more
cruel than was just; others called her act worthy of her austere virginity;
both sides found good reasons for their judgment.

It might be argued that Ovid protests too much on behalf of
Actaeon's blamelessness; *error* (142) can imply fault as well as
accident, and the same might be true of *errans* later ('non certis
passibus errans / pervenit in lucum', 175–6 [wandering with unsure

footsteps he enters the grove]). But the question is ultimately a blind alley. To see the goddess is inherently transgressive and dangerous, regardless of the spectator's intention. Looking is often regarded as an intrinsically predatory activity, with the predatoriness conveyed through hunting metaphors. Thus in Gottfried's *Tristan*, when Isolde appears with her mother before King Mark's court, 'gevedere schâchblicke / ... vlugen dâ snêdicke / schâchende dar unde dan' (10957–9). [Rapacious feathered glances flew thick as falling snow, ranging from side to side in search of prey (p. 185).] In Ovid a similar effect is implied by the gory hunting context in which Actaeon's fatal look is set. The story begins 'on a mountain stained with the blood of many slaughtered beasts' (143), and Actaeon reminds his companions that their 'nets and spears ... are dripping with our quarry's blood' (148). Nets and spears (or arrows) are common images for looks, and Diana too has been hunting and is equipped with 'her hunting spear, her quiver, and her unstrung bow' (166). She lays them by to bathe, and then, when Actaeon's presence is made known by her nymphs' ululations and their attempts to conceal her body, wishes that she had not done so: 'vellet promptas habuisse sagittas' (188) [she would fain have had her arrows ready]. At this moment she returns Actaeon's look, with an obliquity that momentarily suggests feminine coyness: 'in latus obliquum ... oraque retro / flexit' (187–8) [she stood turning aside a little and cast back her face]. But the glance is as dangerous as the gaze; the water-drops take its place as a transforming power, and the hunter becomes the hunted, as bloodily mangled as his former prey.

What is it that Actaeon sees? Here, as in *A Pistil of Susan*, landscape is a metaphor for the female body. The setting is one of secrecy and privacy at their most numinous, the 'most secret nook' (157) of a thickly wooded valley of Gargaphie, 'succinctae sacra Dianae' (156) [sacred to high-girt Diana]. As Theresa Krier puts it, 'Geographical boundaries are continuous with personal boundaries, and the transgression of the grove continuous with transgression of her selfhood.'[15] In this sense, then, the transgression is ours too: in 'seeing' the landscape Ovid describes, we are in effect seeing the forbidden body of the goddess, penetrating the secret valley, and thus sharing in Actaeon's offence. The offence involves seeing a deity, but before death it leads to a kind of self-recognition: Actaeon's look into the pool and his unspoken 'Actaeon ego sum!'. One scholar goes so far as to claim that

Actaeon and Diana are both hunters, and so, in perceiving the naked goddess, the young man is looking in a sort of mirror and seeing a transfigured, sacred form of his own identity ... Diana and the stag are both mirror images of the young hunter; but more than these Ovid emphasizes the fact that what Actaeon sees in the mirror after his transformation is for the first time a sense of his own identity.[16]

To put it like this seems misleading. For one thing, Actaeon sees himself in the pool not as himself but as the stag into which he has been transformed; he cannot even utter 'me miserum!' – 'vox nulla secuta est!' (201) – and though he tries to say 'Actaeon ego sum!', 'verba animo desunt' (231) [words fail his desire]. He loses rather than gains his selfhood; he sees not identity but an unspeakable difference. Correspondingly, it is important that when he sees Diana he sees not a mirror image of himself but a female being. Knowing herself seen, the goddess blushes violently:

> qui color infectis adversi solis ab ictu
> nubibus esse solet aut purpureae Aurorae,
> is fuit in vultu visae sine veste Dianae.   (183–5)

And red as the clouds which flush beneath the sun's slant rays, red as the rosy dawn, were the cheeks of Diana as she stood there in view without her robes.

The chaste goddess might be thought above blushing, but she is not; she feels not just anger but shame at being seen naked by a mortal male. The blush is an index of vulnerability; naked before a man's gaze, even a goddess finds her transcendent subjectivity momentarily compromised. Blushing is no more under the will's control than sexual arousal, with which it is connected.[17] Though we do not see Diana's body, her splendidly cosmic flush is revealed because 'altior illis / ipsa dea est colloque tenus supereminet omnis' (181–2) [the goddess stood head and shoulders above all the rest]. It is as if she were the only adult among children, and this suggests that the human experience underlying the myth is not just the male's gaze at the female and his recognition of sexual difference, but the son's curiosity about the naked body of his mother, a sight forbidden by the incest taboo.[18]

Seeing and telling are closely connected. This will be important in many texts we shall examine: how can what is private or secret be told if it has not been seen? Here Diana's angry 'nunc tibi me posito visam velamine *narres*, / si poteris *narrare*, licet!' (192–3) stresses by repetition a verb that means to tell stories – the poet's activity. The question is not explicitly raised, but is perhaps sensed hanging, how can Ovid tell Actaeon's story unless he too has seen the forbidden sight? The punishment is to be silenced.

The watchers in these examples have all been male: Walther's nightingale, the 'I' of Heinrich von Morungen, the Elders, Actaeon. But it is also possible for the look to be returned and submitted to a critique by a woman, as may be illustrated from a pair of poems written early in the sixteenth century by Henry Howard, Earl of Surrey. Surrey is conspicuously a poet of male chivalry and friendship, but he also composed several poems in the persons of women, showing remarkable empathy with the situations and feelings of their imagined speakers. The first of this pair is spoken by a man:

> Wrapt in my carelesse cloke, as I walke to and fro,
> I se how love can shew what force there reigneth in his bow;
>   And how he shoteth eke, a hardy hart to wound;
> And where he glanceth by agayne, that litle hurt is found.
>   For seldom is it sene he woundeth hartes alike;   5
> The tone may rage, when tothers love is often farre to seke.
>   All this I se, with more; and wonder thinketh me
> Howe he can strike the one so sore, and leave the other fre.
>   I se that wounded wight that suffreth all this wrong,
> How he is fed with yeas and nayes, and liveth all to long.   10
>   In silence though I kepe such secretes to my self,
> Yet do I se how she somtime doth yeld a loke by stelth,
>   As though it seemd, 'Ywys, I woll not lose the so',
> When in her hart so swete a thought did never truely go.
>   Then say I thus: 'Alas, that man is farre from bliss   15
> That doth receive for his relief none other gayn but this.
>   And she that fedes him so, I fele and finde it plain,
> Is but to glory in her power, that over such can reign.
>   Nor are such graces spent but when she thinkes that he,
> A weried man, is fully bent such fansies to let flie.   20
>   Then to retain him stil, she wrasteth new her grace,
> And smileth, lo, as though she would forthwith the man embrace.
>   But when the proofe is made to try such lokes withall,
> He findeth then the place all voyde, and fraighted full of gall.
>   Lorde, what abuse is this! who can such women praise   25
> That for their glory do devise to use such crafty wayes!
>   I that among the rest do sit, and mark the row,
> Fynde that in her is greater craft then is in twenty mo.
>   Whose tender yeres, alas, with wyles so well are spedde,
> What will she do when hory heares are powdred in her hedde?'[19] 30

The speaker purports to be a detached observer of the scene of courtly sexual politics. He walks about wrapped in his careless cloak (1), the conventional mark of the melancholy lover but also here a cloak concealing his secret observation; or he is one 'that among the rest do sit, and mark the row' (27) – the women neatly lined up for observation, as passive objects waiting to be mastered by the male gaze. What he sees – and 'I see' is repeated four times – is Cupid's demonstration of the 'force' that 'reigneth in his bow'. This 'force' is deployed unequally: some victims are wounded to the heart (3), while others suffer only a glancing blow and receive 'little hurt' (4). Not by accident, the first group is represented by a man, and the second by a woman.

Women, according to this widely held theory, inflict desire on men as a form of suffering; apparently victims of the look, they actually victimize the looker. The woman herself sometimes 'doth yeld a loke by stelth' (12), to keep her admirer on the boil, but this is unconnected with her true feelings, the thoughts 'in her hart' (14). Thus a second kind of looking is introduced: there is the penetrating but supposedly entirely objective male gaze, that can even see into the female heart; and there is the female glance, designed to keep male desire alive, and having as its sole end 'to glory in her power, that over such can reign' (18). The smile serves the same purpose as the glance: it seems to promise an embrace (22), only to deny what has apparently been offered. The woman is seen as 'feeding' the man (10, 17), as if she were the all-powerful mother, whose refusal to grant full satisfaction to the son's longing can only be construed as malice. And yet, as we learn from line 29, this is a woman 'of tender yeres'! And the poem has a further surprise for us. It does not offer the common argument, found in Wyatt's 'My lute, awake' or Ronsard's 'Quand vous serez bien vieille', that when she becomes old and undesirable she will be repaid for her cruelty; instead, this speaker imagines her as a kind of Cleopatra, becoming still more cunning and causing still more male suffering when she is grey-haired.

The speaker is an exaggerated version of the lover of courtly and Petrarchan tradition, locked in his own egoism; he sounds like a parody of Wyatt, though Surrey probably admired Wyatt too greatly to have been able to read him consciously in this critical way. The poem shows admirably how the idealizing love of the courtly tradition, seeming to worship women, is really misogynistic, because incapable of empathy with women's own feelings and wishes. It assumes that male desire is the helpless product of a female guile that has power as its sole end: women 'for their glory do devise to use such crafty ways' (26). This tradition projects on to women the *will* to produce the frustration that men experience in their relations with them. In reality, women of course do play at sexual politics; but this poem, like the tradition to which it belongs and which (along with the next) it diagnoses, sees the power-struggle only from one side. The speaker is not really the disinterested, 'careless' (1) observer he pretends to be. The male gaze is as much an exercise of power as the female glance, and as likely to have its hidden and disreputable motives.

> Gyrtt in my giltlesse gowne, as I sytt heare and sowe,
> I see that thinges are not in dead as to the owtward showe.
> And who so lyst to looke and note thinges somwhat neare,
> Shall fynde, where playnesse seemes to haunte, nothing but craft
>   appeare.
> For with indifferent eyes my self can well discearne   5
> How som to guyd a shyppe in stormes styckes not to take the
>   stearne;
> Whose skill and connynge tryed in calme to steare a bardge,
> They wolde sone shaw, yow shold sone see, it weare to great a
>   chardge.
> And some I see agayne sytt still and say but small
> That can do ten tymes more than they that say they can do all.   10
> Whose goodlye gyftes are suche, the more they understand,
> The more they seeke to learne and know and take lesse chardge in
>   hand.
> And to declare more playne, the tyme flyttes not so fast
> But I can beare right well in mynd the song now sung and past.
> The auctour whearof cam, wrapt in a craftye cloke,   15
> In will to force a flamyng fyre wheare he could rayse no smoke.
> If powre and will had mett, as it appeareth playne,
> The truth nor right had tane no place, their vertues had bene
>   vayne.
> So that you may perceave, and I may saflye see,
> The innocent that giltlesse is condempned sholde have be.   20
> Muche lyke untruth to this the storye doth declare,
> Wheare th'elders layd to Susans chardge meete matter to
>   compare.
> They did her both accuse and eke condempne her to,
> And yet no reason, right, nor truthe did lead them so to do.
> And she thus judged to dye, toward her death went forthe   25

Fraughted with faith a pacient pace, taking her wrong in worthe.
　But he that dothe defend all those that in hym trust,
Did raise a Childe for her defence to shyeld her from th'unjust.
　And Danyell chosen was then of this wrong to weete
How, in what place, and eke with whome she did this cryme
　commytt.   30
　He caused the Elders part the one from th'others sight,
And did examyne one by one and chardged them bothe say right.
　'Undra a Mulberye trye it was', fyrst sayd the one;
The next namde a pomegranate trye, whereby the truth was
　knowne.
　Than Susan was dischardged, and they condempned to dye,   35
As right requeares and they deserve, that framde so fowll a lye.
　And he that her preserved, and lett them of their lust,
Hath me defendyd hetherto, and will do still I trust.

The companion-piece is spoken as if by a woman, and the first
impression is of a breath of fresh air after the self-enclosed obsession
of the previous poem. This speaker is also a watcher, and references
to seeing are found in lines 2, 3, 5, 8, 9 and 19, and in the summary of
the story of Susanna and the Elders in line 31. 'Gyrrt in [her]
giltlesse gowne' (1), she sits sewing and watching among the row of
ladies whom the previous speaker observed when 'Wrapt in [his]
carelesse cloke'. And what she sees is the self-interested bias
underlying his purported objectivity. Her eyes, she claims, are truly
'indifferent' (5), disinterested; and they enable her to note the
discrepancy between male boasting and male performance. Some
men boldly offer to steer a storm-tossed ship (a metaphor in the
Petrarchan tradition for the lover's state) when they would be hard
pressed to control a barge; others say little, yet 'can do ten tymes
more than they that say they can do all' (10).

The speaker recalls a recent occasion when the 'auctour' (15) of
the previous poem, 'the song now sung and past' (14), made sexual
advances unsuccessfully to a certain lady. He was wrapped not in a
careless but in a crafty cloak (15); he wanted 'to force a flamyng
fyre', but in fact 'could rayse no smoke' (16). 'If powre and will had
mett' (17) he would have raped or at least seduced her, but, whether
through her resistance or his impotence, he did not succeed. It is this
frustration of his will that motivated the first poem's false accusations; and she goes on to draw a parallel with the story of Susanna.
The parallel is of course an extremely unflattering one to the first
poem's speaker, because it puts her in the position of the virtuous

object of desire and him in that of the old, frustrated voyeur; it may also imply that she is married, so that his attempt on her virtue was still more dishonourable. His male gaze is not just less objective than it seems, it is also a substitute for the sexual goal he is unable to obtain – scopophilia in the sense of Freud's *Three Essays*. And then the Scriptural story implies a transcendent watcher who will defend women against the false accusations of men. The woman's superiority is confirmed in the way she ends by talking about God, whereas the man ended by talking about women.

Finally, we may deduce, if we choose, that the woman whom the speaker of the first poem attempted to seduce is the speaker of the second. If so, her claim to be seeing with impartial eyes and revealing the truth that he has cloaked can equally be seen as self-interested. The guiltless gown may be as much a means of concealment as the careless cloak; and only God, the concealed watcher of human hearts, knows the truth of the matter. In these poems, unlike *A Pistel of Susan*, the reader is not invited to share God's gaze.

The next example also belongs to the sixteenth century, and is intended to illustrate in its most straightforward form the representation of the male gaze as predatory. I know of no extended medieval treatment that shows this predatoriness with comparable clarity; hence my choice of an extract from Book VI, Canto viii, of Spenser's *Faerie Queene*, which will, I hope, aid in the interpretation of the less clear-cut treatments to be encountered in medieval narratives. While rescuing a baby from a bear, Sir Calepine has had the misfortune to lose his lady Serena in the forest; and this extract recounts an unpleasant experience that Serena undergoes when she is wandering helplessly through the wilderness and is captured by a tribe of cannibals who follow no trade but 'on the labours of poore men to feed'.

36 Thereto they vsde one most accursed order,
   To eate the flesh of men, whom they mote fynde,
   And straungers to deuoure, which on their border
   Were brought by errour, or by wreckfull wynde.
   A monstrous cruelty gainst course of kynde.
   They towards euening wandring euery way,
   To seeke for booty, came by fortune blynde,
   Whereas this Lady, like a sheepe astray,
  Now drowned in the depth of sleepe all fearelesse lay.

37   Soone as they spied her, Lord what gladfull glee
        They made amongst them selues; but when her face
        Like the faire yuory shining they did see,
        Each gan his fellow solace and embrace,
        For ioy of such good hap by heauenly grace.
        Then gan they to deuize what course to take:
        Whether to slay her there vpon the place,
        Or suffer her out of her sleepe to wake,
     And then her eate attonce; or many meales to make.

38   The best aduizement was of bad, to let her
        Sleepe out her fill, without encomberment:
        For sleepe they sayd would make her battill better.
        Then when she wakt, they all gaue one consent,
        That since by grace of God she there was sent,
        Vnto their God they would her sacrifize,
        Whose share, her guiltlesse bloud they would present,
        But of her dainty flesh they did deuize
     To make a common feast, and feed with gurmandize.

39   So round about her they them selues did place
        Vpon the grasse, and diuersely dispose,
        As each thought best to spend the lingring space.
        Some with their eyes the daintest morsels chose;
        Some praise her paps, some praise her lips and nose;
        Some whet their kniues, and strip their elboes bare:
        The Priest him selfe a garland doth compose
        Of finest flowres, and with full busie care
     His bloudy vessels wash, and holy fire prepare.

Serena wakes and vainly cries aloud for help; the cannibals remove her jewels and clothes, and gaze on her nakedness 'with lustfull fantasyes'.

42   Her yuorie necke, her alablaster brest,
        Her paps, which like white silken pillowes were,
        For loue in soft delight thereon to rest;
        Her tender sides, her bellie white and clere,
        Which like an Altar did it selfe vprere,
        To offer sacrifice diuine thereon;
        Her goodly thighes, whose glorie did appeare
        Like a triumphall Arch, and thereupon
     The spoiles of Princes hang'd, which were in battel won.

43   Those daintie parts, the dearlings of delight,
        Which mote not be prophan'd of common eyes,
     Those villeins vew'd with loose lasciuious sight,

And closely tempted with their craftie spyes;
And some of them gan mongst them selues deuize,
Thereof by force to take their beastly pleasure.
But them the Priest rebuking, did aduize
To dare not to pollute so sacred threasure,
Vow'd to the gods: religion held euen theeues in measure.

As Theresa Krier's recent work has shown, Spenser is intensely interested in watching.[20] When we first encounter Serena, in Canto iii, she is lying embraced by Sir Calepine in a 'couert shade' 'far from enuious eyes' (stanza 20). It is a paradox of language that any such mention of the absence of watchers alerts us to the possibility of their presence; and in this case, as we read the words, we are made aware of the imaginative intrusion of our eyes, and of course of Spenser's, and indeed those of Sir Calidore, who embarrasses the couple and himself by accidentally discovering them making love. In this later adventure in Canto viii, Spenser offers a lively analysis of the male gaze as defined by John Berger. The gazers are indeed male; they are subjects and Serena merely their female object – she is asleep when they start looking at her. Their cannibalism brings out the voracious nature of the looks they direct upon her 'dainty flesh' (38:8); they literally wish to devour her, and 'Some with their eyes the daintest morsels chose' (39:4).

Behind such a scene lies a long tradition of poetry in which a male subject describes his lady's beauty by dividing her into parts and praising each separately. The technique of *effictio* or minute enumerative description, one of the principal means of amplification taught by the medieval *artes poeticae*, inevitably produces effects of this kind when applied to the female body. To take one example, in the *Poetria nova* of Geoffroi de Vinsauf, a thirteenth-century rhetorical manual, *descriptio* is illustrated as follows:

Let the compass of Nature first fashion a sphere for her head; let the colour of gold give a glow to her hair, and lilies bloom high on her brow. Let her eyebrows resemble in dark beauty the blackberry, and a lovely and milk-white path separate their twin arches. Let her nose be straight, of moderate length, not too long nor too short for perfection. Let her eyes, those watch-fires of her brow, be radiant with emerald light, or with the brightness of stars. Let her countenance emulate dawn: not red, nor yet white – but at once neither of those colours and both. Let her mouth be bright, small in shape – as it were, a half-circle. Let her lips be rounded and full, but moderately so; let them glow, aflame, but with gentle fire. Let her teeth be snowy, regular, all of one size, and her breath like the fragrance of incense . . .[21]

The specimen description continues through another twenty lines of Latin verse, eventually arriving at the lady's foot. The effect is precisely that of fetishization: 'to place the woman outside the (narrative) flow of action and event, flatten the verisimilitude of the representation of woman, and turn her into an icon'.[22] No speaker is defined, but a male subject is clearly implied, as performer of the activities of looking, dividing, assessing and comparing. On her more elevated level, this nameless lady is as much a passive object of delectation as the photographic models whose nude bodies, frequently divided and depersonalized – here a breast and there a buttock – decorate the pages of *Playboy* or *Penthouse*.

It must not be supposed, however, that *effictio* requires a male gaze directed upon a passive female object;[23] on the contrary, the gender roles may be reversed even in medieval romances. The matter is sufficiently important to warrant a digression. We have seen how Lavine gazes at Eneas and is wounded through her eyes, but a more striking instance occurs in the thirteenth-century prose *Lancelot*, which eventually became part of the Vulgate Cycle, 'the most widely read and the most influential group of Arthurian prose romances'.[24] Here the first *effictio* (an extremely full one) is not of Guenevere but of the young Lancelot. It passes systematically from face through neck, shoulders and chest. Of this last the storyteller remarks,

an lui ne trova onques nus hom plus que reprandre, ainz disoient tuit cil qui lo devisoient que s'i fust un po mains garniz de piz, plus an fust atalantables et plaisanz. Mais puis avint que cele qui desor toz autres lo devisa, ce fu la vaillanz reine Guenievre, dist que Dex ne li avoit pas doné piz a outraige, de grant ne de gros ne d'espesseté qui i fust, car autresin estoit granz li cuers en son endroit, si covenist que il crevast par estovoir, s'il n'eüst tel estage o il se reposast a sa mesure. 'Ne se ge fusse, fist ele, Dex, ja an Lancelot ne meïsse ne plus ne mains.'

that was the one thing about him that anyone ever found to criticize, and everyone who observed him said that if he had had a little less chest, he would have been more pleasing and attractive. Later on, though, the person who observed him more closely than anyone – that is, the excellent Queen Guinevere – said that God had not given him too much chest, however big or deep or broad it was, for his heart was just as big, proportionately, and it would surely have burst, if it had not had a space that size to reside in. 'And if I were God,' she said, 'I should have made Lancelot just as he is.'[25]

By now it has become clear that the observer implied by the *effictio* is Guenevere herself, and that she is envisaged as subject, not object, and as exercising precisely that analytic mastery usually attributed to the 'male gaze'. Here it is the male body that is fetishized; and while Guenevere's high rank no doubt makes it easier for her to be represented as the bearer of the gaze, she is by no means the only female gazer in the romance. Though the prose *Lancelot* as a whole is dominated by its hero's fetishization of Guenevere as *the* woman, the one being who can make good the lack from which he suffers, there are powerful countercurrents. Among other scenes in which Lancelot is the object of female looks is one where the Lady of Malohaut gazes at him while he is asleep and is with difficulty restrained from kissing him, arguing that 'one could not have shame from something one did for such a valorous man' (p. 254).

Many medieval poets followed the instructions of the *artes poeticae*, and the method passed down to Petrarch and his Renaissance followers – indeed, by those unfamiliar with its medieval background it has often been thought distinctively Petrarchan. Nancy Vickers writes of the *Rime sparse*,

given an entire volume devoted to a single lady, the absence of a coherent, comprehensive portrait is significant. Laura is always presented as a part or parts of a woman ... Her textures are those of metals and stones; her image is that of a collection of exquisitely beautiful disassociated objects.[26]

The same effect is produced by the passage from Geoffroi quoted above, though with the important difference that in the *Rime sparse* and the many lyric sequences derived from it the speaker is more sharply defined as a specific male subject, with whose emotional needs the reader is encouraged to identify. In Spenser's Serena episode the division of the male subject into a swarm of savages, and the identification of that subject's desire as not just carnal but cannibalistic, produce a distancing and sharply diagnostic effect. (The voracity underlying the *effictio* of a woman is already implied in the *Poetria nova*: Geoffroi introduces his specimen description by explaining that its elaboration serves to make it *cibus* ... *et plena refectio mentis* [the food and ample refreshment of the mind]).[27] The 'religion of love' now appears as a savage cult, which may restrain gross acts of prying into 'Those daintie parts ... Which mote not be prophan'd of common eyes' (43:1–2), but which still has as its goal the literal division of the victim's body. The suspense in which the

'saluage nation' (35:2) halt their mutual congratulations to debate
whether to eat Serena immediately, to let her continue sleeping and
then consume her in a single feast, 'or many meales to make' (37:9),
is gruesomely comic, as is their final prudent decision to let her sleep
longer and thus grow fatter. Their imaginative dividing of her body
into its 'daintest morsels' for separate praise in stanza 39 casts them
precisely as poetic 'blazoners'; and this stanza is then paralleled in
stanza 42, where Serena's bodily parts are commodified with similes
converting them into luxury goods. And the whole passage is
pervaded with gloating looks that turn a woman into a carcase by
anticipation.

What is *our* role in such a scene? Do we share in the cannibalistic
gaze even as it is being wittily diagnosed, or can we somehow
respond to it non-voyeuristically? Such questions will arise recurrently as we examine medieval narratives; they do not necessarily
have single and simple answers, for a text may allow for a variety of
subject-positions (this is in the very nature of fantasy and thus of
fiction, and no text can *compel* the reader to adopt a single role), and
'we' do not compose a monolithic body of readers. Among the
pleasures available to the predominantly male audience of 'slasher
films', it has been suggested, may be 'the pleasure of identifying with
helplessness';[28] and something comparable may be true for the
readers even of narratives that press the objectivization and fetishization of female characters to an extreme.

My last example may seem out of place, because it is from a novel
of the 1980s, *Rates of Exchange* by Malcolm Bradbury; yet it throws
interesting light, from an unexpected angle, on some of the questions
raised by looking and its implications in medieval narratives. Like
not a few other contemporary novels, *Rates of Exchange*, besides
telling a story, is designed to make us think about narrative and its
conventions, about the nature of fiction, and about language. In
principle, therefore, it should be relevant to fictional narratives of
periods other than its own. Its story concerns Dr Petworth, an
academic sent by the British Council on a lecture tour to an
imaginary Eastern European country, one where, despite the social-
ist régime (the novel is set in 1981), 'heavy nineteenth-century
bourgeois realist rain' tends to fall incessantly (109).[29] Petworth, an
expert on linguistics, is visiting Mitteleuropa, a part of the world
where real history has happened. In this strange unEnglish setting
Petworth has assigned as his official guide an attractive young

woman, Mari Lubijova. In the scene with which I am concerned, to Petworth's surprise, delight and embarrassment, Mari joins him in his hotel room, and the following conversation takes place.

'And you know those who watch us and listen to us, they would like us to make some love.'

'What do you mean?' asks Petworth.

'Oh, please, you know them, they are always there,' says Mari, 'But I do not think it is their business. I think we disappoint them, yes?'

'Yes,' says Petworth.

'But I cannot go now,' says Mari. 'I think we turn out the light and be together very quiet for a bit. And if we say nothing, no one can tell anything of us.'

'Who would tell?' asks Petworth.

'Of course,' says Mari, 'Someone is always telling of you and me. So we are quiet together, and we make no words.'

Outside the window there is the noise of the rushing river, and there is a scent of trees in the air. But it is totally quiet and entirely dark in the little bedroom, and there is absolutely nothing to hear or see. A clock ticks, but one cannot tell how much time is passing; certainly it is some time later when Mari, in the dark, says:

'Comrade Petwurt, now I go. You must sleep very nicely, don't forget you must make an early wake, to go on that train to Nogod. Thank you for the drink, thank you to be with me, thank you to be quiet. And perhaps even we did make some love, if not in the usual way.'

'Yes,' says Petworth.

'But there is nothing to know, nothing to tell,' says Mari.

'Someone is always telling of you and me.' In one sense, that refers to the spies, the informers, members of the secret police, who we may imagine are always present, reporting to the authorities on the behaviour of the visiting lecturer and his guide. But in another sense, that someone who is always telling is the novelist; and 'those who watch us and listen to us' are also in one sense spies and in another ourselves, the novel's readers. This may seem a more sophisticated piece of narrative than Walther von der Vogelweide's lyric, because it does not simply embody the paradox of conceal-ment and disclosure; it makes one of the characters seem to be conscious of the paradox, and it incorporates the morally ambigu-ous roles of author and reader, teller and watcher, into the fiction. A perspective opens up in which the world of every novel that deals with intimate relations is a kind of police state, where the most private activities are conducted under the eyes and cameras of hidden watchers. As D. A. Miller remarks, 'Whenever the novel censures policing power, it has already reinvented it, in the *very practice of novelistic representation*.'[30] He is referring to the French nineteenth-century novel, but his statement seems equally true of every kind of fictional narrative that offers a public representation of private activities. How can those watchers be overcome? Only by the extreme and self-defeating means adopted in the second half of this passage. The privacy of the space shared by Petworth and Mari is ensured by complete darkness and silence, so that 'there is absolutely nothing to hear or see'. Even the passage of time is immeasurable, and the outcome is that 'there is nothing to know' and therefore 'nothing to tell'. If the whole novel were like this, its narrative element would disappear completely. In the scene under discussion, the readers may have become sufficiently aroused to be eager for a climax to occur, but the characters cheat them: we do not know whether they make love or not. Yet the novelist's reticence is suggestive: 'perhaps even we did make some love, *if not in the usual way*'. The text erotically teases and seduces its readers, inciting them to become voyeurs once more, and to imagine for themselves exactly what Mari and Petworth did in the darkened space and unmeasured time. Bradbury is not just playing a joke at our expense; he is also mocking the exchange and slippage of meaning between textuality and sexuality that plays such a prominent part in some late-twentieth-century discussions of literature. (This book, for example.) Bradbury's novel is called *Rates of Exchange*, and this is one of the kinds of exchange, between words and bodies, that it deals with.

Late-twentieth-century novelists are notoriously self-conscious about themselves as narrators and about their audiences as readers; but some medieval poets, for whom oral delivery was still a normal situation, were perhaps even more so. And that self-consciousness or reflexivity is especially likely to emerge when, as in the scene from *Rates of Exchange*, their subject is sexual love. As we shall find in the following chapters, medieval storytellers are no less sophisticated than twentieth-century novelists in their dealings with looking and listening, secrecy and privacy.

CHAPTER 3

The Tristan story

The most obvious motive for both secrecy and spying in medieval romance is an adulterous love-affair; and the first and most influential of the great medieval stories of adulterous love is that of Tristan and Iseult, the 'one great European myth of adultery',[1] which in turn generated, by imitation and reaction, further stories of adulterous triangles, such as the *Cligés* of Chrétien, his *Lancelot*, and the many other versions of the story of Lancelot and Guenevere that succeeded it. The story of Tristan's love-affair with Iseult, the wife of his uncle and liege lord King Mark, probably of Celtic origin, emerges in French in the twelfth century, and survives in several different versions. The most famous in its own time was the Anglo-Norman poem by Thomas, but of this we have only a number of fragments; this version as a whole has to be reconstructed from the thirteenth-century texts that it influenced, including Gottfried von Strassburg's *Tristan* in Middle High German and Brother Robert's *Tristrams saga* in Old Norse. More useful for my purposes is the version of Beroul: representing a less courtly tradition than that of Thomas, and surviving only in a single incomplete manuscript, it nevertheless contains a substantial continuous section of the narrative, sufficient to permit exploration of its marked focus on watching and being watched.

Beroul's poem presents numerous scholarly and critical problems. It is not clear whether 'Beroul', about whom nothing is otherwise known, was indeed a single poet. The date of composition is uncertain, though the 1190s (up to a century earlier than the manuscript) are most widely accepted. The poem's milieu is also unclear, and it has been questioned whether it is a literate composition rather than a transcription of an orally composed narrative. One way of interpreting the apparent narrative inconsistencies would be to suppose that the manuscript contains material for

alternative performances on different occasions. Certainly Beroul's
Tristan as it stands is a text of striking generic looseness: we expect
medieval genres to be related to social class, but here, within a
love-story set among the nobility, we find strikingly divergent
material, for instance in the scene in which Tristan, disguised as a
leper and unrecognized by King Mark, tells the king that he caught
his 'ugly sores' from love-making with a lady whose husband had
leprosy (3761–73). One scholar has written of this scene that it
'breaks every convention of courtly narrative';[2] but the conventions
may not yet have existed in Beroul's time and milieu. Narrative
genres were in flux in the twelfth-century vernaculars, and what we
confidently call 'courtly romance' may not yet have crystallized as a
recognizable genre. For Beroul Tristan's disguises as leper and
beggar do not derogate from his rank (unlike the hero's willingness
to ride in a cart in Chrétien's *Lancelot*); nor does his prowess with the
unknightly bow. The cohesiveness of the narrative is also open to
question, especially in the episodes concerning Mark's horse's ears
(1306–50) and Tristan's dog (1437–636). This text does not lend
itself to interpretation according to classical criteria for well-formed
narrative; on the other hand, its narrative syntax is no more peculiar
than that of Joyce or Lawrence, not to mention William Burroughs
or Kurt Vonnegut, Thomas Pynchon or Alasdair Gray. Those
familiar with the methods of twentieth-century narrative will probably have little difficulty with it.

Whatever the problems of interpretation, there can be no doubt
that voyeurism plays a major part in the story Beroul tells. It has to
do so, for the poem concerns a prolonged illicit love-affair, secret not
just because lovers prefer privacy but for reasons connected with
feudal law. It is vitally important first that the affair should not
become known to Iseult's husband and Tristan's uncle, King Mark;
and then that, whatever Mark's private suspicions, it should not
become public knowledge and thus force him into public action
against his wife and nephew. Many incidents concern attempts by
Mark and his informants literally to *see* whether Tristan and Iseult
are committing adultery, dramas devised to catch them in the act,
because merely circumstantial evidence of adultery would not be
legally sufficient.[3] Such dramas form a major part of Beroul's
story-material.

The first surviving scene offers a clear illustration. Mark's
suspicions have been aroused by a group of his barons, who have

their own reasons for wanting Tristan, their rival for the king's paternal favour, to be disgraced; and Tristan has been banished from the court but has continued to have secret meetings with Iseult, arranged by throwing twigs into a stream as messages. A dwarf has told Mark about this, and has advised the king to conceal himself in a tree near the stream, so that he can overhear the lovers' conversation. The image of the king as voyeur, hiding in the tree, secretly spying on the lovers' secret behaviour, is a memorable one, often represented in medieval art;[4] it captures the essence of a story in which shameful suspense is the constant accompaniment of romantic love. But the incident as recounted by Beroul is more complicated than that. Mark is not an unseen spy, because, although it is night-time, Tristan sees by moonlight his reflection in the stream; then Iseult sees it too; and the two lovers play out for Mark's benefit a scene intended to deceive him as to their relationship. Iseult rebukes Tristan for summoning her there, saying that it will only encourage Mark to believe those villains who allege that they love each other wickedly, when really she treats Tristan kindly only because he is her husband's nephew. What she says conveys to Tristan that she too realizes that Mark is spying on them, and he answers in the same way:

> Qar j'ai tel duel c'onques le roi
> Out mal pensé de vos vers moi
> Qu'il n'i a el fors que je meure...
>
> Ne deüst pas mis oncles chiers
> De moi croire ses losengiers –
> Sovent en ai mon cuer irié!   (109–11, 143–5)

for I am so saddened to think that the king ever thought badly of you on account of me, that there is nothing left for me to do but die! ... My dear uncle should not have believed what his informers have said about me! I am constantly enraged by it!

He asks Iseult to speak well of him to Mark. That would be a great mistake, she answers, given Mark's existing suspicions, and she makes to leave, saying,

> Grant poor ai que aucun home
> Ne nos ait ci veü venir.
> S'un mot en puet li rois oïr
> Que nos fuson ça asenblé,
> Il me feroit ardoir en ré.   (188–92)

I greatly fear that someone may have seen us come here. If the king heard even a hint that we were together here, he would have me burned on a pyre.

Tristan calls her back, begging her to advise him: should he ask the king to release him from his service, so that he could go elsewhere and end the unpleasant situation? Heavens, no, exclaims Iseult; that would just make Mark certain that Tristan was disloyal to him! She leaves, and Tristan ostentatiously soliloquizes about his misfortune, unjustly suspected of a liaison he would never dream of entering into. Then he too leaves; and Mark is left to climb down from his tree, convinced that the dwarf has misled him with his 'outrageous rumors' (306), and determined to make peace with Tristan and invite him once more to sleep in his private apartment.

In this scene Mark is a concealed voyeur, but so are we, spying on him spying on the lovers; and the fact that the story is *about* an act of voyeurism surely encourages us to become aware that we too are voyeurs, only more sharp-eyed ones than the king. We share the indignity of his position, knowing what the lovers are saying only because we too are spies; but at the same time we are admitted by Beroul into the lovers' knowledge of Mark's presence and into their motives for saying what they do. This means that we are morally implicated too. The deception the lovers practise on the king is acceptable only if *we* wish it to be so. And I think we do: we wish Mark to be deceived, we delight in the ingenuity with which he is manipulated, and we are thus manipulated ourselves into sharing the extraordinary view expressed by Brangain, Iseult's maid, in the following scene, that the deceit's success is a miracle wrought by God himself for the benefit of 'buen et loial' lovers (380)! Who is watching whom? Who is manipulated by whom? The apparent naïveté and inconsistency of Beroul's storytelling may well have the effect of supreme sophistication for readers or listeners who are conscious of their own morally questionable role. At every point a supposedly impregnable secrecy is penetrated and exposed: Mark watches the lovers; the lovers watch him watching them; we watch them watching him watching them; and Beroul, whose motives are truly secret (at least to us, eight centuries later – but perhaps they always have been), watches us, exposing the disreputable motives of voyeurs who interpret what they see in accordance with their own preconceptions, while unaware until too late that our own interpretation is shaped by the poet's cunning.

The following scene reveals yet another level of voyeurism. Iseult goes to the *chanbre* she shares with her husband and confides to Brangain what has just happened. But Mark now joins them, and Iseult tells him what she and Tristan said to each other by the stream, and then feigns surprise when Mark confesses to overhearing it. Mark sends Brangain to find Tristan; she pretends reluctance, claiming that Tristan hates her, and Beroul comments, implicitly urging us to nod a delighted assent to her deceptiveness,

> Oiez que dit la tricherresse!
> Molt fist que bone lecherresse;
> Lores gaboit a esscïent
> Et se plaignoit de mal talent. (519–22)

Listen to the cunning woman! She was the perfect deceiver. She intentionally lied and complained about his resentment.

But as soon as Brangain leaves the room, Beroul reveals that Tristan has been hidden just outside, secretly listening to the conversation with the king.

> Brengain a par les braz saisie,
> Acole la, Deu en mercie:
> ... [line missing]
> D'estre o Yseut a son plaisir. (531–4)

He seized Brangain by the arm, embraced her, and gave thanks to God [that the king was going to allow him] to be with Iseut whenever he wished.

After a suitable delay Tristan and Brangain return, and Mark forgives Tristan and gives him permission once more to visit his private apartment, thus making it easier for the adulterous relationship to continue. Once again, we have become implicated as watchers and listeners to what is supposedly secret. The concealment on which the story depends is possible, it should be noted, because of the existence of (supposedly) private *places*: the pine tree overlooking the stream, and especially the king's private apartment, the *chanbre*, containing the bed where he sleeps with Iseult. As was noted in Chapter 1, private bedrooms were possessed in the early Middle Ages only by those of the highest rank, and the room and the bed have a powerful emotional and symbolic charge, embodying simultaneously King Mark's public status and his most intimate being. It is from this *chanbre painte* (549) (room with painted hangings) that Tristan is temporarily banished, here that he sleeps in a bed at the foot of the king's, and here too that he abuses his loyalty to his uncle and feudal lord by sleeping with Iseult in Mark's bed whenever he can.

Privacy and enclosure are relative rather than absolute. The royal court or palace is enclosed, and it is a place of comfort and safety, good food and drink and fine clothes, by contrast with the hovels where the lepers live, and still more with the forest of Morrois, to which the lovers flee from Mark's anger. The public opening of the palace doors signifies hospitality, as when Iseult is temporarily restored to Mark:

> Onques porte n'i fu veee:
> Qui vout entrer si pout mengier,
> Onc a nul n'i fist on dangier.   (3000–2)

No door was closed to anyone; all who wanted to come in were fed, and no one was refused.

The court is essentially a place of company; its ruler, in his public role, is always 'surrounded by a great crowd' (2766). For this very reason, the court is no place for private life, and especially for private experience at its most intense, in the form of love. Thus love must at times be reduced to a secret code, which enemies strive to interpret. Beroul generalizes:

> Ha, Dex! Qui puet amor tenir
> Un an ou deus sanz descovrir?
> Car amors ne se puet celer:
> Sovent cline l'un vers son per,
> Sovent vienent a parlement,
> Et a celé et voiant gent.   (573–8)

Oh, God! Who could love for a year or two and still keep it secret? For love cannot be hidden: often one lover nods to the other; they often meet to speak together, both in private and in public.

Within the court, the royal *chanbre* is distinguished from the hall (680, *sale*), where the household in general sleep, and where public business is transacted: at one point, we are told,

> Et li rois Marc en son palais
> O ses barons tenoit ses plaiz;
> Des barons ert plaine la sale.   (1863–5)

King Mark was holding court in his palace with his barons; the hall was filled with his men.

The *chanbre*, by contrast, is an area of royal privilege and intimacy shared only with a favoured few. It may stand by metonymy for the whole sphere of royal or courtly status and civilization, at the opposite extreme from the forest: in Morrois, Tristan reproaches himself for Iseult's sufferings, referring to

> la grant soufraite
> Que vos soufrez et avez faite
> Toz dis, por moi, par desertine.
> Por moi perdez non de roïne.
> Estre peüses a anor
> En tes chanbres, o ton seignor . . .   (2253–8)

the deprivation that you endure and have endured for a long time, on my account, in the wilderness. Because of me, you have lost the title 'Queen.' You could have lived a life of honor in your royal chambers with your lord . . .

And what of the wilderness, the forest? This is where the lovers take refuge; it is outside civilization's walls, yet it is also a place of privacy – greater privacy than the *chanbre*, inhabited as it is by watchers such as the dwarf Frocin and potential watchers such as Iseult's squire Perinis. It is described paradoxically as being as safe as a walled castle (1278, *chastel o mur*), yet it is repeatedly associated with hardship and with the lack of civilized food: 'Il n'avoient ne lait ne sel / A cele foiz a lor ostel' (1297–8) [They had neither milk nor salt in their lodging]. At times the lovers are even short of bread (1425, 1769); when they are on the move, they have no fire for cooking; and when Tristan says he would rather 'live on herbs and acorns' with Iseult than possess the richest kingdom (1404–6), he is speaking not rhetorically but literally. In romantic accounts of the Tristan story, such as that of Denis de Rougemont[5] (based not on any authentic medieval text, but on Bédier's nineteenth-century reconstruction, which introduces it as 'a high tale of love and of death'),[6] love in its transcendence is associated with the death-wish; in Beroul it is associated rather with the hardship of living rough, by contrast with the material comfort of the court and especially of the *chanbre*. Within the forest, Tristan makes a bower, a *loge* or *fullie* (1290–1), which is no more than a parody of the bedchamber that is the proper setting for those of noble birth; and when the effect of the love-potion wears off, he declares,

> Et poise moi de la roïne,
> Que je doins loge por cortine.

> En bois est, et si peüst estre
> En beles chanbres, o son estre,
> Portendues de dras de soie.   (2179–83)

And I am distressed for the queen, to whom I gave a hut instead of a curtained chamber. She lives in the forest, when she could be in beautiful rooms decorated with silk, in the company of her attendants.

Beroul's poem belongs to a world of scarcity, and its treatment of love is ballasted throughout with material considerations; love's effect is to make the lovers' flesh pale and weak (2132), not because love is a sickness but because it brings harsh exile and malnutrition. The most touching evidence of love's power is given by the detail that, when the forester sees the two lying asleep, their bodies apart, Iseult has become so thin that her gold wedding ring set with emeralds is almost slipping off her finger; and thus when Mark in turn comes to spy on them he can remove the ring without waking her and replace it with his own.

Both at court and in the forest, the story is full of further acts of voyeurism. Three of the king's barons – 'Ainz ne veïstes plus felons' [never have you seen such evil men] (582), says Beroul – often see the lovers lying together naked in King Mark's bed (594). The dwarf Frocin peers through the window at night when Mark is absent; it is completely dark, 'Cirge ne lanpë alumez' [no candle or lamp lit] (726), just as in the scene from Bradbury's *Rates of Exchange*; but by moonlight he watches Tristan and Iseult making love, and he quivers with joy at what he sees (738, 'De joie en trenble'). Beroul, with the partisanship that pervades his telling of the story, encourages us to hate and despise the dwarf; but in this scene Frocin's is the only consciousness opened towards us, and it is inevitable that we should at least temporarily share this contemptible figure's point of view and participate in his voyeuristic pleasure. It is impossible to tell whether the quivering of Frocin's body is provoked by joy at the thought of having trapped the lovers or by a more directly sexual thrill.

Sometimes we as readers or listeners seem to be invited to participate in a male gaze directed specifically at Iseult. When she has been condemned to death and is being led to be burnt, Beroul pauses to describe her appearance:

> En un bliaut de paile bis
> Estoit la dame estroit vestue
> E d'un fil d'or menu cosue.

> Si chevel hurtent a ses piez,
> D'un filet d'or les ot trechiez.
> Qui voit son cors et sa fachon,
> Trop par avroit le cuer felon
> Qui n'en avroit de lié pitié.
> Molt sont li braz estroit lïé. (1146–54)

The lady was dressed in a fitted tunic of dark silk, finely stitched with gold thread. Her hair reached to her feet and was held by a gold net. Anyone who saw her face and figure would have to have a very cruel heart not to feel pity for her. Her arms were tied very tightly.

This brief *effictio* clearly implies someone looking, and in doing so focusing on Iseult's physical beauty, 'son cors et sa fachon' – literally, her body and her countenance. Her figure is set off to advantage by her closely-fitting tunic, and the theme of the whole passage is of a female body displayed and bound: not just her tightly bound arms, but the gold thread that binds her silk tunic so revealingly to her body, and the gold net that confines her hair. Any reader who declined the invitation offered by *Qui voit* to turn her into an object of sight (as perhaps a female reader might) would find a masochistic subject-position the only alternative. The element of display is striking; Iseult's role here is to be offered to public gaze within the fiction as a female sacrifice to a justice that belongs to the masculine realm. There is a similar element of exhibitionism in the later ceremonies in which she is formally returned to Mark, when she swears the ambiguous oath exculpating herself of adultery with Tristan; and indeed it will always tend to be so in medieval scenes of this kind, for a woman has no intrinsic public status, and her appearance in a public setting will expose her to male gazes that are charged with gender-difference. The poet is invariably complicit with this non-innocent gazing; in the return scene, for example, he describes how Dinas helps Iseult off with her cloak:

> Ele out vestu une tunique
> Desus un grant bliaut de soie.
> De son mantel que vos diroie?
> Ainz l'ermite, qui l'achata,
> Le riche fuer ne regreta.
> Riche ert la robe et gent le cors:
> Les eulz out vers, les cheveus sors.
> Li seneschaus o lié s'envoise. (2882–9)

She was wearing a tunic over a silk chemise. What can I tell you of her mantle? The hermit who bought it never regretted the great cost! The robe was rich, and her body was beautiful. Her eyes were green, her hair golden. The seneschal enjoyed her company.

When Tristan takes his leave, Iseult blushes, for 'Vergoigne avoit por l'asenblee' [she was embarrassed because of the crowd] (2916). We cannot forget that the poet and ourselves are among that crowd.

More commonly, though, where looking occurs on non-ceremonial occasions, its object is not Iseult alone but the lovers as a pair. A striking example is the later scene in which the lovers are exiled in the forest, and, after Tristan returns from hunting for their food, they lie down together in their *loge*, and Tristan places his sword between them. They are half-clothed, and Beroul explicitly invites us to become imaginative voyeurs: 'Oez com il se sont couchiez' [Notice how they were lying] (1816), he says, and he gives a detailed description of their postures:

> Desoz le col Tristran a mis
> Son braz, et l'autre, ce m'est vis,
> Li out par dedesus geté;
> Estroitment l'ot acolé,
> Et il la rot de ses braz çainte.
> Lor amistié ne fu pas fainte.
> Les bouches furent pres asises,
> Et neporquant si ot devises
> Que n'asenbloient pas ensenble.
> Vent ne cort ne fuelle ne trenble.
> Uns rais decent desor la face
> Yseut, que plus reluist que glace.   (1817–28)

She had put one arm under Tristran's neck, and had thrown the other one, I believe, across his body; she was embracing him closely, and he also had his arms tightly around her. Their love was not feigned! Their mouths were close together, and yet they were lying in such a way that their bodies were not touching. No breeze was blowing, nor any leaf stirring. A ray of sunshine fell on Iseut's face, which shone more brightly than glass.

The means used to create this moment of enchantment are extremely complex. As readers,[7] we are held at a distance from the text that precisely corresponds to voyeurism, inhabiting a space separate from that of the fictional characters, as a cinema audience, unlike one in the theatre, occupies a space segregated from the performance it is witnessing. As Christian Metz has written,

If it is true of all desire that it depends on the infinite pursuit of its absent object, voyeuristic desire ... is the only desire whose principle of distance symbolically and spatially evokes this fundamental rent.

The situation recalls the primal scene, and in that way too is familiar to us as that of cinematic spectatorship:

For its spectator the film unfolds in that simultaneously very close and definitively inaccessible 'elsewhere' in which the child *sees* the amorous play of the parental couple, who are similarly ignorant of it and leave it alone, a pure onlooker whose participation is inconceivable.[8]

Our participation is inconceivable, yet it is as though our very absence is embodied in the scene: the lack of breeze is because we are holding our breaths, the stillness of the leaves reflects our stillness, the ray of sunshine is our glance cast on the sleeping Iseult. And our distance is also part of the scene, reflected in the distance that separates the lovers' mouths and bodies. The look we are invited to cast is by no means the dominating 'male gaze', nor even the crudely lascivious voyeurism of Frocin: when he witnesses Tristan and Iseult's love-making, 'de joie en trenble', but here 'Vent ne cort ne fuelle ne trenble', and the scene's eroticism, incorporating us in our very absence, has a peculiar purity.

In what follows, there are two successive scenes in which the lovers are watched by characters within the fiction. First a forester discovers the bower where they have slept, follows their tracks, and finds them sleeping:

> Vit les dormanz, bien les connut:
> Li sans li fuit, esmarriz fut.
> Molt s'en vest tost, quar se doutoit. (1843–5)

He saw the sleeping couple and recognized them. He turned pale and was frightened; he left quickly because of his fear.

Here perhaps the forester's lack of personal interest in the lovers is what causes the apparent opportunity for a voyeuristic scene to be passed up. But then the forester tells Mark what he has seen, and leads him secretly to the place. Mark draws his sword, intending to kill them (which, if he found them *in flagrante delicto*, would be justifiable by customary if not by ecclesiastical law); but he finds he cannot do it, and the piercing sword is commuted into a piercing gaze:

> Li rois en haut li cop leva,
> Iré le fait, si se tresva.
> Ja decendist li cop sor eus,
> Ses oceïst, ce fust grant deus.
> Quant *vit* qu'ele avoit sa chemise

> Et q'entre eus deus avoit devise,
> La bouche o l'autre n'ert jostee,
> Et qant il *vit* la nue espee
> Qui entre eus deus les desevrot,
> *Vit* les braies que Tristran out:
> 'Dex!' dist li rois, 'ce que peut estre?'   (1991–2001)

The king raised his sword high in anger, but he could go no further. If he had struck them and had killed them, it would have been a tragedy! When he saw that she was wearing her chemise and saw that there was a space between them and that their mouths were not touching, and when he saw the naked sword which was separating them and saw the breeches that Tristran wore, the king said: 'God, what can this mean?'

The distance between the characters is once more juxtaposed with the distance that belongs to sight itself, but this time it is Mark's sight, a gaze that implies in its very nature the question of meaning and thus the possibility of misinterpretation. As an art-historian has written, distinguishing between the gaze (*regard*) and the glance (*coup d'œil*),

> The *regard* attempts to extract the enduring from fleeting process; its epithets tend toward a certain violence (penetrating, piercing, fixing), and its overall purpose seems to be the discovery of a second (re-) surface behind the first, the mask of appearances.[9]

Unlike ourselves, Mark can touch too; but he does no more than attempt to transform the scene's meaning, placing his gloves to block the ray of light that falls on Iseult's face and replacing her ring and the separating sword with his own; then he departs, leaving them still asleep, having marked the scene with signs of his presence, and leaving the way open to further misinterpretation.

One testimony that the voyeuristic potential of this scene is not a twentieth-century invention but was recognizable in the Middle Ages is provided by the way it is expanded by Gottfried von Strassburg in his *Tristan*. The chief form taken by literary interpretation in medieval culture is rewriting,[10] and here we have a fascinating example. In Gottfried's much fuller version, the lovers, lying on the bed of Venus in an elaborate grotto of love, are spied on through a little window, first by a huntsman and then by Mark. (The window, part of Gottfried's more elaborate architectural and allegorical setting for the scene, may also involve an ironic allusion to Song of Songs 2:9 – 'Behold, he standeth behind our wall, looking through the windows, looking through the lattices' – where the wall separating God the spouse from his bride was interpreted as marking the purely spiritual nature of their union.[11] Gottfried's poem is permeated with erotic adaptations of religious motifs, of which this may be one.) Gottfried's Mark too asks himself, 'Merciful God, … what can be the meaning of this?', and then proceeds to gaze in entrancement less at the couple than at Isolde alone:

> er schouwete ie genôte
> sînes herzen wunne Isôte,
> diun gedûhte in ouch dâ vor und ê
> nie sô rehte schoene mê.
> ine weiz von welher arbeit
> diz maere spellet unde seit,
> von der si erhitzet solte sîn,
> und lûhte ir varwe unde ir schin
> als suoze und alse lôse
> als ein gemischet rôse
> hin ûf allez wider den man.
> ir munt der viurete unde bran
> rehte alse ein glüejender kol.
> jâ ich erkenne mich nu wol,
> waz dirre arbeite was.
> Îsôt was, alse ich iezuo las,
> des morgens in dem touwe
> geslichen zuo der ouwe
> und was dâ von enbrunnen.
> sô gieng ouch von der sunnen
> ein cleinez straemelîn dar în,
> daz gleste ir ûf ir hiufelîn,
> ûf ir kinne und ûf ir munt...
> ir kinne, ir munt, ir varwe, ir lîch
> daz was sô rehte wunneclîch,
> sô lieplîch und sô muotsam,
> daz ir Marken gezam:
> in gelangete unde geluste,
> daz er si gerne kuste.
> Minne diu warf ir vlammen an,
> Minne envlammete den man
> mit der schoene ir lîbes.
> diu schoene des wîbes
> diu spuon im sîne sinne
> z'ir libe und z'ir minne.
> sîn ouge stuont im allez dar.
> er nam vil inneclîche war,

wie schône ir ûz der waete schein
ir kele unde ir brustbein,
ir arme unde ir hende.
si haete âne gebende
ein schapel ûfe von clê.
sine gedûhte ir hêrren nie mê
sô lustic und sô lustsam.   (17557–607)

He gazed and gazed at his heart's delight Isolde, who never before had seemed to him so very lovely as now. I do not know of what exertions the tale romances here that might have flushed her cheeks, whose radiance glowed up at the man with the sweet freshness of a rose in which red and white are mingled. Her mouth burned with fire like a red-hot ember. Yes, I recall what her exertions were. Isolde, as I said just now, had sauntered through the dew to the meadow that morning and this is what had given her her colour. And now a tiny sunbeam, too, had found its way inside and was shining on her cheek, on her chin, and on her lips ... Her chin, her mouth, her colour, her skin were so exquisite, lovely, and enticing that Mark was captivated and filled with the desire to kiss her. Love threw on her flames, she set the man on fire with the charm of the woman's form. Her beauty lured his senses to her body, and to the passion she excited. His eyes were fixed upon her. His gaze dwelt with ardour on the beauty of her throat, her breast, her arms, and her hands where they shone out from her robe. She wore a chaplet of clover, but was without a headband – never had she seemed to her lord so bewitching and alluring! (pp. 272–3)

In this intensely erotic passage, it is made explicit that Mark is more excited by gazing on Isolde, by devouring with his eyes the beauty he cannot now possess, than he has ever been before as her husband. The scene would scarcely be out of place in *Venus in Furs*. Moreover, Gottfried ensures that we shall participate in the king's masochistic-voyeuristic excitement by encouraging us to imagine a version of the story in which Isolde's flushed cheeks and burning lips would have been caused by recent love-making – only to 'recall' that they were in fact the result of an innocent stroll through the dew! Thus we are forced to grant our complicity in Mark's voyeuristic pleasure, by recognizing that it is *our* fantasies that are responsible for any pornographic element in the scene.

In the final surviving episode of Beroul's version, Tristan emerges from hiding to visit Iseult yet again in Mark's *chanbre*, while the king is out hunting. But the three malicious barons are warned of this by a spy. One of them, Godoïne, gets there before him, and once more we are in the position (one entirely familiar to modern readers from cinematic manipulations of point of view) of peering with a concealed watcher through a gap in an enclosure.

> La cortine ot dedenz percie;
> *Vit* la chanbre, qui fu jonchie,
> Tot *vit* quant que dedenz avoit,
> Home fors Perinis ne *voit*.
> Brengain i vint, la damoisele,
> Ou out pignié Yseut la bele:
> La pieigne avoit encor o soi. (4413–19)

He had pierced the curtain inside; he could see the room, which was strewn with rushes. He saw everything in the room, and Perinis was the only man he saw. The maid Brangain came in. She had just combed Iseut's hair, and she still had the comb in her hand.

When Tristan arrives, with Godoïne still watching, 'He removed his cloak, revealing his handsome body [thus perhaps permitting the female reader or listener to share in the voyeur's role]. The beautiful, blonde Iseut rose and came to greet him' (4425–7). But yet again the watcher is watched; Iseult glimpses Godoïne's shadow, she subtly hints to Tristan that she has seen a spy, he too sees Godoïne's head 'Contre le jor, par la cortine' [Against the light, through the curtain] (4461), and he draws his bow and shoots him dead. He shoots him, significantly, through the eye; thus voyeurism receives its appropriate punishment, and perhaps at this moment, by vicariously suffering the punishment, we may feel temporarily absolved from our share in its shame.

Though, as has often been noted, Beroul's romance lacks the formal analyses and self-analyses of the characters' inner lives that are found in Chrétien's poems, it nevertheless imagines these lives quite richly. The subjectivity of the lovers, living their life of deception, is realized all the more sharply by contrast with what they reveal to others; their processes of thought and feeling are sometimes conveyed, for example, in speech 'to themselves', distinguished from deceptively intended speech to those keeping them under observation. Thus when Mark, having banished Tristan, then banishes the three barons for their continued criticism of the queen, he returns, still upset, to Iseult at Tintagel:

> Aperçut soi qu'il ert marriz,
> Venuz s'en est aeschariz.
> 'Lasse,' fait ele, 'mes amis

> Est trovez, mes sires l'a pris!'
> (Souef le dit entre ses denz.)
> Li sanz de li ne fu si loinz,
> Qu'il ne li set monté el vis,
> Li cuer el ventre li froidist.   (3161–8)

She realized that he was angry and that he had come alone. 'Alas,' she said, 'my friend has been discovered, and my lord has captured him!' (She said this under her breath [literally 'between her teeth'].) Her blood rushed to her face, and her heart froze within her.

Mark explains that he is angry with the barons, and says that Tristan will return and avenge him on them.

> La roïne l'a entendu;
> Ja parlast haut, mais ele n'ose:
> El fu sage, si se repose
> Et dist: 'Dex i a fait vertuz,
> Qant mes sires s'est irascuz
> Vers ceus par qui blasme ert levé.
> Deu pri qu'il soient vergondié.'
> Souef le dit, que nus ne l'ot.
> La bele Yseut, qui parler sot,
> Tot sinplement a dit au roi:
> 'Sire, que mal ont dit de moi?'   (3200–10)

The queen heard him and almost cried out, but did not dare. Wisely, she composed herself and said: 'God has worked a miracle, arousing my lord's anger toward those who made the accusations against me. I pray to God that they may be shamed.' (She said this softly, so that no one could hear.) The fair Iseut, who knew how to choose her words, asked the king directly: 'Sir, what evil have they said of me?'

Here the marking of inner speech may seem heavy-handed, yet on other occasions Beroul lightly indicates the reflection of one subjectivity in another, evidently assured that his audience will grasp his purpose. In the first surviving scene, we are told that Tristan understands the true meaning of Iseult's deceptive speech: 'Qant out oï parler sa drue, / Sout que s'estoit aperceüe' (97–8) [When he heard his mistress speak, he realized that she understood]. In the scene of Iseult's oath, secret meaning is conveyed by smiles and winks, so that Dinas 'knew the queen's thought' (3875). In the last surviving scene, the quickness with which Tristan seizes the implication of Iseult's suggestion that he should test his bow is underlined by tongue-twisting repetitions of sound:

Tristran s'esteut, si s'apensa,
Oiez! En son penser tensa;
Prent s'entente, si tendi l'arc.   (4441–3)

Tristran drew it and began to think. Listen well! He considered matters carefully [or perhaps 'grasped her meaning'] and drew the bow with all his strength.

Such interpretation of ambiguous signs plays a major part in the action, reaching its climax in the ambiguous oath by which Iseult exculpates herself from the accusation of adultery. The public world is governed by honour and shame, what is believed to be true and can be publicly made good, by contrast with the inner truth of the lovers' relations. Hence the importance of the *escondit*, the 'action de se justifier dans les formes légales',[12] a term frequently repeated (along with associated terms such as *deraisnier* and *esligier*) throughout the text. Tristan, returning Iseult to Mark, states publicly,

Ci voi les homes de la terre
Et, oiant eus, te vuel requerre
Que me sueffres a esligier
Et en ta cort moi deraisnier
C'onques o lié n'oi drüerie,
Ne ele o moi, jor de ma vie.   (2853–8)

I see here the men of your land; and in their presence, I wish to ask your permission to establish my innocence and prove before your court that never in my life was I her lover or she my mistress.[13]

The 'proof' would be by means of judicial combat, which Tristan would doubtless win, but the three barons persuade Mark not to allow it. A woman cannot make her *escondit* by combat, but she can swear a public oath, and this Iseult does, once more avoiding literal falsehood by arranging for Tristan, disguised as a crippled leper, to carry her on his back over a marsh, and then solemnly swearing,

entre mes cuises n'entra home,
Fors le ladre qui fist soi some,
Qui me porta outre les guez,
Et li rois Marc mes esposez.
Ces deus ost de mon soirement,
Ge n'en ost plus de tote gent.
De deus ne me pus escondire.   (4205–11)

no man has ever been between my thighs, except the leper who made himself a beast of burden and carried me over the ford and my husband

King Mark. I exclude these two from my oath, but I except no one else. I cannot swear it about those two.

But it is not only words that are ambiguous; in this world obsessed with looking, visual signs are especially important and, paradoxically, open to misinterpretation. The penetrative gaze appears to lay bare the truth, yet all too often it leads to deception, as here, where the supposed cripple is really Tristan in disguise. Beroul's aristocratic leading characters are illiterate, and thus reliant for private communication on devices such as the twigs thrown into the stream to arrange their assignations. They are skilled at creating deceptive appearances, and Tristan in particular is a master of disguise, appearing not only as a leper (with even his horse disguised) but, outside Beroul's fragments, as the minstrel Tantris. Their enemies are usually deceived, but the lovers are also open to visual deception, the most striking instance being the scene in which Mark spies on them in the forest. Here Mark misinterprets the facts that they are clothed and have Tristan's sword between them as meaning that they have not committed adultery – a meaning he has manufactured out of mere accident – but Tristan equally misinterprets what Mark intends to convey by his gloves, ring and sword, seeing them as signifying threat rather than compassion.

Private life survives in an inimical public world only by concealment and deception, yet it needs the enmity of a jealous husband and malicious spies to give it relish. To evade and deceive the gazes of others is a way of life that loses its meaning if those gazes are removed. Life in the forest, as we have seen, is painful; it is also boring – Tristan has nothing better to do than train a dog to hunt without barking.[14] If Mark finds the lovers lying apart, it is surely because the intensity of their passion has subsided; and it is significant that Beroul should then intervene with the surprising new information that the magic potion that originally caused their love is only of limited duration, and is now about to wear off. Gottfried's much fuller and more magnificent version of the story (which I can only glance at here) confirms the fragility and vulnerability of secret love, however extreme its intensity.

The court world of Gottfried's poem, still more than of Beroul's, is criss-crossed with gazes and glances, expressions of a diffused scopic eroticism not reducible to a gendered gaze. At an early stage in the story of Tristan's parents, Mark holds a festival that is described as a visual feast, in which Blancheflor, Mark's sister, who will be Tristan's mother, is the culminating delicacy:

> und swes der gerne *sehende* man
> ze *sehene* guoten muot gewan,
> daz lie diu state dâ wol geschehen;
> man *sach* dâ, swaz man wolte *sehen*:
> dise vuoren *sehen* vrouwen,
> jene ander tanzen schouwen;
> dise *sâhen* bûhurdieren,
> jene ander justieren. . . .
> Und Marke . . .
> âne ander vrouwen schônheit,
> die er haete an sînen rinc geleit,
> sô haete er doch besunder
> ein sunderlîchez wunder,
> Blanscheflûr sîne swester dâ:
> ein maget, daz dâ noch anderswâ
> schoener wîp nie wart *gesehen*.
> wir hoeren von ir schoene jehen,
> sine *gesaehe* nie kein lebende man
> mit inneclîchen ougen an,
> ern minnete dâ nâch iemer mê
> wîp und tugende baz dan ê. (613–40)

And if a man who loved a spectacle took a fancy to seeing anything, opportunity was there to indulge him. One saw what one wanted to see: some went to note the ladies, others to see dancing; some watched the bohort, others jousting. . . . And Mark . . . had a rare marvel of his own apart from the beauty of other ladies, whose pavilions he had placed in his ring – his sister Blancheflor, a girl so lovely that you never saw a lovelier, there or anywhere. It is said of her beauty that no man of flesh and blood had ever gazed at her with enamoured eyes and not loved woman and noble qualities better ever after. (pp. 49–50)

The young Tristan is as much the object of admiring gazes, when he plays his harp – 'the strangers kept looking at him as one man and confessed in their hearts that they had never set eyes on any young person adorned with so many excellences' (2274–8; p. 71) – or when he demonstrates the technique of woodcraft before King Mark, a scene where looking crystallizes into an *effictio*:

> sîn munt was rehte rôsenrôt,
> sîn varwe lieht, sîn ougen clâr.
> brûnreideloht was ime daz hâr,
> gecrûspet bî dem ende.

sîn arme und sîne hende
wol gestellet unde blanc.
sîn lîp ze guoter mâze lanc.
sîne vüeze und sîniu bein,
dar an sîn schoene almeistic schein,
diu stuonden sô ze prîse wol,
als man'z an manne prisen sol.
sîn gewant, als ich iu hân geseit,
daz was mit grôzer höfscheit
nâch sînem lîbe gesniten.
an gebaerde unde an schoenen siten
was ime sô rehte wol geschehen
daz man in gerne mohte sehen.   (3334–50)

His mouth was as red as a rose, his colour radiant, his eyes clear; his hair fell in brown locks, crimped at the ends; his arms and hands were shapely and dazzling white; his figure was tall to the right degree; his feet and legs (in which his beauty most appeared) deserved such praise as a man may give a man. His clothes, as I told you, were most elegantly cut to his figure. He was so well favoured in presence and manners that it was a joy to watch him. (p. 85)

General gazing gives rise to gossip, as mutual gazing to love; and as the story comes to focus on the specific relationship of Tristan and Isolde, Gottfried cunningly implicates his readers in a more phallic gazing which only gradually and indistinctly emerges from the general play of looks. A particularly striking passage describes Isolde as she appears in public with her mother when Tristan makes good his claim to have killed the dragon:

diu sleich ir . . .
lanc, ûf gewollen unde smal,
gestellet in der waete,
als sî diu Minne draete
ir selber z'einem vederspil,
dem wunsche z'einem endezil,
dâ vür er niemer komen kan.
si truoc von brûnem samît an
roc unde mantel, in dem snite
von Franze, und was der roc dâ mite
dâ engegene, dâ die sîten
sinkent ûf ir lîten,
gefranzet unde g'enget,
nâhe an ir lîp getwenget
mit einem borten, der lac wol,
dâ der borte ligen sol.

der roc der was ir heinlîch,
er tete sich nâhen zuo der lîch.
ern truoc an keiner stat hin dan,
er suohte allenthalben an
al von obene hin ze tal.
er nam den valt unde den val
under den vüezen als vil,
als iuwer iegelîcher wil. . . .
die rehten haete sî gewant
hin nider baz, ir wizzet wol,
dâ man den mantel sliezen sol,
und slôz in höfschlîche in ein
mit ir vingere zwein.
vürbaz dâ viel er selbe wider
und nam den vat al z'ende nider,
daz man diz unde daz dâ sach,
ich meine vederen unde dach.   (10890–948)

The girl glided gently forward . . . tall, well-moulded, and slender, and shaped in her attire as if Love had formed her to be her own falcon, an ultimate unsurpassable perfection! She wore a robe and mantle of purple samite cut in the French fashion and accordingly, where the sides slope down to their curves, the robe was fringed and gathered into her body with a girdle of woven silk, which clung where girdles hang. Her robe fitted her intimately, it clung close to her body, it neither bulged nor sagged but sat smoothly everywhere all the way down, clinging between her knees as much as each of you pleases. . . . She had brought her right hand farther down, you know, to where one closes the mantle, and held it decorously together with two of her fingers. From here it fell unhampered in a last fold revealing this and that – I mean the fur and its covering. (p. 185)

The reader, especially if male, is enticed and teased, stimulated to exercise his imagination upon the body that is so nearly yet not quite revealed by the clinging and precariously fastened garment; at the same time, he cannot avoid recognizing – 'you know' (*ir wizzet wol*) – that it is *his* desire, *his* 'gevedere schâchblicke' [rapacious feathered glances] (10957) (as Gottfried puts it of the watchers in the scene), that give the description its *raison d'être*. And yet Gottfried keeps this voyeuristic drive within bounds. There are many such moments of visual appetite in the poem, but they become more frequent only as spies and watchers become more prominent in the fiction, and he is generally careful to avoid voyeuristic effects implicating himself and the reader alone – that is, in scenes that do not occur in public. Thus Brangane watches as Tristan and Isolde are affected by the love-potion, and encourages them to fulfil their desires. Tristan steals to Isolde's cabin at night (for in this wealthier world than Beroul's, a private chamber is available even on board ship), and we perhaps expect to be drawn in for a keyhole view of their love-making. Gottfried tells us that

> den zwein gelieben waere wol
> und sanfte in ir muote,
> dô sî die leiden huote,
> die wâren suht der minne,
> den Minnen vîendinne
> von ir stîgen haeten brâht.   (12194–9)

these two lovers were in a happy and contented mood at having got out of their way Love's enemy, cursed Surveillance, that veritable plague of Love!

Huote, surveillance, is a concept frequently invoked in the poem, but Gottfried proceeds to get rid of *our* surveillance too, substituting 'kurz rede von guoten minnen' [a short discourse on worthy love] (12185) for an account of the consummation. Earlier he has declined to describe Tristan's knighting and has instead inserted the famous 'literary excursus' on German poets; thus the climaxes first of chivalric and then of erotic initiation are both replaced by discourses that have to do with poetry. What is not said may be more suggestive than what is; but in any case, Gottfried is more conscious than Beroul, and makes us more conscious, of the power and limits of narrative fiction.

Gottfried's Tristan is himself essentially a maker of fictions, a poet who is his own subject,[15] and who uses this deceptive role-playing power as a way of manipulating the looks constantly directed upon him and Isolde and thus of creating a private life unsullied by *huote*. The roles he adopts include merchant's son, pilgrim, court minstrel, married man, Norman merchant, knight, and harpist, and his playing of many parts and telling of many stories forms a rehearsal for his performance as Isolde's lover – the versatile acting, as himself and in still other parts, which alone enables a secret and illicit love to survive in the public world. Isolde, Tristan's pupil, turns out to be as accomplished an actor as her master. Gottfried remarks of the colour-shifting dog Petitcrieu that

> sone wart nie kein sô wîse man,
> der sîne varwe erkande.
> si was sô maneger hande
> und sô gâr irrebaere,
> als dâ kein varwe waere.   (15840–4)

no one, however discerning, could have told you its colour. It was as bewilderingly varied as if there were no colour at all. (p. 250)

It seems quite irrelevant, yet it is an effective figure of the lovers' life, where outward appearances vary so constantly that we become unable to tell what the truth is about anything. The forest to which the lovers flee from *huote* is a more idyllic setting than in Beroul; they hunt for recreation, not survival, and their bower is the sumptuously allegorical *Minnegrotte*, a perfect substitute for 'Artûses tavelrunden / und alle ir massenîe' [King Arthur's Round Table ... and all its company] (16900–1), a place where they live on each other's looks and have all they need:

> waz solte in bezzer lîpnar
> ze muote oder ze lîbe?
> dâ was doch man bî wîbe,
> sô was ouch wîp bî manne.
> wes bedorften si danne?
> si haeten daz si solten,
> und wâren dâ si wolten.   (16902–8)

What better food could they have for body or soul? Man was there with Woman, Woman with Man. What else should they be needing? They had what they were meant to have, they had reached the goal of their desire. (p. 263)

Yet even there the lovers are not really secure from Mark and his court; they fear discovery, and that, Gottfried explains, is why they lie with the sword between them. Their love and the private life it creates is essentially unstable.

One reason is that, as in Beroul's version, love's intensity depends on the existence of obstacles: the unstable equilibrium between desire and the barriers to desire cannot be permanently sustained. But another reason, peculiar to Gottfried, is surely that the obstacles can be overcome only by incessant acting, incessant fictionalizing; and these activities attenuate the private selfhood that feeds the mutuality they seek. A comparison suggests itself with Hamlet, another nephew locked in combat with his uncle, plagued by constant surveillance in a court of outward shows, and determined to assert the reality of 'that within which passes show'. Hamlet, in a self-analysis more searching than would be depicted by any medieval poet, reaches a depth where he fears that even 'that within' is no more than an unstable theatricality that unpacks the heart with words; but he eventually comes to feel that his inner life and vision

are guaranteed by an all-seeing providence. For Gottfried's Tristan
there can be no such conviction of a transcendent destiny, because
Gottfried has seen, as Beroul did not, the metaphysical implication
of the false oath that preserves love's privacy:

> der vil tugenthafte Crist
> wintschaffen als ein ermel ist.
> er vüeget unde suochet an,
> dâ man'z an in gesuochen kan,
> alse gevuoge und alse wol,
> als er von allem rehte sol.
> erst allen herzen bereit,
> ze durnehte und ze trügeheit.
> ist ez ernest, ist ez spil,
> er ist ie, swie sô man wil.   (15735–44)

Christ in His great virtue is as pliant as a windblown sleeve. He falls into
place and clings, whichever way you try Him, closely and smoothly, as He
is bound to do. He is at the beck of every heart for honest deeds or fraud. Be
it deadly earnest or a game, He is just as you would have Him. (p. 248)

'As pliant as a windblown sleeve', falling into place and clinging –
just like Isolde's seductive garment, one might say, that covers or
uncovers whatever the voyeuristic reader chooses. The implication
is that there is no transcendent panoptic vision to guarantee the
inner world. The lovers' bid to arrive at transcendence through
role-playing is doomed to failure, and indeed the attempt carries
within itself the necessity of dissolution, of the fragmentation of the
role-playing self into the roles it plays. Gottfried's great poem is
unfinished, and we are left to suppose, if we will, that some such
implication might have emerged in his version of Thomas's Hall of
Statues scene.

CHAPTER 4

Chrétien de Troyes

Chrétien de Troyes is the most innovative of the great French poets of the twelfth century. He did not invent courtly romance, which has its origins in the *romans d'antiquité* of the mid-century and in versions of the Tristan story such as that of Thomas; but he brought it to perfection, and in doing so experimented with virtually all the storytelling techniques that were to be employed throughout the history of medieval romance. To discuss him adequately in a single chapter is impossible, but watching and the questions it raises are so central in his work that I cannot leave him out. In this chapter I shall first examine two specific scenes from *Yvain* and *Lancelot* in which looking is of particular importance; then I shall attempt a more general study of *Cligés* in its relation to *Tristan*.

The scene from *Yvain* consists of lines 961–1540.[1] Yvain, pursuing the adventure of the magic spring proposed by his cousin Calogrenant, has fought fiercely with Esclados, the lord of the spring, and has chased him into his castle. Once he is inside the main keep, the portcullis clangs down behind him, slicing his horse in half and cutting off Yvain's spurs. Yvain is trapped inside the castle of his mortally wounded enemy. A charming damsel – Lunete, the waiting-gentlewoman of Laudine, Esclados's wife – emerges and points out his danger, but because Yvain once treated her kindly she rewards him by giving him a ring of invisibility, which he hastens to use. Esclados's bewildered household search in vain for his killer, and his widow bitterly laments his death and the killer's escape. Lunete places Yvain by a window from which he can watch the lady, and she is so beautiful that he instantly falls in love with her. Chrétien devotes some 260 lines (1282–540) to Yvain's situation and feelings as an invisible watcher.

The material setting would seem to be of crucial importance in this episode, but the division and arrangement of spaces are difficult to reconstruct rationally. Yvain has been trapped between two gates (956–60), apparently in a narrow passage (1101, *triege*); and yet now he is 'dedanz la sale anclos' (963), shut up in the castle's richly decorated and comfortably furnished public room. It is complete with gilt-nailed ceiling, painted walls, and beds and benches, with the bed or couch on which Lunete invites him to sit 'covered by a quilt so costly that the Duke of Austria never had its equal' (1041–2). And off this *sale* opens Lunete's private room, called her *chanbre* or (at 970) *chanbrete*, with its own door. Chrétien may be improvising, and may lack an unambiguous plan: this is an impression often given by the more fantastic parts of his romances, as though he relied on his quick wits and fluent pen to deal with such trifles as magic.[2] Or perhaps his intention, in a scene of voyeuristic wish-fulfilment, was to create a dreamlike effect, one of bewitchment or diabolic influence, as Esclados's people suggest (1130, *anchanté*; 1202, *mervoille et deablie*), a scene in which an event might occur that 'ne fu escriz an livre' (1176). Later medieval translators of Chrétien's poem attempt to rationalize this effect of unreality. Hartmann von Aue in his thirteenth-century *Iwein* has the knight clearly trapped in the space between two portcullises, which Hartmann never calls a hall. And the anonymous author of the fourteenth-century *Ywain and Gawain* has the damsel hiding Ywain in her room, later called 'þe maydens hall',[3] where it is *her* bed he sits on.

In this setting, invisibility conferred by Lunete's ring permits Yvain to be a perfectly secret and secure voyeur. That is also our position and Chrétien's too (though Chrétien does not explicitly realize it as such): he and we can watch the agitated action and emotional disturbance without being involved or detected. Yvain then is in a situation of 'grant avantage' (1321): previously he was caught by the portcullis as if in a trap which 'agueite / Le rat' (914–15) [lies in wait for the rat]; now the same word *agueite* (1286) is used to describe how he spies the lady of the castle, Esclados's wife Laudine, through his window. But his position of advantage is also one of disadvantage. Like the reader or cinema spectator, he is 'a pure onlooker whose participation is inconceivable'[4] – he can *only* admire Laudine and suffer the pangs of love for her, the usual wounds which strike the heart through the eyes:

> Bien a vangiee, et si nel set,
> La dame la mort son seignor.
> Vanjance an a prise greignor,

Qu'ele prandre ne l'an seüst,
S'Amors vangiee ne l'eüst,
Qui si doucemant le requiert,
Que par les iauz el cuer le fiert.   (1362–8)

The lady, without knowing it, has fully avenged her husband's death. For it she has taken a greater revenge than she would have found possible had not Love avenged her by attacking him so gently and, through his eyes, striking him to the heart.

These metaphorical wounds are added to the literal wounds of the combat in which he has just engaged, and, as Chrétien observes, they are worse than physical wounds: they last longer and the physician's presence only makes them more painful (1369ff.). Yvain's disadvantage is that Love's arrows can travel in only one direction, because Laudine cannot see him. (Since he has just killed her husband, it would in any case be too soon for her to respond to his feelings with any propriety.) Within the fictional world, his adoring gaze at Laudine would seem to have nothing in common with the 'male gaze' as usually defined, because she does not know that she is being watched; thus she cannot 'watch herself being looked at', and her behaviour cannot be affected by the invisible watcher's presence. Yvain remains trapped in a new sense: he is 'a la fenestre ... pris' (1424) [caught ... at the window] by Love. He is now metaphorically as well as literally imprisoned, and 'to him it makes no difference whether [the portcullises] are closed or open' (1523–4). Chrétien as storyteller is similarly trapped, a perfect voyeur, unable to share any relationship with the persons of his fiction.

In another perspective, though, it is less clear that Laudine's behaviour is completely unaffected by Yvain's gaze. Within the fiction it must be; but Chrétien has arranged things so that Yvain's view through the 'fenestre petite' (1283) is also his and ours. What we see in this scene is how Yvain constructs the figure of Laudine; as Chrétien puts it, 'Einsi mes sire Yvains devise / Celi, qui de duel se debrise' [Thus my lord Yvain represents the lady who is torturing herself with grief] (1507–8).[5] And this representation has a distinct bias. Isn't there an element of theatrical exaggeration in the way Laudine plays the part of the newly widowed wife of a matchless lord even when she is left alone (alone, that is, except for Yvain, and Chrétien, and ourselves), 'often clutching at her throat, wringing her hands and slapping her palms, and reading her psalms from a psalter illuminated with gold lettering' (1412–15)? It is as if she were unconsciously following Ovid's instructions in the *Ars amatoria* to widows who hope not to remain widows for long.[6] And, after all, she does soon let herself be argued by Lunete and her own retainers, who are only 'urging her to do what she in fact wishes' (2108), into marrying Yvain. In retrospect, shall we think that total sincerity in her role as grieving widow is compatible with the ease with which she is persuaded to marry her husband's slayer? What is involved here is no doubt partly a male conception of femininity as histrionicism, a sustained and internalized performance for the benefit not just of any man known to be watching but of the male 'surveyor of woman in herself'.[7] But this general cultural phenomenon is here given a further twist. The act of watching turns what is watched into a performance, a spectacle, altogether regardless of the 'real' motives or consciousness of the person under surveillance. At this moment in a narrative in which 'trapping' of various kinds is crucially important,[8] *we* have been trapped: we cannot help watching Laudine with Yvain's eyes through that window, admiring her beauty in an appraising, comparative way – 'Onques si bien taillie ne vi / Ne si fres ne si coloré' (1476–7) [Never have I seen one so shapely or so freshly complexioned] – thinking what a pretty picture she makes as she reads her psalms from the elegant, gold-illuminated psalter (herself like one of its illuminations), wondering whether she was not created by God rather than Nature, and so on. The frame imposed on her by the narrative's adoption of Yvain's voyeuristic position, a position in this case gendered as male, inevitably turns her into a picture.

The scene from *Lancelot* conveys a different but equally powerful point about looking. Chrétien's romance, of which he claims that both *matiere et san* (26)[9] were imposed on him by his patroness Marie de Champagne, is one of many reworkings of that of Tristan: here the members of the adulterous triangle are Arthur, his wife Guenevere, and Arthur's vassal and Guenevere's lover Lancelot. Guenevere has been abducted by Meleagant, the son of King Bademagus, who disapproves of his irresponsible behaviour and puts the queen under guard to protect her from his son. Lancelot, whose love for Guenevere has so far been only at a distance, has undertaken various tasks in order to rescue her, but has hesitated briefly before suffering the indignity of stepping into a cart. Lancelot and Guenevere have each supposed the other to be dead, but in the passage under consideration (lines 4441–5038) they are reunited, and first consummate their love.

Even though they are not under the eyes of Guenevere's husband, their union must be secret, to preserve Guenevere's reputation, which Meleagant, thwarted in his desire for her, would gladly destroy. They first meet in Guenevere's *chanbre*, but evidently in the presence of others, including perhaps Bademagus. Guenevere declares that she forgives Lancelot for his hesitation in entering the cart; then, when he says he would like to speak to her more privately, she 'indicates to him a window with her eyes, not her finger', and tells him to visit her that night, when the household is asleep (4524–8).

As so often in narratives of adulterous love, the precise details of the material setting are of great importance, and here they are specified with almost obsessive exactitude. Lancelot will be able to approach the window of Guenevere's *chanbre* through a garden (*vergier*), but he must take care not to be spotted by any lookout (*espie*). Guenevere is prepared to stay up all night with him, but no greater intimacy will be possible because (and here once more we encounter the startling limits on medieval privacy)

> an ma chanbre devant moi gist
> Keus li seneschaus qui languist
> Des plaies don il est coverz.
> Et li huis ne rest mie overz,
> Ainz est bien fers et bien gardez.   (4539–43)

opposite me in my room lies Kay the seneschal, suffering from the wounds with which he's covered; and as for the door, it's not left open but is shut tight and well guarded.

Lancelot returns to his lodging (4570, *ostel*), and, when night falls, pretends that he wishes to sleep. Chrétien explicitly invites our complicity with his deceptiveness:

> Bien poez antandre et gloser,
> Vos qui avez fet autretel,
> Que por la jant de son ostel
> Se fet las et se fet couchier.   (4568–71)

You, who have done as much yourselves, can understand and supply the reason for his shamming tiredness and going to bed with an eye to the people in his house.

Thus our imaginative presence in the fictional scene is acknowledged. Lancelot is able to enter the garden easily because 'a piece of the garden wall has recently fallen down' (4590–1); he passes through this *freite* unnoticed and waits at the window until Guenevere appears. They can converse in secret; but between them remains 'the window with its massive iron bars' (4602–3), through which they can speak, kiss, and touch, but no more.

Darkness is important throughout:

> il ne luisoit lune n'estoile,
> N'an la meison n'avoit chandoile,
> Ne lanpe ne lanterne ardant.   (4579–81)

there was no moon or star shining, and in the house no candle, lamp or lantern burning.

It is the guardian of secrecy for the lovers, but it also affects our relation to the scene as readers. We and Chrétien are secret witnesses (perhaps, we may vaguely sense, concealed by the darkness ourselves) of what the participants suppose to be an entirely private encounter; Kay is also present, and this indicates a position for us too, but he is alseep. Our awareness of the encounter is mediated less by sight than by the more material and less 'noble' senses, which develop new sharpness as sight falls into abeyance. When Guenevere first appears, she is discernible only as a white shape in the dark, because she is wearing 'une mout blanche chemise' (4597) – and there is doubtless a subdued irony in the association of whiteness with moral purity – and over it 'a short mantle of fine cloth and marmot fur' (4600), already textures that appeal to touch rather than sight. And touch is especially important in the imaginative realization of the barrier and of the fleshly contact that it prevents. 'They were full of desire, he for her and she for him' (4606–7): we recall the importance of obstacles in heightening love's intensity, but also important is the contrast between the iron bars' rigidity and toughness – 'Can't you see how stiff this iron is to bend and tough to break?' (4620–1) – and the tender vulnerability of the flesh they separate. Lancelot determines to force his way through the window; Guenevere retires to her bed, in case any noise should waken Kay. And then

> As fers se prant et sache et tire
> Si que trestoz ploiier les fet
> Et que fors de lor leus les tret.
> Mes si estoit tranchanz li fers
> Que del doi mame jusqu'as ners

La premiere once se creva
Et de l'autre doi se trancha
La premerainne jointe tote;
Mais del sanc qui jus an degote
Ne des plaies nule ne sant
Cil qui a autre chose antant.   (4654–64)

He takes hold of the bars, which he pulls and tugs until he bends them all and drags them from their sockets. But the iron was so sharp that he split the tip of his little finger to the nerve and cut the end joint of his second finger right through. However, with his mind on another matter, he feels neither the wounds nor the blood that drips down from them.

This feat of male strength, like the shedding of blood in a bodily encounter, establishes the knight's worth and both reveals the power of his desire and in turn makes him more desirable. At the same time, Chrétien's very denial that Lancelot notices the wounds and the blood may make us feel them all the more.

Excited by Lancelot's demonstration of power and love, Guenevere eagerly draws him into her bed. Unabashed, the narrative follows the lovers; the cinematic metaphor comes naturally, and I am tempted to say the camera draws in for a close-up, yet in the darkness this is a non-visual voyeurism, holding us (as always when we are only reading a book) at the distance associated with sight, but evoking instead the sensations that belong to bodily touch:

Or a Lanceloz quanqu'il viaut
Quant la rëine en gre requiaut
Sa conpeignie et son solaz,
Quant il la tient antre ses braz
Et ele lui antre les suens.
Tant li est ses jeus douz et buens
Et del beisier et del santir,
Que il lor avint sanz mantir
Une joie et une mervoille
Tel qu'onques ancor sa paroille
Ne fu öie ne sëue;
Mes toz jorz iert par moi tëue,
Qu'an conte ne doit estre dite.
Des joies fu la plus eslite
Et la plus delitable cele
Que li contes nos test et cele.   (4687–702)

Now Lancelot has all that he desires, when the queen welcomes his company and intimacy, with him holding her in his arms and she embracing him. He finds her love-making so sweet and splendid as they kiss and fondle that they truly come to experience such joy and wonderment that its equal was never heard or known; but of that I shall keep silent, since it should not be told in a story. The supreme and most exquisite of joys was that which the tale conceals from us and leaves untold.

The climax then is omitted, in a way that veils the storyteller's responsibility; it is *li contes*, not Chrétien, that declines to reveal the lovers' supreme joy. The final sentence can be read not just as a statement about this (bashful or tactful or teasing) story, but about storytelling in general: desire is intensified by refusal, narrative desire by the refusal to tell, and the 'most exquisite of joys' is defined precisely by its exclusion from the field of the visible and narratable.

When Lancelot leaves after the night of love, he is careful to replace the window bars, thus apparently removing the evidence of adultery. But unknowingly he has left behind different evidence, for Guenevere's sheets are now 'tachié et taint / Del sanc qui li chëi des doiz' [soiled and stained with the blood that dripped from his fingers] (4718–19). In her weariness, she fails to notice this; but when Meleagant visits her in the morning (accompanied, it emerges, by 'companions' and 'guards' – though for Chrétien this is so inevitable that he feels no need to make a point of it), he immediately sees the blood on her bed and also on Kay's, 'for, you understand, his wounds had opened during the night' (4772–3). 'S'an a ses conpeignons botez' (4768) [he nudged his companions] – a perfect instance of how vulgarly what Gottfried calls *huote* bears upon private relations in a world where true privacy is almost unattainable – and leaps to a false conclusion, accusing Guenevere of adultery with Kay. The terms of the accusation are those of detection and law: the blood testifies to the offence (4789, 'le tesmoingne') and provides conclusive evidence (4794, 'ansaignes bien veraies'). This sudden intrusion of the public into the private sphere, this opening up of the *chanbre* to the looks of a crowd, as the police cast their chilling gaze upon the scene of a *crime passionnel*, serves to crystallize the surveillance under which *li contes* has always been keeping the lovers' intimacies; but it also introduces a contrast. The public evidence upon which the public accusation rests is what can be seen; the private experience belongs to darkness and is beyond the grasp of sight.

The explanation that occurs to Guenevere is that the blood on her sheets has come from a nose-bleed – and indeed, Chrétien adds, 'ele cuide dire voir' (4804) [she thinks she is speaking the truth]. Meleagant dismisses this with contempt, orders his guards to ensure that the evidence remains in place, and goes in search of his father, for 'I want the king to do me justice once he's seen how things are' (4814–15). Justice is the responsibility of the ruler in his public role, and, whatever his personal feelings, he cannot refuse to perform it without dereliction of duty.[10] Bademagus is unwilling to believe that his son's accusation can be true, but agrees to come and look, for, he says, 'Le voir m'an aprandront mi oel' (4848) [my eyes will teach me the truth of the matter]. When he enters the *chanbre* (4849), Guenevere indignantly repeats her denial, backed by Kay, who offers, despite his wounds, to exculpate her and himself by judicial combat. Guenevere, however, has secretly sent for Lancelot, who now returns with 'such a great crowd of knights that they filled the entire hall' (4934). We have not been told of any change of setting from *chanbre* to *sale*, but in Chrétien's imagination the spatial change is evidently induced by the conceptual shift from private to public. Lancelot takes up from the wounded Kay the responsibility of making good his and the queen's innocence, but first he says,

> 'Je sai de causes et de lois
> Et de plez et de jugemanz:
> Ne doit estre sanz seiremanz
> Bataille de tel mescreance.'
> Meleaganz sanz demorance
> Li respont mout isnelemant:
> 'Bien i soient li seiremant,
> Et vaingnent li saint or androit,
> Car je sai bien que je ai droit.'   (4964–72)

'I have some knowledge of trials, laws, disputes and judgments: with such allegations no combat should be fought without oaths being taken.' Unhesitatingly Meleagant quickly replies: 'Let oaths be taken, then, and the holy relics be brought at once, for I'm quite sure I'm in the right.'

The relics are produced, and this is the opportunity for the precise terms of the dispute to be repeated: Meleagant swears that Kay has committed adultery with Guenevere, and Lancelot that this is not so.

The Tristan story also includes a memorable scene in which the hero's blood in the heroine's *chanbre* is claimed as legal evidence of adultery, but Chrétien has skilfully reworked it so as to shield Lancelot against Tristan's unscrupulous willingness to make good a lie (that *he* has not committed adultery with Iseult);[11] instead, he creates the paradoxical situation in which Lancelot fights a judicial duel to exculpate *Kay* of the offence of which Lancelot is secretly guilty himself. A trail of blood, far thicker than that in *Tristan*, runs through the whole scene; the blood-stained sheets are mentioned again and again, almost always as objects of sight:

de son cors tant i remaint
Que li drap sont tachié et taint
Del *sanc*   (4717–19)

De ses dras ne se gardoit mie
Que il fussent tachié de *sanc*   (4758–9)

les dras voit
De fres *sanc* tachiez et gotez   (4766–7)

voit ses dras tachiez
De *sanc*   (4771–2)

J'ai trové
Sanc an voz dras, qui le tesmoingne   (4788–9)

Que an voz dras et es suens truis
Le *sanc* qui chëi de ses plaies   (4792–3)

la rëine vit
Et an l'un et an l'autre lit
Les dras *sanglanz*   (4795–7)

C'est *sanc* que an mes dras esgart   (4800)

Les dras et la coute *sanglante*
Des plaies Ke vos mosterrai   (4844–5)

Les dras *sanglanz* an son lit voit
Et el lit Ke tot ansemant   (4852–3)

Mes de mes plaies itant sai
Qu'anuit m'ont seignié a planté
S'an sont mi drap *ansanglanté*   (4890–2)

Li *sans* d'anbedeus parz le prueve   (4902)

por ce qu'il a vëu
Mes dras et les suens de *sanc* tainz.   (4944–5)

... enough of himself remains behind for the sheets to be soiled and stained with blood ... she did not notice how her sheets were blood-stained ... he saw the sheets stained and spotted with fresh blood ... he saw that his sheets were blood-stained ... I've found blood on your sheets as evidence

... by finding on your sheets and his the blood that ran from his wounds ... the queen saw the bloody sheets on both of the beds ... this blood I see on my sheets ... I'll show you the sheets and bedspread stained with the blood from Kay's wounds ... He sees the blood-stained sheets on her bed and also on Kay's ... But this much I know: that my wounds bled profusely during the night, and that has made my sheets blood-stained ... the blood in both places is proof ... he's seen my sheets and his stained with blood.

The blood provides sensational and apparently unequivocal visual evidence of the crime committed; yet there are three possible explanations as to its source – Lancelot's finger, Guenevere's nose, and Kay's wounds. 'My eyes will teach me the truth of the matter', says Bademagus, but what emerges from the scene is precisely the unreliability of sight as a guide to truth. This opposition between the visible and the true is underlined by a recurrent verbal play, especially in the lines leading up to Bademagus's statement, on forms of *veoir* (to see) and *voir* (true):

> Et ele cuide dire *voir*   (4804)
>
> Et bien sera li *voirs* provez   (4809)
>
> Je vuel que li rois droit me taingne
> Quant la chose *veüe* avra   (4814–15)
>
>   Sire, venez *veoir*
> Ce don garde ne vos prenez.
> La reïne *veoir* venez,
> Si *verroiz* mervoilles provees
> Que j'ai *veües* et trovees   (4818–22)
>
> Sire, or venez *veoir* les dras   (4840)
>
> 'Or alons, et si le *verrai*',
> Fet li rois, 'que *veoir* le vuel:
> Le *voir* m'an aprandront mi oel.'   (4846–8)

What is seen, and thus apparently unquestionable, turns out to require interpretation; it belongs to the field of signs, along with Lancelot's deceptive pretence that he is tired and is retiring to sleep, which only we with experience of such matters can 'antandre et gloser', or even Guenevere's presence at the window of her *chanbre*, which she says Kay could 'nul bien noter' (4643) [not construe favourably] if he became aware of it – it might seem unequivocal, but it would still be open to explanation. For this medieval romance,

the true truth about private life and private relations[12] lies beyond
what can be grasped by sight.

It has been stated of the romance as it emerges in twelfth-century
France that 'Il est la première forme littéraire en langue vulgaire
destinée à être lue, et non chantée. Et son ambition initiale est d'être
une traduction du latin, une "mise en roman."''[13] The nature of the
romance reflects these origins. The written text implies the possibility of distance – that between the eye and its object, and that
involved in private, non-participatory reading – and the French
courtly romance of the twelfth century might be defined as a
narrative that pries from a distance into private life, attempting to
bring it under surveillance, and in doing so turns storytellers and
their audiences into spies. We now take it for granted that this is a
natural subject for narrative (not of all kinds – not of war stories or
westerns, for example – but of the kinds that readers of the present
book are likely to find most interesting); and this very naturalness
may make it seem less strange and less exciting for narrative to deal
with such subject-matter at all than it probably did in Chrétien's
time. Late-twentieth-century readers have become accustomed to
narratives that offer verbal representations of intimate feelings,
intimate discussions, intimate relations – a whole field of experience
not available to public observation outside fiction, and into which
storytellers intrude without our even noticing that they are being
intrusive. Moreover, we have become used not only to verbal but to
photographic and cinematic representations that enable us literally
to *see* such material in fictional forms: that is, to see as observers
material that is normally available in real life only to participants.
In other words, through the fiction of our age we have become
thoroughly inured to being voyeurs. If we could cease to take all this
for granted, we would surely notice how strange, exciting, and
perhaps disturbing such subject-matter, and the penetration of
secrecy necessary to reveal it, are likely to have seemed in the twelfth
century. (A similar strangeness and excitement emerge in twelfth-
century religious writings too, as they begin to represent verbally,
for private reading, the intimate relations between the soul and
God.)

To focus closely on how the field of private life was represented in
some medieval romances, even down to such banal details as the
material enclosure of private spaces and the means by which such
enclosure can be penetrated by eye or body, is valuable, I believe, as

a way of defamiliarizing this type of representation. Even in a romance such as *Cligés*, to which I am about to turn, one which repudiates adultery as its theme, the poet still takes us momentarily into the *chanbre*;[14] he does not, as Augustine says of the bridegroom, 'turn all others out of his chamber' when intimacy is about to take place. And the voyeuristic strangeness of such moments is focused more sharply by associating it with *representations* of voyeurism within the fiction (scenes of spying, watching, listening), and also by a variety of narratorial devices that make us as readers or listeners realize *our* position as voyeuristic. (We catch ourselves imagining intimate details that have not been narrated, misinterpreting the nature of the exertions that brought a flush to Isolde's cheeks, or wishing that the poet would tell us things about which he is determined to remain silent . . .) In Chrétien, a more self-conscious storyteller and artist than Beroul (though not than Gottfried), this process further tends to raise the question of the poet's point of view and source of knowledge. Here too we may need to learn to overcome the 'natural' assumptions of our age.

We tend to assume that 'the narrator' of a story tells it – and here the inevitable visual metaphor comes in – from a consistent 'point of view'. The assumption has been especially dominant since Henry James's development of the 'dramatic method' of telling a story from the limited viewpoint of one of its participants, and since James's method was further theorized by critics from Percy Lubbock to Wayne Booth. Modernist and, still more, post-modernist storytelling methods may differ from this, and may sometimes be closer to medieval methods, but the assumptions appropriate to the classic novel are still generally dominant. The medieval situation is different, partly because of the medieval assumption that stories exist outside the volition of any particular storyteller; stories have an autonomous existence in some virtually transcendent realm, though they may be recorded in different ways by individual storytellers and their sources. Romances, as noted above, emerge with the claim to be translations *an romanz* (*Cligés* 3) from previously existing writings. This claim continues long after the development of narratives that must have been known to be fictional. Chrétien and his ideal readers or listeners knew perfectly well, I take it, that his stories were inventions,[15] and delighted in the inventiveness involved in telling them; nevertheless, the pretence is still maintained that the stories exist outside Chrétien himself. *Cligés* was

manifestly composed as a witty revisionary commentary on the
Tristan story, but Chrétien nevertheless assures us in his prologue
that

> Ceste estoire trovons escrite . . .
> An un des livres de l'aumeire
> Mon seignor saint Pere a Biauvez.
> De la fu li contes estrez,
> Don cest romanz fist Crestiiens.
> Li livres est mout anciiens,
> Qui tesmoingne l'estoire a voire; .
> Por ce fet ele miauz a croire.   (18–26)

This story . . . we find written down in one of the books in the library of my
Lord Saint Peter at Beauvais. That was the source of the tale which
Chrétien turned into this romance. The book that is the authority for the
truth of this story is very ancient, which makes it all the more worthy of
belief.

The issue is not 'belief' (a red herring with which Chrétien neatly
distracts us from his trail as a creator of fictions) but rather
autonomy: the story is presented as originating and subsisting
outside the storyteller's mind.

This means that the storyteller need not occupy a consistent
position, whether fixed or developing, in relation to the story. In
some medieval narratives, the storyteller is scarcely present at all:
the story seems to tell itself, unfolding into empty space and then
simply stopping. The narratorial process is as completely occluded
as in a classic Hollywood movie with its seamless editing.[16] That is
not the case with *Cligés*; there Chrétien is present not just in the
prologue but recurrently throughout, explaining his narratorial
methods – 'D'Alixandre vos dirai primes, / Comant il se plaint et
demante' [I shall tell you first how Alexander gives vent to his grief
and despair] (616–17) – commenting on the story as he tells it –
'Mout cuideroit bien esploitier, / – Cuideroit? et si feroit il' [he
would think he acted very well. Think? He would in fact do so]
(96–7) – and so on. But it would be a mistake to jump from
recognizing this presence of the storyteller within the storytelling to
assuming that he has a fixed, interpretable point of view from which
he sees and tells. The storyteller is an observer and presenter as
mobile as the movie-camera. In other words, with medieval narratives, we need to distinguish between narratorial *presence* and a single
narratorial *point of view*.

Narratorial presence may be very lively indeed, as it often is with Chrétien, but it does not necessarily imply any particular viewpoint. The narrator is present in a space separate from that of the story and not fixed in relation to it, a space that he shares with us, his listeners and readers, and in which he may operate as no more than a master of ceremonies or a means of creating local immediacy of effect. But – and this will emerge more clearly as we continue our investigations – the very concern with voyeurism in the subject-matter of romances, the concern with the means by which secrets are brought to light and can be told, exerts some pressure towards a realization of the narrator's position as itself voyeuristic in relation to his story. Questions begin to arise, such as: how does he know this? did he actually witness the intimate relations he recounts? In *Cligés*, however, such questions are not yet pressing; more striking is the way Chrétien looks from many positions, corresponding to the many attitudes this romance adopts towards the Tristan story.

Chrétien claims in his prologue that he himself had written 'Del roi Marc et d'Iseut la blonde' (5), though this work does not survive. The macrostructure of *Cligés* is identical with that of the Tristan story as told by Gottfried, by Brother Robert, and presumably by Thomas: the first third of the narrative concerns the love-story of the hero's parents, while the remainder concerns a love-triangle involving the hero (Cligés), his uncle (Alis, the emperor of Constantinople), and his uncle's wife (Fenice). The parallels go further, involving 'structural transposition and transformation, in a dazzling variety of ways'.[17] The uncle had promised to remain unmarried and make his nephew his heir; he nevertheless marries a fair-haired woman whom his nephew wins for him from an enemy, but the nephew and the bride fall in love before the marriage. A magic potion is administered by the wife's attendant and confidante, but in *Cligés* this motif becomes more complicated: there are two potions, one given to the uncle to make him imagine he is making love to his wife (so that a deception such as that by which Brangain takes Iseult's place on her wedding-night is unnecessary), and one given to the wife later to produce the appearance of death, thus enabling her to escape her husband's anger. A lady's single golden hair plays a part in the plot, but it belongs not to the heroine of the main part but to her mother, and instead of being dropped by a bird it is sewn into her future husband's shirt. The lovers enjoy a period of secret happiness in a place of concealment, with a strong emphasis on the skilled artistry of its construction, as in Thomas's *salle aux images* and Gottfried's *Minnegrotte* (this element is missing from Beroul's *Tristan*); the idyll ends in discovery by an act of voyeurism in which the hero's sword plays an important part (but in *Cligés* it is used not to separate the lovers but to amputate the voyeur's leg!). There are even parallels to some of the most striking verbal devices associated with Thomas's *Tristan*: a threefold pun on *amer* (meaning 'love' and 'bitter') and *la mer* (meaning 'the sea'),[18] and a pun on *poison*, meaning 'potion' and 'poison'.[19]

Moreover, Chrétien includes several explicit references to the earlier story, all of them in the Cligés–Fenice part of the romance. Cligés

> sot plus d'escremie et d'arc
> Que Tristanz, li niés le roi Marc,
> Et plus d'oisiaus et plus de chiens.   (2789–91)

knew more of swordsmanship and archery than Tristan, King Mark's nephew, and more than he of birds and dogs.

Fenice indignantly tells her nurse Thessala,

> Miauz voldroie estre desmanbree
> Que de nos deus fust remanbree
> L'amors d'Iseut et de Tristan,
> Don tantes folies dit l'an,
> Que honte m'est a reconter.
> Je ne me porroie acorder
> A la vie, qu'Iseuz mena.
> Amors an li trop vilena;
> Car ses cors fu a deus rantiers
> Et ses cuers fu a l'un antiers.
> Einsi tote sa vie usa,
> Qu'onques les deus ne refusa.   (3145–56)

I'd rather be torn limb from limb than have people in referring to us [herself and Cligés] recall the love of Iseut and Tristan, about whom such nonsense is talked that I'm ashamed to speak of it. I couldn't reconcile myself to the life Iseut led. With her, love was too debased, for her body was made over to two men, whilst her heart belonged entirely to one. In this way she spent her whole life without ever rejecting either one.

And when Cligés suggests that they elope to Britain, she answers,

> Ja avuec vos einsi n'irai;
> Car lors seroit par tot le monde
> Aussi come d'Iseut la blonde

> Et de Tristan de nos parlé,
> Quant nos an seriiens alé;
> Et ci et la, totes et tuit
> Blasmeroient nostre deduit. (5310–16)

I shall never go away with you like that; because then, once we had left, people throughout the world would speak of us as of the fair-haired Iseut and Tristan; and on every side one and all would heap blame on our enjoyment of our love.

Cligés is involved, then, in an intricate intertextual relation with the Tristan story, which Chrétien probably knew in both the traditions represented by Thomas and by Beroul.[20] The relatively simple structure of settings, opposing *chanbre* to *sale* and court to forest, is greatly complicated by the introduction of a broader international scope and a more realistic geography, culminating however in the technological artifice of the tower built by Jehan and used to conceal Fenice, with many *chanbres* and *cheminees* and also secret rooms in the basement – a kind of Constantinople Hilton, furnished with fine pictures, painted vaults, and bathrooms with hot running water. Even the familiar settings, such as the bed as the most private and most dangerous place, tend to frame actions that are variants on those we expect: Alixandre goes to bed, 'Mes bien se garde qu'an nel voie' (1636) [taking good care that nobody sees him], to enjoy kisses and embraces not with his beloved Soredamors but with his shirt with her hair sewn into it; and after Alis's marriage-bed has been blessed and he retires to it with Fenice, he does not make love to her but (thanks to Thessala's potion) only dreams that he is doing so:

> Mes de neant est an grant eise:
> Neant anbrace et neant beise,
> Neant tient et neant acole,
> Neant voit, a neant parole,
> A neant tance, a neant luite. (3359–63)

But he finds great enjoyment in nothing at all, embracing nothing and kissing nothing, holding nothing and caressing nothing, seeing and speaking to nothing, struggling and striving with nothing.

These variants, and especially the second with its repeated *neant*, reflect back the reader's own voyeuristic experience, knowing love only in imagination, enjoying kisses and caresses not bodily but only with the mind's eye, in a fiction, in a dream of passion. A similar

point might be made about the strangest variant of all, at the very
end of the romance, where we are told that, whereas Fenice escaped
from Constantinople to live happily ever after with Cligés, every
succeeding emperor, to avoid any repetition, has kept his wife in a
chanbre (6778) under lock and key and accompanied only by
eunuchs! This final vision of the *chanbre* as a barren prison once more
reflects back at us our experience as romance-readers.

The elements of myth and magic in the Tristan story are generally
transmuted by Chrétien into current affairs and science: here are no
giants or dragons but only the manoeuvrings of international
diplomacy, the anti-love potion is represented as a product of
advanced pharmaceutical technique, and Iseut's deceptive oath and
ordeal give way to a scientific deception that employs urine-analysis
to indicate that Fenice is on the brink of death. Yet within this highly
rational 'modern' world, mystery remains: from Jehan's tower one
can get through a door 'Tel que ne vos sai ne ne puis / La façon dire
ne retreire' (6386–7) [made in a way I am quite incapable of telling
or describing] into a garden 'clos antor / De haut mur qui tient a la
tor' (6421–2) [enclosed all round by a high wall connected to the
tower], containing a grafted and trained tree with a bed beneath it,
where Bertrand sees Cligés and Fenice sleeping together. The
relation of *Cligés* to *Tristan* is a matter both of repudiation and of
outdoing: it rewrites the 'one great European myth of adultery' so
that adultery is avoided, for the heroine's marriage is never consum-
mated and it is questionable whether it counts as a marriage at all.
Thus the legal justification for voyeurism also becomes
questionable.

By contrast with *Tristan*, indeed, *Cligés* is singularly lacking in
scenes where secret looking or listening is represented in the
narrative. The one literal and explicit act of voyeurism is that just
mentioned, occurring late and briefly, when Bertrand on his
hawking expedition (like the huntsman in *Tristan*) 'vit dormir a
masse / Fenice et Cligés nu a nu' (6450–1) [saw Fenice and Cligés,
both naked, sleeping in a close embrace]. They are beneath the tree,
of which we have been told,

> Ne ja n'iert li solauz tant hauz
> A midi, quant il est plus chauz,
> Que ja rais i puisse passer.   (6413–15)

however high the sun is at noon when it is hottest, not one of its rays can
penetrate ... the branches.

The huntsman's predatory visual rays are more piercing; but it is amusing that, unlike the several voyeurs in *Tristan*, when he tells what he has seen he is not believed, even though it is true, but is taken for a *jeingleor* (6512), a mere poet – like Chrétien.

In Chapter 1 I quoted from Alixandre's soliloquy a textbook example of the heart-and-eyes topos. This continues with an ingenious extended metaphor identifying the arrow that has wounded his heart with the body of Soredamors (770ff.). Thus an *effictio* turning a woman into an enumeration of glittering bodily parts is combined with a similar enumerative description of Love's arrow. Chrétien writes:

> La coche et li penon ansanble
> Sont si pres, qui bien les ravise,
> Quë il n'i a qu'une devise
> Aussi con d'une greve estroite. (778–81)

The nock at the shaft-end and the feathers are so close together, if one examines them closely, that they are separated by no more than the width of a narrow parting in the hair.

What is a simile so far as the arrow is concerned leads into the literal description of Soredamors's hair, identified with the arrow's feathers. Then Alixandre moves downward through the parts of her body, separated and fetishized by the brilliant objects with which most are compared: brow ('mirror or emerald or topaz'), eyes ('two burning candles'), nose and face (lily and rose), the mouth, teeth ('ivory or silver'), chin, ears, throat (crystal), neck (ivory), and exposed bosom ('freshly fallen snow'); but at this point the description has to come to an end, because the rest of Love's arrow is concealed in its quiver, namely Soredamors's 'tunic and shift', and

> Ne la *vi* pas, n'an moi ne peche,
> Se la façon dire ne sai
> De chose, que *veüe* n'ai. (850–2)

I didn't see it, and it's not my fault if I can't give a description of something I haven't seen.

Chrétien's adoption of Alixandre's fixation on the visual – in his case only temporary (what Freud would call an 'intermediate relation to the sexual object ... which lies on the road to copulation')[21] – produces a realization of his 'point of view' in a more general sense: the rhetorical device of *effictio* cannot be completed by a timid lover, and the reader is left to imagine what the tunic and shift conceal. Yet after all the poet *could* describe what Alixandre cannot see, and our awareness of this possibility stimulates our imaginations and invites us to construct a position for the poet, whose role as creative artist is of special importance in *Cligés*.

With the notable exception of spying scenes, *Cligés* contains most of the kinds of looking and implied looking that are normal in medieval courtly treatments of love: looking as an expression of initial admiration, visual descriptions of the beloved (both male and female), the female gaze in the chivalry-topos, the exchange of secret glances between lovers in public places, and so on. The love of Cligés and Fenice is long concealed, as much by their modesty as by its illicit nature. It is betrayed by their eyes:

> Et neporquant des iauz ancuse
> Li uns a l'autre son panser,
> S'il s'an seüssent apanser.
> Des iauz parolent par esgart;
> Mes des langues sont si coart,
> Que de l'amor qui les justise
> N'osent parler en nule guise.   (3832–8)

Yet, had they realized it, they both reveal their thoughts through their eyes. The looks in their eyes are eloquent, but with their tongues they are so cowardly that they dare not make any reference to the love that holds them in its sway.

Yet their love is concealed from the eyes of others, even at the moment when Cligés leaves Constantinople,

> Qu'ains nus n'ot tant les iauz overz
> Ne tant n'i oï cleremant,
> Qu'aparcevoir certainnemant
> D'oïr ne de veoir seüst,
> Quë antre aus deus amor eüst.   (4330–4)

so that there was never anyone with his eyes so wide open or his hearing so sharp that he was able to tell positively from what he heard or what he saw that there was any love between these two.

We and the storyteller thus have the advantage over the curious onlookers and listeners of whom the fictional world is assumed to be full. As in so many romances, the effect of concealment and of this opposition between what is secretly true and what is publicly known is to define individual consciousness more sharply. We glimpse this on Cligés's return to Constantinople:

son panser descovrir n'ose
A celi, por cui ne repose,
Et s'a bien eise et leu del dire,
S'il ne dotast de l'escondire;
Que tote jor la puet veoir
Et seul a seul lez li seoir
Sanz contredit et sanz deffanse;
Que nus mal n'i antant ne panse.   (5149–56)

he does not dare reveal his thoughts to her through whom he finds no rest.
Yet he has every chance and opportunity to speak them, were he not afraid
of being rejected; because all day long he can see her and sit beside her in
complete privacy without being denied or forbidden, since nobody sees or
thinks there is any harm in that.

Here we have two private subjectivities, set in relief against public
suppositions, open to the poet but closed to each other. The space of
individual consciousness is being marked out not just by soliloquy or
interior monologue or dialogue, but by these explorations of the
scopic interface between private and public.

Subjectivity is what cannot be seen, but in *Cligés*, unlike *Tristan*, it
is measured against publicly accessible values. Chrétien rejects
adultery as the basis of romantic love – hence his later difficulties in
Lancelot, when Marie de Champagne evidently required of him a
romance where adultery was unavoidable. In *Cligés*, composed
earlier, there is no suggestion that Guenevere has been connected
with adultery, and there is no reason for scepticism about her advice
to Alixandre to seek 'mariage ... et enor' (2304). Thus Chrétien
arranges that the relationship between Fenice and Cligés is not
strictly adulterous, because Fenice's unconsummated marriage to
Alis would have been liable to annulment. The ideal *Cligés* sets up
seems quite clear: a love which is entirely mutual, and which is also
honourable in rejecting adultery in favour of marriage. The happy
ending is summarized as: 'De s'amie a feite sa fame' (6753) [Of his
sweetheart he has made his wife].

The ideal is noble, but the question is, how can it be put into
effect? The poem lays repeated emphasis on various forms of skill
and artistry.[22] Fenice and Cligés, however fine their principles and
feelings, would be unable to make their complicated way to a happy
ending without the assistance of Thessala and Jehan; and Jehan's
ingeniously constructed tower and tomb hold a climactic position in
the narrative. As with Gottfried's *Tristan*, a Shakespearean analogy,

though inexact, may be helpful. In *Cligés*, as in Shakespeare's middle and late comedies, an analogy is implied between the artistic skill represented in the fiction and that of the poet who creates the fiction.[23] There is a hint of something similar in the parallel implied by Gottfried between the artistry of the *Minnegrotte* and his own artistry. But Chrétien and Shakespeare are closer together in offering reworkings of myth as fiction: in *Much Ado About Nothing* and *The Winter's Tale*, a myth of death and rebirth is so presented that, as with Fenice, the death is a cunningly constructed fiction, though one that involves suffering for the heroine: Fenice suffers a version of Christ's passion. Fenice is not a real phoenix; but then in stories what is real? To put it in grossly simplified terms, one message of Shakespeare's later comedies is that the problems that lead to tragic outcomes can be solved, but only in plays, only by the exercise of the writer's skill. And similarly, I suggest, *Cligés* implies that the moral ambiguity and tragic outcome of the Tristan story can be averted; but only by the artist's *engin*, only in fiction, however ingeniously that fiction draws on historical reality for its material. Alis's convenient death is manifestly a product of the storyteller's intervention; and Alis's sustained, potion-induced dream of love might be read as another emblem of the power of fictional artistry, for in fiction all sexual consummations are wish-fulfilling dreams. It is then a final irony that in the 'reality' outside the fiction, as the closing lines tell us, this story of a woman's liberation from a loveless pseudo-marriage has moved the emperors of Constantinople to keep their wives in prison, guarded by eunuchs. Chrétien is present throughout as a secret watcher, even over what occurs when his characters are *seul à seul*, even over their most secret thoughts, but his 'point of view' is not fixed. His artistry lies in mobility, in shifts of perspective, in unpredictable movements from what can be seen to what cannot. This artistic perspective, with its secret power to transform as well as to watch, is ultimately the most satisfying form of voyeurism.

CHAPTER 5

The Lanval story

The main part of this chapter will be concerned with two versions of the same story, a Breton lay or short romance whose plot turns on two scenes where a woman manifests her magical power by displaying her beauty to the male gaze. The versions differ interestingly, not only because one is in twelfth-century French and the other in fourteenth-century English, but also because the first, *Lanval*, is by a woman, Marie de France, and the second, *Sir Launfal*, by a man, Thomas Chestre. As a postscript, I add a brief discussion of another short romance, this time from thirteenth-century France, *La Chastelaine de Vergi*, that tells a somewhat similar story, but in a secularized and tragic form; here the supernatural is entirely absent, and the question of looking is displaced on to the epistemology of narrative.

Marie de France, one of the few identifiably female authors to have written secular poems in an early medieval vernacular language, probably belonged to the highest Anglo-Norman aristocracy. *Lanval* is the only Arthurian tale in a collection of twelve lays which she claims to have adapted from stories sung by the Bretons; from this it was extracted and twice translated into Middle English. One version is the anonymous early fourteenth-century *Sir Landevale*, a close translation, surviving in five manuscripts, in the octosyllabic couplets of the original.[1] *Sir Launfal*, the second version, from the later fourteenth century, survives in a single manuscript, and appears to be based not primarily on *Lanval* but on *Sir Landevale* and on consultation or recollection of other sources including the anonymous French lay *Graelent*. It involves a more radical rehandling of Marie's story, along with a metrical reshaping into tailrhyme stanzas. Nothing is known of Thomas Chestre, other than what can be deduced from *Sir Launfal* itself; he probably wrote for a non-aristocratic public.

I begin with a summary of Marie's story, and I do this both

because I shall argue that the story has a meaning and because Chestre changes it in important ways. *Lanval* concerns a knight of King Arthur's who is initially bereft of wealth and love, but is compensated when a lady (evidently a fairy) falls in love with him, makes herself known, and grants her love and an unending supply of wealth on condition that he reveals their relationship to no one. He lives a knightly life of great splendour for some time, during which she comes secretly in answer to this thoughts. One day, though, the queen offers him her love; when he refuses, she accuses him of homosexuality, and he indignantly answers that he has a mistress whose poorest servant is fairer than she. These rash words have two consequences: the queen accuses him of having propositioned and insulted her, so that he is put on trial and can escape banishment only by proving the truth of his boast; and the fairy lady abandons him because he has revealed their relationship. But at last she relents, appears in person to vindicate him at his trial, and carries him off to the island of Avalon. 'Nul hum n'en oï plus parler, / Ne jeo n'en sai avant cunter' (645–6) [no one has heard any more about him, nor can I relate any more].[2]

It would be generally agreed that this story may be seen as one of wish-fulfilment[3] and this doubtless accounts for its widespread popularity. The young knight who is the normal hero of medieval romance, an idealized everyman, here gains without effort what every young man wishes, wealth and love; then he loses them again, but, by sheer force of wishing, regains what he has lost. The story includes events regarded as impossible by modern readers and probably by Marie herself. Several of Marie's *lais* are of this general type, and many modern readers would wish to interpret their supernatural elements in psychological terms; but it would be mistaken to suppose either that Marie intended objective magic to symbolize subjective fantasy or – perhaps more important – that, in the 'mélange indissociable du merveilleux et du rëel'[4] of the whole collection, she and her public would have distinguished between objective and subjective precisely as we do. In *Lanval* she brings magic and wishes unusually close together. When Lanval first encounters the fairy world, though 'La mot de fée n'est jamais prononcée',[5] there are explicit indications of the supernatural: he dismounts by a stream (the usual river-barrier between this world and the other) and his horse trembles violently. At the same time, he is alone, lying as if asleep with his head resting on his cloak, and is thinking of his troubles, when the solution to them emerges dream-like, with the appearance of the fairy lady's maidens to summon him to her. In his unhappiness, 'Il ne *veit* chose ke li pleise' (52) [He saw nothing that might please him], but the maidens offer visual pleasure:

> *Garda* aval lez la riviere,
> [Si] *vit* venir deus dameiseles,
> Unc n'en ot *veü*[*es*] plus beles. (54–6)

He *looked* downriver and *saw* two damsels coming, more beautiful than any he had ever *seen*.

The fairy lady herself is encountered in a luxurious tent beyond the price-range of Semiramis or Octavian:

There was a golden eagle placed on the top, the value of which I cannot tell, nor of the ropes or the poles which supported the walls of the tent. There is no king under the sun who could afford it, however much he might give. (87–92)

In a strictly psychoanalytic interpretation this fetish, this object beyond male grasp, would doubtless be recognized as standing in place of the mother's absent phallus.[6] More obviously, the fairy lady corresponds to a familiar male erotic fantasy, lying as she does half-naked, exposed and displayed to Lanval's gaze:

> Ele jut sur un lit mut bele . . .
> En sa chemise senglement.
> Mut ot le cors bien fait e gent;
> Un cher mantel de blanc hermine,
> Covert de purpre alexandrine,
> Ot pur le chaut sur li geté;
> Tut ot descovert le costé,
> Le vis, le col e la peitrine . . . (97–105)

she lay on a very beautiful bed . . . clad only in her shift. Her body was well formed and handsome, and in order to protect herself from the heat of the sun, she had cast about her a costly mantle of white ermine covered with Alexandrian purple. Her side, though, was uncovered, as well as her face, neck and breast . . .

'Il l'*esgarda*, si la *vit* bele' (117) [He looked at her and saw that she was beautiful]. 'Thus she turns herself into an object – and most particularly an object of vision: a sight'.[7] On the bed in the tent – a space enclosed to form a kind of countryside *chambre* – the lady gives words and then deeds to the message implied by her seductive appearance: 'I love you above all else' (116).

There are also elements of female fantasy involved in the lady's self-display, and more generally in her role as wealthy, self-pleasing and successful seductress. To be looked at is in one sense to submit to a dominant male gaze, but, within the given framework of sexual politics, to attract the gaze is a source of female power, and Lanval immediately succumbs: 'I shall do as you bid and abandon all others for you' (127–8). It is significant that at this moment Marie gives a brief glimpse of the lady's point of view. She is nameless throughout, which confirms that in general she exists as the named hero's fantasy, but here we are allowed to glimpse the possibility that she is also a subject and he also an object:

> Quant la meschine oï parler
> Celui que tant la peot amer,
> S'amur e sun cors li otreie. (131–3)

When the maiden heard these words from the man who loved her so, she granted him her love and her body.

The boon she grants him is universal – 'henceforth he could wish for nothing which he would not have' (136–7) – but it is hers to give; she promises to be present to him whenever he wishes, but only where a man may 'aver s'amie / Sanz reproece, sanz vileinie' (165–6) – that is, when no one else is present – and he is forbidden to disclose their love.

The continued fulfilment of his wishes depends on solitude and separation from the socially constructed reality of the court. This is one reason why the tension of the trial scene is so powerful: it is hard to believe that Lanval's secret love is anything *but* a fantasy, and we do not really expect the lady to return once he has allowed public reality to impinge on his fantasy-world. What could be more damagingly literal than the forensic interrogation to which his fantasy is submitted? Yet the lady does return, in a scene in which male looking at the female body receives the heaviest possible stress. Arthur presses his barons to find against Lanval, and they are about to give their verdict when

> Deus puceles *virent* venir
> Sur deus beaus palefreiz amblanz.
> Mut par esteient avenanz;
> De cendal purpre sunt vestues

> Tut senglement a lur char nues.
> Cil les *esgardent* volenters. (472–7)

they saw two maidens approaching on two fine ambling palfreys. They were extremely comely and dressed only in purple taffeta, next to their bare skin; the knights gazed at them with pleasure.

The juxtaposition of luxurious garment and bare skin, more provocative than complete nudity, is a recurrent element in descriptions of female seductiveness.[8] Lanval is asked whether his beloved has come but denies it, and the maidens demand that *chambres* hung with silken curtains, the appropriate setting for femininity in both its power and its weakness, should be made available for their mistress. Arthur agrees, and then once more requires the barons' verdict. Instead comes another female intrusion into the scene of male justice:

> Deus puceles de gent cunrei –
> Vestues de deus pailes freis,
> Chevauchent deus muls espanneis –
> *Virent* venir la rue aval.
> Grant joie en eurent li vassal. (510–14)

they saw two finely accoutred maidens coming along the street, dressed in garments of Phrygian silk and riding on Spanish mules. The vassals were glad of this.

The maidens repeat the booking of *chambres*, and are greatly admired by the watching barons: 'many praised them highly for their bodies, faces, and complexions' (529–30). Urged on by the queen, Arthur yet again demands that judgment should be given; and now there is a culminating interruption, a female witness whose appearance constitutes the evidence that settles the case. The passage is worth quoting at length:

> Ele iert vestue en itel guise:
> De chainsil blanc e de chemise,
> Que tuz les costez li pareient,
> Que de deus parz laciez esteient.
> Le cors ot gent, basse la hanche,
> Le col plus blanc que neif sur branche,
> Les oilz ot vairs e blanc le vis,
> Bele buche, neis bien asis,
> Les surcilz bruns e bel le frunt
> Et le chef cresp e aukes blunt;
> Fil d'or ne gette tel luur

> Cum si chevel cuntre le jur ...
> Il n'ot al burc petit ne grant
> Ne li veillard ne li enfant
> Que ne l'alassent *esgarder*.
> Si cum il la *veent* errer,
> De sa beauté n'iert mie gas.
> Ele veneit meins que le pas,
> Li jugeür, que la *veeient*,
> A [grant] merveille le teneient;
> Il n'ot un sul ki l'*esgardast*
> De dreite joie n'eschaufast.   (559–85)

The lady was dressed in a white tunic and shift, laced left and right so as to reveal her sides. Her body was comely, her hips low, her neck whiter than snow on a branch; her eyes were bright and her face white, her mouth fair and her nose well-placed; her eyebrows were brown and her brow fair, and her hair curly and rather blond. A golden thread does not shine as brightly as the rays reflected in the light from her hair ... There was no one in the town, humble or powerful, old or young, who did not watch her arrival, and no one jested about her beauty. She approached slowly and the judges who saw her thought it was a great wonder. No one who had looked at her could have failed to be inspired with real joy.

As when first seen by Lanval, the lady consciously displays herself as a sight, moving slowly and wearing what will reveal enough of her beauty to stimulate the imagination to supply what is unseen; the description is detailed enough to amount to a formal *effictio*. The effect is such as to imply that the lady *wishes* to be fragmented by the onlookers' eyes, wishes that each of her parts should be fetishized as a means to power. Lanval of course recognizes her, and exclaims, 'gariz sui, quant jeo la *vei*' (600) [my cure is in *seeing* her]. She enters the palace and mounts a final, triumphant display of her body, like the climax of a striptease performance,

> Si que de tuz iert bien *veüe*.
> Sun mantel ad laissié chaeir,
> Que meuz la püissent *veer*.   (604–6)

in such a way that she could be seen by all, [she] let her cloak fall so that they could see her better.

Here, by contrast with the bedroom scene in *Lancelot*, the visible and the true are identical, and the lady has only to reveal herself for Lanval's case to be recognized as unanswerable. Contrary to all expectation, his wish-fulfilling dream comes true not just for himself but for the whole court, and whereas in *Tristan* and *Lancelot* the hero intervenes to save the heroine from judicial punishment, here, in this poem by a woman, female power manifests itself to rescue the male hero. It does so not in the bedroom – the lady never enters the splendid *chambre* that has twice been booked for her – but in the court of law. Lanval is publicly vindicated (623, *aquitez*; 628, *desrainié*), and he then disappears for ever into the world of his dream, carried off to Avalon, an island cut off from everyday reality by the water surrounding it.

This is a story, then, in which fantasy plays an unusually strong part: not just a fantasy, but a fantasy about fantasy, a wish-fulfilment about wish-fulfilment. Marie tells a story about what seems to be a story that Lanval tells himself; in her story his story comes true, and he ends by being absorbed into the realm of story, the realm of what 'nus *recuntent* li Bretun' (642). She ends by saying, 'Ne jeo n'en sai avant *cunter*' (646). But this account may not go far enough in recognizing the fantasy element in *Lanval*. Wish-fulfilling fantasy may seem to be offered as compensation for an unpleasant reality; but the 'reality' in which the hero begins can equally be interpreted as a fantasy, not of wish-fulfilment but of persecution. Lanval is a knight of 'valur, ... largesce, ... beauté, ... prüesce' (21–2), whose very virtues cause him to be envied and singled out for disregard when Arthur is distributing 'Femmes et tere' (17) to everyone else.

There were those who pretended to hold him in esteem, but who would not have uttered a single regret if misfortune had befallen him. He was the son of a king of noble birth, but far from his inheritance. (24–6)

Suppose I were to go about saying that I was a king's son, but inexplicably severed from my inheritance; that my virtue and beauty made everyone envy me; that I was surrounded by people who pretended to respect me but would really be delighted if misfortune befell me; and that everyone else was being given valuable presents, with myself as the sole exception? I would surely be diagnosed as a victim of persecutory paranoia – that is, unless I were a little child, because such feelings of persecution are common childhood fantasies, regarded as paranoid only if persisting into adult life. It is normal for children to feel themselves unjustly neglected or persecuted by their parents; Freud writes in his 1916 paper 'Some Character-Types Met with in Psychoanalytic Work' that 'We all think we have reason to reproach Nature and our destiny for congenital and infantile disadvantages; we all demand reparation for early wounds given to our narcissism, our self-love' (*SE*, XIV, p. 315). Arthur's court may be seen as symbolizing the family, with Arthur as father and the knights as his sons;[9] and it is a normal part of growing up for a child to feel that his siblings are unjustly favoured against himself, and to fantasize about having a parent different from the one who actually has the power to give or withhold love. Freud begins an earlier paper, 'Family Romances', by stating that 'The liberation of an individual, as he grows up, from the authority of his parents is one of the most necessary though one of the most painful results brought about by the course of his development' (*SE*, IX, p. 237). He goes on to explain how, once children become capable of criticizing their parents, 'the child's imagination becomes engaged in the task of getting free from the parents of whom he now has a low opinion and of replacing them by others, who, as a rule, are of higher social standing' (pp. 238–9). Normal fantasies of this kind, translated into fictional terms, would account for Lanval's lost royal inheritance in Marie, and also, as we shall see, for the role of Guenevere as wicked stepmother in Chestre.

If Arthur is father then obviously his queen is mother; and just as there are two versions of father (bad and good, Arthur and Lanval's 'real' but absent father) so there are two versions of mother (good and bad, the fairy lady and the queen). The fairy lady offers Lanval everything he could possibly want, and especially what father denies him, wealth and sex. And Lanval, like a baby, is not required to *do* anything to receive mother's bounty: no knightly enterprises are necessary, she simply offers herself, saying, 'jo vus aim sur tute rien' (116). It is as if, like mother to baby, the fairy lady manifested herself as food to be devoured. That indeed is how Marie puts it, in describing their first meeting:

> Od s'amie prist le super:
> Ne feseit mie a refuser ...
> Un entremés i ot plener,
> Que mut pleiseit al chevalier:
> Kar s'amie baisout sovent
> E acolot estreitement.   (181–8)

He took his supper, which was not to be disdained, with his beloved ... There was one dish in abundance that pleased the knight particularly, for he often kissed his beloved and embraced her closely.

This re-enactment as fantasy of what for the baby is reality inevitably causes confusion in human relations. If Lanval's relationship with the fairy lady is pre-Oedipal and guiltless, his relationship with the queen is post-Oedipal and guilty. She too offers herself to him without any initiative on his part. But she is a seductive mother, wickedly proposing to take the son in her husband's place (or, put differently, this scene is a repetition of the earlier seduction by the fairy lady, but now transformed by post-Oedipal awareness). Hence Lanval's horrified repudiation of the betrayal that would be involved, and his reaffirmation of his earlier, more innocent fantasy. The story might now take either of two turns: on this contact with post-Oedipal consciousness, the child's fantasy of total, passive possession of mother might be repressed, leaving Lanval to make his way to maturity, like so many romance heroes, by performing worthy deeds and thus gaining a wife and land; or the original wish-fulfilment might take over completely. The latter is what happens; after agonizingly intense wishings, the fairy lady, the good version of mother, returns.

This may fairly be called a regressive fantasy, an avoidance of the painful but necessary liberation of the son from dependence on the mother. The stories of many medieval romances can be interpreted as offering reassurance about the possibility of growing up: despite all obstacles, the son *can* separate himself from his parents, make his own way in the world, and become a husband and father in his turn. (As Derek Brewer puts it, 'most medieval romances are essentially stories of the successful *rite de passage*'.)[10] That is not the message of *Lanval*. Its message is rather: life is hard, but never mind, you can go back instead of forward, you can be reunited with mother. So when the fairy lady ultimately returns, Lanval has still performed no knightly deeds, and when she leaves, even though he has been publicly vindicated, he does not resume his place in the world but 'leapt in a single bound on to the palfrey behind her' (639–40). To be riding a palfrey behind a lady, rather than riding a warhorse on one's own, is not a very knightly situation;[11] rather, it is that of a child. And Avalon is analogous to the water-surrounded womb; the son is reunited with mother for ever by ceasing to have an independent existence of his own.

It is not easy to interpret Marie's attitude towards the events of her story. She initially invites our sympathy for Lanval in terms that may indicate the fellow-feeling of one who, as a Frenchwoman in

England, had also been a stranger in a foreign court:[12] 'Now he was
in a plight, very sad and forlorn. Lords, do not be surprised: a
stranger bereft of advice can be very downcast in another land when
he does not know where to seek help' (33–8). Later, though, she
appears to stand at a certain distance from his retreat into the fairy
world, and to emphasize that only in stories are such possibilities
available. The hero is overwhelmingly central and the narrator's
presence is attenuated, felt chiefly as an intangible but pervasive
coolness; yet the hero's role is unheroic, and our last glimpse does
not show him in a knightly posture. The story embodies a male
fantasy, that of the son who gets mother all to himself. If Marie's
attitude towards it is somewhat detached, that may be partly
because her gender made it easier for her to see her hero from
outside; thus she is less committed to Lanval's fantasy of erotic
fulfilment than, for example, to that of the young wife in *Yonec*. If
Marie has a role in the Lanval story, it is not as Lanval but as the
fairy lady who confines him to the world of fiction. He may imagine
that he is devouring her; actually she, as storyteller if not as mother,
is devouring him.

  Sir Launfal is a revealingly dissimilar case. Many of its differences
from *Lanval* reflect the general stylistic differences between French
and English romances: the English style is more concrete and
dramatic but less capable of elegance and abstraction, and (because
in England even up to the late fourteenth century the courtly public
wanted its reading in French) it reflects a lower level of courtly
manners and a narrower understanding of courtly values. Other
differences betray Chestre's lack of poetic craftsmanship compared
with Marie de France: the tailrhyme stanza is a technically demanding form, and the effort to fulfil its requirements leads Chestre
repeatedly into formulaic banality and sometimes into absurdity.[13]
But beyond this, *Sir Launfal* appears to express attitudes that belong
specifically to its author. To put it briefly and dogmatically, Chestre
either failed to grasp or failed to value the true nature of the Lanval
story. He loved it, and that was why he devoted so much effort to
elaborating it (*Sir Launfal* is nearly twice as long as its immediate
source, *Sir Landevale*); but he loved it in a way involving total
commitment to the fantasy from which Marie remained at least
partly detached. It became *his* fantasy, and he attempted to live it in
writing as fictive reality. The result is a fascinating disaster.

  Chestre identified passionately with his hero in his wish-

fulfilment, his humiliations, and his final victory. He evidently
recognized that the story was one in which the hero's part was
remarkably unheroic, and attempted to remedy this defect. Some of
Chestre's major additions evidently aim to 'epicize' Launfal's role.
He introduces him as the culminating figure in a catalogue (13–24)
of the knights of 'Douȝty Artour' (7),[14] and raises him to the status
of royal seneschal. Then, after Launfal has received the fairy lady's
bounty, Chestre adds a long section not derived either from *Sir
Landevale* or from *Graelent*, in which he wins the prize at a tournament held in his honour by 'Alle þe lordes of Karlyoun' (433).
Next he receives a challenge from the fifteen-foot-high knight Sir
Valentyne. They fight, and at the first course Valentyne knocks off
Launfal's helmet, 'Jn tale as hyt ys telde' (576), and then rudely
laughs at him. All is not lost, however, for Gyfre, the servant
provided by Launfal's fairy mistress, now becomes invisible
(without our having received any warning that this is among his
powers) and puts the helmet on again; and when Valentyne makes
Launfal drop his shield, Gyfre retrieves it in mid-air. At the third
course, Launfal instantly slays Valentyne; and when 'Alle þe lordes
of Atalye' (601) attempt vengeance, Launfal slays them too 'as lyȝt
as dew' (608), and returns cheerfully to Britain. This section of *Sir
Launfal* is so absurd as to encourage the thought that, like Chaucer's
brilliant parody of tailrhyme romance in *Sir Thopas*, it may be
intentionally comic; but there is really no evidence for that. It is far
more likely to be a serious attempt to provide Launfal with a display
of knightly prowess, rendered inept first by his advantage in having
an invisible assistant, then by the ridiculous ease with which he
defeats everyone, and overall by the dependence of his victory on the
fairy lady's guarantee that

> Jn werre ne yn turnement
> Ne schall þe greue no knyȝtes dent,
> So well y schall þe saue. (331–3)

Chestre wants Launfal to be a true hero, but he is reliant on his
lady's favour even for his success in battle. Moreover, even if
Chestre's attempt at epicizing Launfal had succeeded, it would
necessarily have remained irrelevant to the story's original core.
The narrative hinge is the requirement that Launfal should keep his
fairy mistress secret, and this means that no knightly deeds of his
could in any real sense be performed in her honour. Sir Valentyne

challenges him to joust for his lady's love (523–8, 538), but Launfal may not mention the lady in accepting the challenge, and Chestre is unfortunately incapable of turning that enforced silence into a drama of inward heroism. Finally, Chestre employs Gyfre again to prevent our last sight of Launfal from showing him behind the lady on her palfrey. Gyfre hurries up with Launfal's own horse (1012–14), and Launfal and the lady ride away together.

For all Chestre's modifications, the story remains essentially a child's fantasy of persecution and reward; the more so because Chestre cannot allow himself to see it as that. The role of Arthur's court as family is brought nearer the surface by another of his changes, which draws in Arthur's marriage to Guenevere as the story's first event. Thus Guenevere is introduced as a stepmother figure, an intruder into the family whose promiscuity makes her disliked by the knights from the beginning. And Chestre resolves the ambiguity in Arthur's role by making Guenevere responsible for driving Launfal from court by singling him out as the knight who receives no gifts:

> Euerych kny3t sche 3af broche oþer ryng,
> But Syr Launfal sche yaf noþyng:
>   Þat greuede hym many a syde.   (70–2)

The discrepancy between this initial enmity and Guenevere's later claim to have loved Launfal 'More þan þys seuen 3ere' (678) has been noted by several critics as a psychological oddity.[15] Chestre, however, regards Guenevere exclusively from Launfal's point of view, and the discrepancy is further evidence of his identification with his hero's fantasy rather than a sign of any interest in the queen's psychology. (Indeed, I suspect that in this version Guenevere's promiscuity has come to symbolize the general problem of the mother's sexuality, which makes her both desirable and frightening to the son; and the later encounter between her and Launfal, in which he perceives her as having attempted to seduce him while her story is that he has attempted to seduce her, is another way of treating the ambivalence of the son's desire for the mother.)

As with *Tristan*, a comparison with *Hamlet* is tempting. Like Shakespeare's play, Chestre's story begins with a jealous and rejected son at a parental wedding-feast; and the situation is brought still closer to *Hamlet* when Chestre introduces the death of Launfal's father as his reason for leaving court. The child's feeling that no one loves him and everyone is jeering at him (Valentyne's laughter when he knocks Launfal's helmet off being a further example of this) is developed still more fully in Chestre's version through another addition, the episode with Arthur's nephews and the mayor of Karlyoun, to which I shall return shortly. Just as this persecutory paranoid fantasy emerges in a cruder, less censored form in *Sir Launfal* than in its predecessors, so does the wish-fulfilment that compensates for it. Both are connected with looking, and to that I now turn.

Launfal's first encounter with the fairy lady, now identified as 'Þe kynges douȝter of Olyroun, / Dame Tryamour' (278–9), is narrated in a way that both stresses a greedier looking than in Marie's version and defines the value of what is being looked at more unequivocally in material terms. The whole scene is imagined in fuller, more concrete detail. To the attendant damsels' 'closely fitting tunics of dark purple' are added green velvet mantles with gold borders and trimmings of two kinds of fur, and also tiaras 'Wyth syxty gemmys & mo' (240). One small sign of Chestre's total identification with the compensatory fantasy is found at this moment of its first emergence. *Sir Landevale* had said about the fairy maidens, 'Fayrer women neuer he see' (63); Chestre takes the fantasy as his own and writes, '*J* sawe neuer non swyche' (243). The eagle on the tent is now an even more striking fetish, with eyes made of carbuncles that weirdly glow like moonlight. If the damsels were somewhat over-dressed, Tryamour displays herself to Launfal's eager gaze in unsubtle *déshabille*:

> For hete her cloþes down sche dede
> Almest to her gerdylstede:
> Þan lay sche vncouert.
> Sche was as whyt as lylye yn May,
> Or snow þat sneweþ yn wynterys day –
> He seygh neuer non so pert.   (289–94)

What she offers (besides herself) is imagined even more materialistically. She begins by declaring that she loves Launfal, but her first promise is:

> Yf þou wylt truly to me take,
> And alle wemen for me forsake,
> Ryche J wyll make þe.   (316–18)

She promises him an inexhaustible supply of gold marks, her horse Blaunchard, her servant Gyfre, a pennon bearing her arms, and invulnerability in battle.

As in *Lanval*, she will come to him only in private; but Chestre, anxious to remove any possibility that this is a mere dream, insists that Gyfre also sees her (502–4). There is some potential for embarrassment in a fairy servant who is also a voyeur; but, more important, the less possible it becomes to regard the fairy mistress as Launfal's wish-fulfilling fantasy up to the very end, the more naïve Chestre's view of her appears. Launfal regularly withdraws to the privacy of his *bour* or *chaumber* (374, 728) to enjoy her favours,[16] but Chestre is determined that her material gifts should receive the greatest publicity. The wealth she has promised Launfal is delivered in weighty and ostentatious form: ten men arrive on packhorses laden with silver, gold, 'ryche cloþes & armure bryȝt' (382), followed by Gyfre on Blaunchard; they loudly ask where Launfal lives, and explain that all this is for him. Correspondingly, when Tryamour withdraws her favours, the emptiness of Launfal's purse and the disappearance of Gyfre and the horse are given more emphasis than her own absence (733–41). Until then, Launfal has thrown his wealth about with an excess that suggests a non-aristocratic conception of the nature of aristocratic *largesse*. He overtips Sir Valentyne's messenger grossly in giving him 'A noble courser, & a ryng, / And a robe of ray' (545–6), and the insistence that once Launfal comes into the money his debts are paid 'be tayle & be score' (419) suggests commercial calculation rather than the knightly generosity that is supposed to be his great virtue.[17]

Tryamour's final appearance loses the shock-effect it had in *Lanval* because it is no longer the first time she has been seen by anyone but Launfal himself; but, like her first appearance, it has an added concreteness and a stronger emphasis on gazing. The first damsels to arrive are not two but ten in number – 'Þe barouns *sawe* come rydynge / Ten maydenes, bryȝt of ble' (848–9) – and as before they requisition 'A fayr chamber' (863) for their mistress; Arthur indeed orders 'Þe fayryst chaunber' (869) in his palace to be made ready. The next set of damsels are also ten –

> Þo *saw* þey oþer ten maydenes bryȝt,
> Fayryr þan þe oþer ten of *syȝt* . . .
> Ech man hadde greet desyre
> To *se* har clodynge   (883–91)

– and their demand that Arthur, rather than preparing a *chamber*, should

> Þyn halle agrayde, & hele þe walles
> Wyth clodes & wyth ryche palles,
> Aȝens my lady Tryamour, (904–6)

may indicate Chestre's resistance to the opposition between public and private on which Marie's story turns.[18] When Tryamour herself arrives, she is equipped with the utmost gaudiness – a crown of gold and precious stones, a purple dress, an ermine-furred saddle, green velvet saddle-cloths bordered with gold bells, 'stones of Ynde' (956) on her saddle-bows, a falcon, white greyhounds with gold collars, and all, Chestre insists, of the greatest material value: why, even her horse's breast-trappings were 'worþ an erldome, stoute & gay, / Þe best yn Lumbardye' (959–60). Availability to sight is stressed repeatedly:

> Þe barouns *seyȝ* come rydynge (926)
>
> Þey *saw* neuer non so gay (929)
>
> Þat semely was of *syȝt* (945)
>
> Þat any man myȝte *aspye* (954)
>
> Þat men her schuld *beholde* (963)
>
> And whan Launfal *sawe* þat lady (967)

Tryamour rides into Arthur's hall, and then 'Sche dede of her mantyll on þe flet / (Þat men schuld her *beholde* þe bet)' (979–80). This is of particular interest to the ladies, and above all to Guenevere, her rival for Launfal's affections:

> Vp stode þe quene & ladyes stoute,
> Her forto *beholde* all aboute,
> How euene sche stod vpryȝt. (985–7)

Their brilliance is entirely eclipsed, and Arthur acknowledges, 'Ech man may *yse* þat ys soþe, / Bryȝtere þat ye be' (1004–5). That might seem conclusive, but Chestre has made the opposition between the good and bad versions of mother considerably more vindictive than in his source. Guenevere longs to punish Launfal for his rejection of her seduction attempt; indeed she told Arthur, 'But y be awreke, y schall dye! / Myn herte wyll breke aþre!' (713–14). At that point Chestre added her rash vow: if Launfal succeeds in bringing forward 'a fayrer þynge' than herself, 'Put out myn eeyn gray!' (809–10). Sure enough, and with entire appropriateness to this story of gazing (compare Tristan's punishment of Godoïne), Tryamour's last act before departure is to blow at Guinevere 'Þat neuer eft myȝt sche *se*' (1008). Launfal was put on trial, but Guenevere is punished. Apt though it is, the act is one of private vengeance; in his eagerness to ensure the visible punishment of the wicked, Chestre has again failed to grasp the relation between private fantasy and public justice on which the story depends.

Chestre's overall aim is to ground and conceal his fantasy (which means concealing from himself that it *is* a fantasy) in a solid social and material reality, and it is in his evocation of the social dimensions of a materialistic way of life that he shows his greatest strength. This element in *Sir Launfal* also turns on looking, now experienced from the other side: the motive for action is the sense of being looked at by others, which gives rise to honour or, more often, to shame. As Stanley Cavell writes,

> shame is the specific discomfort produced by the sense of being looked at, the avoidance of the sight of others is the reflex it produces ... Under shame, what must be covered up is not your deed, but yourself. It is a more primitive emotion than guilt, as inescapable as the possession of a body, the first object of shame.[19]

Chestre's own social insecurity may reveal itself in the way his hero is more concerned with avoiding shame in others' eyes than with gaining honour.[20] In a passage derived from *Graelent*, Launfal, accompanied from court by Arthur's nephews, meets his former servant the mayor of Karlyoun, and what follows shows some shrewd observation of human behaviour. The mayor, thinking Launfal is still in royal favour, politely asks after Arthur; but immediately Launfal reveals that he has left court, the mayor changes his tune, with the implausible excuse that he is expecting seven knights from Brittany at any moment, and proposes that Launfal should lodge in the orchard instead. But then later, when the mayor sees the first instalments of Launfal's magic wealth being delivered, he changes back again, and invites him to dinner, adding that just yesterday he had wanted him to come to a feast, if only Launfal had not been out. Launfal rejects his hospitality, and the mayor slinks away to escape the eyes of one who knows his unworthiness: 'Þe meyr for schame away ȝede' (415).

Between these two encounters with the mayor has come a full treatment of the social consequences of poverty. As *Havelok* bears witness, a Middle English romance could include a realistic yet dignified account of what it really means for the hero to be poor (labour, hunger, unemployment, violent competition for jobs ...); *Sir Launfal* is different, representing not just poverty but a descent from wealth, a social fall involving humiliation before others. Arthur's nephews tell Launfal that they must leave because 'our robes beþ torent, / And your tresour ys all yspent' (139–40). When they return to court in their 'totore & thynne' robes (156), they cover up for him by saying that they happened to depart on a rainy day and had gone hunting in their old clothes. The rainy day is an amusing English touch (it rarely rains in French romances);[21] and there is something unaristocratically prudential about wearing old clothes for hunting, that quintessentially aristocratic activity. (The medieval English aristocracy may really have worn old clothes when hunting in the rain,[22] but mention of this custom would surely have seemed inappropriate in a genuinely courtly romance.)

Left alone, Launfal is not asked to the Trinity feast at Karlyoun because he is poor and therefore despised; the mayor's daughter, taking pity, invites him to dinner; he says he has no heart for it, and tells her pathetically how he could not even go to church because he lacked 'hosyn & schon, / Clenly brech & scherte' (200–1). What matters above all is evidently what the neighbours think, and that is based on what they see. Finally, when Launfal is on his way to the fateful meeting with Tryamour, the shamefulness of his situation reaches its depth: he is riding 'wyth lytyll pryde' (213), his horse slips and falls in the mud, 'Wherfore hym scornede many men / Abowte hym fer & wyde' (215–16), and he rides off 'Forto dryue away lokynge' (218) – the accusing eyes that mark his intolerably low social worth. It is for this reason, no doubt, that Tryamour, having met Launfal, makes a remark that is otherwise hard to understand: 'J wot þy stat, ord & ende: / Be nauȝt aschamed of me!' (314–15). She must mean 'Don't be ashamed that I know of your poverty' – and she immediately announces steps to remedy it.

The epicizing additions are intended to wipe out this shame. When Launfal mounts to fight Valentyne, it is before the eyes of many spectators –

> All þat *sawe* hym yn armes bryȝt
> Seyde þey *sawe* neuer swych a knyȝt,
> Þat hym *wyth eyen beheld*   (568–70)

– and when Valentyne laughs at knocking off his helmet, it produces a correspondingly intense shame:

> Syr Valentyn logh, & hadde good game:
> Hadde Launfal neuer so moche shame
> Beforhond, yn no fy3t.   (577–9)

The shame must be obliterated, and so it is, with Gyfre's assistance,
which however 'Noman ne segh wyth sy3t' (582). If Gyfre were not
present, Launfal would be shamed by defeat, but if Gyfre were not
invisible, Launfal would be shamed by his inability to overcome
Valentyne without magic assistance. What Chestre seems to forget
is that he and we see everything, and the effect is of transparent
self-delusion or what Freud calls *Verleugnung* (disavowal),[23] which
translates into a statement turning on *dennoch* ('nevertheless' or 'all
the same'). 'I know that Launfal, with whom I identify so strongly,
isn't really an epic hero; I know that he is really as ridiculous and
contemptible as I fear I would seem if my inner being were open to
others' eyes; but all the same ...'. To tell the Lanval story while
identifying so exclusively with Lanval as hero is to embark on
unavoidable self-defeat. It is rare to find a medieval text so strongly
marked by its author's wishes, and lending itself so readily to a
diagnostic reading.

   La Chastelaine de Vergi, an anonymous verse-narrative, is another
version of the Lanval story,[24] but one which is entirely desuperna-
turalized. The lady has no magical power, and the outcome is that
she, her lover, and the character corresponding to Guenevere all
die. The setting is the court world of gossip, curiosity, jealousy,
secrecy carefully guarded but broken by spying, and there is no
escape to Avalon. The wish-fulfilling fantasy that underlies the
magic in *Lanval* and *Sir Launfal* is absent, and so is the corresponding identification, with the hero or his fairy mistress: *La Chastelaine
de Vergi* seems impersonal compared with Chestre's treatment of
the story and even with Marie de France's. It is a tale told with
feeling but with a cool artistic detachment that forbids the reader
to enter into the experience of any one character: we can only
contemplate the elegant inevitability of the patterning that leads
the characters to death and exile. And the author seems on the
verge of recognizing that the very breaking of secrecy that produces
the tragic outcome is also what makes it possible for the tale to be
told.

   The tale tells of an unnamed knight who serves the Duke of
Burgundy; he is conducting a passionate but secret love-affair with
the Duke's niece, the Chastelaine of Vergi, and

> la dame li otria
> par itel couvenant s'amor
> qu'il seüst qu'a l'eure et au jor
> que par lui seroit descouverte
> lor amor, que il avroit perte
> et de l'amor et de l'otroi
> qu'ele li avoit fet de soi. (22–8)

the lady granted him her favours on condition he understood that, at the day and hour of his divulging their love, he would lose both her love and the enjoyment of it.[25]

The affair's beginning is concealed from us, and no reason is offered for the requirement of secrecy; it is simply a narrative *donnée*.[26] The couple meet frequently in the Chastelaine's *chambre* (37), the signal for their meetings being given by the lady's dog, which is allowed to run into an orchard where the knight is waiting. 'Et fu lor amor si celee / que fors aus ne le sot riens nee' (41–2) [and their love was so well concealed that not a soul knew of it but themselves]. Thus we begin with a situation that raises in its purest form the question peculiar to love-narrative: how can this story be told? – how can the story be told of a love that is secret? The whole poem constitutes an answer to this question; the story is an explanation of its own existence as a story. The prologue has already touched on the same issue, plunging into generalizations about the danger of revealing a secret love and into repetitions of the opposing verbs, to conceal and to reveal, *celer* and *descouvrir*:[27]

> Une maniere de gent sont
> qui d'estre loial samblant font
> et de si bien conseil *celer*
> qu'il se covient en aus fier;
> et quant vient qu'aucuns s'i *descuevre*
> tant qu'il sevent l'amor et l'uevre,
> si l'espandent par le païs,
> puis en font lor gas et lor ris.
> Si avient que cil joie en pert
> qui le conseil a *descouvert*,
> quar, tant com l'amor est plus grant,
> sont plus mari li fin amant
> quant li uns d'aus de l'autre croit
> qu'il ait dit ce que *celer* doit. (1–14)

There exists a class of people who make so good a pretence of loyalty and of concealing secrets that one cannot but trust them; yet when it happens that

someone reveals himself to them, acquainting them with his love and
private affairs, they spread the knowledge abroad and make it a matter for
raillery and mirth. And it happens, too, that he who has revealed his secret
loses his happiness thereby, for the greater the love, the greater the chagrin
that true lovers feel when one suspects the other of telling what he ought to
conceal.

The Duchess of Burgundy falls in love with the knight, and discreetly propositions him; he rejects her advances, and she, lying in
bed with her husband, tells him that the knight has propositioned
her. (This scene is one of many that take place in the secrecy of the *lit*
and/or the *chambre*; it remains to be revealed how the poet can know
what was said or done in this private place.) The Duke summons the
knight, repeats his wife's accusation, and threatens him with banishment. The knight, knowing that this would mean the end of his relations with the Chastelaine, backs his denial by agreeing to give a
truthful answer to any question the Duke asks. The Duke responds
that the knight is unmistakably in love with someone, and demands
to know who it is. In great anguish, after the Duke has promised that
whatever he says will be revealed to no one, the knight confesses his
affair with the Chastelaine. The Duke then wishes to know how it has
been successfully kept secret, and asks to witness the operations of
their scheme with the dog; and the knight is obliged to agree. Thus
what the Chastelaine has been promised should never be told is told
to the Duke, on condition that it should never be told: love becomes
narrative, the private takes a step on the road to becoming public.

In the next scene, the Duke becomes a voyeur and *écouteur*, and the
story is so told that we share his position of undignified curiosity,
seeing and hearing exactly what he does. Somewhat like King Mark,
he takes care to hide (391, *celer*) himself not in but behind a large tree
'pres de la chambre' (387), and there he sees the couple meeting and
hears their passionate greetings: 'Tout oï li dus a l'entree, / qui mout
pres d'aus apoiez fu' (420–1). [All [they spoke] before going in was
heard by the duke, leaning [against the tree] close by.] There is no
indication that the knight's behaviour is affected by his knowledge of
the Duke's presence; and once the lovers have entered the *chambre*, the
door closes, and we continue to share the Duke's situation, now
unable to see or hear their doings, but waiting patiently for them to
reappear:

> Ilueques s'est issi tenu
> toute la nuit, endementiers

que la dame et li chevaliers
dedenz la chambre en un lit furent
et sanz dormir ensamble jurent,
a tel joie et a tel deport
qu'il n'est resons que le recort,
ne nus ne l'entende ne n'oie
s'il n'atent a avoir tel joie
que Amors aus fins amanz done,
quant sa paine reguerredone.   (430–40)

He stayed positioned there all that night, while the lady and the knight lay in one bed within, together but not asleep, enjoying such pleasure and delight as it neither befits me to describe, not any man to hear about unless he hopes to have such joy as Love gives to true lovers when he requites love's pains.

Only true lovers, not mere spies like the Duke and ourselves, are worthy even to hear of love's bodily pleasures; and the poet, somewhat as in scenes we have examined from Gottfried's *Tristan* and Chrétien's *Lancelot*, substitutes a discourse *about* love for the climax we are forbidden to witness but are surely encouraged to imagine.

Night passes, and the lovers re-emerge, once more to be witnessed by the waiting Duke; the restriction of the voyeur's position we share with him is underlined by the poet's comment that when the knight leaves,

la dame l'uis clot;
mes tant comme veoir le pot,
le convoia a ses biaus ieus,
quant ele ne pot fere mieus.   (473–6)

the lady shut the door, but as long as she could see him her lovely eyes accompanied him on his way, since she could do nothing better.[28]

We too can do nothing better. The Duke repeats his promise to 'keep this secret [him]self' (499, 'cest conseil celer'). Next day in his *chambre*, having 'ordered everyone else to leave the room' (523–4) (but this time not ourselves, for it is not love-making that is to be witnessed), the Duke informs his wife that he knows she has lied and tells her, 'you are never to ask me any more about it' (549). The Duchess, though, is eager to know more of this story, and plans to wait until night and use her feminine wiles to lure her husband into satisfying her longing. Again we are not forbidden the *chambre*,

which is to be the scene not of sexual but of narrative desire and its
fulfilment. After prolonged discursive foreplay, turning on the
concealment and uncovering of secrets, the Duke gives way and
'related ['a la verité contee'] the lovers' entrances and exits, and
finally kept back nothing of what he had seen and heard' (655–8).
The Duchess promises to conceal (665, 'celer') what he has told her,
and says he may hang her if she reveals it (666, 'le descuevre'); but
she inwardly vows that when the opportunity arises she will mention
it to the Chastelaine, 'and will spare ['celera'] no venomous detail'
(679–80).

Next Whitsun, when the ladies are in her *chambre* preparing for the
dance, the Duchess drops a hint to the Chastelaine about how
cleverly she has trained her dog; the other ladies 'overheard the
exchange' (719, 'ont oï le conte') without understanding it, but the
Chastelaine understands well enough, and, sick and angry, remains
behind:

> Dedenz une garderobe entre
> ou une pucelete estoit
> qui aus piez du lit se gisoit,
> mes ele ne la pot veoir.   (726–9)

She entered a closet where a young girl, unseen by her, was lying at the foot
of the bed.

In this most private of rooms the story's climax is to occur; but the
poet takes care to arrange that here too there will be an unseen spy,
indicating a subject position for his listeners, and providing an
explanation for the possibility of telling the story. The Chastelaine
soliloquizes, arguing that only the knight, whom she had thought
truer to her 'que ne fu Tristans a Yseut' (760) – a telling instance of
the intertextuality of courtly romance – could have revealed this
private detail to the Duchess, whose lover he must be. She laments
bitterly that he should have disclosed their secret (809–10, 'des-
couvert / nostre conseil'), and ends by dying of grief. Meanwhile the
knight, missing her at the dance, asks the Duke where his niece is;
the Duke leads him to the *chambre*, and, finding it empty, urges him
to enter the *garderobe* alone, kindly thinking to allow the lovers a
private embrace. The knight finds his lady dead, and at this moment
the girl who had been concealed all along reveals herself and tells
him what the Chastelaine had said in her soliloquy. Blaming himself
for what he had told the Duke, he stabs himself to death. The girl

rushes out, finds the Duke, and tells him 'ce qu'ele a oï et veü' (905) [everything she had seen and heard]. He in turn draws the sword from the knight's body, hastens back to the dance, and kills his wife on the spot. He does this 'in the sight of all' (923, 'voiant toz') and then, 'oiant toz, qui oïr le vost, / dist tout l'afere en mi la cort' (928–9) [in the hearing of all who cared to hear, related the whole affair in open court].

Thus the private becomes entirely and officially public, open to the sight and hearing of all, the story having passed from the knight to the Duke to the Duchess to the Chastelaine to the girl in the closet and thus back to the knight and the Duke and finally to the whole court. All that stays concealed from us is its hero's name: he is referred to only as *li chevaliers*, even after the Duchess has named him to her husband (126). The Duke flees to the Holy Land, where he becomes a Templar, and it remains only for the poet to remind us, in the tale's closing lines, that

> li descouvrirs riens n'avance
> et li celers en toz poins vaut.
> Qui si le fet, ne crient assaut
> des faus felons enquereors
> qui enquierent autrui amors.   (954–8)

disclosure gains us nothing, while concealment has everything to commend it. He who observes this rule is proof against the attacks of those false prying knaves who pry into the loves of other folk.

Yet if this rule had been observed, there would have been no story for the poet to tell. Only in a world of devouring curiosity, of 'faus felons enquereors' who conceal themselves to watch and listen in secret, would there be any courtly romances – narratives that 'pry into the loves of other folk' and that are about people who do just that. *La Chastelaine de Vergi*, this perfect and tragic narrative machine, ends, then, with a pointed reflection on its own nature, and leaves us to meditate on the motives of those who tell and listen to such stories. We perhaps may identify with the girl in the closet, the most innocent of all the poem's voyeurs; but the poet has no such excuse.

CHAPTER 6

Troilus and Criseyde and *The Manciple's Tale*

Chaucer's *Troilus and Criseyde* belongs to the tradition of French courtly romance that we have been exploring in poems by Beroul, Chrétien de Troyes, Marie de France, and the anonymous author of *La Chastelaine de Vergi*.[1] It too is one of the poems that 'enquierent autrui amors', and it pushes the tradition still further, prying in greater depth and more detail than its predecessors into a secret love-affair and into the inner lives of its characters, creating a world that is pervaded with human subjectivity. Yet interwoven with this subtler and more intense curiosity there is also its apparent opposite, a stronger sense of distance. This has two causes. One is Chaucer's habitual self-presentation as a bookish translator, a naïve, non-participant intruder into a world that he knows only in writing, not from personal experience:

> Forwhi to every lovere I me excuse,
> That of no sentement I this endite,
> But out of Latyn in my tonge it write.　　　　(II 12–14)

Courtly romances characteristically claim to be based on written sources; to take an especially clear example, Gottfried von Strassburg writes in the prologue to his *Tristan* (lines 149ff.) that he searched through many Latin and vernacular books till he found the only authentic version of the story, that by Thomas of Britain, which he now offers to his readers. But Gottfried claims at least to have entered the *Minnegrotte*, even though he has not shared Tristan and Isolde's supreme experience (lines 17100ff.), and I know of no romance earlier than Chaucer's that emphasizes so strongly the poet's clerkly separation from his human material. The other cause of the sense of distance is that the immediate source of *Troilus and Criseyde* is neither a French romance nor the supposed Latin work by 'myn auctour called Lollius' (I 394), but the *Filostrato* of Boccaccio;

and Chaucer's contact with the more advanced culture of *trecento* Italy enabled him to add a new and apparently contradictory dimension to the French tradition, for it led him to set his love-story in a classical antiquity imagined as remote in time and religion from the medieval present.[2] Curiosity and distance together create the possibility of voyeurism, but in *Troilus and Criseyde* they also add complexity to the notion of romances as narratives 'that pry into the loves of other folk', because the claims to personal inexperience and historical remoteness lead to a sharper and more explicit problematization of the means by which the private lives and loves of others can be known and told, brought under surveillance and reduced to narrative.

All too much has already been written about *Troilus and Criseyde*; some of its voyeuristic elements have been discussed with considerable insight,[3] and in this chapter I can hope to disentangle only a few threads from the almost intolerably complex fabric woven by Chaucer and his collaborating readers. This means that I shall not focus on looking, important though it is in the poem's action (Sarah Stanbury notes that '*Troilus* is built on a system of private and reciprocal gazes that are centrally directed to the ends – and control – of Pandarus, the poem's supreme voyeur').[4] I shall be concerned rather with the *presence* of others (Pandarus, the poet, his readers) at supposedly private moments; these others are aware of what is happening, but their awareness is often not specified as visual, and may belong to the ear at least as much as the eye.

My initial aim is to examine the nature of privacy and its violation within the poem's fictional world, but this demands some prior discussion of fictional space. In *Troilus and Criseyde* as in earlier romances we find two kinds of underlying spatial opposition, one between the enclosed and the unenclosed (its extreme form being the opposition between the *chambre* and the unbounded forest or wilderness), the other between the private and the public. In *Troilus*, however, these oppositions are realized with a new specificity and complexity. Most of the poem's action occurs in a Troy besieged by the Greeks, so that the whole walled city is felt to be enclosed in a way that signifies both security and danger. Private transactions occur in the palaces and streets of this city, and within the palaces the focus of secrecy and intimacy is provided by curtained beds in private rooms, places not only for sexual union but for solitary thought, for bodily comfort, and for friendly confidences and plans.

The public world impinges on the private not just through the ultimate threat of the siege (and we know that historically Troy must fall) but more immediately through the political decisions taken by its rulers in the public spaces of *consistorie* and *parlement* (IV 65, 143). Outside the walls, where we might expect forest or wilderness, the place of adventure in which threatened lovers could take refuge, is the Greek camp. This is no physical wilderness, and it offers no danger of hardship or starvation: Calchas's 'faire brighte tente' (V 1022) is a luxurious dwelling with seats and beds, and servants offering wine and spices; yet it proves to be a moral wilderness, a place of fear, betrayal and crumbling principle. The world Chaucer imagines belongs to a naturalistically and humanistically conceived history, entirely lacking in magic or marvel; the landscape conventionally associated with wilderness and adventure is located only in the human mind – for example in the forest of Troilus's nightmare, where 'a bor with tuskes grete' (V 1238) is embracing and kissing Criseyde.

The settings within the city walls include a greater and more minutely distinguished variety of spaces than we have found in earlier romances. Since this aspect of the poem has been well analysed by H. M. Smyser,[5] I need not enter into much detail here, but it is worth noting that, besides the various bedrooms, both permanent ones and those created temporarily by drawing a *travers* or curtain (III 674), there is also the special privacy of the 'litel closet' (III 663) in which Criseyde sleeps at Pandarus's house and the *stewe* (III 601), a room with its own fireplace, connected with the *closet* by a trapdoor, where Troilus awaits his opportunity to join her. More private still is the fragile enclosure Criseyde makes by pulling the bed-sheets over her to hide her blushes at III 1055–7 and again at III 1569–70. To know what happens inside such a space is to achieve an astonishing degree of intimacy with her. Domestic spaces are intricately divided with trapdoors, stairs, windows, window embrasures, and fireplaces; and then there are spaces intermediate between private and public, such as the garden, the street, the temple, the city wall and its gatehouse. The effect is of an almost novelistic realism, at times even of fabliau-like farce, where human ingenuity is exercised and human possibility limited by the sheer materiality of the world.

Realism is enhanced, and we are drawn deeper into the fiction, by the way that the settings' sensory qualities are specified in detail.

Darkness and light, as we have seen, often bear significantly on secrecy and looking, but here they are treated with an evocative delicacy that far exceeds their relevance to spying. In Book II, 'whan that it was eve' (1301), Pandarus returns home from visiting Criseyde, and there 'Troilus he fond allone abedde' (1305). He first pretends to be unable to see who it is in the bed, and then offers his friend a light by which to read the letter he has brought from Criseyde. Heat and cold too can be significant; later in the same book, when Troilus, supposedly sick, is in bed in Deiphebus' house, Pandarus is able to arrange that he should be visited only by Deiphebus and Helen, and then by Criseyde, on the grounds that 'the chaumbre is but lite, / And fewe folk may lightly make it warm' (1646–7). Noise and silence play important parts, especially throughout Book III: when Pandarus secretly manages to manoeuvre Troilus and Criseyde into the same bed amidst a houseful of sleeping people, the wind and rain that have caused Criseyde to stay overnight are frequently mentioned as muffling other noises, and finally are the subject of Pandarus's private joke the next morning, when he remarks to his niece that

> 'Al this nyght so reyned it, allas,
> That al my drede is that ye, nece swete,
> Han litel laiser had to slepe and mete.
> Al nyght,' quod he, 'hath reyn so do me wake,
> That som of us, I trowe, hire hedes ake.'   (III 1557–61)

By now, as in Hollywood films under the Hays Code, the storm has become not just a means of concealing intimacy from public curiosity but a metaphor of passion itself.

In admiring Chaucer's novelistic skills, we may need to remember that *Troilus and Criseyde* is not in fact a novel. For one thing, Chaucer accepts no obligation to sustain unambiguous consistency of material setting.[6] More important, the range of spaces extends beyond the physical to the metaphysical, from the chambers, beds, windows and walls of Troy to the heavenly spheres through which Troilus's spirit passes after death on its way to its final destination. Then there is a great variety of private psychological or imaginative spaces not identified with or confined to physical space. These include memories of the past and plannings or imaginings of possible futures, such as Criseyde's optimistic proposals for returning to Troilus after she has been exchanged for Antenor (v 1275ff.), unconvincing plans because they involve too many alternative scenarios; or Troilus's response, a different imagining of the outcome (IV 1464ff.) that creates the pathos of 'foreseeing' the wrong future and draws its full meaning from the unchangeable history into which this fiction is inserted:

> But Troilus, now far-wel al thi joie,
> For shaltow nevere sen hire eft in Troie! (v 27–8)

There are dreams, opening up other imaginative spaces than the forest in which Troilus sees Criseyde with the boar, for example Troilus's nightmares of lamenting alone 'In place horrible', of being captured by his enemies, and of falling from high places (v 246–60). Many of these imaginative spaces – 'memories, dreams, reflections' usually referred to by the term *fantasie* – themselves open on to metaphysical space: Troilus's nightmare falling sensations might be glimpses of hell, and dreams, though open to multiple interpretation, may be sent by gods and grant a divine power to foresee the future.

Especially important are the spaces opened up by written texts, for the world of this poem is at the opposite extreme to the booklessness of Beroul's *Tristan*, and its inhabitants, male and female, are not only literate but habitually measure literature and life against each other. Examples are 'the geste / Of the siege of Thebes' read to Criseyde and two of her ladies as they sit 'Withinne a paved parlour' in her palace (II 81ff.), and the love-lyric sung by Antigone in Criseyde's garden (II 827ff.), about which Criseyde asks who wrote it and whether its praise of love is true. Especially important is the book to which Pandarus apparently turns in the middle of the consummation scene in Book III. He provides a cushion for Troilus to kneel on, notes with satisfaction that Criseyde kisses him and invites him to sit, and urges her,

> 'Now doth hym sitte, goode nece deere,
> Upon youre beddes syde al ther withinne,
> That ech of yow the bet may other heere.'
> And with that word he drow hym to the feere,
> And took a light, and fond his contenaunce,
> As for to looke upon an old romaunce. (III 975–80)

The context emphasizes the need to overcome the difficulties of hearing and seeing – Troilus must sit inside the bed-curtains if he and Criseyde are to hear each other, and Pandarus needs a light to read by – but within this context the focus is a book. The intertextuality that we have noted as characteristic of courtly romances now assumes solid form as a written text within the fiction, an 'old romaunce' whose events the lovers are re-enacting.[7] Pandarus becomes a reader just like ourselves[8] – or does he? On reflection, given that Middle English *as* is notoriously vague in function and often redundant,[9] it is unclear whether 'As for to looke' implies that he was really looking or only behaving as if doing so; and then looking is not identical with reading: the relation between the two is one theme of *my* book. As so often, Chaucer's 'elusion of clarity'[10] ultimately leaves it to us, if we choose, to achieve an imaginative disambiguation of his apparently simply text.

Within this complex articulation of material and imaginary spaces, the story of a secret love-affair is played out. Barry Windeatt has demonstrated that comparison of *Troilus* with the *Filostrato*

reveals that Chaucer consistently draws a society that allows much less privacy to his lovers, while at the same time he gives his characters a much increased sense that their love affair must be kept secret ... the English poet is putting back the events of the Italian poem into the more communal society of great medieval households. In Chaucer's conception, the private life of the individual still has to be won from a surrounding society, and this emphasizes the difference between the private and public lives of the English characters much more sharply than is done in the *Filostrato*, where Boccaccio assumes a greater degree of private life.[11]

There are of course practical reasons for the secrecy of the love-affair in *Troilus and Criseyde* beyond a general concern for the privacy of intimate relations in a society where privacy is difficult to attain. The situation is not, as in the Tristan story, that there is a royal husband to be deceived, for Criseyde is a widow. This is not a romance of adultery, and the legal issues raised in such romances, with the accompanying need for evidence from spies who have personally witnessed the lovers' relations, do not arise. It is important, though, that Troilus is a Trojan prince and Criseyde the daughter of a traitor who has fled to the besieging Greeks; Troilus's father would certainly not permit him to marry or even abduct her, especially given (as Troilus himself points out) that the war was provoked by 'ravysshyng of wommen so by myght' (IV 548). (Boccaccio emphasizes that Criseida is of unacceptably lower social rank than Troiolo,[12] but Chaucer leaves that out. As was noted above,[13] Boccaccio further has Criseida making the Ovidian point that secrecy heightens the intensity of desire, but that too Chaucer omits.) If marriage is unimaginable (and it is never mentioned as a possibility), then it becomes essential to preserve Criseyde's honour, her *name*, and the lovers are greatly influenced by the need to avoid gossips and scandalmongers. This concern for secrecy is repeatedly represented as the story is told, in ways that encourage us to question how it can have been told at all. Repeatedly, the characters gain privacy with some effort, and the effect of the effort is to call attention to the voyeuristic nature of Chaucer's position and ours as unseen witnesses.

In Book II, for example, when Pandarus, visiting Criseyde, takes his leave, she tells him to sit down, because she wishes 'to speke of wisdom er ye go' –

> And everi wight that was aboute hem tho,
> That herde that, gan fer awey to stonde,
> Whil they two hadde al that hem liste in honde.   (II 213–17)

As if we too had politely taken the hint to move out of earshot, the serious business they have to discuss concerning Criseyde's position in Troy fades into a blur; but as Pandarus again makes to depart, he begins to talk more frivolously to his niece:

> Whan that hire tale al brought was to an ende,
> Of hire estat and of hire governaunce,
> Quod Pandarus, 'Now tyme is that I wende.
> But yet, I say, ariseth, lat us daunce ...'.   (II 218–21)

This frivolity is carefully calculated to lead into his real purpose, which is to reveal Troilus's love and encourage her to accept it; Pandarus does not in fact leave for another 370 lines, and we witness the following conversation in great detail. The important and the unimportant change places, and in the confusion we become *enquereors* without noticing what has happened. Once Pandarus has really departed, Criseyde 'streght into hire closet wente anon' (II 599), to think over what he has said;

> And wex somdel astoned in hire thought
> Right for the newe cas; but whan that she
> Was ful avysed, tho fond she right nought
> Of peril why she ought afered be.
> For man may love, of possibilite,
> A womman so, his herte may tobreste,
> And she naught love ayein, but if hire leste.   (603–9)

The act of entering her *closet*, her private room, is clearly designed to exclude others, so that she can think without distraction. Smyser convincingly sets out the general context in which such a moment must be interpreted:

In modern narrative, when the actions or thoughts of a character are being described and there is no allusion to the presence of any other person, we assume, without being told, that nobody else is present. In *Troilus and Criseyde* we can almost say that the opposite is the case: unless it is otherwise stated, everybody is assumed to be in company.... Solitude is decidedly the exception, the presence of retainers is the rule. We may go a step further and say that not only is the presence of retainers the rule but that gaining an exception to the rule can involve a certain amount of difficulty.[14]

Criseyde must retire to her *closet* to gain solitude; yet Chaucer and we follow her there, not only keeping her under surveillance but, even though she sits 'as stylle as any ston' (600), entering into her most secret thoughts. In lines 607–9, indeed, it is as though Chaucer's thoughts and ours mingle with hers: in this early instance of 'style indirect libre' it is unclear *who* is offering the generalization (so reassuring to a woman afraid that her freedom of choice may be slipping away) that a man may love a woman desperately without her reciprocating, unless she so chooses.

Criseyde's thoughts are interrupted by shouts from the street; Troilus goes riding past from the battlefield, heroically battered yet modestly blushing; and then Criseyde too blushes 'of hire owen thought' (652) and resumes her meditation 'Ther as she sat allone' (690).

> And, Lord! So gan she in hire thought argue
> In this matere of which I have yow told,
> And what to doone best were, and what eschue,
> That plited she ful ofte in many fold.
> Now was hire herte warm, now was it cold;
> And what she thoughte somwhat shal I write,
> As to myn auctour listeth for t'endite.   (694–700)

The question how 'myn auctour' could know what Criseyde thought 'as she sat allone' is of a recurring type; here it is enough to note that, among the intricate folds of her consciousness, is the thought that she is one of the most attractive women in Troy, and also the thought that she wishes no one to know this thought:

> For wel I woot myself, so God me spede –
> Al wolde I that noon wiste of this thought –
> I am oon the faireste, out of drede ...   (744–6)

Yet we know what she wishes no one to know about her most secret thoughts.

Later still in Book II, Pandarus once more visits his niece, and claims that he has 'newe thinges' to tell her concerning information brought by a 'Greek espie' (1112). He continues,

> 'Into the gardyn go we, and ye shal here,
> Al pryvely, of this a long sermoun.'
> With that they wenten arm in arm yfeere
> Into the gardyn from the chaumbre down;
> And whan that he so fer was that the sown
> Of that he spak no man heren myghte,
> He seyde hire thus, and out the lettre plighte.   (1114–20)

The letter is from Troilus, and as before, with the excuse of having public affairs to discuss in private, Pandarus draws Criseyde away from her attendants to speak of more intimate matters. Also as before, we hear what 'no man heren myghte', entering more silently and invisibly into the position of spies than the Greek spy who was so easily recognized. We have become accustomed to think of the *chaumbre* as a private place, but the garden may be more private; and Pandarus now uses it to present Criseyde with Troilus's declaration of love. At first she declines to receive it, and her uncle expostulates with her:

> 'Refuse it naught,' quod he, and hente hire faste,
> And in hire bosom the lettre down he thraste,
>
> And seyde hire, 'Now cast it awey anon,
> That folk may seen and gauren on us tweye!'
> Quod she, 'I kan abyde till they be gon';
> And gan to smyle.   (1154–9)

The pair are distant enough from others within the fiction to escape hearing though not sight; but Chaucer and we can see as well as hear, and Criseyde will have to wait till the poem's end if she wants to wait till we have gone. And indeed shortly after this we are present throughout when she

> gan some of hire wommen to hire calle,
> And streght into hire chambre gan she gon;
> But of hire besynesses this was on –
> Amonges othere thynges, out of drede –
> Ful pryvely this lettre for to rede.   (1172–6)

It might be suspected that the function of such scenes was to invite the penetration of a male gaze into the mysteries of the feminine – Criseyde's *closet* or *chaumbre*, her bosom, her inmost thoughts and feelings. This would seem especially likely if, as has been argued, the real audience of *Troilus and Criseyde*, as opposed to its internally implied audience, was 'primarily, if not exclusively, male'.[15] In fact, though, it is not only Criseyde's privacy that is exposed to the reader's curiosity: Chaucer creates similar effects with Troilus. Book III provides some examples. Troilus is lying in bed, allegedly sick and really love-sick, when Pandarus comes to visit him,

> And on a paillet al that glade nyght
> By Troilus he lay, with mery chere,
> To tale; and wel was hem they were yfeere.   (229–31)

Others are evidently present at first, and Pandarus does not feel able to move to his friend's bedside to talk privately until 'every wight was voided but they two, / And alle the dores weren faste yshette' (232–3). We however are not *voided*: we remain inside the closed doors, and thus hear Pandarus's long speech to Troilus, in which he admits to having acted as go-between on his behalf, claims that his motives have been purely altruistic, and urges Troilus to take the utmost care to preserve Criseyde's reputation. He twice refers to God's knowledge of his motivation – 'God woot, and thow,' (240) that he pitied Troilus, and 'God, that al woot, take I to witnesse' (260) that nothing mercenary was involved – thus reminding us that author and readers share that omniscience. 'Were it wist' (274) that he had persuaded his own niece to accept Troilus as her lover, 'al the world upon it wolde crie' (277), and he therefore begs Troilus 'That privete go with us in this cas' (283); the *privete*, however, embraces the circle of the poem's readers. He reminds Troilus of the many proverbs against being a *labbe* (300), and deplores the excessive freedom of *tonge* (294, 302) that ruins women's reputations. Then he politely explains that his remarks about the folly of boasting are not meant for Troilus personally:

> I sey nought this for no mistrust of yow,
> Ne for no wis-man, but for foles nyce,
> And for the harm that in the werld is now,
> As wel for folie ofte as for malice.   (323–6)

Since, within the poem, Troilus is the only person present to hear these remarks, they must be directed at the fools among the poem's audience: it is uncannily as though Pandarus can see *us* through the fiction's semi-transparent boundaries, watching and listening to everything that goes on, and speculating about the answers to the many questions the narrative raises. When Pandarus has finished, Troilus expresses his gratitude for what his friend has done, reminds him how reluctant he was to reveal his love even to him, and asks,

> How dorst I mo tellen of this matere,
> That quake now, and no wight may us here? (370–1)

Yet we hear what nobody can hear.

Scenes where the words or action relate to love are not the only ones represented as involving a voyeuristic penetration of privacy. Another kind of voyeurism occurs in scenes of solitary grief, where we may feel sympathy but also embarrassment at the exposure of undignified behaviour the person concerned would restrain if aware of our presence as readers. A striking example occurs in Book IV. After the exchange of prisoners has been agreed and Troilus has with difficulty kept silence 'Lest men sholde his affeccioun espye' (153), he hurries from the public forum of the Trojan *parlement* to the privacy of his *chambre*,

> faste allone,
> But if it were a man of his or two
> The which he bad out faste for to go
> Bycause he wolde slepen, as he seyde,
> And hastily upon his bed hym leyde. (218–24)

To be alone, he has to dismiss his one or two attendants with the excuse that he wishes to sleep; once they have gone, 'He rist hym up, and every dore he shette, / And wyndow ek ...' (232–3); and only after these extreme efforts to guarantee complete secrecy does he give vent to a violent fit of passion, leaping, roaring, beating his breast, throwing himself to the ground, and sobbing. His behaviour is like that of a child in a tantrum; we know that he would no more act like this in public than he would make love in public; and we are surely moved and fascinated, but also embarrassed by our own invisible presence in his *chambre*. If the scene were differently handled, the question of our presence might never occur to us; but it is precisely Troilus's explicit precautions to achieve privacy that make us aware that he has failed to do so. There is a similar scene after the lovers' separation, when Troilus goes alone to his *chambre* in order to give unrestrained expression to 'his sorwes that he spared hadde' (v 204) when in public: once more his curses, tears, and restless wallowing in bed arouse embarrassment. His behaviour would be shameful if displayed publicly; and because it is displayed to us, and shame is infectious, it makes us ashamed too.

One consequence of the poem's persistent violations of the characters' privacy is that the very story in which a leading impulse is to protect Criseyde's reputation becomes the means of destroying it, and the role of the poet and his listeners becomes indistinguishable from that of the spies who watch and tell, however different their motives may be. The concern Pandarus expressed about wagging tongues is found throughout. When Criseyde was inwardly debating in Book II whether to allow herself to fall in love with Troilus, an important argument against doing so was that 'thise wikked tonges ben so prest / To speke us harm' (785–6). And she goes on to envisage

> How bisy, if that I love, ek most I be
> To plesen hem that jangle of love, and dremen,
> And coye hem, that they seye noon harm of me! ...
> And who may stoppen every wikked tonge,
> Or sown of belles whil that thei ben ronge?   (799–805)

Here the tongues of malicious gossips merge into the clappers (also known as tongues) of loudly ringing bells. When Pandarus finally suceeds in bringing the lovers together in his house in Book III, we need assurance that none of these dangerous gossips knew anything about it:

> Dredeles, it cler was in the wynd
> Of every pie and every lette-game.   (526–7)

The two kinds of storyteller eventually merge into one, as the lovers foresee and the poet condemns those malicious repeaters of their story, the *olde clerkis* themselves, who will present it as one of shame and betrayal, not love and fidelity. At the very moment of committing herself to Diomede, Criseyde soliloquizes,

> Allas, of me, unto the worldes ende,
> Shal neyther ben ywriten nor ysonge
> No good word, for thise bokes wol me shende.
> O, rolled shal I ben on many a tonge!
> Thorughout the world my belle shal be ronge!
> And wommen moost wol haten me of alle.   (v 1058–63)

Here the pun on *tongue* is repeated. The plays on words help to create an image of the babbling human tongue as large, noisy and alarming, even when what is being stated is that secrecy is perfect and there will be no gossip. Chaucer, unlike the earlier romance-writers we have examined, makes fully explicit the paradoxes involved in the public reporting of private and secret matters.

The poem's historical dimension gives a special complexity to its investigation of private life, the more so because the coexistence within it of public and private is not a matter of stable equilibrium. The two opposites define themselves more sharply through their constantly shifting relationship: our sense of the privacy of sexual consummation is established precisely in its violation by the presence of the historian and the go-between, and the great public issues of war and empire are shown to depend on private desire, fidelity, and betrayal. At times Chaucer emphasizes the historical distance of the events he recounts, but in ways that occlude the problems of narration. In the proem to Book II, for example, he addresses Clio, the muse of history, as his poem's inspiration, and claims that the only art he needs to employ is that of putting into rhyme the material that history supplies. He was not present during the events of his story, which happened in pagan antiquity; and he is no lover himself, not a servant of Cupid, as he puts it in the first proem (I 15), but only a servant of Cupid's servants; he therefore cannot write on the basis of *sentement*, or personal feeling, personal experience of love. This narratorial guise as an unworldly scholar struggling to make sense of learned and remote sources gives him his excuse for leaving conspicuous gaps in the story: how old was Criseyde? had she any children by her late husband? did she eventually, having betrayed Troilus, give her heart or only her body to Diomede? 'Men seyn – I not – that she yaf hym hire herte' (v 1050): such gaps invite our imaginative participation to fill them.

It might be expected that the gaps would include the lovers' intimate relations, but that is not so. Their first night together is recounted in exquisite detail, in some of the most beautiful poetry of erotic love in English:

> Hire armes smale, hire streghte bak and softe,
> Hire sydes longe, flesshly, smothe, and white
> He gan to stroke, and good thrift bad ful ofte
> Hir snowissh throte, hire brestes rounde and lite.
> Thus in this hevene he gan hym to delite,
> And therwithal a thousand tyme hire kiste ...   (III 1247–52)

Chaucer's language is frank in these descriptions of the lovers' secret activity, but he uses none of the medieval equivalents to four-letter words; those belong to the language of fabliau rather than that of courtly romance. Instead, metaphor plays its appropriate part: they embrace each other as closely as the honeysuckle twisting round a tree-trunk, Criseyde is first as silent as a frightened nightingale and then opens her heart like a nightingale when it sings, and so on. One such metaphor is introduced in a way that is particularly interesting for my purposes. After the bashful Troilus, having swooned and been brought round, finally gathers courage to embrace Criseyde fully, Chaucer asks what could the hapless lark say when seized by the sparrowhawk? And he goes on,

> Criseyde, which that felte hir thus itake,
> As writen clerkes in hire bokes olde,
> Right as an aspes leef she gan to quake,
> When she hym felte hire in his armes folde . . .

(III 1198–201)

Somehow, then, the *clerkes* who wrote the *bokes olde* were in a position to know exactly how Criseyde trembled when Troilus clasped her; and the invocation of clerkly authority is very deliberate on Chaucer's part, since he scarcely needed it to account for a simile found elsewhere in Middle English romance.[16] Pandarus has made elaborate preparations. Criseyde is to go to bed, separated from her waiting women, in a 'litel closet' (III 663) provided with a 'secre trappe-dore' (759) through which first he and then Troilus can come to her when everyone else is asleep. But these precautions must have been unavailing, if the *clerkes* (presumably celibate?) got to be so well informed about what happened. And further the lovers' privacy has literally been broken, indeed has never existed, because Pandarus is not merely in the know all along, he is in the room all along, throughout this climactic love-scene.

Pandarus's role is of special importance for consideration of voyeurism in *Troilus and Criseyde*. It was a role that Chaucer greatly expanded from the *Filostrato*, and it corresponds in many ways to that Chaucer attributes to himself, as one who serves lovers without having known success in love. Moreover, Pandarus takes over inside the poem the complicated planning and manipulation necessary to bring two by no means forward young people together in the same bed without anyone else's knowledge; hence the predominance of scenes in which he is shown intruding into private spaces.[17] Like

Chaucer, too, Pandarus becomes 'an artificer of situations, a deviser of fictions'.[18] Thus in answer to Criseyde's questioning as to how he discovered Troilus's love for her, Pandarus invents a scene in which he heard Troilus groaning 'In-with the paleis gardyn, by a welle' (II 508), acted as a spy – 'Tho gan I stalke hym softely byhynde' (519) – and listened to him soliloquizing about love. He constructs another story in Book III to explain how Troilus comes to be present in his house when Criseyde is staying overnight; and he seems to enjoy his indispensable role as much as Chaucer must have done, and to be as downcast as Chaucer appears when the outcome of all his plotting is the exchange of prisoners, the lovers' separation, and Criseyde's infidelity. But he is not only a fiction-maker and a go-between, he is also, whenever possible, a spy on the love-affair he devises. There is little emphasis on watching, with all that it may imply of dominance; but just as Chaucer or his clerkly authorities are in some imaginative sense actually present throughout the lovers' dealings – or how else could he tell us about them? – so Pandarus is literally present as an interested observer. Unlike hostile watchers such as Frocin or the barons in Beroul, Pandarus is manifestly benevolent, doing what he does out of friendship; yet he also gains vicarious satisfaction – of sexual, not just narrative desire – from bringing the lovers together.

First he persuades Criseyde to allow Troilus into the *litel closet* to receive her assurance that he has no cause for his alleged jealousy of her alleged love for his alleged rival Horaste (III 797); but then, having got Troilus sitting on her bedside, he does not leave the room himself, but, as we have seen, turns or seems to turn to that 'old romaunce' – presumably something about love written by one of the surprisingly knowledgeable *olde clerkis* of Trojan times. It is fortunate that Pandarus stays, because the outcome of Criseyde's long and moving speech against jealousy is that she covers her head with the sheet and falls silent, at which Troilus faints. Pandarus presumably notices the sudden quiet; but, however he knows there is an emergency, he immediately leaps up, pushes Troilus into Criseyde's bed, pulls off all his clothes except his shirt (just what one would do if someone fainted, no doubt), helps Criseyde to chafe his hands and moisten his temples, does not discourage her from giving him mouth-to-mouth resuscitation (which leads Troilus to come round exclaiming, 'O mercy, God, what thyng is this?' [1124]); and finally, saying that too much light is bad for sick people's eyes, Pandarus returns to the fireplace, taking his candle with him.

There he apparently stays all night; at any rate, Chaucer does not mention his departure, indeed does not mention him at all until next morning. The normality of a situation in which a bedroom, even that of a married couple, is shared with others must have made clarification unnecessary.[19] There is none of the peering through bedroom windows that we have encountered in the Tristan story; the love-scene itself is described with the greatest beauty and delicacy. But when morning arrives, there is that extraordinary episode in which Pandarus returns to Criseyde's bedside before she rises, makes his joke about rain keeping people awake and giving them headaches, pries under the sheet, thrusts his arm beneath her neck, and kisses her. There are scholars who manage to persuade themselves that at this point Pandarus commits incest with his own niece.[20] The episode at least makes it unmistakably clear that Pandarus, whose lack of success in love has become a standing joke among his friends, has gained and is still gaining a vicarious sexual pleasure from the encounter between his niece and her lover. He is sexually aroused by having witnessed their love-making.[21]

Readers notoriously disagree about the effect of Pandarus's presence during the love-scene. Some would argue that his avuncular benevolence, with the cosy assurance he brings that whatever happens between the lovers is permitted and will not be allowed to go wrong – 'I wol myself be with yow al this nyght' (III 914) – defuses the shame that might otherwise accompany the scene. He is like the voyeurs included within the fiction of a soft-porn movie, as a way of making the movie's own voyeurism seem normal. Others feel that his evident arousal serves to remind us of the shamefulness of our own imaginative presence during such scenes. And we are not only present, we are also given a far larger share of responsibility for what happens in *Troilus and Criseyde* than we are as readers of, say, Beroul's *Tristan*. Beroul never explicitly raises the question how he or we can know what happened in private and in the dark; but Chaucer constantly raises such questions, precisely by admitting that there is so much he does not know. And he keeps on telling us, as he does in the middle of the love-scene in Book III, that *we* know or can guess what is unknown to him:

> Of hire delit or joies oon the leeste
> Were impossible to my wit to seye;

> But juggeth ye that han ben at the feste
> Of swich gladnesse, if that hem liste pleye! (1310–13)

Thus the responsibility for imagining further details of the lovers' play becomes ours; and this is a point Chaucer re-emphasizes a few lines later, when he tells us that we should do as we please with any words he may have added to what he found in his source. He goes on,

> For myne wordes, heere and every part,
> I speke hem alle under correccioun
> Of yow that felyng han in loves art,
> And putte it al in youre discrecioun
> To encresse or maken dymynucioun
> Of my langage, and that I yow biseche. (1331–6)

We cannot really alter Chaucer's wording, but we respond imaginatively to such appeals, entering into the scene described and filling the gaps he leaves. Thus we too become pandars; and in the strange episode when Pandarus comes to his niece's bedside after Troilus has left her, if we imagine that Pandarus has intercourse with her, then that too is our responsibility. Chaucer has said no more than that he passes over what 'chargeth nought to seye' (1576), and if we choose to construct a scene that would be truly shocking, it is our voyeurism, not his, that is to blame.[22]

Troilus and Criseyde is an extraordinary achievement in many ways, but perhaps especially in the way that it acknowledges and even foregrounds the element of voyeurism in medieval romance, while sustaining a treatment of love that is beautiful and reverent without being solemn. In a later work, Chaucer returns to the theme of the poet as voyeur, but now in a spirit of sour disillusion. This is *The Manciple's Tale*, the last but one of the *Canterbury Tales* – in a sense the last of all, because *The Parson's Tale* is no tale, but a treatise whose teller austerely rejects both fiction and verse. In his prologue the Manciple shows his contempt for the Cook, whom the Host has called on to tell the next tale, but who is so drunk that he can scarcely keep awake. The Host warns the Manciple not to reprove the Cook too openly, in case he should take vengeance another day by revealing some of the unpleasant truths he knows about the Manciple's creative accounting procedures; and the Manciple beats a hasty retreat, and gives the Cook yet another drink. The outward jollity of *The Manciple's Prologue* is strikingly unfunny, and it becomes

hard to know whom to regard with the greater contempt, the Cook
for his swinish drunkenness or the Manciple for his jeering mockery
when he thinks it safe combined with cowardice when he thinks it is
not. These are human beings degraded below the level of animals,
and *The Canterbury Tales* as a whole seems to be entering a phase of
terminal degeneration. In its sarcastic way, the prologue concerns
the danger of speaking freely of what one knows and the greater
wisdom of expedient flattery or silence; and this theme, of the
subordination of truthful speech to expediency and self-interest, is at
the centre of the tale that follows and is put foward with wearying
repetitiveness in the moral the Manciple draws from it.

The tale is about Apollo: the god of poetic eloquence, but now
almost completely demythologized and deglamourized, dwelling
not in heaven but 'in this erthe adoun' as a 'lusty bachiler' (IX 105,
107)[23] famed for his skill in archery. He possesses a pet crow, as
white as a swan, which he has taught to speak, so that 'countrefete
the speche of every man / He koude, whan he sholde telle a tale'
(134–5). As many readers have observed, it is as though Chaucer, in
the crow, is describing himself as poet of *The Canterbury Tales*, taught
by Apollo to imitate the voices of all the pilgrims.[24] But Apollo has
another possession that he cherishes even more, a wife whom he
loves dearly and does his utmost to please – in vain, however,
because she secretly takes a lover,

> A man of litel reputacioun,
> Nat worth to Phebus in comparisoun.   (199–200)

In Apollo's absence, the wife sends for her lover, and 'Anon they
wroghten al hire lust volage' (239). They are not alone, however,
because

> The white crowe, that heeng ay in the cage,
> Biheeld hire werk, and seyde never a word.   (240–1)

They think they are in privacy and safety, but the crow (whose cage
is presumably in the *chambre*, and who must therefore have had
plenty of opportunity to witness the sexual act legitimately performed) is present as an impotent voyeur – precisely the role in
which Chaucer so often places himself in his courtly poems about
love.[25] The crow might be thought of as a degraded version of the
nightingale in Walther von der Vogelweide's 'Under der linden', or
of the Pandarus of *Troilus and Criseyde*; but unlike them he does not

keep secret the secret things he sees, but plays instead the part of the 'wikked tonges' or 'faus felons enquereors' so feared by lovers in courtly literature. At the same time, the narrative is quite lacking in eroticism, and beyond the moralizing phrase 'lust volage' there is nothing to evoke the love-making the crow witnesses and thus to involve *us* in the shame of voyeurism.

When Apollo returns, the crow hints at what has happened, in a line which, in its tactless and cynical way, is surely one of Chaucer's funniest: 'This crowe sang "Cokkow! Cokkow! Cokkow!"' (243). Cuckoo means cuckold – even the crow seems to have been infected by the prologue's malice – but at first Apollo does not understand what he is being told:

> 'What, bryd?' quod Phebus, 'What song syngestow?
> Ne were thow wont so myrily to synge
> That to myn herte it was a rejoysynge
> To heere thy voys? Allas, what song is this?'   (244–7)

And now the crow tells him, in words of one syllable, indeed using one word that Chaucer never employs in his courtly poems, that his wife has taken a worthless lover, 'For on thy bed thy wyf I saugh hym swyve' (256). And he adds that it has continued for a long time, and that 'ofte he saugh it with his yen' (261). One might ask why in that case the crow did not tell Apollo about it before; but perhaps the pleasure of watching outweighed the pleasure of telling. Apollo's immediate response is to set an arrow to his bow and slay his wife on the spot. Next he demythologizes himself even further, breaking his bow and arrows and his various musical instruments; and then he rounds on the crow.

> 'Traitour,' quod he, 'with tonge of scorpioun,
> Thou hast me broght to my confusioun.'   (271–2)

Now he turns aside, to speak with operatic and self-deceiving sentimentality about his wife; she lies dead, he exclaims, 'with face pale of hewe, / Ful giltelees, that dorste I swere, ywys!' (276–7). Like the crow, we know perfectly well that she is not guiltless; Apollo prefers to think otherwise, and he therefore rounds on the crow with renewed anger, calling him false thief and traitor. He pulls out all the bird's white feathers, turns him black, deprives him of his powers of song and speech, 'and out at dore hym slong / Unto the devel' (306–7). 'And for this caas,' adds the Manciple, turning it

into a Just-So story, 'been alle crowes blake' (308). The tale ends
with a lengthy moral, in which the Manciple explains that it is an
exemplum teaching his listeners, as his mother taught him, the
wisdom of holding one's tongue. As the moral continues, for line
after line, until it is eventually fifty-four lines long (by far the longest
in *The Canterbury Tales*, though the Manciple's is the shortest tale of
the collection), it inevitably undoes itself. It recommends silence in
an intolerably verbose way, and it mentions the tongue that is to be
restrained so often that one is left with a mental image of a gigantic
tongue incessantly babbling. The tongue, frequently mentioned in
Troilus and Criseyde as the danger the lovers had to fear, has now
swollen up till it seems to fill the whole space of the poem.

Critics have found it irresistible to speculate about Chaucerian
self-reference in *The Manciple's Tale*. The voyeur-poet is rebuked and
shamed for telling what he sees, even though it is the truth; and he is
eventually stripped of his feathers and deprived of his poetic power
by an angry and foolish god. There is of course no possibility of
knowing what real experience, if any, underlies the self-punishing
comedy of this fiction. Had Chaucer really reached a state of
self-disgust with his role as poetic voyeur? At any rate, within *The
Canterbury Tales*, the end of *The Manciple's Tale* leads in all manuscripts of any significance into *The Parson's Prologue*, and there the
whole box of tricks is hastily shut up as the evening shadows
lengthen, and the Parson hurries to deliver the poem's last words in
the short time left.[26] He firmly rejects the Host's proposal that he
should tell a *fable* (x 29, 31), and offers instead 'Moralitee and
vertuous mateere' (38) in plain prose. His tale, as I remarked, is no
tale at all, but a penitential treatise; and after it we do not return to
the fiction of the pilgrimage and the tale-telling competition, but are
left instead with the voice of Geoffrey Chaucer, 'the makere of this
book', speaking from outside the book he has made, and regretting
the composition of nearly all his most famous works, including *The
Canterbury Tales*. The other works he lists as being revoked in these
retractions are precisely those courtly poems in which his role has
been that of Apollo's crow, spying and reporting on a sexual love
from which he is excluded. The first mentioned is 'the book of
Troilus'; and among the others is *The Parliament of Fowls*, which will
be considered in Chapter 11 as an example of poetic voyeurism in
first-person narrative.

CHAPTER 7

Partonope of Blois

Chaucer was the most influential of medieval English poets. Much of his influence involved matters of style and tone unrelated to the theme of this book, but, not surprisingly, his successors' reception of *Troilus and Criseyde* sometimes stimulated further developments in the treatment of looking and listening. One of the most interesting cases is *Partonope of Blois*, a romance dating from the early fifteenth century – evidently quite a popular one, surviving in at least five manuscripts, with some marked differences among the versions. It is translated, often freely, from *Partonopeus de Blois*, an even more popular twelfth-century French romance – one scholar describes it as being, for its contemporaries, of equal importance to the stories of Tristan and of the Grail.[1] The translator's identity is unknown, but it is unmistakably clear that he had read and learned from Chaucer, and especially from *Troilus and Criseyde*.[2] Besides many recollections of Chaucerian phrases, the translator had learned from Chaucer a way of representing himself as a translator: that is, as a secret intruder in and commentator on the often private world of the French narrative. In doing so, he takes up Chaucer's contrast between *sentement* and written sources, observing that while the French poet

> tellyth hys tale of sentament,
> I vnder-stonde noȝth hys entent,
> Ne wolle ne besy me to lere. (2347–9)[3]

I must add that in *Partonopeus* the storyteller's self-presentation is already full, sophisticated and extremely interesting: he appears as a lover, but one who lacks his hero's initial and ultimate success with his lady, and he frequently intervenes in the narrative to draw wry contrasts between his own story and Partonopeus's.[4] One is tempted, anachronistically, to call this narratorial technique 'Chaucerian';

and a full study of *Partonope of Blois* would need to take account of a complex situation in which Chaucer learned from French romances, possibly including *Partonopeus*, some of those very techniques of self-presentation which the English translator learned from Chaucer and then re-applied to his source. By means especially of his intrusion into the text *as a translator*, the English poet opens up its private spaces, enables us to follow him into them, and thereby intensifies the privacy he violates.

Partonope of Blois is a poem of over 12000 lines in the fullest English version, and it tells a complicated story. In this chapter I shall confine myself to one early episode of some six hundred lines, which is of special interest because it offers such a strange transformation of the themes of looking and telling. This episode, relating a love-affair that begins in complete darkness, can be recognized as a version of the story of Cupid and Psyche, but with reversed genders; we shall also see that it has something in common with the episode from Chrétien's *Yvain* examined in Chapter 4, and indeed the author of *Partonopeus* clearly belongs to the same cultural world as his great contemporary and was probably influenced by him. I shall discuss some of the translator's changes to his French original, but sharp distinctions between the effects produced by the two versions cannot always be made. The translator added many passages to this episode, ranging in length from one to 85 lines, but he also engaged in a general absorption and re-imagining of his source, responding to effects already found in it while making innumerable small changes of phrasing, order and emphasis. This English translator was a far subtler reader of his French source than Thomas Chestre was of Marie de France, and as a result, in passing from twelfth-century French to fifteenth-century English, *Partonope* became more fascinatingly complicated.

The romance begins with a legendary history of France, in which, somewhat as in the opening stanzas of *Sir Gawain and the Green Knight*, a tale of European chivalry is shown to have a Trojan origin and a myth is recounted of the founding of civilization. After the fall of Troy, Marcomiris, one of Priam's many sons, flees to France, a land almost entirely forested and inhabited by wild beasts, where there 'was neyther Erle, duke, ne kynge; / Eche man was lorde of hys owne thynge' (326–7). He is made 'chyffe Iustyce' (377) and encourages the building of 'Cytees and castelles' (375). His descendants in turn become kings of France and establish *lawes*

(400, 402, 404, 407) 'For batellus, for customys, and ffrauncheses' (405). The third king, Clovis, is converted to Christianity, and he does justice 'To euery manne, after hys state were' (444). Thus degree has an origin (though only in contradiction, for what is it to be lord of one's own property when there are no lords and no property?), but thereafter it is inherited. It receives considerable emphasis once the story begins.

Clovis takes his adolescent nephew Partonope out boar-hunting in the dangerous forest of Ardennes. After slaying one boar, the young prince gets lost in the forest at night while pursuing another. The hunting party seek him in vain, and he is left completely alone. The following night, by moonlight, he makes his way to the seashore and there discovers a splendid ship. He boards it, finds it empty, and falls half-asleep; meanwhile the ship sets sail 'Wythe-owten helpe of mannus honde' (821) and carries him out to sea and eventually to an unknown shore. On it is a walled city containing a castle which, though it is night, is 'as bryghte / As thowe hyt had be day lyghte' (848–9). The adventure is described in a pleasantly eerie way, and crossing the water no doubt marks some new stage in the process of the young hero's growing up. He disembarks and enters the city, which also turns out to be completely deserted. He wanders from one empty palace to another, finally entering the hall of a marble tower. This public space is empty of people, but unseen hands bring him water for washing, burning torches, and rich food and wine in magnificent vessels. After a delicious meal, of which he eats plentifully because he is now very hungry, 'To chamber the torches toke þe waye' (1128), and, with a prayer to God, he follows. He is now in the *chambre* that, as we have seen, in medieval romances signifies private space and intimate yet often dangerous experience. Here a male hero can expect an encounter with the feminine – for this youth, a first encounter. Partonope, feeling tired after his adventures, moves towards the blazing fire and is looking longingly at the splendid curtained bed when he notices that the torches are beginning to depart. He sits on a bench beside the bed and starts removing his spurs, but they and his clothes are mysteriously taken off for him. He gets into the bed. Now the chamber becomes completely dark, and Partonope, a very young hero indeed (thirteen in the French, which becomes eighteen in the English – but then the English have always attributed an unsuitable sexual precocity to the French), is frightened. The remainder of the scene takes place in total darkness.

To put it briefly, a lady, described as *une fee* in French[5] but only 'A yonge mayde' in English (1193), gets into the same bed. There is a lengthy period of manoeuvring and discussion between the two young people, with her urging him to leave and him saying how tired he is and how difficult departure would be in the dark; and it ends with each of them taking the other's virginity. From one viewpoint, what happens can be described as a rape; the episode's underlying assumption is the time-honoured male belief that 'no' means 'yes'; for all his inexperience, Partonope apparently knows this by instinct or cultural formation. It must be admitted that he uses some force; but it must also be admitted that she offers little more than verbal resistance. This becomes more intelligible after the consummation, when she explains that she is the Empress of Constantinople, that her barons wished her to marry, and that she sent envoys round the world to choose a suitable husband – especially, says the French poet with that national self-confidence that has long been so delightful a part of the French character, to France, where God has put such excellent people. The envoys selected Partonope as the best possible choice, the lady (called Melior) went to look for herself, agreed, and used the magical powers she possesses to cause the boy to get lost while hunting, to transport him to this deserted city (called Chef d'Oire), and to bring him ultimately to this very bed. The 'rape', then, is the intended outcome of Melior's enterprise. They are now to continue to spend their nights together, but he must not attempt to see her for two and a half years, after which they will be married. The long remainder of the story tells of his attempt to see her at his mother's behest, her anger, his madness, and their ultimate reconciliation and wedding.

The scene in the bedchamber is an account of sexual initiation as a turning point in the process of growing up. Regarded in the male perspective that generally belongs to romance, it is an encounter with the feminine; and here, we learn, an encounter brought about by feminine ingenuity. What is of special interest for my purpose is that it takes place in darkness. Can love begin in the dark? The answer might seem to be obvious; but *Partonopeus* probably dates from the same decade as Andreas Capellanus's *De amore*; and Andreas, it will be recalled, begins by insisting on the crucial importance of sight for falling in love, and even goes on to argue that 'Blindness is a hindrance to love because a blind man *has not the faculty of sight* to provide his mind with objects provoking uncontrolled thought.'[6] The bedchamber scene in *Partonopeus* might almost have been designed to disprove Andreas's doctrine.

We have examined the special significance attributed to sight in modern as well as medieval theories of desire and power; but there are some modern theorists who would claim that this way of thought is not simply a reflection of human nature, but is a symptom of an obsession with the visual that belongs to the history of male dominance. Let me quote some sentences by Luce Irigaray, a critical follower of Freud and Lacan:

Female sexuality has always been conceptualized on the basis of masculine parameters. ... Woman, in this sexual imaginary, is only a more or less obliging prop for the enactment of man's fantasies. ... As Freud admits, the beginnings of the sexual life of a girl child are so 'obscure,' so 'faded with time,' that one would have to dig down very deep indeed to discover beneath the traces of this civilization, of this history, the vestiges of a more archaic civilization that might give some clue to woman's sexuality. ... Woman's desire would not be expected to speak the same language as man's; woman's desire has doubtless been submerged by the logic that has dominated the West since the time of the Greeks.

Within this logic, the predominance of the visual, and of the discrimination and individualization of form, is particularly foreign to female eroticism. Woman takes more pleasure from touching than from looking, and her entry into a dominant scopic economy signifies ... her consignment to passivity: she is to be the beautiful object of contemplation.[7]

(The archaeological metaphorics here attributed to Freud is that of his 1931 paper 'Female Sexuality', where he writes of the emergence of the girl's pre-Oedipal attachment to her mother as 'like the discovery ... of the Minoan–Mycenean civilization behind the civilization of Greece' and of the attachment itself as 'grey with age and shadowy and almost impossible to revivify'.)[8] Many would object to the essentializing of 'woman' involved in such generalizations; but that essentializing is characteristic of medieval thought too, and is embodied in the recurrent story-patterns of medieval romances. For my purpose, it is enough that such beliefs, associating male desire with sight and female desire with less distancing senses such as touch, should be available as ways of thinking that may help to illuminate the medieval text.

Partonope's solitary, dreamlike journey into darkness corresponds perhaps to a quest into the mysterious, archaic depths of 'female sexuality'. Seeing depends on the presence of light; and one way to derange what Irigaray calls the 'dominant scopic economy' must be to create darkness. Woman is for Freud (in another of those essentializing phrases that express his construction of femininity as mystery) 'the dark continent';[9] and by creating darkness at Chef d'Oire, Melior more effectively draws Partonope into that continent and enables him (and thus also us) to experience its mystery. In the absence of looking, and of the 'discrimination and individualization of form' that it permits, the poet's account of events in the bed gives unusual prominence to touching and also to hearing – unusual, that is, given the predominant pictorialism of medieval poetry and what we have seen to be the scopic bias of its descriptive conventions. In *Partonope*, of course, there is no possibility of an introductory *effictio* of Melior, because she is not available to sight. Whereas sight is usually conceptualized as penetrative and dominating, hearing is always receptive and passive, and therefore in conventional terms feminine, and touch may be so. We habitually speak of a piercing gaze, but hardly of a piercing touch; and I can think of no term that is to hearing as 'gaze' is to sight. It is striking, too, to what extent the English translator of *Partonope of Blois* intensifies the sensory effects already present in the French.[10] This is partly a consequence of the shift of language, for medieval English translations of French narratives almost invariably make them more concrete, as we have seen with *Lanval* and *Sir Launfal*. But in this case, I think, the English poet also responded imaginatively to promptings he found in a specific and unusual French text.

Melior explains that she first fell in love with Partonope not through seeing him but through what she *heard* from her ambassadors. This idea is strengthened in a passage entirely added by the translator, where Melior develops an unusual variant of the heart-and-eye topos – Cupid shot his fiery arrow through her *ear* into her heart:

> And gode of loue þer-wyth a-none
> So sharpely shotte hys fyr[é] flone
> Thorowte myne ere in-to myne herte. (1627–9)

Nowhere else have I encountered this strange variant, which surely indicates the translator's awareness of transmitting a scene in which the accepted predominance of sight no longer operates.

In the bedchamber scene, once the light disappears, sight becomes impossible, and the resulting confinement to hearing and touch stirs the imagination to produce a delightful and more diffused eroticism. It does so for us as well as for the participants, for, as we have noted, distance is a prerequisite for sight; touch on the other hand demands contact. Just this point is made by Irigaray:

More than the other senses, the eye objectifies and masters. It sets at a distance, maintains the distance. In our culture, the predominance of the look over smell, taste, touch, hearing has brought an impoverishment of bodily relations. It has contributed to disembodying sexuality.[11]

In responding imaginatively to the tactile elements in the scene, we are drawn in rather than distanced. When Partonope is left in bed in the dark, 'Þe cloþes to hym fulle softe he drowe' (1170). (*Softe*, with its ambiguous appeal to touch and to hearing, is a word used frequently in this scene.) Then Melior enters, and instead of the detailed pictorial description that would be normal at this moment, we have something far vaguer and more suggestive:

> In þe flore he herde comynge
> A þynge fulle softely what euer hyt were.　(1181–2)

Even the gender of this 'thing' is uncertain, and the last phrase beautifully evokes Partonope's speculation and incites ours. In response,

> Vnder þe cloþys he can hym hyde,
> And drow hym to þe beddys syde;　(1188–9)

and, in due course,

> wyth hyr hondes vppe she nome
> The cloþys alle, and In dyd crepe,
> For þer she wolde, she þoȝte, slepe.
> Whether she were fayre or ellys no,
> Nere þe chylde she dressyd here tho.　(1197–201)

By this point we have been informed (but Partonope has not) that the 'thing' is a 'young maid', but now we are offered further matter for speculation – was she beautiful or not? In the dark, it is impossible to tell.

In what follows, there are references to more bodily parts than is common in love-scenes in English romances – but, contrary to what might be expected, they are not the private parts that usually get named only in fabliaux. Book III of *Troilus* was the most powerfully erotic writing in English before *Partonope of Blois*, and it was a major influence on the English translator. In *Troilus*, of parts below the neck, arms, hands, sides, back and breasts are mentioned (and knees, but only for kneeling, not in bed); and of these, sides, back and breasts are named only in the single stanza quoted in the last chapter.[12] In *Partonope*, as the two shy young people manoeuvre in the same large bed, unexpected bodily conjunctions occur, for example of legs and heels:

> Thys fayre lady þat was so hende,
> Streyghte forþe here legge, and happed to ffele,
> Trewly þe ffrenshe boke seyeth þe hele
> Off þys wofulle Partonope. (1297–300)

The inserted reference to the source causes pleasing suspense, making us wait to discover *which* part of Partonope Melior happened to feel when she stretched out her leg; it also encourages us to recognize an unEnglish naughtiness in the very mention of such a bodily part in such a conjunction. The heel may not usually be thought of as an erogenous zone; but everything is different in the dark.

Even when the pair are not moving, hearing comes into play: Partonope 'syked softely, he lyethe fulle stylle' (1481), Melior hears him and feels her heart quivering like a leaf in a high wind, and 'Here body was colde, yette dyd she swete' (1488). (Thus bodily awareness is once more suggested.) Later, movement resumes, and there is a long passage (1520–71) in which bodies and bodily contact are beautifully evoked. Melior 'fulle softely' turns away from Partonope from 'here ryghte syde' to 'þe lyfte syde' (1520–3). He reaches out, and

> Fro hym he putte forthe hys honde.
> He soghte faste, tylle þat he fonde
> Thys yonge lady, I yowe ensewre. (1529–31)

He never felt such another creature 'of flesche and bonne' (1533); he laid his arm over her, and 'So softe, so clene she was to fele' (1537) that he did not know where he was. She felt his hand on her and pushed it away; then by silent agreement – 'be on a-corde' (1549) – they lie still almost all night, but at last

> After hys lady he gan to graspe
> Wyth hys honde full cowardely, (1552–3)

and then he moves right next to her. He once more lays his arm over her; this time she endures it 'pasyentlye' and 'full mekely' (1559–60)

– words that jokingly attribute 'feminine' virtues to her desire – even while begging him not to.

> And wyth þat worde a-none ganne he
> In hys armes her faste to hym brase.
> And full softely þen sho sayde, 'Allas!'
> And her legges sho gan to knytte,
> And wyth hys knees he gan hem on-sh[yt]te.
> And þer-wyth-all she sayde: 'Syr, mercy!'   (1562–7)

The ambiguity of her remark is amusing: it could equally mean 'Please don't!' or 'Thanks very much!' If the poet entered into more detail he would take the already stretched decorum of Middle English romance to breaking point; but he sums up rather tenderly by saying that thus 'a-way her maydenhede / Haþe he þen rafte, and geffe her hys' (1570–1). Partonope gives as well as takes: he too is a virgin, and in his aggressiveness there has been nothing cruel or knowing, and nothing beyond what Melior herself appears to desire. The boar-hunt on which Partonope got lost also concluded in darkness; it is renarrated twice, and quite gratuitously, in the course of this love-scene, first by Partonope and then by Melior as part of her explanation of how she brought him there; and these renarrations are considerably fuller in English than in French. The repetitions serve as a reminder that love too is a hunt, but in the dark it is far from clear who is the hunter and who the hunted.

The French and English writers both refer to themselves as male, and the story told in this scene originates no doubt as a male fantasy: one scholar has concisely observed that in stories of this type, where (as in *Lanval* too) a young man encounters a willing fairy mistress, 'the cause of the [hero's] reward seems to be the need for it'.[13] Yet (again like *Lanval*) it can also be read as a female fantasy of secret power; the crude male fantasy of the willing female victim is richly elaborated into a complex, dreamlike experience, and the poet has devised a fiction in which it can plausibly be believed that the woman really does mean 'yes'. In the English version we learn at an early stage (1221ff.) that Melior intends to get Partonope as her husband; the progressively more gruesome punishments with which she threatens him if he disobeys her commands to leave – being killed (1316ff.), cut to pieces with knives (1323ff.), fettered and perpetually imprisoned (1334ff.), and pulled apart by wild horses (1461ff.) – must therefore be devised as a test for him; and presumably the magic powers by which she drew him to Chef d'Oire would enable her to protect herself against his hesitant advances if she chose. What Partonope gains is ultimately sexual possession of a phallic, penetrative kind, and his subsequent determination to *see* Melior shows that he cannot escape this wish for mastery; but on the way he has shared (and so have we) in what Luce Irigaray would regard as a characteristically feminine eroticism: a 'sexual multiplicity', involving a 'plurality of erogenous zones' – even the heel! – not grouped under 'the primacy of the phallus'.[14] For a while at least, first in the night-time forest and then in the darkened bedchamber at Chef d'Oire, Partonope has become an explorer of the 'dark continent' of the feminine; and indeed one might say that in the bedroom he too has *become* a dark continent, *participating* in 'sexual multiplicity', hunted as well as hunter, rather than being fixed in a single role as one who explores and exploits.

There is a further way in which both he and the reader experience the story as an exploration of feminine darkness. The poet tells his story according to what medieval rhetoricians call the *ordo artificialis*; that is, events are narrated in an order other than that in which they occur.[15] Melior's desire for Partonope and the magic by which she draws him into her bed precede their encounter in that bed but are narrated afterwards. (In the French her intentions are completely concealed; in the English we are told soon after they enter the bed that Melior intends to have Partonope as her husband, but we do not know why or how she brought him there.) The *ordo artificialis* is brought about by feminine wiles; the narrative is given not only its substance but its shape by Melior's magic art of deception, and in this respect the poem is a literal enactment of the metaphors of rhetorical theory. Art, writes Geoffroi de Vinsauf (meaning specifically that which produces the *ordo artificialis*),

> ludit quasi quaedam praestigiatrix,
> Et facit ut fiat res postera prima, futura
> Praesens, transversa directa, remota propinqua ...

plays, as it were, the conjuror: causes the last to be first, the future to be present, the oblique to be straight, the remote to be near ...[16]

and it is as though Melior, with her magic powers, were that *praestigiatrix* or female conjuror exercising control over the shape of the narrative. The French poet calls her skill *engin*;[17] the English translator calls it *crafte*. When she explains things to Partonope, she proudly claims, 'Alle thys dyd I þorowe my crafte' (1659), and again

> Alle þys was made by crafte of me.
> Thys crafte I dyd, yette more I can.   (1672–3)

The *crafte* of the romance writer is attributed by him to Melior; the plot's twists and mysteries may encourage us to see romance itself as a feminine genre, but in any case it is characterized by a cunning and deceptiveness that are among the qualities traditionally attributed to woman.

The absence of sight from the bedchamber scene, and thus of the 'male gaze' in any literal sense, puts the two virgin lovers on equal terms. 'Point of view' (a term we cannot help using even when nothing is to be seen) is handled with great subtlety. This too is a feature intensified by the translator, who adds much detail about the characters' thoughts and feelings, and in doing so also inserts himself into the narrative and invites us to follow suit. Until Melior enters, we experience events through Partonope's consciousness (and thus, as in *Lanval*, we might take the adventure to be only his fantasy, a hallucination induced by weariness and disorientation). As soon as she gets into the bed, her consciousness is interposed: we are told that she lies still and says nothing, 'For she ne herde ne felte no-þynge' (1204). But between the two comes a narratorial passage explaining who this intruder is, and referring further to what a reader of the French original would *see*: she was a 'yonge mayde', and

> ho so luste to rede
> The story in frenshe, þer shalle he se
> She was a laydy of grette degre,
> That homely to hyr owne bedde come.   (1193–6)

Thus there are evoked both a narratorial consciousness and the consciousness of a possible reader of the French source (who, unlike the characters, would not be deprived of sight, but would see only words, not bodies); this hypothetical reader of the French would presumably be different from the actual reader of the English; and then, behind the translator and however many readers there may be in both categories, must be the writer of the 'story in frenshe', since after all stories in French do not write themselves. Moreover, an indefinite number of still other persons are apparently waiting in the narrative's wings. Beings of some kind presumably provided Partonope with food, drink, and light, led him to the bedchamber, removed his spurs and clothes. When Melior issues her threats of

punishment to Partonope, she informs him that 'I haue men / Þat
wol a-raye the fulle Ille' (1424–5) and that

> I haue knyghtes faste me be-syde
> That shulle a-bate alle thy pryde.   (1441–2)

That way of putting it makes it sound as though they too might be in
the bed; in the dark it would be hard to tell. Throughout the scene
these multiple consciousnesses shift places so rapidly that we can
scarcely distinguish among them: the effect is stereoscopic – again
the inescapable visual metaphor! – but it is a stereoscopy of
consciousness and imagination.

Suspense is heightened in the English version by the storyteller's
frequent interventions, holding up the actual telling of his story for
various reasons. He offers his own judgments on the characters'
behaviour, telling us that when Melior begins to pity Partonope
after hearing him sigh,

> Nowe me þynketh, so Gode me saue,
> She owte of very [w]omanhede
> Off hys desese to take grette hede.   (1508–10)

He sometimes invites an audience of listeners to offer *their* judgments
– fictional listeners, no doubt, since a long fifteenth-century poem is
more likely to have attracted private readers. 'What sey ye loueres,'
he asks about Melior's willingness to risk her honour to gain
Partonope as her husband, 'was hyt not thys / A gentylle herte?'
(1231–2). He anticipates the future course of events; sometimes this
can be explained by a characteristically English concern for moral
propriety – he wants us to know in advance that Melior got into bed
with Partonope not promiscuously but because she intended to
marry him – or sometimes it is to arouse our pity for her: Partonope
is going to be untrue to her eventually, and

> Alle here lyffe she myghte welle rewe
> Vppon hyr-selfe, and eche man haue rowthe,
> That euer so fayre on for here trowþe
> Falssely shulde deseyued be.   (1237–40)

Sometimes again the narrator invites us to decide what should
happen next: when Partonope sees the bed and sits down beside it,
he asks, 'What shulde he do?' (1164); and later, since the young
people are both so bashful,

> Lette se nowe ho can beste deuyse
> Þes tweyne to make a-quentyd to be.   (1287–8)

He intervenes to invoke the assistance of Venus:

> But to þat lady I clepe and calle
> That Venus is called, goddas of loue,
> Þat in heuen sytteste a-boue,
> Brynge þys lady to here desyre,
> Þat haste so sore sette on ffyre
> In here serues þys her trowbell herte,
> Þat she here-after fele no smerte
> For here trowþe, ne for here kyndenes.   (1245–52)

Yet another occasion for narratorial intervention occurs when the translator, in a particularly Chaucerian manner, refers apologetically to his source for details he claims to think questionable: when Melior's leg touches Partonope's heel,

> 'Owte! allas þen!' sayde she,
> And In a maner gan to crye,
> For sothe I wolle not lye,
> Myne auctor seyethe hyt was not lowde.   (1301–4)

He proceeds to offer his own defensive explanation for the inaudibility of her cry: it was so that there should be 'No grette a-ffray, ne no sterynge' (1308). To find fault with such prudence would surely be churlish.

Many of the English additions refer to celestial beings of one kind or another. It is normal for characters in English romances to be more pious than those in French; it is so in *Sir Landevale* and *Sir Launfal*, and equally in *Partonope of Blois*. The translator naturally reproduces Melior's prayer to the Blessed Virgin (1326), which he found in his source and which convinces Partonope that his invisible partner is not, as he has feared, a devil. But he also adds several prayers to God by both Partonope (1112–21, 1131, 1141–5) and Melior (1274–5). The translator himself, as we have seen, prays to Venus on Melior's behalf (1245–52); he makes Partonope bless Fortune for bringing him into Melior's power (1411–17); and, as we have also seen, he makes Melior explain that Cupid shot his arrow into her heart through her ear (1627–32). Melior concludes,

> I se þat hyt ys the ordynauns
> Off gode of loue, howe sore me smerte.
> Hyt was me shape or then my [sherte].   (1714–16)

That last turn of phrase occurs in *The Knight's Tale* in connection
with a reference to Cupid;[18] and all these added classical allusions
are unmistakably influenced by the English poet's Chaucerian
reading. The Chaucerian sources, though, have classical pagan
settings, not the Christian setting of *Partonope of Blois*, and this
Chaucerian imitator shows none of Chaucer's concern to distinguish between pagan and Christian or to represent the supernatural
as a matter of science or planetary influence. We simply have
Christian piety, magic, Fortune and pagan mythology side by side
within a fictional realm where metaphysical consistency is of no
concern.

In general, though, the English translator read Chaucer intelligently and resourcefully, and the result is the creation of a multi-
dimensional imaginative space inhabited by a huge variety of actual
and potential points of view – though in the absence of sight they are
better called 'points of consciousness'. If we pause to consider who is
or may be present in the darkened bedchamber besides Melior and
Partonope, we shall surely have to mention at least Melior's knights,
God, the Blessed Virgin, the possible devil, Venus, Cupid, Fortune,
the translator, the author of the French book, the readers of that
book, Geoffrey Chaucer, and of course ourselves. That seems like
rather a lot of voyeurs peering through the darkness at the supposedly private relations of the two participants. As the young
couple jostle against each other in bed and nervously start aside, so
we may imagine these many additional consciousnesses elbowing
each other in the dark as they compete for position. Presumably only
the supernatural beings can see anything; the rest of us are voyeurs
in imagination only, and it is hard to say whether we should feel
more ashamed of intruding as observers into a fictional representation of what in reality we could experience only as participants or
at imagining for ourselves sights that in the fiction are decently
veiled in obscurity. As we read this section of the poem, especially in
its English version, our experience is surely very like that of people
suddenly plunged into darkness. Deprived of sight, we find our
tactile and auditory sensations heightened, but are unable to
organize them into any consistent spatial perspective or to set them
in an unambiguous hierarchy of significance.[19] We find ourselves as
readers not adopting any particular 'point of consciousness' – I do
not imagine that female readers will find themselves identifying
consistently with Melior or male readers with Partonope – but

shifting restlessly from one subject-position to another. We even find ourselves shifting temporal position, as we respond to the translator's tantalizing anticipations of the outcome. As readers of the French, we would adopt Partonope's point of view throughout, and then undergo a single disorienting shock as we learned that everything had been planned by Melior, and that what we had taken to be a rape was really part of the victim's magical plan; but as readers of the English we start getting partial glimpses of this as soon as the lights go out, and the possibility of reading events backwards from the end unsettles us from the beginning. The narrative method itself, then, replicates the experience it describes: we enjoy a double exploration of the dark continent. I do not suppose this to be the fulfilment of any conscious programme on the English poet's part; it is rather that his imaginative engagement with a fascinating scene in his French source leads him, with Chaucer's help, to turn it into an experience so mobile and complex, so subversive of all fixed subject positionings, that it can scarcely be called voyeuristic at all.

CHAPTER 8

The Knight's Tale and The Merchant's Tale

Chaucer's *Knight's Tale*, like *Troilus and Criseyde*, is set in classical antiquity – 'the pagan past at its most noble and dignified, imagined from within'.[1] It was a remarkable feat for a fourteenth-century English poet to construct in words, within the limits of his historical knowledge, a culture systematically different from his own and intended to represent that of pagan antiquity, and it seems unlikely that Chaucer could have succeeded in something that none of his contemporaries even thought of attempting had he not had both the opportunity to encounter the Italian *trecento* and the imagination to respond to that opportunity. Chaucer grasped something of the attempt by *trecento* poets and thinkers to re-enter a pagan past envisaged as constituting an autonomous sphere of values, and to restore it to life in a modern vernacular.[2] Like *Troilus and Criseyde*, *The Knight's Tale* is translated from a poem of some classical learning by Boccaccio – in this case the *Teseida*, 'in many ways ... an archaeological reconstruction of the world of classical antiquity'.[3] But in their imaginative reworkings of the past, these two Chaucerian narratives differ significantly, especially in their representations of the roles of the sexes. Both poems, products of a patriarchal medieval culture, are set in societies where power is ultimately in male hands; but whereas in *Troilus and Criseyde* there is a sphere of private life within which women interact socially and sexually with men on an equal footing and themselves possess a margin of freedom for their inner lives, in *The Knight's Tale* no such social interaction of the sexes and no such margin of female freedom exist. In *The Knight's Tale* public and therefore masculine considerations dominate entirely over private: Chaucer's Athens and Thebes are structured by male bonding, the positions occupied in them by women are emotionally as well as politically subordinate, and women's chief function is to be the objects of rivalry and exchange among men.[4]

When Emelye prays in the temple of Diana that she may remain a virgin, the goddess can only reply:

> Among the goddes hye it is affermed,
> And by eterne word writen and confermed,
> Thou shalt ben wedded unto oon of tho
> That han for thee so muchel care and wo,
> But unto which of hem I may nat telle. (I 2349–53)[5]

Above as below, decision-making is a male prerogative.

As Irigaray would lead us to expect (and her adaptation of Freud's metaphors from classical archaeology now seems peculiarly apt), this homosocial Greece imagined by Chaucer is marked by a 'predominance of the visual'. My discussion must reflect this, and so, while in *Troilus and Criseyde* I was often concerned with the presence of secret observers whose awareness was not specifically associated with looking, my account of *The Knight's Tale* will be partly concerned with forms of the visual that are not connected with secret observation. Far more than in *Troilus and Criseyde*, large elements of the world represented in *The Knight's Tale* are designed to convey philosophical and cultural meanings emblematically, through what can be publicly seen. The elaborate *descriptiones* of the temples of the gods in Part III fall under this heading. The gods personify the great cosmic and/or instinctual forces that the poem envisages as working on and through human beings; the interiors of their temples are described predominantly in pictorial form, and from the first line of the first temple – 'First in the temple of Venus maystow *se* . . .' (1918) – are referred to almost twenty times as being *seen* or capable of being seen. They are even mentioned many times as being seen by the storyteller –

> Ther *saugh* I first the derke ymaginyng
> Of Felonye . . . (1995–6)

> Ther *saugh* I Dane, yturned til a tree . . . (2062)

– for, though he is describing a remote past that he cannot really have laid eyes on, the Knight[6] participates in the 'scopic economy' of his tale. Cultural meanings are represented in the form of spectacle; under this heading would come the tournament and Arcite's funeral in Part IV. The tournament with its preliminaries, eagerly watched by the Athenian populace, is 'a lusty sighte for to *see*' (2116); it is also a demonstration of ducal power, with Theseus sitting above 'as he were a god in trone', displaying himself to his people who press forward 'Hym for to *seen*' (2529–31); and the theatre where it occurs emblematizes harmonious social order, with its tiers arranged

> That whan a man was set on o degree,
> He letted nat his felawe for to *see*.   (1891–2).

At the funeral, Arcite's corpse is displayed in the *halle* (2880) 'for the peple sholde *seen* hym alle' (2879), and the magnificent pagan ritual is a pictorial lesson in the acceptance of mortality. Again, sight functions as the means by which philosophical truth is demonstrated; in Theseus's final speech, where he attempts to establish the meaningfulness of earthly events, including Arcite's death, he repeatedly argues from what we can *see* –

> The grete tounes *se we* wane and wende.
> Thanne may *ye se* that al this thyng hath ende.
> Of man and womman *seen we* wel also . . .   (3025–7)

– to what we cannot see, from the mutability of earthly things to the stability of the heavenly order behind them.

The 'predominance of the visual' in *The Knight's Tale* is accompanied by what Irigaray calls 'discrimination and individualization of form', and this manifests itself particularly in the action's material setting. The symbolic landscape of romance appears in *The Knight's Tale* in an especially clear, almost diagrammatic shape. On the one hand there is the ordered civic and courtly area of Athens, protected and constrained by walls; on the other there are open landscapes where adventurous and/or chaotic activity takes place, such as the battlefield where the Thebans are defeated and the forest only 'a myle or tweye' from the court (1504). In the forest occur hunting and the rites of May (1510–12); it is also where Palamon and Arcite fight like savage beasts or like those 'hunters in the regne of Trace' (1638) who seek to kill savage beasts before they are killed by them. At the same time, as we have found in the Tristan story, the forest can function as a parodic version of court life or a reminder of its predatory potential: it is where Palamon as voyeur and *écoutour* stalks Arcite, cowering fearfully in a bush (1516–27) and listening to what his cousin says secretly to himself.

Yet this sharp discrimination is shadowed by unexpected ambiguity. The ambiguous value of civilized order is stressed more

strongly in *The Knight's Tale* than in any other romance we have
studied. It is conveyed for instance in the way that the same wall
encloses both the tower where Palamon and Arcite are imprisoned
and the garden where Emelye wanders gathering flowers:

> The grete tour, that was so thikke and stroong,
> Which of the castel was the chief dongeoun
> (Ther as the knyghtes weren in prisoun
> Of which I tolde yow and tellen shal),
> Was evene joynant to the gardyn wal
> Ther as this Emelye hadde hir pleyynge.   (1056–61)

Civilization at its darkest and its brightest are physically bound
together.[7] Yet however 'thikke and strong' their walls, cities offer no
ultimate security: what happens to a city taken by assault is
horrifyingly exposed when Theseus (albeit justly) conquers Thebes
'And rente adoun bothe wall and sparre and rafter' (990) and again
in the depiction in Mars' temple of 'The toun destroyed, ther was
no thyng laft' (2016). A similar ambiguity is conveyed by the 'noble
theatre' (1885) constructed by Theseus for the tournament. Like
Gottfried von Strassburg's *Minnegrotte*, it is an allegorical building
erected in the forest; not a celebration of love, but a manifestation at
once of order and of disorder, a place where even within the rules of
chivalry Palamon and Arcite fight as much like beasts from savage
places – the cruel tiger 'in the vale of Galgopheye' (2626) and the fell
lion 'in Belmarye' (2630) – as they did earlier in the grove where it
stands. It is a symmetrical architectural celebration of cosmic
forces, but those forces, male and female alike, make for destruction.
The most to be hoped is that these destructive powers, at once
planets and gods, should be contained by the devices of civilization:
there is no possibility of overcoming or abolishing them. Even a
noble ruler such as Theseus can do justice only at the cost of
destroying cities and heaping up corpses; he can order the tournament to be fought without loss of life, but he cannot prevent
Saturn from slaying the winner; and the highest wisdom he can offer
is to make the best of what the gods decree, 'to maken vertu of
necessitee' (3042). Arcite's funeral also takes place in the grove: the
place 'Ther as he hadde his amorouse desires' (2861) now becomes
the place of death, and the local gods themselves are 'Disherited of
hire habitacioun' (2926).

One other feature of the tale's spatial setting is a consequence of
its total absence of private life. Erotic contact and the sexual act play

no part in the action, and the *chambre* is therefore not a place of intimacy but a mere symbol of rank: Arcite in disguise becomes 'Page of the chambre of Emelye the brighte' (1427) and then squire of the chamber to Theseus (1440). Later, when Theseus is woken from sleep by the preparations for the tournament, he does not emerge immediately but 'Heeld yet the chambre of his paleys riche' (2525) until Palamon and Arcite are summoned; then he shows himself at a window. It is our only glimpse of the ruler's private quarters, yet it is not really an instance of private life, especially by comparison with scenes in Mark's or Arthur's *chambre*, scenes that may lack dignity but at least possess human warmth. Hippolyta goes unmentioned, and Theseus's holding himself back from the public eye is evidently as calculated an enactment of ducal power as is his subsequent self-display at the window or in procession through the city 'Ful lik a lord' (2569). Still more than the *chambre*, the bed lacks its usual richness of human meaning; here it is only a place for solitary sleep, broken by an ambiguously prophetic dream of Mercury (1383ff.), or, in the end, for a squalidly painful death, 'Allone, withouten any compaignye' (2779). In other romances, including Chaucer's own *Troilus*, we have encountered in the *chambre* and the bed a realm of shared privacy that gains emotional richness from its tension with the opposing realm from which it strives to shield itself, that of public law and public gazes; here privacy is reduced to a calculated or imposed solitude. One other mention of the *chambre* is as the privilege extended to a noble prisoner, the 'chambre an heigh' (1065) from which Arcite gazes down at Athens and Emelye's garden; yet it is only a cell with a view, holding him at a voyeur's distance from all human contact. And as the tale proceeds, that is how its vision of the whole of human life, or perhaps of pagan life, ultimately takes shape – 'this foule prisoun of this lyf', as Theseus describes it in his closing speech (3061).

In Irigaray's view, the functions and importance of looking will be closely connected with the power-relations of the sexes; and in *The Knight's Tale* this proves to be so. Important indications of the position of women in the tale are given in its opening lines. The subordination of women in the poem's world has been established by an event that has already occurred when the story proper begins: Theseus's conquest of the Amazons. The 'regne of Femenye' (866, 877) has already been overcome by the *wysdom* and *chivalrie* of the 'lord and governour' (861) of Athens. Here Chaucer has made a

major change from the *Teseida*. Boccaccio deliberately constructed
the *Teseida* as an epic in twelve books, in imitation of Virgil's *Aeneid*,
and Teseo's war against the Amazons had been the subject of Book
I. Having completed the poem, Boccaccio went still further in his
epic imitation, adding to it a collection of prose glosses or *chiose*, so
that it would appear in the form in which classical epics were read in
the Middle Ages, surrounded by a medieval commentary on its
meaning. In a gloss to Book I he defends himself for having spent so
long on Teseo's war against the Amazons, something apparently
irrelevant to his story of Arcita and Palemone; he did so, he says,
because the behaviour of the Amazon women 'is rather strange
[*alquanto pellegrina*] to most people, and therefore more interesting' (I
6:1, gloss).[8] Scholars disagree as to whether Chaucer knew the
chiose,[9] but in any case he apparently felt the force of the criticism
against which Boccaccio defended himself, and therefore summarily
discussed Theseus's victory in an *occupatio*, the rhetorical figure that
mentions what is *not* going to be treated in detail:

> And certes, if it nere to long to heere,
> I wolde have toold yow fully the manere
> How wonnen was the regne of Femenye
> By Theseus and by his chivalrye.   (875–8)

Nevertheless the victory over the Amazons remains the only one of
Theseus's many conquests to be specified, and it still holds first
place in the tale. We are not intended to forget that *Femenye* – that
imagined 'rather strange' Other World in which women live, rule
themselves and fight without men – has been overcome only by an
extreme exertion of masculine *wysdom* and *chivalrie*; nor perhaps to
forget that Theseus's wedding of Hippolyta was itself the outcome of
siege warfare:

> And how asseged was Ypolita,
> The faire, hardy queene of Scithia;
> And of the feste that was at hir weddynge,
> And of the tempest at hir hoom-comynge ...   (881–4)

   Perhaps too that tempest (unmentioned either in Boccaccio or in
Statius, the genuine classical source for the Theban epic) has
something of the symbolic force of the storm that provokes and
accompanies Aeneas's union with Dido in Book IV of the *Aeneid*, the
sea-storm accompanying the arrival of Othello and Desdemona in
Cyprus in Act II, scene 1, of Shakespeare's play, or, in its different

way, the 'smoky reyn' in *Troilus and Criseyde* Book III. The tempest, that is, may offer a glimpse of the disruptive power of sex itself, a disruption which, from the dominant masculine viewpoint, is associated specifically with female sexuality. This disruptive power has been mastered by the defeat of the Amazons, but it remains a hovering threat in the minds of men. This may explain Theseus's initially harsh response to the Theban widows who approach him when he is about to enter Athens: his first assumption is that they are motivated by 'envye / Of myn honour' (907–8), as if they were rival warriors like the Amazons, though he immediately proceeds to ask if he can right any wrong done them. What the tale goes on to show is male rivalry as the real disruptive force, whether motivated by desire for power (as in the Theban story of a war between brothers which Theseus brings to an end) or by desire for women as passive sexual objects (as in the story of Palamon and Arcite, which continues the fratricidal Theban rivalry). In *The Knight's Tale* the Otherness of women is represented as being under male control on earth as in the heavens. Their only effective weapon is tears, whether those of Theban or Athenian ladies on earth or those of Venus above, begging Saturn, 'Til that hir teeres in the lystes fille' (2666), to fulfil her promise that Palamon shall gain Emelye. There is no role for women as rulers or as sources of philosophical wisdom: it is striking that Pallas Athene, the goddess of rational wisdom, mentioned by Boccaccio as the presiding deity of Athens,[10] remains unmentioned by Chaucer.

In an earlier account of *The Knight's Tale* I stressed its 'classical simplicity and rationality of structure',[11] which I associated with the general project of Chaucer's 'philosophical romances' (*The Knight's Tale*, *Troilus and Criseyde*, and *The Franklin's Tale*), the Renaissance enterprise of imaginatively reconstructing pagan antiquity. That classicizing project involved the rejection of much of what *we* mean by romance (though Chaucer possessed no term corresponding to 'romance' in its modern range of senses): structural extravagance, unrealism, unconcern with historical probability, magic and mystery unresolved into science and philosophy. Chaucer, I claimed, despised those qualities; and indeed they are conspicuously absent from *Troilus and Criseyde*, by contrast with romances such as those of Chrétien or Marie de France, Thomas Chestre or either author of the Partonope story. Susan Crane has recently argued that this view underestimates the importance of 'romance illogicalities

. and marvels'[12] in *The Knight's Tale* and thus elides its acknowledg-
ment of 'feminine difference'. Benefitting from her observations, I
would now say that, in pursuit of his classicizing project, Chaucer
has *repressed* the feminine in *The Knight's Tale*. (As the term 'repression' implies, my assumption is that this was an unconscious process
– that is, that, though Chaucer of course knew that he was omitting
most of Boccaccio's account of the Amazons, he was not fully aware
why he did this. But there is no way of achieving certainty about
Chaucer's motives.) To apply to a literary text the terminology
applied to the mind by psychoanalysis, the conscious of *The Knight's
Tale* consists of the general world of the tale, an imagined classical
antiquity dominated by men. That world, however, attempts to
exclude the possibility of female power, and the moment of repression of this possibility is represented on the 'historical' level by
Theseus's victory over the Amazons and on the textual level by
Chaucer's excision of virtually all information about them.

Book I of the *Teseida* tells of the Amazons' successful rebellion
against patriarchy, when they killed their husbands and fathers,
finding it intolerable to be kept in a subjection which they denounce
as unjust, 'For they did not treat us as if we had been born of the
same kind of seed as they were' (1 29:5–6). It goes on to describe
their exclusion of all men from their territory, their rejection of
sexual love except for procreation, and their heroic defence of their
land against the Athenians' attack, a defence so successful at first
that 'Even the bravest of [the Greeks] took cover . . . so fearful were
they of the women's arrows' (1 56:5–7). Even when the Athenians
establish a beachhead, the Amazons continue to battle to the death.
Forced to abandon the shore, they take refuge in their castle and
hold out for several months, during which Teseo 'accomplished
little, or rather, nothing except terror and painful humiliation,
because very often the women within risked death by preying on
them boldly, so confident were they that they could not be van-
quished' (1 94:3–8). The Amazons agree to surrender only when
shown that Teseo has undermined the castle walls, a tactic on which
Ipolita comments contemptuously that 'fighting in dark places is
neither the craft nor the art of a good knight' (1 106:7–8). Teseo's
marriage with Ipolita is part of the treaty by which the war is
brought to an honourable conclusion.

This fascinating material, sometimes presented misogynistically,
but always conveying forcefully what a danger women would

represent to men if they should 'perform manly, rather than womanly, deeds' (1 24:8) (thus rejecting male definitions of sexual difference), is omitted by Chaucer. The omission has itself been repressed by modern scholars, for one seeks in vain for any comment on its significance not only in my own earlier account of *The Knight's Tale* but in the best and fullest studies of its relation to the *Teseida*.[13] Yet it is as if what is omitted continues to exist within the tale itself, though relegated to its unconscious. From time to time the repressed returns in ways that disturb the conscious surface of the narrative; it returns, however, not in its original form as female heroism but as the more insidious danger and fascination represented by 'the feminine', the female as Other. Freud insists that

The process of repression is not to be regarded as an event which takes place *once*, the results of which are permanent ... repression demands a persistent expenditure of force, and if this were to cease the success of the repression would be jeopardized, so that a fresh act of repression would be necessary.[14]

Occupatio might be envisaged as the product of a continuing tension between the repressing force or 'censorship' and what it attempts to exclude: by not telling, it functions as a symptom of the existence of what it does not tell. Freud observes that repression may operate either by refusing to admit the unwelcome guest to the house or by ordering him out of the drawing room once he has entered;[15] *occupatio* is a figure comparable to the latter process, because it gives a brief, tantalizing glimpse of what is being excluded.

It may not be by chance that the unconscious of *The Knight's Tale* can be identified with 'the regne of Femenye', because some developments in psychoanalytic theory propose a general analogy between the concept of the feminine (that is, of woman seen by man as other) and the concept of the unconscious itself. Luce Irigaray is asked in an interview whether, having deconstructed the Freudian theory of femininity, she can elaborate an alternative theory, with a different concept of the unconscious. She answers,

the first question we have to ask is whether there is something in the unconscious as it is currently designated that might belong to the repressed feminine. In other words, before asking about elaborating an unconscious that would be *other* with respect to the unconscious as it is now defined, it is appropriate, perhaps, to ask whether the feminine may not be to a large extent included in that unconscious ... whether the feminine does not, in part, consist of what is operating in the name of the unconscious.[16]

Irigaray's question offers at least a suggestive formulation, and one that is helpful in trying to understand how *The Knight's Tale* works.

In the romances examined so far, voyeurism has most often been a matter of a secret view of the private activities of a pair of lovers, and, though most watchers have been male, their gender has apparently been largely indifferent. In the imagined pagan, epic past of *The Knight's Tale*, there is a more complete sexual segregation than within the medieval courtliness of most romances, and, as I have noted, love-making has no place. Neither has the darkness within which touch and hearing assume special importance; the sexes are separated by a visible space bridged only by sight. This leads to a fuller development of the kind of voyeuristic scene encountered in the stories of Diana and Actaeon and of Susanna and the Elders: a concealed man or men watches a naked woman or women, curious about their otherness and motivated by a kind of fearful fascination. The way towards this in *The Knight's Tale* is prepared by an unusually emphatic development of the recurrent romance scene in which the sight of a woman wounds a man with love.

No woman could be more unAmazonian than Hippolyta's younger sister Emelye: sweet, flowerlike (1038–9), virtuous, dutifully observant of pagan religious customs, she sings angelically, and, though her hair (always perilous to men) may be long, it is firmly controlled by being 'broyded in a tresse / Bihynde hir bak' (1049–50) rather than hanging enticingly loose over her cheeks. Her disruptive effect in provoking murderous male rivalry is plainly not her fault or wish; it is a consequence of the projection on to her of the repressed sexual desires of the imprisoned knights, with their dangerously fratricidal ancestry. The tale makes us see her voyeuristically from Palamon's viewpoint, framed by the stoutly barred prison window –

> And so bifel, by aventure or cas,
> That thurgh a wyndow, thikke of many a barre
> Of iren greet and square as any sparre,
> He cast his eye upon Emelya,
> And therwithal he bleynte and cride, 'A!'
> As though he stongen were unto the herte   (1074–9)

– but not until we have first seen her as a free-standing figure, unaware of the knights' existence and of her effect on them. The male gaze may turn her into an object, but the narrative insists that she does not respond by behaving as one who is conscious of being looked at. In the scene from *Yvain* where Yvain is an invisible watcher of Laudine's grief, I suggested that, although within the fiction she cannot know that he is watching her, the framing of the fiction by his gaze presents her as if her function were to be a spectacle. In *The Knight's Tale* the two Thebans are not magically invisible, but for Emelye they might as well be. Here Chaucer differs interestingly from Boccaccio. Boccaccio describes this scene as a classic case of the male gaze in Berger's terms: that is, 'Women watch themselves being looked at' and the woman who is conscious of being watched by men 'turns herself into an object – and most particularly an object of vision – a sight'. In the *Teseida* Emilia hears the *omè* ('alas') uttered by Palemone when Cupid's arrow strikes him, looks up to the window, sees the two young men there, blushes, and leaves the garden. 'But', adds Boccaccio,

as she went she was not unmindful of that *omè*, and although she was a maiden as yet unready for love's fulfilment, she was nonetheless aware of what it implied. And thinking that she knew the truth of the matter, she rejoiced in being found attractive and thought herself lovelier and made herself fairer the next time she went into that garden. (III 19)

In Chaucer there is none of this. Palamon makes the usual complaint of being 'hurt right now thurghout myn ye / Into myn herte' (1096–7), but there is no indication that Emelye has looked at him. The male tendency to extend the mastery signified by the penetrative gaze by projecting meaning on to the female is immediately revealed when he guesses that Emelye is Venus – that is, the source of sexual desire, that is, the source of *his* sexual desire. Arcite too is 'hurt' and 'wounded' (1115–16), and even, he asserts, slain (1118) by Emelye's beauty, again without her wish or knowledge;[17] and this instantly produces deadly rivalry between the two cousins. The beast-fable quoted by Arcite (1177–80) shows how totally Emelye is regarded as an object: she is merely the potential food of the hounds and the kite, and the ground of their savage rivalry.

A second female intervention, not found in Boccaccio, occurs when Theseus condemns Palamon and Arcite to death, and the Amazonian sisters and their attendant ladies beg, as the Theban widows did, for pity and mercy (1748ff.). In both cases, the intervention may at first seem disruptive, but it turns out not to be so, because it pleads for an appropriate male enactment of justice or tempering of justice with mercy; indeed in the second case, though the women are moved by the thought that 'no thyng but for love was this debaat' (1754), it is Theseus's *resoun* (1766) that urges him to do what they ask, and this in turn involves him in making a logical distinction between pride and humility. The women weep, but the man does not.[18] Theseus proceeds to speak of Cupid, not Emelye or Venus, as responsible for the knights' folly, pointing out bluntly that Emelye has known nothing of their rivalry, 'namoore . . . than woot a cokkow or an hare!' (1809–10). Without consulting her, speaking on behalf of one who has no voice in public affairs (1833), he announces that the question which knight is to marry her shall be settled by a tournament:

> Thanne shal I yeve Emelya to wyve
> To whom that Fortune yeveth so fair a grace.   (1860–1)

Emelye will have no choice, though female fickleness will have a part in the decision, because Fortune, described as *chaungeable* (1242), is a female deity.[19]

Susan Crane states that 'Both Emelye and Diana contradict the tale's governing ideals and structures',[20] and locates the contradiction especially in the scene where Emelye prays to Diana in the goddess's temple. In the earlier description of Diana's temple, unlike the parallel descriptions of those of Venus and Mars, a moment of voyeurism plays an important part, and it is one that we have already encountered in an Ovidian version: Actaeon, turned into a hart and devoured by his hounds as punishment for seeing the goddess naked. But there is an odd disturbance of continuity. Chaucer writes:

> Ther *saugh* I Dane, yturned til a tree –
> I mene nat the goddesse Diane,
> But Penneus doghter, which that highte Dane.
> There *saugh* I Attheon an hert ymaked,
> For vengeaunce that he *saugh* Diane al naked;
> I *saugh* how that his houndes have hym caught
> And freeten hym, for that they knewe hym naught.   (2062–8)

The gratuitous informativeness of the distinction between Daphne and Diana attracts attention as a symptom of the speaker's contradictory feelings: he prefaces his account of Diana's vengeance on Actaeon by, as it were, hiding his eyes, and denying that *he* saw what Actaeon is about to see. This is the passage in the whole tale where references to seeing cluster most thickly, and it is also one of the places mentioned above where the storyteller breaks decorum by becoming a watcher of the scene he is supposed only to be chronicling: he watches Actaeon watching Diana.

This dangerous theme of the male secretly watching the female culminates in the account of Emelye's sacrifice in Diana's temple. Chaucer imagines this in exotically pagan terms, claiming to have authentic classical sources 'In Stace of Thebes and thise bookes olde' (2294), even though he actually adapted it from Boccaccio. He needs a pagan setting for what follows, where the male storyteller shows an uneasy fascination with female religious rites involving nakedness:

> This Emelye, with herte debonaire,
> Hir body wessh with water of a welle.
> But hou she dide hir ryte I dar nat telle,
> But it be any thing in general;
> And yet it were a game to heeren al.
> To hym that meneth wel it were no charge;
> But it is good a man been at his large.   (2282–8)

The exact meaning of these lines is hard to specify, because they are written in such vague terms; and the vagueness, I think, is significant: it betrays the storyteller's embarrassment at how exciting he finds the thought of these female rites. Here the repressed seems to return briefly in a disturbing form. A rough translation might run as follows:

This Emily, with modest heart, washed her body with water from a well. But how she performed her rite I dare not tell, unless it should be in somewhat general terms; and yet it would be fun to hear everything. It would be no burden to any man who means well; but it is a good thing for a man to be free to imagine it.

Even 'Hir body' is revealing: Chaucer might have written 'Hirselven wessh', but he chooses to mention the female body that he does not describe.[21] The washing occurs in Boccaccio, but this narratorial response to it does not. Boccaccio says that it happened 'in a place revealed to few women [*a poche manifesto*]' (VII 72), and that may be the germ of Chaucer's voyeurism. Chaucer's narrator is a kind of Actaeon, spying on Diana's followers, uneasily defensive about his position, and fearing perhaps the possibility of Actaeon's punishment. (We shall see further identifications of voyeuristic storytellers with Actaeon when we examine post-Chaucerian first-person narratives.) The pagan setting is essential for this effect; sexual segregation was of course the norm in medieval monasticism, but for nuns there were no rites involving nakedness.

Emelye's speech is heard only in the feminine space of the temple of Diana – the tale reports no other words of hers – and her prayer to the goddess is again specifically pagan. She wants to 'ben a mayden al my lyf' (2305), but this does not mean being shut up in a nunnery: it means having a jolly Amazonian time hunting and wandering with Diana's other virgin followers through the wild woods, the place of romance adventures. And she particularly specifies that she does *not* want 'to ben a wyf and be with childe' (2310). In practical terms this is sensible; pregnancy and childbirth really were among the gravest dangers to the health and indeed life of medieval women, and avoiding them could be among the inducements to virginity held out in medieval devotional treatises for female readers.[22] But Diana is the goddess of childbirth as well as of chastity and hunting – and indeed her many different roles, which also include being goddess of the underworld and of the changeable moon, seem to define her, much more than Venus, as the goddess of the feminine itself, woman as elusive Other, escaping male classifications.[23] (Venus, it might be said, personifies the man's woman, Diana the woman's woman, a more dangerous threat to patriarchy.)[24] For this reason alone, Emelye's prayer is unlikely to be granted. As we have seen, Diana can tell her that the gods have decreed that she shall be married, but not to whom. She has no choice but to acquiesce in being an object of male desire. In the conscious of *The Knight's Tale*, pagan though it is, there is no room for the disruptiveness of women who are subjects rather than objects and who live their own lives; Theseus put a stop to that when he defeated and married Hippolyta. The tale briefly opens up the prospect of a female world, and the storyteller finds it unexpectedly exciting; but then it immediately closes it down again.

Emelye watches the tournament with the other ladies (an example of the 'chivalry-topos') and when Arcite wins, with the changefulness always attributed to women, 'she agayn hym caste a freendlich ye' (2680). In response to Arcite's moving speech when he is dying in agony as a result of Saturn's intervention, Emelye as usual says nothing at all. She weeps with the other women when he is dead, and here the storyteller intervenes again, almost as if he were punishing women for the way that thoughts of their Otherness excited and confused him earlier: he trivializes their grief, minimizing its disruptive power in a world that he wants to be safely under male control:

> What helpeth it to tarien forth the day
> To tellen how she weep bothe eve and morwe?
> For in swich cas wommen have swich sorwe,
> Whan that hir housbondes ben from hem ago,
> That for the moore part they sorwen so ...   (2820–4)

> 'Why woldestow be deed,' thise wommen crye,
> 'And haddest gold ynough, and Emelye?'   (2835–6)

Emelye does speak at Arcite's funeral, but her words and her *desir* are excluded in the course of another *occupatio* – 'Ne how she swowned whan men made the fyr, / Ne what she spak, ne what was hir desir' (2943–4) – and are thus once more repressed to the level of the feminine as unconscious.[25] At a certain stage in the funeral, she is 'lad ... homward' (2956), and the funeral games that follow, unwatched by women, are a pagan ceremony involving male nudity that corresponds to the female ceremony in Diana's temple. Here, though, there is nothing to excite the unambiguously male, heterosexual storyteller; for, if desire and the look are to remain male, desirability must belong only to the repressed 'regne of Femenye'. Finally, Theseus marries Emelye to Palamon in a public ceremony with a political purpose: it is a means to 'have fully of Thebans obeisaunce' (2974) by uniting the surviving Theban prince with Theseus's sister-in-law. Once more, Theseus speaks for Emelye in this public place, 'With al th'avys heere of my parlement' (3076), not consulting her own wishes; and once more she says nothing. The tone of the conclusion is not, in my view, intended to be cynical, as some critics have suggested;[26] it was by just such a dynastic marriage that the peace-party at Richard II's court hoped to bring an end to the destructive war with France that had begun so long before. Peace is to be wished for, and so is the triumph of Athenian wisdom over Theban crime. But we may note, and if we choose note with sadness (but the sadness is not Chaucer's), how completely 'the regne of Femenye' has now been subdued and silenced.

The Merchant's Tale is another story set in pagan antiquity, though it is less carefully distinguished from medieval Christianity than in The Knight's Tale. Like The Knight's Tale and Troilus and Criseyde, it frequently fuses pagan myth with scientific astrology (a technique

learned from the *trecento* poets) to bring the classical past back to life
in a modern vernacular:

> Bright was the day, and blew the firmament;
> Phebus hath of gold his stremes doun ysent
> To gladen every flour with his warmnesse.
> He was that tyme in Geminis, as I gesse,
> But litel fro his declynacion
> Of Cancer, Jovis exaltacion.   (IV 2219–24)[27]

The tale tells of a knight whose wife has an adulterous love-affair
with his squire, and the outcome is determined by the intervention
of the pagan god Pluto and his spouse Proserpina. So far I might
have been describing another of Chaucer's philosophical romances.
The Merchant's Tale is in fact a fabliau, but one whose distinctive
effect is created by the incorporation of many of the elements of
romance in an unstable and potentially explosive equilibrium with
brutal comedy. My interest in it here is to examine how the
voyeuristic tendencies of courtly romance can be retained and
transformed in a narrative designed to provoke cruel laughter. The
role of watching for the characters, the teller, and the audience in
Chaucerian fabliau might be the theme of another book, but here I
treat it briefly and simplistically as a coda to my discussions of
Troilus and *The Knight's Tale*.

Voyeurism in *The Merchant's Tale* takes three main forms. First
there is that of Januarie. This aged and lecherous bachelor, having
belatedly decided that it is better to marry than to burn and that he
needs a legitimate heir, applies himself 'T'*espien* where he myghte
wedded be' (1257). There follows a woundingly ironic 'digression on
marriage' (1267–392) and then the same verb is repeated, when he
says he will 'fonde t'*espien*' (1410) a suitable bride, and asks his
friends to help because 'Ye shullen rather swich a thyng *espyen* /
Than I' (1413–14). The verb places women as objects of a furtive yet
dominating and penetrating male gaze that can accurately assess
their worth; and the noun *thyng* envisages the prospective bride
solely as an object – fodder to be devoured ('bene-straw and greet
forage', 1422) or a 'yong thyng' (1429) to be moulded like wax to fit
Januarie's purposes. His bride will be the means by which the old
man can avoid fornication, at once pleasing his flesh and saving his
soul. This initial objectifying of women leads into imaginative
voyeurism, as Januarie lingers nightly over mental images of 'Many
fair shap and many a fair visage' (1580), trying to decide which

maiden to marry – thinking not only, it must be admitted, of their physical appearance but also of their reputation and wealth. This voyeuristic gloating continues even after he has made his choice, when 'in his bed' (1599) he fantasizes about May's 'fresshe beautee and hir age tendre, / Hir myddel smal, hire armes longe and sklendre' (1601–2) – and also about the qualities of character he supposes himself able to see in her. For him the crucial motives are 'hir yowthe and hir beautee' (1626), while we are left to infer from some later lines about the marriage settlement that for her the attraction is the acquisition of real estate:

> I trowe it were to longe yow to tarie,
> If I yow tolde of every scrit and bond
> By which that she was feffed in his lond,
> Or for to herknen of hir riche array.   (1696–9)

She is to gain property by herself becoming Januarie's property; but until the wedding she remains for the narrative so much the visual object she is for Januarie that the question of her motives, or indeed whether she has any choice, is never raised.

Januarie's goals are unquestionably genital copulation and pro-creation, but so far the bed is the place not for sexual union but for solipsistic sexual fantasy. As the wedding night approaches, this fantasy is heightened. It is stimulated by the treatment of May as an object of sight – 'Hire to biholde it semed fayerye' (1743), and Januarie was 'ravysshed in a traunce / At every tyme he looked on hir face' (1750–1) – so that while bodily Januarie is 'With othere worthy folk upon the deys' (1711) at the wedding feast in his hall, 'in his herte' (1752) he is alone with May in bed, threatening her with his 'sharp and keene' (1759) sexual potency. (Meanwhile the squire Damyan is instantly struck with love for May, 'And to his bed he wente hym hastily' [1779], presumably so that he too can engage in some preliminary fantasizing.) Januarie dismisses the guests as soon as he decently can, drinks fortifying potions 't'encreessen his corage' (1808) (a sad echo of the love-potion of the Tristan story), and has the house voided and the 'travers drawe' (1817), just as in the preparations for bed in Pandarus's house in Book III of Troilus. The bed is blessed by the priest; and now the second kind of voyeurism is introduced.

Up to this point, Januarie's voyeuristic fantasies have been exhibited with cool irony; now, as they give way to reality, it is we who become voyeurs. The guests are ushered 'Out of the chambre' (1820), just as in Augustine's account of wedding ceremonies, so as to preserve the privacy of the shameful act that is to follow. But we do not leave with the guests; we remain in the *chambre* and see what happens in the bed in far sharper detail than ever we do in *Troilus*. What we see is fascinating and repellent: a close-up shot of the 'thikke brustles of his berd unsofte, / Lyk to the skyn of houndfyssh, sharp as brere' (1824–5), rubbing against May's 'tendre face' (1827).[28] The impression is not only visual but also tactile; we are imaginatively close enough to *feel* the friction of his skin against hers. There is no mention of darkness, as in *Partonope of Blois*, and the effect is of supplementation of sight by the more material senses, not of substitution. The sexual act itself is mercifully omitted, except that a strong impression is given of the labour (1842) paradoxically involved in this play (1835, 1841); and then the close-up returns to catch Januarie's jubilation at having completed the act successfully:

> The slakke skyn aboute his nekke shaketh
> Whil that he sang, so chaunteth he and craketh.   (1849–50)

Until now, May's subjectivity has been excluded and even denied – 'The bryde was broght abedde as stille as stoon' (1818) – but now we are specifically invited to imagine the scene from her viewpoint:

> But God woot what that May thoughte in hir herte,
> Whan she hym saugh up sittynge in his sherte,
> In his nyght-cappe, and with his nekke lene;
> She preyseth nat his pleyyng worth a bene.   (1851–4).

There is a similar close-up the next time we see them in bed: Januarie, woken by his troublesome cough, requests that she should 'strepen hire al naked' so that he may 'han som plesaunce' (1958–9) of her. The stripping is more suggestive than nudity would be; and the Merchant, telling us that he will not describe what happened next lest any prudish readers should be offended, makes sure that we shall be unable to avoid imagining it, and imagining it not merely as voyeuristic spectators but, as before, from May's own intimate point of view:

> But lest that precious folk be with me wrooth,
> How that he wroghte, I dar nat to yow telle,
> Or wheither hire thoughte it paradys or helle.   (1962–4)

She is close enough to feel, not just see; perhaps too close to see.

It will be recalled that Freud's definition of scopophilia as a perversion included the wish to 'look on at excretory functions'.[29] Urination and defecation also are activities normally conducted in private, as is witnessed by the use of the word *privee* to refer to the place where they happen. It is striking that in *The Merchant's Tale* the narrator uses the same method of refusal-to-specify to make us imagine ourselves as watchers in the *privee* too. After Damyan has passed his love-letter to May, she goes to bed with Januarie, waits till he is asleep, and then uses the *privee* as the place to read the letter and to dispose of it:

> She feyned hire as that she moste gon
> Ther as ye woot that every wight moot neede;
> And whan she of this bille hath taken heede,
> She rente it al to cloutes atte laste,
> And in the pryvee softely it caste.   (1950–4)

J. S. P. Tatlock, in what remains one of the best accounts of *The Merchant's Tale*, remarked that 'All possibility of glamor in the *amour* is destroyed by the fact that the place she needlessly selects for reading their first love letter is a privy'.[30] Perhaps, though, 'needlessly' goes too far: where else could a medieval knight's wife hope to be alone and undisturbed if her husband was already occupying the marital bed in the *chambre*? It is the very plausibility of the choice that makes it so offensive.

Nothing could be more vulgarly intrusive than the nudge the Merchant gives us in line 1951 to make sure we know to what his euphemism refers; and there is also surely something disgusting in Chaucer's use of *softely* to describe how May threw the fragments of the love-letter into the privy. Its primary meaning is 'quietly' – she wants to avoid attracting attention – but it also transfers to the place of excretion an adverb that more properly belongs to love-making. Freud observed that 'The excremental is all too intimately and inseparably bound up with the sexual; the position of the genitals – *inter urinas et faeces* – remains the decisive and unchangeable factor'.[31] That 'Love has pitched his mansion in the place of excrement', as Yeats more elegantly put it, is a physiological truth that must be repressed in order to make erotic idealization possible. Fabliaux tend to lift the repression, and thus to release the psychic energy it demands. In *The Merchant's Tale* it is precisely the confusion of idealization with what it normally represses, or of courtly romance with fabliau, that produces so disturbing an effect.

The passage under discussion further indicates the importance of

the tactile as well as the visual in *The Merchant's Tale*. Chaucer's
language frequently stimulates us to imagine textures, which may
be soft, as when Januarie remarks that 'a yong thyng may men gye, /
Right as men may warm wex with handes plye' (1429–30), or, to
adopt Chaucer's unusual and telling word, *unsofte* like the bristles of
Januarie's beard (1824–5).[32] The chief organs for judging texture
are the hands, and these are mentioned in the tale with unusual
frequency, as in line 1430 just quoted, or in the passage (like a
parody of the love-intrigues in *Troilus*) where May visits the
supposedly sick Damyan with a letter in reply to his,

> And sotilly this lettre doun she threste
> Under his pilwe; rede it if hym leste.
> She taketh hym by the hand and harde hym twiste
> So secrely that no wight of it wiste,
> And bad hym been al hool.   (2003–7)

Here May's hand first thrusts the letter *sotilly* under Damyan's
pillow and then, with a contrasting effect, squeezes his hand *harde* to
convey a further message to him. It has often been noted how May's
cunning act of taking an impression of the garden key 'In warm wex'
(2117) ironically literalizes the simile in Januarie's confident assertion that a young thing can be moulded like warm wax; but the
parallel is particularly striking in this poem where the tactile is so
strongly foregrounded. Once Januarie loses his sight, touch
becomes even more important (just as darkness makes it important
in *Partonope of Blois*) and so do the hands which are its instruments.

> He nolde suffre hire for to ryde or go,
> But if that he had hond on hire alway,   (2090–1)

and the same point is repeated in 'That hadde an hand upon hire
everemo' (2103). He enters the garden 'With Mayus in his hand'
(2157), and when she urges him to let her climb the pear-tree she
suggests that he should take its trunk not just in his hands but
'inwith youre armes' (2342) in a parody of a marital embrace.
Almost the last event mentioned in the tale is how 'on hire wombe he
stroketh hire ful softe' (2414), an intensely tactile moment, and also
marvellously ironic, since her belly is presumably now quick with an
heir of uncertain paternity. All these suggestions of the manual and
the tactile draw us in close to the narrative events, closer than we
ought or want to be, and thus create an embarrassment that is part
of the tale's harsh comedy.

A third kind of voyeurism occurs in Januarie's garden, 'walled al with stoon' (2029), a place as private as the bedroom, and deliberately constructed for the performance of unspecified 'thynges whiche that were nat doon abedde' (2051). The rich symbolic potential of gardens – pagan, Biblical, exegetic, courtly – is called up in references to him 'that wroot the Romance of the Rose' (2032) and to Priapus as 'god of gardyns' (2035) and in the multiple recollections of the Song of Songs in Januarie's painfully beautiful speech beginning 'Rys up, my wyf, my love, my lady free!' (2138). As in *A Pistel of Susan*, this *hortus conclusus* or 'gardyn ... enclosed al aboute' (2143) is not only a material enclosure but an evocation of the female body, the object of desire which the husband claims as his exclusive possession. From this too all others including ourselves ought to be excluded, and Januarie's key is intended to ensure as much. But, quite apart from Damyan, the Merchant, and ourselves (not to mention Priapus and Jean de Meun), there are now concealed watchers and listeners in the text, in the form of Pluto and Proserpina. They are first mentioned casually, alongside the allusion to Priapus, as visitors to the garden, so that they may seem mere literary decorations, like the mythological figures present at the wedding feast. But after Damyan has been placed in the pear-tree, we learn that they are present in material reality, sitting solidly 'Upon a bench of turves, fressh and grene' (2235). Their purpose is not to spy but simply to enjoy the fresh air and a marital dispute; nor do they seem to gain any pleasure from what they see. The human characters merely serve as handy exempla to prove their respective points: Pluto says, 'Ne se ye nat this honurable knyght ...' (2254), as though he has just noticed what is happening. Having noticed, he and Proserpina intervene to control the course of events, restoring Januarie's sight and giving May a bold excuse to explain away what her husband is then able to see happening in the pear-tree. Apart from the planetary gods in *The Knight's Tale*, this is the first time we have encountered watchers with supernatural power to change what they watch; Pandarus's interventions were minor by comparison. One of the objects of their gaze is Damyan – 'Lo, where he sit, the lechour, in the tree!' (2257) – and if Januarie's aphrodisiacs are parodic versions of the love-potion in the Tristan story, this is surely a comic inversion of the most famous scene in that story, in which King Mark sits in a tree to watch his wife with her lover. Now it is the lovers in the tree and the cuckold on the ground.

What happens is again described with an apology that makes sure
we cannot fail to visualize it:

> Ladyes, I prey yow that ye be nat wrooth;
> I kan nat glose, I am a rude man –
> And sodeynly anon this Damyan
> Gan pullen up the smok, and in he throng.   (2350–3)

Pluto and Prosperina see it; we see it; and now Januarie sees it, what
he sees yet again being presented with a sly apology:

> Up to the tree he caste his eyen two,
> And saugh that Damyan his wyf had dressed
> In swich manere it may nat been expressed,
> But if I wolde speke uncurteisly.   (2360–3)

It may not be expressed, but it surely has to be imagined; and to
help us we get more suggestive details such as ' "Strugle?" quod he,
"Ye, algate in it wente!" ' (2376) and 'thy smok hadde leyn upon
his brest' (2395).

Januarie, however, is persuaded that what he has seen does not
correspond to the truth. We may think of scenes in courtly romances
where the question is raised of *veoir* and *voir*, but here it is not a
matter of signs requiring interpretation. May argues that it is –

> Ful many a man weneth to seen a thyng,
> And it is al another than it semeth.
> He that mysconceyveth, he mysdemeth   (2408–10)

– but in fact the evidence is unambiguous. Januarie, however,
prefers to revert to his situation at the beginning, where the mastery
conferred by sight belongs to the realm of fantasy. *The Merchant's
Tale* turns on sight and blindness; Januarie's physical blindness
appropriately matches and completes the moral blindness with
which he has entered upon marriage; yet the restoration of his
physical sight marks no gain of insight, but leaves him in a state of
utter confusion, willing to believe what May tells him, and complacently kissing her and stroking her belly. He might as well be still
blind; and we too have seen so much that blindness may seem
preferable. The voyeurism so cunningly imposed by the narrative on
its audience holds us fascinated while the tale lasts, but in the end
leaves us horrified, as if we too had suffered a version of Actaeon's
punishment. We can be grateful for the Host's epilogue, with its
briskly uncomprehending application of the tale to his own, reassur-
ingly 'normal', nagging wife, and the consequent swerve away from
sight to hearing: 'But of hir tonge, a labbyng shrewe is she!' (2428).

CHAPTER 9

The Squyr of Lowe Degre

Of the English romances there is perhaps none in which secrecy, spying, storytelling, and the relationship among them are of such importance as in *The Squyr of Lowe Degre*. This anonymous late romance, surviving in its complete form only in a sixteenth-century printed edition, and probably not composed before the early Tudor period,[1] has rightly been seen by its few modern commentators as consciously looking back to a long tradition of preceding Middle English romances. It contains, for example, two passages (lines 77–86 and 614–32)[2] referring explicitly to fourteenth-century romances with well-known stories – *Libeaus Desconus* and *Guy of Warwick* – and taking these as possible models for its hero's career. It would be wrong, though, to suppose either that *The Squyr of Lowe Degre* is a merely derivative work or that its relationship to the tradition of Middle English romance is one of parody or satire.[3] It is much concerned with social mobility and the contribution of wealth to social status, rather than with the transcendent concepts of knighthood and nobility that tend to govern earlier romances, but that is no more a sign of parody than are the similar features of *Sir Launfal*. *The Squyr of Lowe Degre* is engaged, and at a far higher level of literary skill and imaginative intensity than Chestre's poem, with the real interests of the period in which it was written. I shall suggest that, in its generic self-consciousness and its focus on the father–daughter relationship, it has something in common with Shakespeare's romances; and it is no more a parody of romance or an 'anti-romance'[4] than is *Cymbeline* or *The Tempest*. *The Squyr of Lowe Degre* is a poem of haunting and mannered oddity, the work of a poet who was able to infuse popular traditions with his own highly distinctive imaginative power.[5] It would be good to know more about him and his public; but in any case his work's retrospectiveness makes it a fitting conclusion to the part of my book concerned with voyeurism in romances.

In a sense the first act of spying in *The Squyr of Lowe Degre* occurs at
the moment the poem opens. In an abbreviated version of the story
in the seventeenth-century Percy Folio manuscript, some narratorial explanation is offered in the opening lines as to how an English
squire comes to be in the service of the King of Hungary and his
daughter; but the printed version, though generally much ampler,
omits this explanation, and plunges us immediately into a situation
that we have to interpret as if *we* were watchers or listeners: 'It was a
squyer of lowe degré / That loved the kings doughter of Hungré . . .'
(1–2). Within a few lines our curiosity is rewarded, and we join the
poet in gaining a knowledge of the Squire's motives concealed from
all others:

> But ever he was styll mornyng,
> And no man wyste for what thyng;
> And all was for that [fayre] lady,
> The kynges doughter of Hungry.
> There wyste no wyghte in Christenté
> Howe well he loved that lady fre.   (11–16)

References to silence, secrecy and concealment, marked by the
repetition of words such as *styll*, *counsayle*, and *pryvely* or *pryvité*, are
remarkably frequent throughout the poem.

We have observed that the capacity of medieval romance to deal
with private life depends on the availability of private spaces, and
that the possibility of spying depends on the penetrability of these
spaces. The world of *The Squyr of Lowe Degre* is full of enclosed and
private spaces, but equally of *huote*, surveillance, of spies and
opportunities for spying. It is a world, like the early Tudor court as
evoked in the poetry of Skelton, Hawes, or Wyatt, where 'treason
walketh wonder wyde' (520). A vassal's adultery with his lord's wife
had long been counted as high treason,[6] but in this poem differences
of rank and the political implications of secret love-affairs shadow
the story more darkly than was usual in earlier medieval courtly
romances – as darkly as they really did the court of Henry VIII. Of
the poem's many secret enclosures the *chambre* remains the most
important and most often mentioned: the word occurs twenty-eight
times in the Copeland text – more than once every forty lines. When
the Squire wishes to indulge in his solitary sighs, he can go to his
own *chambre*, and from there into an enclosed garden containing the
further enclosure of an arbour:

And evermore whan he was wo
Into his chambre would he goo;
And through the chambre he toke the waye
Into the gardyn that was full gaye;
And in the garden, as I wene,
Was an arber fayre and grene. (23–8)

But giving on to the arbour is also the 'chambre wyndowe' (66) of
the Princess; and when the Squire soliloquizes there about his secret
love, wishing that he were rich, or of high birth, or that he could win
his lady by chivalric contest as in a romance, she overhears what he
says.

In *The Squyr of Lowe Degre* spying is almost exclusively a matter of
listening rather than watching. The poet's focus on the material
means by which privacy and its penetration are made possible is
extraordinarily sharp:

That lady herde his mournyng all,
Ryght under the chambre wall;
In her oryall there she was
Closed well with royall glas –
Fulfylled it was with ymagery.
Every wyndowe by and by
On eche syde had there a gynne,
Sperde with many a dyvers pynne.
Anone that lady fayre and fre
Undyd a pynne of yveré,
And wyd the windowes she open set;
The sunne shone in at her closet.
In that arber fayre and gaye
She sawe where that squyre lay. (91–104)

'Oriel', in this sense of a windowed recess, appears to have been a
rare word in pre-Tudor English.[7] Here the Princess's *oryall*,
elegantly lit with pictorial glass, provides a private space or *closet* for
the lady to sit alone or talk with her intimates; at the same time, by
projecting from the wall, it offers a vantage point for watching and
listening to whatever happens in the arbour below. The vantage
point is secret, because the coloured glazing admits light and sound
but conceals the person behind it from a watcher outside. (The
principle of a point for concealed social observation is neatly
explained in a late-fifteenth-century first-person narrative, *The
Floure and the Leafe*, in relation to an arbour:

> The hegge as thicke as a castel wall,
> That who that list without to stond or go,
> Though he would all day prien to and fro,
> He should not see if there were any wight
> Within or no; but one within well might
>
> Perceive all tho that yeden there without.)[8]

On the other hand, the Princess's window is also capable of being opened (the domestic technology being advanced enough to enable a lady to manage this without difficulty) so as to give a clearer view and make two-way communication possible. The modern reader may take all this for granted, but the details serve to focus attention on the importance of privacy and spying, and it could be suggested that the poet's fascination with such a *gynne* has something in common with the technical interests of modern espionage fiction. The means of surveillance may come to attract the intensity of interest that belongs to surveillance itself.

The Princess reveals herself and addresses the Squire, asking the cause of his grief and promising to keep his *counsayl* (110). He confesses that he loves her, and goes on to mention possible developments for his story, alternative to his earlier fantasy of chivalric triumph. If she had been displeased at the revelation of his love, his story might have had a prompt conclusion: 'Ye might have bewraied me to the kinge, / And brought me sone to my endynge' (125–6). 'My endynge' identifies 'the end of my life' with 'the end of my story'. If however she now rejects him, his story will be prolonged and inconclusive, reaching its *endynge* only at the ends of the earth, for he will abandon 'lande and lede' (135) to wander as a begging hermit to the Holy Land and beyond, 'Tyll I come to the worldes ende' (142). At any rate, unless the Princess assists him, 'There shall no sho come on my fote' (144): he will never be knighted, and thus his story will not be a chivalric romance. One effect of such treatments of life in terms of the morphology of narrative is to remind us that our situation as listeners parallels that of the listeners in the story.

The Squire stands at the lowest level of the poem's hierarchy of listeners and tellers. He overhears no one, but is overheard by the Princess, and though he is a fruitful source of ideas for narrative development, the choice of how his story will proceed lies with her. Her response to his confession consists of detailed instructions as to how he must now behave, amounting to a kind of flow-chart for future narrative, exploring various possible branches of his story and their outcomes, couched in a mixture of command and prophecy. The fundamental axiom is that this will be a love-story, and thus that she will keep his secret:

> By hym that dyed on a tre,
> Thou shalt never be deceyved for me;
> Though I for thee should be slayne,
> Squyer, I shall the love agayne.   (151–4)

(Already one possible branch is glimpsed: a tragic love story, in which the Princess dies rather than reveal the Squire's love. But in that case how could we be hearing the story now?) He is to serve the King and conceal his love-sickness and their present conversation; and the Princess offers advice that has general application to this poem's world (but also to the poem's audience) and that we shall shortly hear repeated: 'If ever ye wyll come to your wyll, / Here and se, and holde you styll' (159–60). The best chance of success, especially for the powerless, is to be a listener and watcher, but to remain silent and passive until the moment for action arrives. The Squire must beware of the Steward, of whom we now hear for the first time; for, if he learns of his wooing, he will betray him to the King; and the outcome of that narrative branch would be arrest, imprisonment, trial, and possible execution. To gain the Princess's love, he is told, 'With chyvalry ye must begynne' (172), winning his spurs by deeds of prowess. This narrative possibility is developed in extraordinary detail, in what amounts to a summary of the materials of chivalric romance so far as these are compatible with life in the natural world (that is, excluding dragons, green knights, and so forth). For seven years he must ride through harsh landscapes and severe weather, sleeping outdoors in his armour if necessary. He must cross the sea many times, undertaking battles throughout Lombardy, but 'Loke that ye stand aye in the right' (194). Then he must go to Rhodes (not captured by the Turks until 1522) and fight on three Good Fridays. This will entitle him to knighthood, and the Princess gives a detailed description of the arms he must bear, including a lady's head surmounted by a motto 'for the love of me' with letters that spell 'AMOR' when rearranged (214–16). She further describes the splendid armour he will wear, and then explains that after Rhodes he must travel further to the Holy Land (but now as a knight, rather than as the hermit of his own narrative speculation, the parallel between the two being marked by repetition of 'To seke where Christ was quicke and dead' at 138 and 'To seke where Christe were dead and quycke' at 238). There he must dedicate his sword at the Holy Sepulchre and offer first five and then three florins,[9] and then at last he will be able to say that he is 'proved a venturous knyght' (250). Now the Princess reverts to an earlier phase in this proleptic story: she will provide him with huge sums of money for his expenses and equipment, so as to ensure his honour. Once this *digressio ad aliam partem materiae*[10] is over, she returns to the conclusion, expressed as dependent not on prophecy but on prayer: 'I pray to God and Our Lady, / Sende you the whele of vyctory' (257–8). If this happens, her father will be pleased, and will make the Squire king in his place, so that the end will be union and lifelong happiness: 'That we might our dayes endure / In parfyte love that is so pure' (265–6). But even this is not the only possibility, for the Princess's energetic narrative imagination envisages that 'if we may not so come to, / Other wyse then must we do' (267–8). Once more she moves to the beginning of the Squire's future romance and back to its end. He must depart promptly, taking leave of king, queen and court; and she will wait for seven years, 'Betyde of you what so betyde' (276). And so the Squire thanks and kisses the Princess and takes his leave to participate in the story she has set down for him.

But now, with the abruptness that this poem characteristically mingles with lavish amplification, we learn that there is a spy superior to the Princess:

> The kinges steward stode full nye
> In a chambre fast them bye
> And hearde theyr wordes wonder wele
> And all the woyng every dele.   (283–6)

In this 'modern' setting, even the Steward can gain the privacy of a *chambre*. How he hears their conversation is not explained; it may be through his own window, or perhaps the poet imagines not the stone walls of a medieval castle but the lath-and-plaster internal divisions of a Tudor house, through which sound might easily carry. Thus the Steward learns of their *counsayle* (300), but the poet also makes us privy to his, informing us that he loved the Princess *pryvely* (297) and that he had his own plans for the Squire's story, according to which it would end with arrest and hanging. There are thus two competing versions of the romance's future course: the Steward's, which, by

means of this act of overhearing, includes knowledge of the
Princess's; and the Princess's, which includes the Steward's as one
possible branch of the narrative flow-chart (lines 159–68) but is
weakened by ignorance that it has itself been overheard.

The Squire begins to enact the role the Princess has devised for
him. He returns to his *chambre* (303), puts on livery and takes up his
staff of office as marshal of the King's hall, and sets about serving
the King and the company. And now we discover that yet another
spy is involved, the King himself:

> The kynge behelde the squyer wele,
> And all his rayment every dele;
> He thoughte he was the semylyest man
> That ever in the worlde he sawe or than.
> Thus sate the kyng and eate ryght nought,
> But on his squyer was all his thought.   (333–8)[11]

Within the public space of the hall, the King can retain the privacy
of what Charles d'Orléans would call 'the chamber of his thought';[12]
and the gaze of the Tudor monarch, because all-inclusive, does not
publicly single out the special object of his private interest. The
consequence of this public and yet secret gaze is deferred, because
now the Steward approaches the King and repeats what he has
learned from his own act of overhearing, but with an addition that
marks his deceptive version of the story and includes yet another
narrative branch, this time based on a negative hypothesis:

> Had I not come in, verayly,
> The squyer had layne her by,
> But whan he was ware of me
> Full fast away can he fle.   (349–52)

The King says that he finds this unbelievable, elaborating his
response into still a further narrative flow-chart. He cannot believe
that the Squire would enter the Princess's *chambre* (363) and seduce
her, even with her consent, unless he could gain her hand in
marriage; and 'yf she [wyll] assent him tyll, / The squyer is worthy
to have none yll' (371–72).[13] The King warns the Steward not to
slander the Squire, for it would be a great pity to harm him or
distress the Princess, or indeed 'to put thyselfe in drede, / But thou
myght take hym with the dede' (389–90). (This of course alludes to
the fact that the only acceptable evidence of illicit sexual relations
was to catch the culprits *in flagrante delicto*.) Next the King narrates

what would happen to the Steward if he made such an accusation and it proved to be malicious – arrest and a twelve-year imprisonment in fetters, followed by drawing and hanging – but the Steward nevertheless reaffirms his accusation, and promises that if the King will grant him 'Strength of men and great power' (408) he will seize the Squire 'In chambre with your doughter bright' (410) that very night.

The King apparently endorses this version of the story's future, though only hypothetically: *if* the Squire comes to the Princess's *chambre* (431), the Steward is to spy on their conversation – 'And here and se and holde you styll' (428) – *even though* the Squire should kiss her, and he is not to intervene '*But yf* he wyl her chamber breke' (437). (Here we may suspect that the chamber, strongly associated with femininity, and the normal setting for sexual relations, licit or illicit, is beginning to acquire its sixteenth-century colloquial sense of a woman's private parts or virginity.) *If* this occurs, the Squire is to be seized and imprisoned; *if* he resists violently, he is to be cut to pieces, but *if* he surrenders he must be brought unharmed before the King. Finally, the King promises that the Squire shall not marry his daughter for seven years, and urges the Steward to 'watche that lady nyght and daye' (454). With this strikingly elaborate covering of every narrative possibility, the King proclaims himself masternarrator of the poem, while the specification of seven years as the delay before marriage hints at a convergence between his version of the story and his daughter's.

The meal once over, the Squire asks the King's leave to embark on his chivalric quest according to the Princess's version; this is readily granted, and he departs immediately. But almost at once, as he and his company take supper on their way, he says that he has forgotten to take leave of the Princess and returns to the castle alone. This sudden decision is one of the few points at which the Squire's motives are left in secrecy: 'he sayd he had forgete' (498), but whether this is really so we cannot tell. The poet's purpose in leaving us in the role of excluded observers may be to let us guess that the Squire does intend to enact the role of seducer in which the Steward has maliciously cast him. A crucial factor, as so often with courtly romances, must be the desire for privacy on the part of those whose duties and/or social status require that they should almost never be alone. The Squire has set off 'With all his meyny by his side' (488), but by this device he can return 'by hymselfe . . . Without strength of

his meyné' (502–3). This also puts him in danger, however, for
though he returns with drawn sword he remains disadvantaged by
being at the bottom of the poem's hierarchy of spies and storytellers:

> He wende in the worlde none had be
> That had knowen of his pryvité;
> Alas! it was not as he wende,
> For all his counsayle the stewarde [kende].   (511–14)

The Steward lies in wait, 'Armed with a great company' (518),
concealed beside the Princess's *chambre*. Once more narrative possibilities are explored, this time past ones: *if* the Squire had known
that he would be ambushed, 'He had not come theder by his owne'
(523), and *if* the Princess had known that he was coming, she would
have arranged protection for him. But the Steward, as it seemed,
stood above them as a designer of narrative; and the Squire,
claiming to be 'beset with many a spy' (536), appeals to the Princess
to 'Undo thy dore!' (539) (using the phrase that gave the poem its
alternative title). The poet strangely fails to narrate the Squire's
realization that he is ambushed, and it has been suggested that, in
appealing to the Princess to open her door, he is at first only
pretending to be in danger.[14] This is possible; but more important is
the fact that this is one of several points at which a ballad-like
abruptness of narration drives us into the position of listeners who
do not hear all we wish and must struggle to interpret what we do
hear. In this we share the Princess's situation: she is woken from
sleep by shouting outside her door, but does not realize who wants
her to open it. She calls back to the intruder to go away, summariz-
ing her earlier narrative design, by which she is promised to one
whom she will marry 'Whan he is proved a venterous knyght'
(558).[15] The Squire responds by explaining who he is and saying
that he has come 'full pryvely' (569) to take his leave; but the
Princess has evidently missed his earlier explanation of his danger,
and she proceeds to talk to him at length before opening her door,
repeating and elaborating the chivalric romance of which he is to be
the hero, and adding a defence of her offer of material support, as
being both practical and 'for the worshyp of us two' (610). This
speech repeats many lines from her earlier narrative projection,[16]
and it also recollects the triumphant exploits of 'Syr Lybyus or Syr
Guy' (614). We may perhaps wonder why the Princess's speech is so
leisurely or why the Squire does not interrupt to explain the mortal

danger he is in; verisimilitude, however, cannot be the prime consideration, and the lack of it does not mean that we have here a parody of romance or, as one scholar suggests, a satirical exposure of the Princess's unconscious wish 'to avoid consummation of the relationship'.[17] As often in late Shakespeare, we may well be suspended between empathy with the emotions a scene arouses and the distancing effect of the means by which they are expressed; but that does not imply parody. In *The Squyr of Lowe Degre* the conflict is not between characters but between stories; at this point it seems that the Princess's version, however attractive, is about to succumb to the Steward's and her defensiveness about her offer of 'golde and fe' (607) prepares us for her story's impending defeat.

The Steward's party attacks (thus apparently overcoming the King's story as well as the Princess's), and the Squire, in his only significant action in the poem, fells seven of them and kills the Steward. Perhaps then he will for the first time succeed in imposing his own narrative pattern? – but now there is another unexplained twist in events, which once more puts us in the role of puzzled overhearers. The remaining members of the ambush seize the Squire, but remove 'his good garmente' (652) and disguise the Steward's body in it, disfiguring the face so that 'she should not know what he ware' (656). The product of this corporeal rewriting of the story is then left outside 'her chambre dore' (657). 'Full pryvely' (660) they carry the Squire unharmed 'to the kynges chambre' (662), and there the King welcomes him, saying, 'Thou hast cast thee my sonne to be; / This seven yere I shall let thee' (667–8). No further explanation is offered, and we are left to deduce that part of the King's narrative design has been concealed from us, and that he had seen through the Steward's treachery even more completely than we had supposed and had issued instructions accordingly. Our sense that the King is the supreme storyteller is redoubled, especially now that the Steward is out of the running, but we still have no idea how the King's narrative can be brought to a completion that will harmoniously incorporate those of his daughter and her suitor when the seven years are up.

The poet returns us to the Princess, who at last opens her door and mistakes the corpse – as her father must presumably have intended, though this too is never explained – for that of the Squire. She disembowels and embalms it, and keeps it as a treasure, each day kissing it and hearing five masses, saying, 'There shall none

knowe but heven kynge / For whome that I make myne offrynge'
(705–6) – a reminder that God is the supreme watcher and listener.
This narrative element is at once improbable and macabre, though
no more improbable than Imogen's mistaking Cloten's headless
corpse for her husband's in *Cymbeline*, and no more macabre than
Filomena's story in Book IV of Boccaccio's *Decameron* of Lisabetta's
adoration of the pot of basil in which she has buried her murdered
lover's head. It appears to be carefully calculated to convey a
horrifyingly extreme test of devotion – so extreme that it does not
pretend to be anything but a fiction, horrifying nevertheless in its
intense single-mindedness, yet not unbearably horrifying both
because we know that, even within the fiction, the corpse is not
really the Squire's and because we must believe by now that the
King's narrative coincides with the poet's own and will have a
happy ending. We are thus able to savour the Princess's devotion at
a certain aesthetic distance.

There follows the poem's passage of greatest virtuosity. The King
asks, 'My doughter, wy are you dysmayde?' (708), contrasts her
present mourning with her former beauty and gaiety, pretends to
assume that she is love-sick, and says he will knight her beloved if he
is below her in birth or offer a sufficient dowry if he is too high. She
refuses to reveal the cause of her grief, and her father proceeds to
deliver a speech of 114 lines (739–852) in which he promises every
conceivable delight of courtly life for her consolation – luxurious
furniture, clothes, music, wine, food, hunting, dancing, singing,
games, sailing, perfumed sleep. Perhaps this fantasy of sensory
fulfilment is touched with Tudor ostentation, but it is an astonishing
demonstration of the power of language to transform reality into the
image of desire (and thus too a demonstration of the King's power as
storyteller). We are overwhelmed by the ingenuity with which detail
after detail is added long after we might expect the imagination to be
exhausted. At last the fantasy seems to be swooning into dream, or
into synaesthetic hallucination, but then it is sharply pulled back
into the material world, where pleasure depends not on the power of
language but on that of commanding others' services:

> Whan you are layde in bedde so softe,
> A cage of golde shall hange alofte,
> With longe peper fayre burnning,
> And cloves that be swete smellyng,
> Frankensence and olibanum,

> That whan ye slepe the taste may come.
> And yf ye no rest may take,
> All night minstrelles for you shall wake.   (845–52)

Yet the ultimate pleasure this section offers is that of renunciation, when the Princess comments simply, 'Gramercy, father, so mote I the, / For all these thinges lyketh not me' (853–4), returns to her *chambre*, and continues her mourning for seven years.

The poet now returns to the Squire. The King visits him *pryvely* (864) in prison, makes him promise never to reveal his *counsayl* (868), and releases him to undertake the travels laid down in the Princess's version of his story (though we never learn how, or whether, the King knows what these are), on the understanding that in seven years he will return, marry her, and take possession of the King's lands. All this he does, including the offering at the Holy Sepulchre; the poet narrates it briefly, and tells us that on his return the Squire narrated it to the King. The King orders him, 'in my chamber holde the styll, / And I shall wete my doughters wyll' (913). Perhaps only God – 'ut vidit cogitationes eorum'[18] – can truly know the will of another; but the King, God's earthly deputy, sets about spying on his daughter. Concealed 'Right under the chambre window' (917), he listens to discover her *counseyle* (918), which, the poet explains, she would not have revealed if she had known her father was present. He hears her addressing the corpse, lamenting that it is falling into dust, deciding to have it buried, saying farewell one by one to all the delights of courtly life – an abbreviated catalogue of those he had promised her earlier – and vowing to become an anchoress and devote her prayers to her dead lover. Thus she plans a quite different narrative from that she originally devised, and one with a tragic conclusion. (Religious values are affirmed here as throughout the poem, but there is no suggestion that they offer any human comfort to the supposedly bereaved Princess, or that she expects them to do so.) At this point she swoons and the King steps forward, finally acknowledging his role as master-narrator in this complex structure of overlapping and competing stories. He promises his daughter that she shall marry a king, and when she denies this possibility, he retells her story and the Squire's, revealing to her some of the truth behind the fiction that has deceived her – the Steward's spying, misrepresentation, and treachery, and the identity of the embalmed corpse. He repeats his promise that she shall marry a king or even an emperor, but he has still not revealed the Squire's survival, and she rejects it. Yet again, she sketches a hypothetical narrative based on supposition about what might have happened if things had been different: *if* her father had warned her of the Steward's enmity, 'My love had never be dead for me' (1046). She swoons again, and now at last the King reveals that her love is alive, and has actually carried out his part in the chivalric romance she had originally devised as the story of their lives.

Not surprisingly, the Princess is sceptical, and demands, 'if it so be, / Let me soone that squyer see' (1061–2). The Squire is brought forth, she swoons a third time, and when she recovers there is music of every kind – 'In chambre revelyng all the lordes' (1078) – until dawn breaks. Their wedding follows. Apart from the feast, this is the only public event described in a poem full of 'behind-door work'[19] – actions conducted in real or intended privacy – and even the feast contained the King's gaze at the Squire and the secret decisions that must have accompanied it. The nobility, knighthood, and 'all the comunalté' (1112) celebrate for forty days, and then, not in *chambre* but 'even in the myddes of the hall' (1119) of which the Squire had begun as marshal (7), the King makes his new son-in-law 'kyng among them al' (1120). With such a ceremonial act, there can for once be no possibility of concealment or spying. Thus 'That yong man and the quene his wyfe' (1127) lived happily ever after, and the poet comments, 'also farre as I have gone, / Suche two lovers sawe I none' (1129–30). These lines serve to reopen an otherwise strongly conventional romance closure, by emphasizing 'the story's distance from reality'.[20] They remind us that the realm of fictional narrative may be quite other than the world we see, and at the same time they place the storyteller as a watcher of lovers. He has had to watch (and listen) in order to be able to tell, and this task has involved a difficult process of reconstruction and co-ordination on the basis of evidence at once fragmentary and excessive: too many stories and not enough of any one of them.

By becoming in my turn a re-narrator of *The Squyr of Lowe Degre* I have tried to demonstrate just how many narrative enterprises and hidden possibilities of intention jostle within it for supremacy. Ultimately, however, it is not enough to say that this poem is 'concerned with narrativity';[21] it is so, but the source of its compelling interest is that it is also concerned with the connection between narrativity and fundamental human relationships. These relationships are of course imagined not absolutely but in forms influenced by the national and familial politics of the poet's age: the father is also a Tudor monarch, the favoured suitor of a squire of low degree elevated by the monarch's choice. Here, however, I focus on what seems most permanent in the poem's representation of human relationships. At one level the story offers a version of the eternal triangle, with two men pursuing the same woman. (In this version they are both of lower social rank, but the Squire is at least 'A gentyll man' [20],[22] while the Steward, like Malvolio, would have to transgress the crucial boundary between gentle and non-gentle in order to win the lady.) They compete, however, not in the terms appropriate to the kind of chivalric narrative that the Squire initially fantasizes –

> And [it] were put in ieopedé
> What man shoulde wynne that lady fre,
> Than should no man have her but I ...   (83–5)

– but in terms of narrative itself: they are not rivals in knightly prowess but rival storytellers. The problem is that the suitor favoured by the Princess is by far the less enterprising and versatile narrator, waiting like Chaucer's Troilus to have his life-story written for him by others, unable on his own initiative to step outside the bounds of *Libeaus Desconus* or *Guy of Warwick*, and readily accepting the role that his lady then assigns him in her own equally chivalric narrative. As we have seen, the power to tell is closely connected with the power to spy on behaviour intended to be private, and whereas the Princess overhears the Squire, the Steward establishes his superiority by overhearing them both. He then carries his story, suitably amended, to the King, is set by him to continue spying, and steps treacherously outside the limited narrative role that the King specifies for him, thus apparently incorporating the King in *his* narrative and becoming the poem's champion storyteller.

The King's role is crucial; and it may be more easily understood from parallels in Shakespearean romance. (Here it may be worth digressing to observe that the analogies between *The Squyr of Lowe Degre* and late Shakespeare are not matters of chance; three likely causes may be suggested for them. One is the place of romances in early Tudor culture, the importance of which for Shakespeare's general formation has been suggestively explored by Emrys Jones.[23] Shakespeare's satirical use of the phrase 'a squire of low degree' in

Henry V v 1[24] may well indicate that he knew this very poem; in any case, his early reading must have included romances of this type. A second is the fascination with absolute rule and its godlike power to penetrate even thought that was a major imaginative focus in Tudor and Stuart England. Ulysses' warning to Achilles in *Troilus and Cressida* III 3 that his 'privacy' is an illusion for

> The providence that's in a watchful state ...
> Keeps place with thought and almost, like the gods,
> Do thoughts unveil in their dumb cradles ...

might equally have been a conclusion drawn from the Hungary of *The Squyr of Lowe Degre*. A third cause is the consciously belated generic self-consciousness that pervades Shakespeare's romances, with their emphasis on narrative and its archaic conventions and on their own fictionality.) One Shakespearean parallel for the King is the Duke in *Measure for Measure*, that 'old fantastical duke of dark corners' (IV 3) who stoops to spying and deception in order to ensure that a romance going desperately astray can be wrenched back to follow the appropriate conventions. (Here, as in *Cymbeline*, a corpse misidentified as that of a heroine's lover is an important device in the tragicomedy.) Another is the King of *Henry VIII*, standing above the play's action as a watcher, and then stepping forward to exercise his irresistible power so as to reshape English history as a romance. But perhaps the closest parallel is Prospero – the poet's manifest surrogate, introduced from the beginning as a storyteller with the magical power to make his stories out of human lives, but also the heroine's father, manipulating her and her chosen suitor with the excuse of testing them both, and then, once they are united, abdicating as both ruler and storyteller.

In *The Squyr of Lowe Degre*, superimposed on the triangle already mentioned is a second, more fundamental triangle of father, daughter, and daughter's suitor. As in *The Tempest* (and in other plays by Shakespeare, *King Lear* being only the most obvious case), the mother is absent, and the essential family relationship is that of father and daughter. (In *The Squyr of Lowe Degre*, the Princess once tells the Squire that he must 'take thy leve of kinge and quene' [271], but the queen is neither seen nor mentioned again.) The power of the King is also the power of the father as perceived by the child – a power to know what the child believes to be secret and to be, in effect, the narrator of the child's life. The figure of the father-king

dominates the whole poem, moving gradually into the acknowledged centre and then abruptly disappearing; and, as I have noted,
the absolutism of Tudor notions of imperial sovereignty is equally
part of the poem's image of fatherhood. Of the King in this romance
might be said what a recent critic has written about Prospero, that,
while 'the agent of benign transformation', he is also 'the brooding
embodiment of patriarchal authority and absolute power, who
dominates everyone ... and determines everything that happens to
them'.[25] The father's authority is beyond question or understanding, and is exercised with what seems unfeeling cruelty: he allows his
daughter to suppose her lover dead and to cherish the wrong corpse
for seven years, he makes her believe that he will force her to marry
another suitor of his own choice, and his ultimate revelation of the
truth seems almost maliciously piecemeal, holding back the knowledge that the Squire is not dead until the last possible moment, as if
his concern were more with narrative climax than with his daughter's happiness. Twice, first when the King explains that he let her
believe the corpse to be the Squire's, and then when she realizes that
he could have intervened to prevent the ambush, the Princess asks,
'Alas! father, why dyd ye so?' (987, 1043). The question is painful
and pressing, but it receives no satisfactory answer: the first time the
King's answer is irrelevant – 'For he [the Steward] wrought you all
thys wo' (988) – and the second time there is no answer at all. It is as
if the daughter must undergo at her father's hands an extreme
emotional and spiritual test (this is. especially the effect of his
enticing catalogue of sensory pleasures) before she is worthy to gain
a husband; she must be made ready to renounce the world as an
anchoress in order that she may become a wife.

But the King's motives remain unstated – since this is not a play,
he is not even allowed any such awkward explanatory aside as
Edgar's 'Why I do trifle thus with his despair / Is done to cure it' or
Duke Vincentio's

> But I will keep her ignorant of her good,
> To make her heavenly comforts of despair,
> When it is least expected[26]

– and we are left to speculate, somewhat as in Prospero's case,
whether the 'trifling' with the Princess and her suitor is truly
intended as an altruistic test or whether it betrays a father's
unwillingness to relinquish his daughter to her future husband. In

the case of *The Squyr of Lowe Degre* we might well conclude that the relevant criteria are neither moral nor psychological but aesthetic. The best storyteller (which means the most penetrating voyeur) wins – but that does not mean that the moral and psychological questions disappear. They are the more haunting because they are never formulated, except as a bewildered 'Why, father?'. The King successfully conceals his *counsayle* from us as well as from the other characters, and his final triumph, like Prospero's, is an act of abdication, writing himself out of his own story. The voyeur's power to see and manipulate is concomitant with his ultimate exclusion from the life he watches. To ask what are the political implications of his making the Squire king is surely vain (does the Hungarian constitution allow for more than one king at a time? can the son-in-law succeed to the throne during his father-in-law's life-time?). It is the story's destined end, and was indeed the conclusion of the narrative originally devised by the Princess for her suitor (see lines 259–64). When the young couple become king and queen, the crowning marks their release from childish subjection to paternal authority and their assumption of adult status; but at the same time the King's disappearance preserves for ever the secrecy of his motivation and his power. We are left as defeated spies, unable to search out the heart of his mystery – or, in this familiar story of all our lives, as children, prevented by our father's death from asking the questions that only his death enabled us to realize that we needed to ask.

CHAPTER 10

The Romaunt of the Rose

The poems discussed in Chapters 3–9 have been romances, along with two *Canterbury Tales* that can be read as disillusioned commentaries on romance; that is, they have been third-person narratives about love in which the storyteller, so far as his role is realized at all, exists on a different plane from the lovers and his other fictive creations. In these poems I have been concerned with two types of voyeurism, though it has emerged that each tends to interact with and influence the other: voyeurism involving the persons within the fiction, and voyeurism involving the storyteller and his audience as watchers of the fiction. Henceforward I shall be concerned with first-person narratives where in principle this distinction collapses, for now the narrating poet is his own subject. In practice what happens is not so simple: I begin with a first-person love-story, where the poet is his own hero, telling of his own dream-experience as a lover, but I then move to a series of narratives by Chaucer and his successors, in which, as in *Troilus and Criseyde*, the poet represents himself as having no such personal experience, even when dreaming, and his role becomes more and more explicitly that of a furtive watcher, debarred by his clerkly status from any enjoyment other than that of watching. The substance of these poems is often allegorical and always doubtless fictional, and, in referring to 'personal experience', I do not mean to imply that Guillaume de Lorris or his successors really had the experiences they describe, whether dreaming or waking. We have no information about such matters, and it is unnecessary to consider the relationship of fiction to reality. Like the poems, I normally draw no distinction between the *sujet de l'énonciation* and the *sujet de l'énoncé*; thus in *The Romaunt of the Rose*, for my purpose, the poet-dreamer Guillaume *is* the lover Amant.

For a different kind of analysis, the distinctions disregarded here may be of considerable importance. In the *Roman de la Rose*, for example, questions of time and tense are of great interest, even though I can overlook them as not affecting the identity of the poem's 'I'. One scholar has valuably drawn a distinction among four aspects or functions of that 'I': the Dreamer, 'the Hero of the Dream', 'the Real-life Hero ... to whom all the dream-events happen afterwards, in reality', and the Narrator who 'remembers all these past events';[1] but this is an analytic tool rather than part of the poem's immediate experience, which is what concerns me here. The dreamer-lover is not a third person whom we join the poem's narrator in watching from a separate plane, even though there are certain 'inconsistent' moments when he presents himself as being unknowingly stalked by the God of Love:

> But I, that nothyng wist of this,
> Wente up and doun ful many a wey,
> And he me folwed fast alwey.   (1344–6)[2]

I need not attempt to disentangle this 'naïve' and perhaps dreamlike self-presentation in which past and present, sleeping and waking, ignorance and knowledge, are fused in a single 'I'; I bracket off such questions, in dealing with *The Romaunt of the Rose* and with later first-person narratives. Problems of the poetic 'I' and the poetic persona have received an adequate (perhaps more than adequate) share of scholarly attention elsewhere.

In the present chapter I examine closely one short section of the Middle English *Romaunt of the Rose*, covering approximately lines 531–1326. This is translated from the French of Guillaume de Lorris, dating from about 1237; the translator may well have been Chaucer, and the translation is close enough for me to take the English version, with a few minor exceptions, as representing the French.[3] (In the current standard edition of the *Roman de la Rose*,[4] it corresponds to lines 517–1298.) The *Roman de la Rose* was probably the most influential of all medieval vernacular treatments of love, and it is the only first-person narrative I shall consider in which the poet represents himself wholeheartedly as a lover rather than a watcher of love. I choose this section for study because it is concerned with the scopic phase in the unfolding of love. It will be remembered that in medieval thought both religious and courtly accounts of love regarded looking as the first stage in a process culminating in sexual union; this was so whether love was seen as dangerous folly or delightful suffering. Guillaume's *Roman de la Rose* is an account of the earlier part of this process, that is, of what may be called 'falling in love'; when it ends, the goal remains unachieved. It forms an allegorical dream in which, he announces, 'al the art of love I close' (40); and the section with which I am concerned comes early in the process, starting when the lover first gains admission to the garden of love and concluding with his rapturous summary of the paradisal life led by those inside, just at the moment when Cupid is about to take aim and shoot him with his arrows. What eventually follows is an enactment of the metaphor with which we are now entirely familiar from romances:

> He streight up to his ere drough
> The stronge bowe that was so tough,
> And shet att me so wondir smerte
> That thorough myn ye unto myn herte
> The takel smot, and depe it wente.   (1725–9)

But it is possible for an allegorical narrative, unlike a romance, to represent the same human experience sequentially in different forms. What precedes this moment at which the lover is shot through his eye into his heart might be imagined as preliminary to it, or it might, perhaps more convincingly, be imagined as one of several alternative representations of the part played by looking on the way to commitment to love: first the series of exemplary events which I shall discuss, then the lover's gaze into the well of Narcissus (on which I shall comment later), finally the wounding by Cupid's arrow.

My concern, then, is the narrative of the dreamer's first experiences inside the garden; but one difficulty in analysing these lies in strong preconceptions about what 'must' be happening imposed by the scholarly commentaries that pre-empt interpretation. Guillaume de Lorris's part of the *Roman*, by contrast with Jean de Meun's much longer continuation (dating from about forty years later), has been widely regarded, especially in the English-speaking world, as sweetly and idealistically courtly, with something of the springtime quality of the season in which it is set. Dissent has come mainly from scholars who regard Guillaume's poem as implying an orthodox clerical viewpoint not explicitly stated but systematically veiled in irony. The choice, it would seem, is between two radically opposed parties. First there are those who see the world of Guillaume's Amant as 'a self-sufficient paradise of wit and love and revelry . . . an enchanted garden',[5] allegorizing 'the life of the court' and/or 'the poet's state of mind when, as a young man ready for love, he sees that joy ... is attainable through courtly virtues'.[6] This interpretation involves seeing Guillaume's and Jean's contributions as fundamentally opposed, and thus produces 'the now conventional judgment' that regards

the earlier part, by Guillaume, as a joyous celebration of 'courtly love,' fresh and lyrical, and the longer second portion, by Jean de Meun, as an 'anti-Guillaume,' a brilliant ... denunciation of the ideals of courtly love and a celebration of a naturalistic doctrine of a sort of philosophical libertinism.[7]

On the other hand are those who see the two parts as doctrinally unified and as offering 'a warning to heed the voice of reason, and to avoid desire that may lead to hypocritical behaviour and adultery in the heart'.[8] For this latter party, Resoun's intervention, advising Amant that love is 'yvell' (3269) and 'foly everydell' (3271) and that his only sensible course is to forget or reject Cupid, conveys Guillaume's true doctrine, which is then massively developed by Jean – only by then it is too late, for the arrow that entered Amant's eye has already lodged in his heart. It is unfortunate that most of the *Roman*'s readers are likely to have met some scholarly account of it before reading any of the poem itself. That was certainly my own case; and I do not think it would have occurred to me to see it in either of the ways indicated if I had not been influenced by previous secondary reading. My aim here is not to strike a balance between the prevailing views, but, after some introductory remarks, to pretend that I am reading the *Roman* for the first time and to give, as best I can, an account simply of what happens in this section of Guillaume's poem. For this reason, I deliberately avoid relating my account to existing scholarly discussions of the poem.

The Romaunt of the Rose is a dream-poem,[9] the dream of a young man, not yet twenty. He dreams that he wakes on a May morning and, walking through a meadow alongside a river, finds a garden enclosed by high stone walls. Considered from a disenchanted viewpoint, the garden may be taken to represent both a particular kind of experience (the arousal and prospective fulfilment of male desire – the nearest approach to paradise on earth, as the young dreamer comes to judge) and the socio-economic and cultural conditions that permit the leisured cultivation of desire as a privileged form of experience (entry to an exclusive circle of youthful, fashionable and wealthy courtiers). The absence of any distinction between the experience and the conditions that make it possible is part of the garden's enchantment. It is important to recognize that what the poem calls love we should be more likely to call male desire. Guillaume's 'love' for the lady symbolized as a rose is not a relationship involving mutuality or even reciprocity; indeed, it is represented in such a way as to imply that, if this is indeed love, Lacan was right in stating that 'the relation between the sexes does not take place. ... There is no sexual relation.'[10] The objection expressed by Bialacoil ('Fair Welcome') to letting Amant kiss the rose is Chastite's fear that

> who therto may wynnen, ywis,
> He of the surplus of the pray
> May lyve in hoope to get som day,   (3674–6)

and Amant's own images for what he wishes to achieve are similarly exploitative:

> For no man at the firste strok
> Ne may nat felle down an ok,
> Nor of the reysyns have the wyn,
> Tyl grapes be rype, and wel afyn
> Be sore empressid, I you ensure,
> And drawen out of the pressure.   (3687–92)

Such, no doubt, is the way many male adolescents think, now as in the thirteenth century. And the same is true of much medieval courtly writing; a human love which is both mutual and erotically founded, such as that represented in Book III of *Troilus and Criseyde*, is relatively rare in medieval texts,[11] and its absence from the *Roman* need not indicate that Guillaume was writing ironically. I find his tone impossible to interpret; one function of Jean de Meun's continuation was perhaps to scratch that particular itch, and fix the tone more precisely as one of radical, Ovidian irony.

To return to the dream: there is something inside the garden. For Amant this is the object of his desire and for us it is the meaning of his dream, concealed within the walls of allegory; but inside also implies outside, the other realm of those excluded, whose exclusion makes what is inside all the more desirable. These may be represented as the images of disagreeable personifications that Amant describes on the wall; we later learn that these images 'ful of sorowe and woo' (611) have been commissioned by Myrthe, the lord of the garden, but we are never told why. The poem's opening lines stress the prophetic power of dreams: they tell in advance, as Macrobius teaches, what occurs subsequently (*afterward* 5 and 29, *after* 13 and 20). This seems to have a double meaning. First, Guillaume's dream foretold his personal history, a love-affair still incomplete; thus the apparent incompleteness of dream and poem may be a matter of tact rather than accident, because to give it an ending would be to pre-empt the decision of the lady addressed, who 'wel ought, of pris and ryght, / Be cleped Rose' (47–8). Guillaume's closing speech, addressed to Bialacoil, is a plea for her surrender. The poem itself is presumably designed to persuade her to respond favourably, by representing her as the object of desire, the Rose. This case has been subtly argued by David F. Hult,[12] who notes that such open-endedness is common enough in medieval courtly lyrics, though less so in extended narratives; we shall see that Chaucer's *Parliament of Fowls* is comparably open-ended. The second meaning of the references to prophecy, I suggest, is that dreams employ personification and myth to define a universal truth belonging to past and present as much as to future. In this sense 'prophecy', the value attributed to dreams by Macrobius, must be reinterpreted as 'statement of general truth'.

Allegory reveals general truth; but it does so by concealing it. The truth of dreams does not become *apparaunt* (5) till afterwards; we dream *covertly* of what later occurs *openly* (19–20); the book recounting the dream is one in which, says Guillaume, 'I *close*' (40) the art of love. It is tempting to connect this dialectic of closing and opening, covering and discovering, with the passage on May with which the dream narrative begins. This repeatedly speaks of Nature's wish in spring to cover its winter nakedness:

> For ther is neither busk nor hay
> In May that it nyl *shrouded* ben
> And it with newe leves *wren*.
> These wodes eek *recoveren* grene ...
> And than bycometh the ground so proud
> That it wole have a newe *shroud*,
> And makith so queynt his *robe* and faire
> That it hath hewes an hundred payre. (54–66)

The passage ends by expounding or uncovering the meaning of its own allegory or extended metaphor, that of the earth's covering robe of grass and flowers:

> That is the *robe* I mene, iwys,
> Through which the ground to preisen is.　　　　(69–70)

Thus covering and uncovering, closing and disclosing, become virtually identical. After this, Guillaume (in his dream-role as Amant) rises, clothes himself, and sews on his sleeves. In doing so he adopts the garb of civilization, analogous to that of allegory: the repression of desire that makes civilization possible enforces both the external clothing of the body and the internal censorship that conceals the latent significance of dreams beneath their manifest significance, thus making them allegorical.

There is a further cluster of covering and uncovering terms somewhat later, when Guillaume intervenes into the dream in order to anticipate the closure of his poem and its meaning, promising that we will learn the 'craft of love',

> If that ye wol so long abide,
> Til I this Romance may *unhide*,
> And *undo* the signifiance
> Of this drem into Romance.
> The sothfastnesse that now is *hid*,
> Without *coverture* shall be *kid*
> Whanne I *undon* have this dremyng.　　　　(2166–73)

Within the dream the idea of enclosure is centrally thematized in the walled garden. We have observed the tendency of such gardens to symbolize the female body (for example in *A Pistel of Susan* and *The Merchant's Tale*), and Guillaume's *Roman* is the chief secular source for this idea, as the Song of Songs with its *hortus conclusus* is the chief sacred source. And within the garden is the rosebush 'That with an hegge aboute enclos is' (1652, cf. 1841–2, 2967–8) and that is subsequently further protected against Amant by the castle ordained by Jealousy 'T'enclose the roses of good savour' (3943, cf. 3919, 3921, 3925, 3936). On the bush is the rosebud that is the final goal of male desire – a delightful self-enclosed object that Amant gazes at and longs to possess, a closed book that we desire to read. But, just as narrative desire belongs not only to its ultimate goal but to the whole process of reading, so the lover's desire is sustained and intensified by the whole process that constitutes the art or craft of love, and that begins with looking. (Even Spenser's cannibals eventually decide not to eat Serena immediately but to allow her to sleep longer to grow more succulent; thus their looking will be prolonged.) To looking I now return.

Amant is naturally eager to enter the garden, the more because he can hear such 'blisful' (496, 500) birdsong from inside. He searches round the wall, until he comes to a little gate, 'So shett that I ne myght in gon' (529). His analyst would have had no difficulty in interpreting the closed gate, even if he did not know that in Jean de Meun's continuation the dream was going to end with a hilariously obscene symbolic account of the sexual act. He knocks, and it is opened, needless to say, by a beautiful young woman. The dreamer's adventure has begun, and it opens with a strong emphasis on watching. He observes the young woman, who is 'semely for to see' (586), in great detail, giving a part-by-part description from hair to throat, followed by garments (539–74), following the conventions of *effictio* laid down in the *artes poeticae*. The implicit scopophilia of such a description and its fetishization of the female body as visual object emerge particularly clearly once they are attributed, as here, to a first-person male narrator. Someone – some desiring male – has to be gazing in order to produce such a description. And here it conveys an especially strong impression of eroticism, with the sense of sight also evoking fantasies of the other senses. Her flesh, he says, is as tender 'as is a chike' (541). (The original, 'la char plus tendre que poucins' [*Roman* 526], through the accident that French is the language of cuisine, still more strongly suggests a menu.) As for her neck, 'Ther nys a fairer nekke, iwys, / To fele how smothe and softe it is' (555–6). In imagination he is already caressing her, and perhaps sinking his teeth into that tender flesh. Spenser's cannibalistic passage is only a further development of the objectification and devouring fragmentation of the female body implied by such descriptions.

The girl says that her name is Ydelnesse (*Oiseuse* in the *Roman*); and what this means, if the allegory is decoded, is fairly obviously that in order to enter the garden of love and enjoy its pleasures, leisure is a prerequisite.[13] One great attraction, and also source of confusion, in the *Roman de la Rose* and other love-allegories is that the characters have allegorical or mythological meanings but also have bodies that may be suffused with a literal eroticism. This is true of the gate-keeper: whatever moral colouring her name implies, she is a delectable creature in her person. She confesses that, like many beautiful young ladies who haunt the night-spots, she cares for nothing 'But to my joye and my pleying, / And for to kembe and tresse me' (598–9). She explains that the lord of the garden is

Myrthe (French *Deduiz*), and that he amuses himself there with a
company of the most beautiful people in the world. The dreamer
says that he is determined to *see* (637) what happens inside 'that
gardyn *fair to see*' (644); and she lets him in. There, the first thing he
notices is the birds singing like angels, making him think of paradise
and intensifying his eagerness so that

> Than myght I not withholde me
> That I ne wente inne for to *see*
> Sir Myrthe, for my desiryng
> Was hym to *seen*, over alle thyng,
> His countenaunce and his manere –
> That *sighte* was to me ful dere.   (723–8)

Then, walking down a little path, he finds Myrthe and his
company, being sung to by a lady called Gladnesse (French *Leesce*).
Next his eye is caught by people dancing everywhere with musi-
cians playing to them. I mentioned night-spots; and it is true that in
the dream this is happening early in the morning and in the open
air. But what is described in the form of a dream is of course the
dreamer's own night-life, experienced 'a-nyght in my sleping' (92) –
and indeed he has told Ydelnesse that he is so eager to see Myrthe's
company that nothing will stop him seeing it 'this nyght' (637). The
'night-spot' he fantazises is devised to represent a garden on a May
morning. Let us suppose then, to clear our minds of existing
scholarly prejudices, that the young man in his dream has entered a
fashionable discotheque called The Garden of the Rose or (if we
may imagine C. S. Lewis as its proprietor) The Enchanted Garden.
The exclusiveness so strongly emphasized by the images on the
outside of the walls fits well with this supposition, because the really
fashionable club has to have crowds of people outside trying to get
in, and being excluded because they look too old, too poor, too ugly,
and so on.

   Among the entertainers, the dreamer sees a remarkable performance, arranged by Myrthe himself: two lithe girls, very young,
dressed 'In kirtles and noon other wede' (778) are dancing together,
and

> That oon wolde come all pryvyly
> Agayn that other, and whan they were
> Togidre almost, they threwe yfere
> Her mouthis so that thorough her play
> It semed as they kiste alwey....   (784–8)

One way to interpret this dance is perhaps as expressing what one scholar calls 'a sense of virtue immune to the vice and tribulations of the world'.[14] That is not what immediately occurs to me, however. It strikes me that Myrthe has arranged a suggestive, quasi-Lesbian performance, involving the corruption of under-age girls: Amant later admits his preference for rosebuds rather than mature roses (1673–90). The word *pryvyly* (added to the French) reminds us, as such words inevitably do, of our own presence and its dubious status: the secret is no secret to us, and what is done secretly in public seems unlikely to be done with even the intention of secrecy. This is a performance designed for Myrthe's delectation and ours; and needless to say, Amant is there, watching the show with great enthusiasm and extremely reluctant to depart: 'Ne bede I never thennes go, / Whiles that I *saw* hem daunce so' (791–2). At this point a lady called Curtesie courteously invites him to do more than watch. He does so, joining in the dance and thus progressing a step further towards the experience of love; yet at this very moment he inserts an even stronger emphasis on watching rather than doing:

> Thanne gan I *loken* ofte sithe
> The shap, the bodies, and the cheres,
> The countenaunce and the maneres
> Of all the folk that daunced there,
> And I shal telle what they were.   (812–16)

He watches, and then he tells. What underlies this is again the normal rhetorical convention of *effictio*, yet, once attributed to this young man, it inevitably has voyeuristic associations. In order to describe, he has to watch carefully, obsessively even, and the act of watching an erotic performance with such enthralment obviously has sexual implications. Next we learn a little more about Myrthe himself and his girl-friend. Myrthe is a handsome, beardless young man, dressed in the height of thirteenth-century fashion, and his face, figure and clothes are the object of another *effictio* (817–46); the 'enchantment' of the whole episode is connected with the way its eroticism is broadly diffused, not focused solely (though it is largely) on female figures. His companion is Gladnesse, the young woman described as singing earlier. She has granted him her love, we are told, since she was twelve; and then there is a passage about her flesh similar to that about Ydelnesse's flesh, only going a little further:

> She semed lyk a rose newe
> Of colour, and hir flesh so tendre
> That with a brere smale and slendre
> Men myght it cleve, I dar wel seyn.   (856–9)

This is plainly a sadistic fantasy on the dreamer's part: he licks his lips over the tenderness of the girl's flesh, and in doing so momentarily fantasizes about what it would be like to whip her. *Brere* is doubtless suggested by *rose*, but the thought's development is unmistakably driven by sadistic desire.

Myrthe and his chief guest, the God of Love himself (whose garments of flowers are described, but not his body), are men, but most of the other dancers mentioned are women; it is hard to decide whether to categorize them as guests or as performers. The dreamer is of course also male, and the night-life he devises for himself in his dream is naturally a male erotic fantasy. His entrance into the garden of love is an encounter with sexuality, defined as perceived by the young male. Thus the God of Love is accompanied by a 'bacheler' (918) called 'Swete-Lokyng' (920) (French *Douz Regart*), who carries two bows and ten arrows. The looks this 'bacheler' personifies must be the messages conveyed by female eyes and intercepted by the male watcher. Swete-Lokyng himself needs to be not a female but a male personification in order that he can appropriately be armed; but the choice of this way of allegorizing female looks, as weapons, used aggressively against the male, is a male choice.[15] And in general (to move temporarily outside the present section of the *Roman*) what Guillaume's allegory does is to fragment the girl who arouses Amant's sexual interest and also to masculinize her, by projecting on to her his male perception of sex as aggression. She is represented in the allegorical fiction not as one person, like Amant himself, but in two other ways: as an object, the rose, and as a cluster of chiefly male personifications. These modes of representation are not neutral: they imply certain attitudes built into the poem's total system of signification and therefore likely to escape notice. (They may well have been occluded for Guillaume himself.) To symbolize a girl as a rose is obviously to evoke her beauty and its transience; it is also to see her as the passive object of male desire, something to be hastily plucked and possessed,

> For brode roses and open also
> Ben passed in a day or two,
> But knoppes wille [al] freshe be
> Two dayes, atte leest, or thre.   (1681–4)

And to divide her into personifications is in a sense to violate her still further: she exists only as perceived by the insecure young male who desires her. Here there is a parallel with the fragmenting external descriptions we have already considered. In medieval rhetoric, alongside the device called *effictio* stands that called *notatio*, or internal description, description of 'the qualities of the inner man such as reason, faithfulness, patience, honesty, injustice, arrogance, dissipation and other characteristics of the inner man, that is, of the spirit, which are set forth either for praise or for censure'.[16] There is a sense in which this kind of personification-allegory is an expansion of *notatio*, opening up still further the analysis of inner qualities and representing them as separate allegorical agents.

In the *Roman* there is none of that empathy with a woman's inner life found at its most generous in Book II of *Troilus and Criseyde*. In the long run one consequence is that the poem does not distinguish between the girl's wishes and those of her absent male proprietors, whoever they may be – *whose* jealousy, for example, is the Jelousie aroused by Wikked-Tonge at line 3820 of the *Romaunt*?[17] The poem's imagining of sexuality and sexual relations is permeated by the assumptions of a society in which males are dominant. The lady's chastity (which in one way the multiple enclosures symbolize) is being defended against Amant and his chief ally Venus by a number of personifications such as Jelousie, Shame and Daunger. What motivates the defence does not appear to be any religious value set upon chastity, so presumably the issue is rather the daughter's exchange value when the time comes for her to be passed by her male relatives to her future husband. The advantage of a personification-allegory that represents faculties, moral principles, feelings, and so on, attributed to the lady, as separate personifications is that it blurs the distinction between internal and external. From the social point of view, the reason for her resistance to Amant must be that her male proprietors wish to preserve her virginity as an essential part of her value. Thus it is appropriate that the resisting forces should be represented as male persons. But, inasmuch as the poem is concerned with her inner life, she has doubtless internalized the resistance to such an extent that she experiences it as one element in the internal struggle between desire and modesty. Thus it is also appropriate that the defenders of her chastity should have the names of psychological components. A modern reader might complain that the *Roman*'s allegory fails to distinguish between the social and the psychological, treating Frend and Daunger and Ydelnesse as if they were all on the same footing; but this apparent confusion is actually a true representation of the phenomenology of the culture that produced such poems. Jean de Meun in his continuation seems to recognize some of the ironies involved in this confusion (for instance, the misrepresentation of self-interest as idealism and of misogyny as woman-worship), but I doubt whether he was capable of standing outside the confusion sufficiently to analyse it systematically, any more than we can fully detach ourselves from the assumptions of our own culture. I see no sign that Guillaume de Lorris even recognized the ironies; but I find his attitude impossible to interpret with any certainty.[18]

I return from this digression to Guillaume's treatment of looking. In Myrthe's company not all the females are performing for the benefit of the male clients. True, the God of Love's partner is a slender-waisted girl called Beaute; she is systematically described, and her body, as we might expect, once more makes the dreamer's mouth water: 'Hir flesh was tendre as dew of flour' (1013). His mental undressing of her affects his memory in terms not just of sight but of 'savour' (taste, or possibly smell):

> A ful gret savour and a swote
> Me toucheth in myn herte rote,
> As helpe me God, whan I remembre
> Of the fasoun of every membre.   (1025–8)

However, 'Biside Beaute yede Richesse' (1033); and Richesse is not a man but a noble, much-esteemed lady, who has power over the whole world; she is expensively dressed, and her belt has a buckle made of a gem with the marvellous power of protecting the wearer against poison, and is trimmed with another that cures palsy, toothache, and blindness. Such magic jewels are common enough in medieval romances, but when they are worn by a lady called Wealth a new meaning emerges: only the wealthy can afford the best medical treatment, and the jewels must be the medieval equivalent to her private health insurance policy. But Richesse has another, even more precious possession; she leads about by the hand 'A yong man ful of semelyhede, / That she best loved of ony thing' (1130–1). Guillaume explains that this young man was given to extravagant purchases of clothes and horses, and that his aim in life was to spend freely without working, 'And therfore he desired ay / To be aqueynted with Richesse' (1138–9). What he did for her in return is not mentioned, but is not difficult to guess. It may be one of the few comforts available for the feminist reader of Guillaume that in the Garden of the Rose a woman does not necessarily have to provide sexual services for men; if rich enough, she can buy a man to serve her. That at least is part of the meaning here; at the same time the seductive and unscrupulous power of wealth is personified as a woman – and that is no more complimentary to women than anything else in the poem.

The other dancers are described in turn. Largesse, appropriately following Richesse, has no difficulty in drawing other folk to her as a magnet draws iron, and this generosity is also associated with scopic eroticism. Her gift of her brooch to another lady has as its consequence the baring of her own bosom, flesh enticingly glimpsed through transparent silk:

> And opened hadde she hir coler,
> For she right there hadde in present
> Unto a lady maad present
> Of a gold broche, ful wel wrought.
> And certys, it myssat hir nought,
> For thorough hir smokke, wrought with silk,
> The flesh was *seen* as whit as mylk.   (1190–6)

As with Ydelnesse, the simile applied to her flesh (an addition by the translator) evokes oral as well as visual pleasure. Next comes Fraunchise, wearing an elegantly pleated loose white garment that 'Bitokeneth that full debonaire / And swete was she that it ber' (1244–5). Then come more briefly described dancers of both sexes; and finally I must mention the last of the garden's clientele, before the dreamer comes to the fountain of Narcissus and moves on from watching. This is a girl called Youthe, 'That nas not yit twelve yeer of age, / With herte wylde and thought volage' (1283–4).[19] Youthe is dancing with her sweetheart, who is no older than she, and of similar disposition. He kisses her when he pleases,

> That all the daunce myght it *see*.
> They make no force of pryvete,
> For who spake of hem yvel or well,
> They were ashamed never a dell,
> But men myght *seen* hem kisse there
> As it two yonge dowves were.   (1293–8)

In interpreting this, we must take account of historical differences in assumptions about the age at which sexual activity becomes proper

and legal; we must also note that what is described is not furtive
behaviour but something Guillaume presumably intends to be the
innocence of the Golden Age. But innocence is a quality difficult to
represent in art, because it implies the absence of artifice; and this
innocence is on display. This pair of eleven-year-olds are performing their erotic dance not innocently but exhibitionistically, and
much to the dreamer's pleasure. Once innocence is consciously displayed, it ceases to be truly innocent; and the same is true once it is
represented even in words. The display within the text only replicates and calls attention to the display of the text, which flaunts
publicly what should be private. Its shamelessness raises the question of shame for us, and, whether or not genuine, is shameful.
Perhaps more generally too, the uncovering of meaning that Guillaume promises when the poem reaches its conclusion is a form of
exhibitionism, a semantic striptease in which, as it happens, the
lights go out before the final garment is removed – because Guillaume's poem survives, by accident or design, in an unfinished
state. Certainly, in the lines just quoted, the mention of *pryvete* and
shame, in order to deny their relevance, unavoidably encourages
us to use them as criteria of judgment. Paedophilia has its place
along with voyeurism in Amant's fantasy-world.

The narrative of his experiences as a watcher is only preliminary; after it, his goal will be not just to see but to possess. The
scopic phase culminates in the discharge of Cupid's arrows and
their penetration 'thorough myn ye unto myn herte' (1728), but
between this moment and the earlier moment at which Cupid
summons Swete-Lokynge to hand him his bow and arrows
(1330ff.) is inserted the episode of the well of Narcissus. This has
proved one of the hardest parts of the poem to interpret, but it is
perhaps worth considering once more in the context in which
Guillaume placed it, of looking as the first stage of love. It takes
place while Cupid is stalking Amant, waiting for the moment to
strike (1449–54). Amant sits down to rest beside a well inscribed
'Here starf the fayre Narcisus' (1468), and Guillaume correspondingly pauses (for after all, he *is* Amant) to retell the story of Narcissus – a story of looking. He was a *bacheler* (1469), who was loved
by 'a fayr lady that hight Echo' (1474), but was so proud of his
beauty that he rejected her. She prayed that he might receive an
appropriate punishment, and, since 'This prayer was but res-
onable' (1499), what happened was that when Narcissus was

returning from a hunt, hot and thirsty, he came to the well and knelt down to drink.

> And in the water anoon was seene
> His nose, his mouth, his yen sheene,
> And he therof was al abasshed.
> His owne shadowe had hym bytrasshed,
> For wel wende he the forme see
> Of a child of gret beaute.   (1517–22)

The content of these lines corresponds precisely to the origin of narcissism as defined by psychoanalysis. Freud observes in his 1914 paper 'On Narcissism: An Introduction' that 'we are bound to suppose that a unity comparable to the ego cannot exist in the individual from the start: the ego has to be developed' (SE, xiv, pp. 76–7). Before this development comes the stage of auto-eroticism, in which the infant, not yet integrated as an ego, takes pleasure in its separate bodily parts. Just that is expressed in lines 1517–18, with the separation of nose, mouth and eyes and the passive and impersonal form of 'was seene'.[20] Narcissism, however, 'differs from auto-erotism in that it involves a concept of one's own person or ego; the infant loves himself *as himself*'.[21] This is conveyed by lines 1521–2, where Narcissus, now the subject of the verb 'to see', sees not bodily parts but a single 'child of gret beaute'. In fact, the *Romaunt* represents him, more exactly, as *supposing* himself to see *the form* of a beautiful child:[22] this is the birth of narcissism as interpreted by Lacan – the *stade du miroir*, in which the infant sees his image and *mis*recognizes it as a unitary self, as the ego.[23]

The *Romaunt*'s Narcissus, then, is not a figure of self-love in any crude sense. What follows is his death, and this is explained as being caused not by self-love but more generally by desire for the unattainable, by a longing to possess and inhabit the wholeness that is only a *forme* or *shadowe* or illusion:

> He lovede his owne shadowe soo
> That atte laste he starf for woo.
> For whanne he saugh that he his wille
> Myght in no maner wey fulfille,
> And that he was so faste caught
> That he hym kouthe comfort nought,
> He loste his wit right in that place,
> And diede withynne a lytel space.   (1529–36)

Having made his own love unattainable to Echo and thus caused
her death, he is requited by himself dying of unattainability: 'And
thus his warisoun he took / For the lady that he forsook' (1537–8).
Guillaume pauses to draw the moral for ladies, and implicitly for his
own lady: if they make themselves unattainable objects of desire and
thus cause their lovers' death, God will know how to requite them
(1539–42).

   We return to the dream-narrative. Amant first draws back from
the well in fear, but then gathers courage, thinking he might
approach it unharmed. He looks into the clear, swelling water, and
sees 'Two cristall stonys' (1568). They brilliantly refract the sun's
light into 'an hundrid hewis' (1577), and they also reflect the garden
and all it contains, half at a time, 'Withouten ony coverture' (1588),
or again 'full openly / A thousand thinges' (1637–8). Unlike
Narcissus, Amant does not see an illusory unity of the self, but the
glittering sensory variety of his dream-world. This, says Guillaume,
is the mirror which caused the death of Narcissus,

> For whoso loketh in that mirrour,
> Ther may nothyng ben his socour
> That he ne shall there sen somthyng
> That shal hym lede into lovyng.   (1605–8)

Again there is no indication here of *self*-love, no indication, for
example, that the 'cristall stones' are, as in the Ovidian version of
the myth, 'geminum, sua lumina, sidus' [his eyes, twin stars].[24]
Whoever looks will see something that will arouse love, because
there Cupid has sown 'of love the seed' (1617) – and, as I remarked
earlier, what the poem calls love we should call desire: this is what
the myth and the fiction have in common. What Amant sees is a
rosebush, which arouses such delight and longing that he instantly
turns towards it, admires the buds especially, and selects one as
more beautiful and fragrant than the rest. At this moment he is
pierced by Cupid's arrow. What has happened in the Narcissus
episode is that looking reveals itself as the means by which one
succumbs to desire – desire whose object is union and is therefore,
by definition, always unattainable in the real world, whether the
subject is male or female, and whether the object is the illusory ego
or the perfect possession of another self.

The Parliament of Fowls and A Complaynt of a Loveres Lyfe

Unlike Guillaume de Lorris, Chaucer never presents himself in his poems as a lover with experience or expectation of success. We have seen this exemplified in *Troilus and Criseyde*, where he appears as a clerkly translator, investigating a love-affair from the remote past, and needing to consult 'clerkes in hire bokes olde' (III 1199) even to discover how Criseyde trembled when Troilus embraced her. The same is equally true of the dream-poems that precede *Troilus*, even though there Chaucer as dreamer cannot avoid being at the centre of his dream. The earliest, *The Book of the Duchess*, comes nearest to presenting him as a participant in the love which is the courtly poet's required subject-matter. In its 43-line prologue Chaucer appears as a melancholy victim of love-sickness (though even there the sickness must be due to failure); but the melancholy leads to a dream and a poem about someone else's success rather than a narrative of his own cure by the 'phisicien but oon' (39) who could assist him. In the dream, Chaucer is a sympathetic but naïve questioner of the poem's true 'Amant', a 'man in blak' (445) who is a figure of John of Gaunt, mourning his first wife's death. Here Chaucer learns about love not from 'myn auctour called Lollius' (*Troilus* I 394) but from a living authority of high rank and thus capacity for romantic feeling.

In Chaucer's next dream-poem, *The House of Fame*, he finds himself inside a temple of Venus, which he recognizes as such through his iconographic learning (129–39) rather than through any natural affinity with the goddess and what she symbolizes. On the wall-decorations he follows the love-story of Aeneas and Dido, in a manner more directly voyeuristic than his reading of that of Troilus and Criseyde: the words of Virgil and Ovid have been transformed into pictures, and his repeated 'I saw' insists on the distance necessary for looking. After this, Chaucer is carried away

by an eagle sent by Jupiter to reward him for his diligent service of
Cupid and Venus; but the service has been only a matter of reading
and writing about love of which 'thou haddest never part' (628), and
the 'disport and game' (664) he is to enjoy is still not to be any
experience but only 'tydynges / Of Loves folk' (644–5) obtained
from Fame's dwelling. Once more, Chaucer only sees and hears
what is reported of love, the insubstantial spoken word turned into
text and images, and what he learns before the poem breaks off
unfinished is that report is utterly unreliable, a matter of 'Thus hath
he sayd' and 'Thus herde y seye' (2052–3).

The Parliament of Fowls, the third of Chaucer's dream-poems, is the
one that most explicitly shows the poet as voyeur, someone whose
writing about love derives from what he witnesses, not what he
experiences. In *The Book of the Duchess* he does not present himself as
a poet until the poem's closing lines, where he proposes to attempt to
become one in future, turning his dream into verse. In *The House of
Fame*, his dream-experience is a reward for his literary services, but
there is no indication that the dream is to become material for
further poetry; perhaps there would have been in the poem's
non-existent conclusion. In the *Parliament*, however, we find a
dreamer fixated on the visual whose dream is explicitly offered as
'mater of to wryte' (168).

The *Parliament* begins with Chaucer meditating on the 'wonderful
werkynge' (5) of Love, whose miracles and fierce lordship he knows
not 'in dede' (8) but only 'in bokes' (10). He has been reading a
book, 'write with lettres olde', in search of 'a certeyn thing' (19–20).
We never discover what this thing is, and the poem ends with
Chaucer still reading books in the hope that they will stimulate him
to dream of 'som thyng for to fare / The bet' (698–9). The goal of
reading, like that of the lover's desire, seems to be unattainable, and
the dream and the poem end in suspension, waiting for some future
consummation. But the poem's general thrust gives some indication
what it is that Chaucer hopes to learn: how to relate the erotic love
that is the source, subject and *raison d'être* of courtly poetry to the
larger systems of thought and value provided by philosophy.
Guillaume de Lorris, as we have seen, enters eagerly into the realm
of 'love' as idealized male desire without attempting any serious
contextualization, and his recurrent use of religious language (paradise, angels, and so on) seems no more than a way of claiming
supreme value for the courtly experience of love by the only means

open to a medieval writer. Yet for any medieval writer who was not content to be a mere entertainer but aspired to the title of poet, a fundamental problem within the secular culture of courtliness and chivalry was to find a way of placing human love in some serious context that would not simply condemn it as lecherous folly. Chaucer struggles with this problem in most of his richest works – above all in *Troilus and Criseyde*. It was one to which no philosophical solution could be provided by the intellectual tools available to him; the poetic solution lay in persistent evasion and ambiguity, in the choice of pagan settings for his narratives, and above all in finding ways of deferring the moment of closure at which human values would be subsumed in or cancelled by divine values. *The Parliament of Fowls* is all postponement; juxtaposing a pagan vision of cosmic asceticism with an exploration of 'love' in the contexts of nature and of culture, it ends with no answer to the *demande d'amour* proposed in the dream, and with the prospect only of a further quest, further reading, further dreams. Here the poet's role as voyeur is of crucial importance. He can be the means of floating this fragile structure of endless deferrals into the world only if he is held at a distance from what fascinates him; but that distancing does not turn him into the heroic artist of modernism, 'refined out of existence, indifferent, paring his fingernails', but leaves him as a clerk peeping at a sex-goddess, the undignified watcher of an unfinished striptease.

The book to which Chaucer turns at the beginning of the *Parliament* is the *Somnium Scipionis*, the final part of Cicero's *De re publica*, preserved in the Middle Ages along with a commentary by Macrobius that was a source of medieval dream-theory. Chaucer summarizes what the younger Scipio learns in it from a dream of his grandfather Scipio Africanus: a pagan philosophical vision of cosmic harmony and of reward and punishment after death, promising heavenly bliss to those who serve 'commune profyt' (47, 75) and mentioning lovers only as 'likerous folk' (79) who will be punished but eventually forgiven and received into 'that blysful place' (83). Chaucer goes to bed depressed,

> For bothe I hadde thyng which that I nolde,
> And ek I ne hadde that thyng that I wolde. (90–1)

This formulation appears elsewhere in his work as the state of the lover, tormented by unattainable desire – 'My peyne is this, that what so I desire / That have I not' (*Complaint unto Pity* 99–100) – but

also as the general state of humanity when unenlightened by
philosophy: Boethius agrees with Philosophia's description of his
angwyse as being 'for that the lakkide somwhat that thow noldest nat
han lakkid, or elles thou haddest that thow noldest nat han had'
(*Boece* III, pr. 3, 33–6). Then Chaucer sleeps, and dreams in his turn
of Scipio Africanus, who promises 'That sumdel of thy labour wolde
I quyte' (112). Africanus takes Chaucer to the gate of a walled park,
a situation reminiscent of Guillaume's as his dream begins in the
Roman; this gate has a double inscription, promising both 'al good
aventure' (131) and the misery of 'Disdayn and Daunger' (136) to
any who enter. These are the two sides of the experience of love, and
Chaucer stands bewildered, unable to decide 'whether me was bet /
To entre or leve' (152–3), until Africanus unceremoniously pushes
him in.

Now for the first time Chaucer explicitly defines the poet as
voyeur. Africanus explains that he need not fear to enter, since the
inscription refers only to Love's servants,

> But natheles, although that thow be dul,
> Yit that thow canst not do, yit mayst thow se.
> For many a man that may nat stonde a pul
> Yet liketh hym at wrastlyng for to be,
> And demen yit wher he do bet or he.
> And if thow haddest connyng for t'endite,
> I shal the shewe mater of to wryte.   (162–8)

Chaucer then can visit the walled park, not as a participant but as a
spectator. Africanus's analogy is suggestive beyond its intellectual
function: it implies that love-making, like wrestling, is a contact
sport that can give pleasure to the attentive watcher. In the very act
of watching lovers, even though lacking the ability to join in,
Chaucer may gain vicarious enjoyment as well as material for his
writing.

His role in what follows is solely that of a passive watcher and
listener: he does not even engage in any dialogue, as he did with the
'man in blak' in *The Book of the Duchess* and with the eagle and the
unnamed man who asked his name (1868ff.) in *The House of Fame*,
and as he would do with Cupid and Alcestis in his last dream-poem,
the Prologue to *The Legend of Good Women*. *The Parliament of Fowls* is
the only one of Chaucer's dream-poems in which he says nothing
within the dream. Once inside, he finds himself in a paradisal
garden where he sees 'Cupide, oure lord' (212) with many alle-

gorical followers, among them 'Beute withouten any atyr' (225). Next he sees a 'temple of bras' (231) surrounded by dancing women with their hair loose. Inside the temple the atmosphere is of steamy eroticism. It is dark, but a dim light is provided by flames on the altars, kept burning by 'sykes hoote as fyr' (246) which are 'engendered with desyr' (248) and provoked by 'the bittere goddesse Jelosye' (252). Then, Chaucer says,

> The god Priapus saw I, as I wente,
> Withinne the temple in sovereyn place stonde,
> In swich aray as whan the asse hym shente
> With cri by nighte, and with hys sceptre in honde.
> Ful besyly men gonne assaye and fonde
> Upon his hed to sette, of sondry hewe,
> Garlondes ful of freshe floures newe.
>
> And in a prive corner in disport
> Fond I Venus and hire porter Richesse. (253–61)

Chaucer's source here is a passage from the description of the temple of Venus in Book VII of the *Teseida*, but there are significant differences of effect, some caused solely by the shift of context. One is that in the *Parliament* we are never told that the temple is dedicated to Venus; thus the impression given by the lines just quoted is that Priapus 'in sovereyn place' is the presiding deity, with Venus 'in a prive corner' not just because love is private but because she is subordinate to him. Priapus's symbolic role is perfectly clear: within the temple he is the god not of the garden but of the phallus, and he is seen at the moment of frustrated desire described by Ovid in the *Fasti*:[1] he attempted to rape the sleeping nymph Vesta, but a braying ass woke her and her companions and his visible priapism was laughed at by all. The 'sceptre' in his hand is the phallus itself, and Chaucer has changed his source to have people attempting to place the garlands 'Upon his hed' – whether of the god or of his organ scarcely matters, since Priapus here is an embodied erection. In Boccaccio the garlands are merely hanging 'throughout the temple' (vii 60); the effect of the change, especially of the doubled verb 'assaye and fonde', is to suggest a vain effort to conceal or prettify the embarrassingly conspicuous truth of frustrated desire. The scene is one of looking in two senses: Priapus is looked at and thereby shamed in the moment recalled from the *Fasti*, and is then looked at again by Chaucer as his gaze penetrates the temple's dimness. In the *Teseida* the second looker is female, because it is

Palemone's prayer that is described as seeing what is in the temple; in the *Parliament* the looker is the male poet scanning the red-light district in search of story-material.

This last change becomes more important when the focus shifts from Priapus to Venus. Chaucer's gaze makes her out through the dim light ('unnethe it myghte be lesse' [264]), reclining languidly on a gold bed, 'Til that the hote sonne gan to weste' (266). The last touch, unEnglishly tropical though it sounds, is also Chaucer's addition, as is the implication of 'in disport' (260) that Venus and Richesse are engaged in erotic play – the kind of wrestling that Africanus promised he could watch. And what Chaucer sees, he tells:

> Hyre gilte heres with a golden thred
> Ibounden were, untressed as she lay,
> And naked from the brest unto the hed
> Men myghte hire sen; and, sothly for to say,
> The remenaunt was wel kevered to my pay,
> Ryght with a subtyl coverchef of Valence –
> Ther was no thikkere cloth of no defense.   (267–73)

Once more, unbound female hair implies a dangerous sexual temptation; but now the goddess's hair and her calculatedly almost-unclothed body tempt only to scopophilia. The fairy lady in *Lanval* and *Sir Launfal* exposed herself so as to arouse a desire that would culminate in sexual union; but Venus is imagined as a striptease artiste. (If this scene is Chaucer's response to Guillaume's *Roman de la Rose*, it suggests that to see the realm of love as a nightclub is less perverse than might be thought.) 'Men myghte hire sen': desire is arrested and sustained at the scopic distance. That is why it is important that Priapus should be seen first, 'in sovereyn place': what is celebrated in the temple is a cult of frustration, of desire never fulfilled but always fixated in the unending moment of the gaze. The impersonality of 'Men myghte hire sen' is not kept up for long; what is revealed underlying it is '*my* pay', the watching Chaucer's pleasure. And his pleasure depends not only on seeing but on there being something he cannot see: he gets a greater thrill from Venus's 'subtyl coverchef of Valence' than he did from 'Beute withouten any atyr', because the goddess's last covering permits a more exciting fetishization of what is concealed and forbidden.

I have been subjecting this short scene to an analysis that may have seemed excessively voyeuristic;[2] but it is surely one of the most remarkable in Chaucer. On one level it offers a diagnosis of a certain kind of 'love' – the courtly cult of desire, self-contained, shut off as the temple is from the garden, exotic, pagan, a cult of pleasure which is also sorrow. Its setting is a perpetual twilight, waiting for a culmination that never comes, for in the dream-world 'nevere wolde it nyghte' (209). The effect arises from the stimulus of Chaucer's encounter with Boccaccio and thus with pagan antiquity imagined with a new sensuousness. On another and complementary level, it offers an exact definition of the poet as voyeur. For a moment Chaucer seems to be among those on their knees before the goddess (278–9), tasting 'the sadness of her night'; but it is only a moment. He is a watcher of the cult of watchers, licking his lips and then passing on to see more: 'But thus I let hire lye, / And ferther in the temple I gan espie ... ' (279–80). The indignity of his role is the price paid for the attempt to write of love from a viewpoint that is not one of commitment.

Having glanced at the temple's wall-paintings with their stories of lovers from Tristan to Troilus, Chaucer returns to the fresher air of the garden; and there he witnesses the poem's main subject, the parliament of the birds on Saint Valentine's day. This offers an alternative conception of love, placed now in the context of the natural and social orders. Now the presiding deity is the 'noble goddesse Nature' (303), before whom birds of all species present themselves to receive judgment on their choice of mates. No 'foul that cometh of engendrure' (306) is missing; and this formulation reminds us that the goal is the procreation of species, a question no more raised in the temple than in *Troilus* or any of the great medieval courtly romances. There are so many birds 'that unethe was there space / For me to stonde, so ful was al the place' (314–15); and from now on Chaucer virtually disappears even as an observer. Voyeurism, the appropriate response to Priapus and Venus, is irrelevant to Nature's concerns. This being so, I shall carry my analysis of the *Parliament* little further.[3] In the realm of Nature, the species of birds correspond to and ratify the human hierarchy of rank; at the same time, within the highest species/rank, that of the noble 'foules of ravyne' (527), three males compete for the hand of a single female. (The poem may have had some topical reference.)[4] Their competing claims are put in terms of courtly absolutism, and are thus rationally undecidable; the bird-species each choose a representative 'by pleyn eleccioun' (528) to express their views, but still no agreement is

reached; finally Nature's decision is that the mating process can go
forward for another year only by means of *eleccioun* (621) on the
female's part. This she declines to exercise, and Nature grants her a
further year, after which she shall have her 'choys al fre' (649). The
poem ends with birds being *chosen* (673) to sing a roundel; the song
wakes Chaucer from his dream, and he proceeds to read still more
books. There is surely a deep paradox in Chaucer's treatment of the
common medieval homology of natural species and human ranks,
for it involves the attribution of choice to birds, whereas the natural
order operates harmoniously (and the poem lays repeated emphasis
on *armonye* and *acord*) precisely because it is not troubled by elective
affinities and enmities, nor is its procreative sexuality disturbed by
sin or perversion, concepts valid only on the assumption of freewill.

In Chapter 9 we saw how a follower of Chaucer could grasp and
develop the voyeurism implied in his role as translator of old books.
A similar development occurs in the post-Chaucerian first-person
love-narrative, and I shall begin to illustrate this from John Lydgate's *Complaynt of a Loveres Lyfe* (also known as *The Complaint of the
Black Knight*). Here the poet's intelligence about what he is doing is
less striking, even while his stylistic and rhetorical skill is more
marked, than that of the author of *Partonope of Blois*. Lydgate
(c. 1370–1450) was in his time the most famous and admired of
Chaucer's disciples, and he was certainly the most prolific, being
commissioned by royalty and nobility to produce such huge improv-
ing works as the *Troy Book*, *The Pilgrimage of the Life of Man*, and *The
Fall of Princes*. He was a Benedictine monk and was ordained priest
in 1397; the *Complaynt of a Loveres Lyfe* is a secular, courtly poem, but
it too looks as though it was written under commission. Like his
other close imitations of Chaucer's courtly poems, it is generally
thought to be among Lydgate's earlier works, probably dating from
before 1412.

In structure, the *Complaynt* is very simple. As its title suggests, its
core is a love-complaint – a distinct form in medieval courtly
literature, sometimes existing as a separate lyric, sometimes as a
lyric moment expressing a character's feelings at a point within a
complex narrative such as *Troilus and Criseyde*, sometimes incorporated into a relatively simple narrative frame – which is the situation
in Lydgate's poem. Here the actual *compleynt* (193)[5] is spoken by a
nameless unhappy lover and consists of lines 218–574 of a poem of
681 lines. It is framed in two first-person sections which I shall call

the prologue and epilogue; in these the poet explains how he came to overhear it and how he then wrote it down. All this is in the seven-line stanzas of rhyme royal, saturated with recollections of the phraseology and syntactical patterning of Chaucer's poetry; but at the very end come two eight-line stanzas forming a double envoy – a common closural device in late-medieval courtly poems, intended to tie and cut the umbilical cord linking the poem with the poet who gave it birth. The first is addressed to 'Princess', the probably imaginary lady whose cruelty has provoked the lover's *compleynt*; the second to the book itself as it leaves the poet behind and sets off to 'my lyves quene' (674), the poem's *destinataire*, who may or may not be identical with the 'princess' of the preceding stanza. The uncertainty results from the parallel established within the poem between the poet and the man whose *compleynt* he reports: they are both sorrowing lovers.

In this respect the chief Chaucerian model for the *Complaynt* is *The Book of the Duchess*, with its obscure opening in which Chaucer represents himself as a melancholy lover suffering from insomnia.[6] Though not a dream-poem like the *Book*, the *Complaynt* in many ways follows the pattern of medieval dream-poetry; it is a first-person narrative, in which everything is reported as having been personally seen or heard by a narrator who has wandered out alone into an idealized springtime landscape. Lydgate does not fall asleep and have a dream influenced by his emotional state, but the core of his poem could well have been framed in a dream. Lydgate's awareness of the dream-poem as model may be indicated by his playful reversal of its framework: instead of beginning with sleep and ending with waking, the *Complaynt* begins with Lydgate waking and ends with him going home to sleep.[7] In *The Book of the Duchess* Chaucer, apparently suffering from love-sickness, dreams of seeing a pale knight dressed in black, also apparently suffering from love-sickness, and overhearing him speak 'a compleynte to hym-selve' (464); in the *Complaynt of a Loveres Lyfe*, Lydgate overhears the lamentation of a love-sick knight dressed 'In blake and white, colour pale and wan' (131). A major difference, however, is that Chaucer, though dreaming, having overheard the brief *compleynte*, then reveals himself and engages in conversation with the knight, while Lydgate, though awake, only overhears his love-sick knight, and in this respect resembles rather the dreamer of *The Parliament of Fowls*. Lydgate, indeed, takes voyeuristic passivity further than Chaucer did in the *Parliament*, and remains in concealment throughout the knight's lamentation, so that the two men never meet. It is precisely the dream that makes possible the face-to-face encounter in *The Book of the Duchess*. In both the *Book* and the *Complaynt* a social gap exists between the knight and the poet; in the *Book* the dream creates an imaginative space in which they can converse on relatively equal terms, as perhaps they could not properly have been represented as doing in waking life.

Behind both the *Book* and the *Complaynt* lies a body of fourteenth-century French courtly poetry in which the founding assumptions of such works generally lie nearer the surface. A typical example is the *Dit de la Fonteinne amoureuse* by Guillaume de Machaut, a first-person narrative incorporating a dream, probably written for the recently married Jean, duc de Berry, on the occasion of his departure as a hostage to England in 1360. Chaucer certainly knew this poem; Lydgate may not have done, but it is worth consideration for the light it throws on the kind of poem he was to write. In a lengthy prologue, Machaut relates how he was lying half-asleep in an unfamiliar bedroom when he heard through the window 'une creature / ... qui trop fort se plaignoit' (70–1) [someone lamenting very bitterly].[8] Imagining that it might be a murderous spirit, he was terrified; and he digresses to excuse his timidity by distinguishing between a knight and a 'clers / Rudes, nices et malapers' (139–40) [ignorant, silly, impertinent clerk], 'plus couars qu'uns lievres' (92) [more cowardly than a hare], such as himself. Listening further, he hears the unseen person say that he intends to compose a *complainte* on his separation from his lady. At this Machaut loses his fear, dresses, lights a candle, takes his portable desk and writing instruments (the markers of his clerkly status and skills), and settles down to transcribe the *complainte*. The next eight hundred lines of the *Dit* consist of the lover's *complainte* itself; it includes a version of the story of Ceyx and Alcyone that is among the sources of *The Book of the Duchess*. At its end the speaker proudly points out to the lady that

> Cent rimes ay mis dedens ceste rime,
>   Qui bien les conte.
> Prises les ay en vostre biauté ...   (1021–3)

I have put one hundred rhymes into this complaint, who ever cares to count them. I was inspired to them by your beauty ...

Machaut stops writing, reads through what he has written, checks the number of rhymes, and, since the *complainte* has occupied the whole night, goes out in the early morning in pursuit of the speaker. He finds him to be a great lord, handsome but pale, for his heart is 'd'amoureuses pointes ... navrez et poins' (1108–9) [pierced and wounded by the arrows of love]. Machaut timidly kneels at a distance, but the lord treats him graciously, shows him the 'Fonteinne Amoureuse' in a beautiful park, explains that he is unhappy because he is obliged to leave his lady, and finally asks Machaut

> Que tant vueilliez estudier
> Que de m'amour et de ma plainte
> Me faciés ou lay ou complainte.
> Car je say bien que la pratique
> Savez toute, et la theorique
> D'amour loial et de ses tours.   (1502–7)

to be so kind as to set yourself to making for me a lay or complaint about my love and my sorrow. For I know very well that you know all the theory and practice of true love in all its aspects.

At this Machaut produces the *complainte* he transcribed earlier, saying, to the lord's amazement, 'vesla ci toute preste' (1520) [here it is, all ready) – and he explains how he came to write down a love that the lord had striven to keep secret. The lord sleeps in the poet's lap, the poet sleeps too, and the second half of the poem consists of Machaut's dream, which it turns out the lord has shared, and an account of the comfort he receives from it.

This charmingly absurd confection reveals with admirable clarity some of the shaping assumptions of late-medieval courtly ideology. There is a fundamental division in rank and way of life between knight and clerk, and yet each is dependent on the other. (The greater intimacy with his lord depicted in the *Dit* than in Chaucer's *Book* doubtless reflects the fact that Machaut, aged about sixty and a canon of Rheims, was already a famous poet and composer, while Chaucer was young and unknown.) The knightly lord's social elevation entitles him to experience the supreme joys and sorrows of love, secret feelings which are the only inspiration of love-poetry. Thus he composes the love-complaint, giving direct expression to his passion, while the humble clerk, after mocking his own fearfulness, can only listen enthralled, concealed behind his window. But it is the clerk who writes what the lord composes, in doing so slyly calling attention to the technical mastery which is really, of course, Machaut's own achievement. The clerk has some knowledge of love (and indeed Machaut begins the *Dit*, as Chaucer begins *The Book of the Duchess*, by touching on his own love),[9] but that is passed over lightly in favour of the lord's deeper and more important feelings. The two eventually sleep and dream together, just as, near the beginning, Machaut incorporated his name and Jean's alongside each other in an anagram; and the clerkly poet's dream offers comfort to his noble patron. Machaut's presentation of the completed poem to the duc de Berry will repeat the message already implied in the fiction: 'These are your feelings and your words; I am no more than the humble scribe who set them down.' A similar message, but one related to a literary as well as a social hierarchy, will be conveyed more directly by Lydgate's *Complaynt*.

The landscape of Lydgate's prologue is much indebted to that of *The Romaunt of the Rose*, though with certain features also borrowed from *The Parliament of Fowls*;[10] but Lydgate has been careful to alter some of its most problematic features in such a way as to dissolve potentially dangerous clashes between courtliness and orthodox morality. The poem begins with him rising from bed, wandering through the woods in May to gain relief from his love-sickness, and following a river

> Til at the last I founde a lytil wey
> Tovarde a parke enclosed with a wal.   (38–9)

As in the *Romaunt*, it has only one small gate; but anyone who wishes can enter, and Ydelnesse is not the condition of entry. Again, there is 'a litel welle' (75) in the *parke*, but Lydgate is careful to explain that it was *not* 'lyche the welle wher as Narci[s]us / Islayn was thro vengeaunce of Cupide' (87–8), and he further simplifies the moral issue by stating that in the fountain of Narcissus Cupid had sown 'The greyn of deth' (90), whereas Guillaume (1617) had said that Cupid 'Hath sowen ther of love the seed'. Thus Lydgate can safely look in it and even drink it, and he finds that doing so assuages the 'bitter languor' (109) that 'Daunger and Disdeyn' (106) have caused him to suffer. The landscape includes some of that imagery of concealment that we observed in the *Romaunt*:

> The soyle was pleyn, smothe and wonder softe,
> Al *ouersprad* wyth tapites that Nature
> Had made herselfe, *celured* eke alofte
> With bowys grene the flo[u]res for to *cure*
> That in her beaute they may long endure
> Fro al assaute of Phebus feruent fere.[11]   (50–5)

Another example occurs in the transformation of a relatively ordinary line from Diana's temple in *The Knight's Tale* – 'Ther saugh I Dane, yturned til a tree' (1 2062) – into a beautiful mythological periphrasis for the laurel tree, suggesting that Daphne is still concealed beneath its bark: 'I saw ther Daphene *closed* vnder rynde' (64). In the *Romaunt* such imagery seemed to be connected with the recurrent references to the meaning of dreams and of allegory as something covered, shrouded, hidden, enclosed. In the *Complaynt*, just as the walled area can be entered freely, so there is no dream or allegory with a hidden meaning to be 'unclosed' or interpreted, and the imagery of concealment can more readily be associated with the poet's own role. Not the meaning but the poet is hidden.

In the *Complaynt of a Loveres Lyfe*, Lydgate is from the beginning the silent watcher and listener that Chaucer becomes once pushed into the garden in *The Parliament of Fowls*. His position as voyeur and *écouteur* is spelt out with great clarity: he accidentally comes upon the man in black and white, sees his pallor and feverish shivers, hears him groaning, and at once hides in the bushes in order not to be observed:

> Wherof astonied, my fote I gan withdrawe,
> Gretly wondring what hit myght[e] be
> That he so lay and had[de] no fel[a]we,
> Ne that I coude no wyght with him se.
> Wherof I had routhe and eke pite
> And gan anon so softly as I coude
> Among the busshes priuely me shroude,
>
> If that I myght in eny wise espye
> What was the cause of his dedely woo. . . .   (141–9)

Lydgate remains concealed among the bushes throughout the *compleynt* until the man in black and white moves beyond observation:

> And al this w[h]ile myself I kep[te] close
> Among the bowes and myself gan hide.
> Til at the last the woful man arose
> And to a logge went[e] ther besyde
> Wher al the May his custom was t'abide,
> Sole to compleyn of his peynes kene. . . .   (582–8)

'*Sole* to compleyn' encourages us to assume that, if the knight had known he was in a spy's presence, he would not have engaged in the

self-revelation that has just been reported. The shamefulness of
Lydgate's role as a concealed watcher and listener is thus confirmed,
and his awareness of this may perhaps be indicated by his insistence
in the prologue that he can properly report what he overheard if it
gives pleasure to his reader(s):[12]

> And for me semeth that hit ys syttyng
> His wordes al to put in remembraunce,
> To me that herde al his compleynyng
> And al the grounde of his woful chaunce,
> Yf therwithal I may yow do plesaunce,
> I wol to yow (so as I can) anone
> Lyche as he seyde reherse[n] euerychone.   (169–75)

Why should he insist on the propriety of what he is about to do
unless he feels that it is not proper, and wants to make us, and
perhaps literary decorum, responsible for making him do it? Lydgate's position is made to seem more unworthy than the comic roles
attributed to Chaucer in his dream-poems – his failure to grasp the
knight's cause of grief in *The Book of the Duchess*, his reluctance to be
carried through the heavens in search of Fame in *The House of Fame*,
and his humble submission to the criticism of his work by Cupid and
Alceste in the Prologue to *The Legend of Good Women*.

The indignity of the voyeur's position is further emphasized by
two mythological analogues that Lydgate brings into the poem,
both apparently quite gratuitously. The first is the now familiar one
of Actaeon, slain by his own hounds for seeing Diana naked. Why do
we need to be told that the spring from which Lydgate drinks in the
prologue is *not*

> lyke the welle of [pure] chastite
> Which as Dyane with her nymphes kept
> When she naked into the water lept,
> That slow Atteon with his ho[u]ndes felle
> Oonly for he cam so nygh the welle?   (94–8)

And it seems significant that Lydgate has guiltily repressed the
reason generally given for Actaeon's punishment – spying on the
naked goddess. More strikingly irrelevant is the passage in the
epilogue in which Lydgate prays to Venus to preserve the love-sick
knight,

> For that ioy thou haddest when thou ley
> With Mars thi knyght wh[en] Vulcanus [yow] founde
> And with a cheyne vnvisible yow bounde

> Togedre both tweyne in the same while
> That al the court above celestial
> At your shame gan[ne] laughe and smyle. (621–6)

This is almost the only laughter in the poem, and John Norton-Smith rightly comments that 'The poet's remark seems a little tactless here.'[13] My guess is that this recollection of the comic shame of both watcher and watched was suggested to Lydgate by the thought of the position *he* occupies in his poem. I do not mean to imply that these two mythological analogues for voyeurism are part of any grand plan on Lydgate's part; only that they were unconsciously suggested to him by his sense of his own position as poetic spy.

Why does Lydgate represent himself in this undignified way in the *Complaynt*? The reason resembles Machaut's, and is indicated in a passage at the end of the prologue, immediately preceding the knight's *compleynt* (lines 169–217). Lydgate has seen the knight and described his position 'Gruffe on the grounde in place desolate' (167) and also his own position, concealed among the bushes (147); but before repeating the knight's words he pauses to beg for his audience's consideration. Borrowing ideas and phrases from the proems to Books I, II and III of *Troilus and Criseyde*, where Chaucer similarly writes of his inability to convey the full intensity of his lovers' feelings, Lydgate explains a fundamental principle of medieval literary courtliness: it is only possible to write of the feelings experienced by lovers if one can do so *felyngly* (188) and *of sentement* (197) – that is, on the basis of having experienced such feelings oneself. Both terms are borrowed from Chaucer's proem to Book II of *Troilus*, where he writes that 'of no sentement I this endite' (13) and 'I speeke of love unfelyngly' (19). Just as Chaucer's claim was that he was writing only what he had read in 'olde bokes', so Lydgate's is that he is copying down only what he has heard a knight say when he thought himself unobserved. Chaucer had contrasted himself with the audience whose servant he was: he was only a historian of love, they were of gentle birth and therefore lovers and experts on love as it were by profession. In the same proem to Book II, he writes that it will be no surprise to him to receive critical comments

> if it happe in any wyse,
> That here be any lovere in this place
> That herkneth, as the storie wol devise,
> How Troilus com to his lady grace. (29–32)

And Lydgate borrows the very same rhyme-phrases –

> And yf that eny now be *in this place*
> That fele in love brennyng or fervence
> Or hyndred were *to his lady grace* ...   (204–6)

– to make a different point but one that still puts him as poet on a lower plane than his audience as lovers.

This repeated self-depreciation of Chaucer's runs too deep in his work to be simply a matter of literary convention. Its origin may lie in his real social inferiority to a courtly public, though he also exploited it skilfully as a way of inciting his listeners and readers to make their own judgments on his subject-matter, rather than relying on any doctrinal authority of his or anyone else's. Chaucer purports, as we have seen, to be no more than a historian or translator, one who knows love not 'in deed' but only from books. Chaucer copies rather than creates, but Lydgate is doubly a copyist. He is excluded from personal experience of love not just by social inferiority but by his profession as celibate priest and monk. He may go through the motions of the unhappy lover's role at the beginning of his prologue, but he is careful to avoid all detail and to represent himself as instantly cured, 'An huge part relesed of my smert' (116), by drinking from the well in the park. And in the epilogue, having prayed to God that each true lover 'may haue such a grace / His ovn lady in armes to embrace' (657–8), he is quick to explain that he did not mean that literally:

> I mene thus, that in al honeste,
> Withoute more, ʒe may togedre speke
> Whatso y[e] list[e] at good liberte.   (659–61)

Lydgate was always conscious of the constraints placed upon him as a courtly poet by his religious profession. At the same time, he is keenly aware that even his literary treatment of love is second-hand, copied from Chaucer. Chaucer may really have been writing *Troilus and Criseyde* in part for an audience of courtly listeners (though he also addresses readers, and always has them in mind); Lydgate was almost certainly writing only for readers, and he refers to his audience as being 'in this place' only because Chaucer had done so. Hence the striking statement of his position as poet when he writes that he cannot adequately convey the knight's *compleynt*,

> But euen like as doth a skryuener
> That can no more what that he shal write
> But as his maister beside doth endyte:
>
> Ryght so fare I, that of no sentement
> Sey ryght noght, as in conclusion,
> But as I herde when I was present.   (194–9)

In comparing himself to a professional copyist, who knows no more of what he must write than what his master sets down beside him, he puts himself on the lowest of four levels of book-making distinguished by medieval scholars. Saint Bonaventure defines them in the prologue to his commentary on Peter Lombard's *Libri sententiarum*: the *scriptor* or scribe 'writes out the words of other men without adding or changing anything', the *compilator* puts together other men's material in his own way, the *commentator* clarifies the writings of other men, and the *auctor* may include other men's materials but only in order to confirm his own.[14] Chaucer had written in the prologue to his *Treatise on the Astrolabe*, 'I n'am but a lewd compilator of the labour of olde astrologiens' (Prologue 61–2), but Lydgate pushes himself one class further down, from *compilator* to *scriptor*. On the level of the poem's fiction, the master whom he copies is the knight whose words he writes as he hears them (and in this respect his position is identical with Machaut's in the *Fonteinne amoureuse*); on the level of the image, the master is of course Chaucer. Lydgate has suppressed Chaucer's name, just as in the prologue to *The Siege of Thebes*, his addition to *The Canterbury Tales*, when he meets the Canterbury pilgrims, everyone is there except Chaucer.[15] Lydgate has this double reason, then, for presenting himself as a concealed spy: as a monk he can know about love only second-hand, and as a belated poet he can know about love-poetry only second-hand. This may also explain why his negative definition of the *welle* in his poem adds that it is not 'lyche the pitte of the Pega[c]e / Vnder Parnaso wher poetys slept' (92–3). The allusion is to the spring sacred to the Muses, the Hippocrene; Lydgate is denying that the fountain from which he drinks is that of poetic inspiration. The source of the *compleynt* which follows is not inspiration but imitation.

It should be added that Lydgate's sense of his own position as one of shameful secondariness and inferiority to his subject-matter derives not only from Chaucer, but from a larger cultural shift of which Chaucer and Machaut were both parts. Late-medieval culture was increasingly inclined to regard the serious vernacular poet as a 'clerk' or *clericus*, rather than a mere entertainer. This gave his position a higher dignity, but, when he was dealing with secular, courtly material, it also set a gap between him and those about whom he was writing. A pictorial illustration may help to clarify this. One iconographic model for the representation of the author in illuminated manuscripts showed him as a concealed reporter. A good example is the frontispiece of Bodleian MS Douce 213, a fifteenth-century French translation of Boccaccio's *Decameron*.[16] Here we see the ten courtly young people who are the storytellers of the *Decameron*, dressed with great elegance, one telling a story to the others, inside a walled enclosure representing (as in the *Roman de la Rose*) the sphere of courtliness; and outside the wall sits Boccaccio, dressed with clerical sobriety, listening intently and writing down what he hears on a scroll which will become the *Decameron* itself. Some words Lydgate uses of himself –

> With al my myght I leyde an ere to
> Euery word to marke what he sayde   (152–3)

– exactly suggest Boccaccio's posture. When the clerkly narrator is represented as a concealed voyeur or *écouteur*, as in Lydgate's poem and several others to be discussed in later chapters, the shamefulness of his position becomes far more explicit.

There is, however, a different aspect of the poet as voyeur that is worth mentioning. Unheard, Lydgate hears the truth about the knight. That truth is precisely *trouthe*: fidelity, integrity. The thought of his *compleynt* turns on the opposition between the true and the false. The knight is a true lover, but his lady rejects him because he has been falsely accused of being false to her. The words true and false are absent from the poem before the *compleynt*, but from line 242 onwards *trouthe* and associated terms such as *trwe*, *vntrwe* and *untrouthe* occur over fifty times, and *fals* and associated terms such as *falshed*, *falsnes*, *falsly*, over twenty times. Like Chaucer's Troilus (v 1706–8), the knight appeals to God, who is Himself Truth, to vindicate his *trouthe*:

> Now God that art of Trouth[e] souereyn,
> And *seest* how I lye for trouthe bounde,
> So sore knytte in Loves firy cheyn ...
> Consider and *se* in thyn eternal *sight*
> How that myn hert professed whilom was
> For to be trwe. ...   (288–90, 295–7)

Later he repeats the appeal to 'God that knowest the thoght of euery wyght / Ryght a[s] hit is, in [al] thing thou maist *se*' (540–1), now asking Him, if he should die of grief, at least to ensure that his lady recognizes his *trouthe*. Lydgate knows the truth about the knight only through the medium of overheard speech, while God, whose gaze penetrates all things including human thoughts, knows it directly; but the parallel is faintly present between the poet's ear and God's all-seeing eye, and, if the poem reaches the 'princess' of the envoy, the knight's prayer will be answered, and his cruel lady will indeed know his *trouthe*. There is an analogy, unlikely but real, between the poet cowering in the bushes and God seeing all things from his concealment in the heavens.

Finally, Lydgate's epilogue is worth one word more. The poem began on a May morning, but by the time the knight's *compleynt* is over evening has fallen, marked by a passage beautifully evoking the effect of evening light, in a verbal equivalent to some of the most exquisite achievements of fifteenth-century manuscript illumination:

> the sunne his ark divrnall
> Ipassed was so that his persaunt lyght,
> His bryght[e] bemes and his stremes all
> W[e]re in the wawes of the water fall,
> Vnder the bordure of our occean
> His chare of gold his course so swyftly ran,
>
> And while the twilyght and the rowes rede
> Of Phebus lyght were deaurat a lyte,
> A penne I toke ...   (590–8)

Like miniaturists such as the Boucicaut Master, the poet combines colouring that imitates nature with gold leaf that reflects light back at the reader so that the page is indeed *deaurat* (a Lydgatean coinage), gilded over. Lydgate explains that he seized a pen and copied down the *compleynt*

> Worde by worde as he dyd endyte,
> Lyke as I herde and coud him tho reporte,   (600–1)

and he emphasizes yet again that he is a mere copyist, apologizing if he has *mys-reported* anything (605). Venus appears as the evening star, and Lydgate prays her to assist the knight by influencing his lady to pity him. The poet goes home to bed, and neatly brings the poem to an end by extending nightfall inside it to nightfall outside it, praying that the true lovers to whom it is addressed may gain their ladies' favour 'er the sun tomorow be ryse[n] newe' (655). There is a kind of cosiness about this conclusion that seems to expunge the poet's earlier shame. Lydgate goes safely to bed in his monastic cell, freed from the unconvincing love-melancholy of the prologue and from the indignity of his role as *écouteur*. The lover may be a secular Saint Sebastian, as he described himself in his *compleynt*, with Cupid's arrows sticking in his side (438), but to Lydgate this is ultimately a matter of aesthetic pleasure rather than personal concern. To describe a Saint Sebastian is surely more comfortable than to be one. The poem is full of sharp, dangerous, potentially phallic weapons, including Phoebus's 'persaunt lyght' (591), Cupid's arrows, and God's penetrating gaze; but as night falls and the sun's rays drop into the ocean, the only such weapon remaining is the harmless scrivener's pen.

CHAPTER 12

The Palice of Honour and The Goldyn Targe

In this chapter I shall examine two Scottish dream-poems, both dating from around 1500, both examples of love-allegory in the tradition of Chaucer and Lydgate, and both written by poets associated with the court of James IV of Scotland who were also clerics bound to celibacy. In both the poet represents himself as hiding in order to spy on a pagan celebration of love, and as being dragged out of his concealment to be ridiculed and punished by female deities. The poet's lowly role as a mere observer is intensified by his clerical status, which forbids him to do more than watch, but this also heightens his sense of the otherness of female sexuality and thus his curiosity about it and his investment of feeling in watching and then in being watched. The first is Gavin Douglas's *Palice of Honour*. Douglas, a younger son of the earl of Angus, was also a *clerk* who received an advanced formal education and took holy orders. The date of his ordination is unknown, but he was dean of Dunkeld by 1497, provost of St Giles' in Edinburgh by 1503, and bishop of Dunkeld in 1515, having narrowly failed to gain the archbishopric of St Andrews. *The Palice of Honour* can be dated fairly exactly to 1501.[1] Though looking is of importance throughout its 2169 lines, I shall concentrate on the first of the three parts into which it is divided. *The Palice of Honour* belongs, and is highly conscious of belonging, to the tradition of dream-allegory going back to the *Roman de la Rose*. The examples that Douglas knew best were probably Chaucer's dream-poems and those of Chaucer's fifteenth-century successors such as Lydgate in England and Henryson and Dunbar in Scotland. In many ways the *Palice* resembles an elaborate revision and completion of Chaucer's unfinished *House of Fame*; both are poems in three books, in which a poet is carried on a heavenly journey to the dwelling of fame or honour, and both focus on the themes of fame and poetry.

Since the *Palice* is not widely known, it may be helpful to begin with a summary.² In a waking prologue, Douglas, entering a paradisal garden, hears a mysterious voice singing in praise of May, is frightened by it, and then falls into an 'extasie or swoun' (106)³ and has a dream. In Book I, we learn more of the hideous desert landscape in which his dream begins: elaborated from the desert Chaucer enters at the end of Book I of *The House of Fame*, it is the very opposite of the garden of the prologue. He sees the company of Minerva, 'the Quene of Sapience' (241), riding by, but also her disreputable hangers-on, the traitors Sinon and Achitophel, who explain that the procession is making for the palace of Honour. Next he sees the company of Diana, goddess of chastity, making for the same goal. Third he sees the court of Venus. Douglas has been hiding timorously in an oak stump, but now he cannot resist singing a song cursing Venus and Cupid. Venus hears it and Douglas is dragged out of hiding and put on trial for blasphemy. His objections to her jurisdiction are overruled, and as he waits in terror for her to pronounce sentence Book I abruptly ends.

At the beginning of Book II, rescue comes, in the form of yet another court, that of rhetoric, headed by the muse Calliope. Just as in the Prologue to *The Legend of Good Women* Chaucer is saved from Cupid's anger with his writings by the intercession of Alcestis, so Douglas is saved by Calliope's intercession. She assures Venus that Douglas is such a fool that he can do nothing to damage her honour, and Venus releases him into Calliope's custody. The rest of the poem is concerned with the poetic vocation and with honour as its goal. With a nymph as his guide, Douglas is sent on a tour of the heavens and then reaches a mountain up which he has to scramble to reach Honour's palace. There he sees Venus again in an outer court, and looking in her mirror he gives an account of all the stories it reflects. Venus hands him a book to translate – presumably the *Aeneid*, since Aeneas was Venus's son, and Douglas's best-known poem is his superb translation of Virgil's poem into Scots. The nymph pushes him through the gate of the palace proper (like Africanus shoving Chaucer through the garden gate in *The Parliament of Fowls*), and he catches a dazzling glimpse of God himself inside the closed hall. The nymph explains that in God's eyes true honour is not earthly fame but virtue. (Perhaps that is Douglas's guess at what the 'man of gret auctorite' who appears in the final line of *The House of Fame* might have said if Chaucer had completed the poem.) Douglas wishes he could see more, but the nymph tells him to take a break first, by visiting a garden where the Muses are gathering the flowers of rhetoric. On the way there, he falls off a log crossing a moat, and the fall wakes him from his dream. He ends the poem by dedicating it to James IV as the source of earthly honour, an act that may possibly have got him made provost of St Giles'.

This strange work is perhaps best understood as a young poet's demonstration of his virtuosity, and especially of the encyclopaedic knowledge of poetic tradition, rhetoric, mythology and science that was regarded as a necessary qualification for the poetic career as defined by scholars from Petrarch and Boccaccio onwards. Douglas read Boccaccio's *De genealogia deorum gentilium*, a manifesto of the Renaissance conception of learned poetry, and both Petrarch and Boccaccio appear among Calliope's followers in Part II of the *Palice* (though, like other learned English poets between Chaucer and Wyatt, Douglas probably knew only their Latin works).[4] The poem thus becomes a dream of the poetic career itself, but one involving much self-mockery. At its centre, inevitably, is Douglas, as poet but also as cleric. What is most interesting for my purpose about *The Palice of Honour* is Douglas's self-presentation, which is, manifestly, a presentation of himself as poet: a poem gets him into trouble with Venus, she refuses to release him to Calliope until he has composed another poem in her praise, and the *Palice* looks forward to the translation of the *Aeneid* that was to be the crown of Douglas's poetic achievement.

In *Troilus and Criseyde*, as we have seen, Chaucer gives us some encouragement to think of him as a voyeur, comparable to Pandarus, the literal voyeur who is his surrogate within the fiction. *The Manciple's Tale* can be read as a sourer and more disillusioned treatment of the love-poet as voyeur, a caged bird hanging in the bedroom, who reports what he sees but can take no part in it. In *The Parliament of Fowls* Chaucer is more explicitly reduced to the role of voyeur in his own dream as, under the sovereignty of Priapus, he watches Venus doing her languorous striptease. In these poems and others, Chaucer deliberately adopts the role of a love-poet who has no personal experience of love; he purports to write for courtiers to whom love is a natural and appropriate activity, but is himself no more than a reader and observer. In Lydgate's *Complaynt of a Loveres Lyfe* we saw how he, as a priest and monk, emphasized more strongly the poet's role as fascinated but excluded and concealed

onlooker, and betrayed a stronger sense of the embarrassing nature
of that role for the poet. Lydgate explicitly insists on the fittingness
of his reporting what he has heard and seen, even while on the level
of mythological allusion he is reminding us – perhaps unconsciously
reminding himself – of what disastrous things can happen to those
who watch or are watched. (Several copies of Lydgate's *Complaynt*
survive in Scottish versions;[5] it is a poem that Douglas almost
certainly knew.) The remaining late-medieval poets I shall discuss –
Douglas, Dunbar, Skelton – were all priests as well as courtiers, and
so all had similar motives for representing themselves as voyeurs in
their relationship to the major theme of courtly poetry: sexual love.

Douglas's situation was a particularly contradictory one: unlike
Chaucer or Lydgate, he was of the high rank for which love was the
appropriate activity, yet it was inappropriate to his priestly profession. This is a possible explanation of his strange and otherwise
unexplained comically shameful behaviour in the prologue to *The
Palice of Honour*. In the springtime landscape of love, with its
dew-covered flowers, sweet scents, singing birds, crystal streams,
grasshoppers and bees, and even olive trees (an index of the
description's literary origin), he hears a voice singing in praise of
May as 'rute and augment of curage [sexual desire]' (82), who
should be praised and honoured by those 'that constranit ar in luifis
rage' (86). Every detail seems governed by the appropriate courtly
decorum, and yet Douglas's response is one of inexplicable unease
and even terror:

> And with that word I raisit my visage,
> Soir affrayit, half in ane frenesie.
>
> 'O Nature, Quene, and O ʒe lustie May,'
> Quod I tho, 'how lang sall I thus foruay,
> Quhilk ʒow and Venus in this garth deseruis?
> Recounsell me out of this greit affray,
> That I may sing ʒow laudis day be day.
> ʒe that all mundane creaturis preseruis
> Comfort ʒour man that in this fanton steruis,
> With spreit arraisit and euerie wit away,
> Quaiking for feir, baith pulsis, vane and neruis.'   (89–99)

These lines might be interpreted as alluding, like the prologues to
The Book of the Duchess and *A Complaynt of a Loveres Lyfe*, simply to the
speaker's lack of success in love, which puts him out of harmony
with the season; but his disturbance seems excessive – almost as if

anticipating the 'neuraesthenia' of *The Waste Land*, with its mixing of memory and desire in spring and its fear of 'The awful daring of a moment's surrender'. The idealized landscape is described in the opening stanzas as Flora's 'tender bed' (4) and 'heuinly bed' (11), and May, the traditional season for the rites of love, the season that brings Venus's triumph over Mars (83), is praised as 'Maternall Moneth, Lady and Maistres' (65). The sound of the song may be 'amiabill' (102), but the effect on Douglas of all these dangerous female influences, stirring his sexual feelings, is to weaken his masculine powers of resistance: 'As feminine so feblit fell I doun' (108). Masculine identity, especially as defined in the clerical tradition, depends on the rejection of female temptation, whether it comes from Venus or Eve; when that rejection is weakened, the consequence for the male is loss of potency. Douglas, 'With spreit arraisit [snatched away] and euerie wit away' (98), collapses into the bushes in a daze that he explains as caused by 'ouir excelland licht' (113), and has his dream. No more in the dream than in this prologue can we forget the poet's own position as watcher and listener, because he cannot forget it: we see and interpret what he sees, but we also see him seeing it – and then being drawn into it in a position of severe disadvantage.

Part I begins with a stanza in which Douglas urges on his barren wit to reveal the shameful content of his vision: 'Schaw now thy schame, schaw now thy bad nystie' (129). The shame and folly defined in these lines are the physical and spiritual weakness revealed in his collapse and its consequences, but also the impotence of poetic craft, the 'beggit termis' (131) and 'dull, exhaust Inanitie' (133) revealed in the poem he makes out of his experience. Behind the parallels lies an unspoken identification of the pen with the phallus, which we shall notice elsewhere in these poems by courtly clerics. Douglas is horrified by the transformation of a paradisal landscape into 'This wildernes abhominabill and waist' (155) and of spring into winter, 'Ver translait in winter furious' (190). Instead of being in a garden by 'beriall stremis' (53) he is now 'Amyd a Forest by a hyddeous flude' (123), and instead of birds 'Melodiously makand thair kindlie gleis' (23) there are now – the height of unnaturalness – 'fisch ʒelland as eluis' in the 'laithlie flude' (145–6). The nightmarish scene, 'In quhome nathing was nature comfortand' (150), nevertheless bears a certain resemblance to Douglas's native landscape and weather at their most inclement, and he

evokes with incomparable force not only the scene itself but its effect
on him, turning him from a man into a cowering animal: 'Out throw
the wod I crap on fute and hand' (160).

In three stanzas set off from the rest of the poem by having ten
lines instead of nine, Douglas laments the change as a typical
product of the turning of Fortune's wheel. Then, awaiting death
(193), he hears a noise 'As heird of beistis stamping with loud cry'
(196), and, overcome by his fears,

> Amid a stock richt priuelie I stall,
> Quhair luikand out anone I did espy
> Ane lustie rout of beistis rationall   (199–201)

– an unexpectedly orderly procession of ladies and gentlemen riding
hackneys 'Full soberlie' (205) and 'with stabilnes ygroundit' (210),
with a gorgeously dressed queen drawn in a triumphal chariot
amidst them. They pass by, 'And I abaid alone within the tre' (228).
Here we have all the essentials of the poet as voyeur: fearful
concealment, secrecy, impotence, and spying. He stays hidden once
the procession has disappeared – 'And I remanand in the tre alone'
(230) – until the two traitors ride up, and then he emerges from his
tree-stump to ask who they are and 'quhat signifieis ʒone rout'
(238). They explain that Minerva is surrounded by sybils and wise
women, including the heroic murderesses Judith and Jael, and by
'Clarkis diuine with problewmis curius' (249), both pagans and
Jews. Her procession is on its way 'throw out this wildernes / To the
Palice of Honour' (263–4); Achitophel and Sinon (again a pagan
and a Jew) accompany it, like storms in May, as men who have used
their wisdom to ill ends; they have no expectation of entering
Honour's palace but hope only to see it. Their final message before
riding off is that the courts of Diana and Venus are approaching.
With this, Douglas goes back into hiding:

> And I agane, maist like ane Elriche grume,
> Crap in the muskane Aikin stok misharrit.   (299–300)

He knows how degraded his position is – 'Thus wretchitlie I maid
my residence' (301) – but is too frightened to do otherwise.

Douglas, 'Remanand thus within the tre all lokkin' (313), looks
eagerly, as any courtly poet would, for the appearance of Venus, but
instead he sees a sign that has become very familiar to us: a 'Hart
transformit' (316) by Diana's anger. The mythological reference is
explicated in detail:

> I knew the signe
> Was Acteon, quhilk Diane nakid waitit,
> Bathing in a well and eik hir Madynnis ӡing.
> The Goddes was commouit at this thing,
> And him in forme hes of ane Hart translatit.
> I saw, allace, his houndis at him slatit.
> Bakwert he blent to giue thame knawledgeing.
> Thay raif thair Lord, misknew him at them batit.   (320–7)

This retelling of Ovid's story identifies Actaeon's offence as that of spying on the naked goddess; now Douglas watches Diana's vengeance on the archetypal watcher. I suggest that, as in Lydgate's *Complaynt*, an apparently gratuitous treatment of Actaeon functions as a figure or symptom of the poet's sense of the shame and peril of his own voyeuristic position in his poem. Diana's procession consists of the goddess herself on an elephant ('an animal ... which has no desire to copulate'),[6] with ladies dressed as foresters, and famous virgins – few in number, as Douglas slyly notes – 'Baith of the new and the auld Testament' (344). Once more, he says, 'All on thay raid and left me in the tre' (345).

Now Douglas further describes the horrors of the landscape and his own dazed condition. He hears distant music, and rambles on about how sound carries over water but not in it, and how few fish have ears. He pulls himself up short – 'Aneuch of this – I not quhat it may mene' (382) – in a way that simultaneously illustrates the encyclopaedic ambition of the Humanist conception of poetry, makes fun of his own unsuitability for the role of visionary poet, and, in doing so, discourages us from taking that role itself too seriously. Chaucer in *The House of Fame* had also expounded the physics of sound, conveying a similar uneasy ambivalence towards Dante as a model for the learned and inspired vernacular poet. Douglas reminds us that he has been relating 'quhat I had hard or sene' (385); now he first hears an angelic harmony and then

> Of the maist plesand Court I had a sicht
> In warld adoun sen Adam was creat.   (401–2)

This is what he has been waiting for, the court of Venus, which seems 'a thing Celestiall' (417). He describes at length the splendour of her chariot, her horses, her person, and the accompanying blind archer who enables him to identify her as the goddess of love. Two elements in this passage are especially significant. One is the emphasis on sight. It is Venus's look, not that of the male watcher, that exercises mastery. Her beauty shines like the sun's, 'castand sa greit ane glance, / All fairheid it opprest baith far and neir' (452–3), and it is so brilliant that

> For to behald my sicht micht not Indure,
> Mair nor the bricht Sone may the Bakkis Ee.   (461–2)

Yet it exercises an irresistible fascination: 'Thair was na wicht that gat a sicht, eschewit' (466), suffering wounds and becoming her servant. The goddess's eyes hold such mastery that

> For blenkis sweit nane passit vnpersewit,
> Bot gif he wer preseruit as thir Sanctis.   (470–1)

The exchange of glances which is the basis of sexual love is ravishing, irresistible, and dangerous. The second element follows from this; once Cupid has been mentioned, and thus Venus herself has been identified, Douglas says much more about the dangers of the love she embodies: Cupid is 'maist dissauabill', Venus's court is 'variabill' and 'eirdly lufe ... sendill standis stabill' (482–5). The attitude Douglas represents himself as holding towards sexual love is deeply engaged but strongly ambivalent: he knows what clerks know about its perils, but he also finds that, just by looking, he is fixed and wounded by Venus's looks.

Next comes another excursus in praise of the music of Venus's choir, with variations 'soung and playit be sair cunning Menstrall / On lufe Ballatis' (497–8). To this music 'baith heuin and eird resoundit' (516); the godly is mixed with the ungodly throughout the whole panegyric. Venus is accompanied by Mars, gazing at her – 'Behaldand Venus, "O 3e, my lufe," he sang' (559) – and, like the Venus of Chaucer's *Parliament of Fowls*, by all the other famous lovers of history and legend, and by a huge courtly company of 'euerie kinde and age' (598), garlanded and singing joyfully. This provokes Douglas himself to sing his opposing song, marked off by a second group of three ten-line stanzas. He urges his heart to 'Complene thy paneful cairis Infinite' (609), and the song is indeed a 'complaint of a lover's life' such as Lydgate overhears, except that it goes beyond lamenting his own misery to condemn all worldly felicity and to curse Cupid and Venus themselves: 'Wo worth Cupyd and wo worth fals Venus!' (634). From a love-complaint it turns into a song such as a disillusioned cleric ought to sing, and yet

Douglas has not escaped from Venus's power. His singing proves to be as much a sign of folly as of courage, because his hiding-place is not impregnable.

By this intervention the voyeur has laid himself open to detection; and, as Sartre puts it, he finds his 'transcendence transcended'.[7] The privileged subjectivity of the watching narrator is stripped from him, the distance that is the price paid for looking collapses, and his vulnerability, his existence as an object for others, is forcibly revealed to him:

> Tho saw I Venus on hir lip did bite,
> And all the Court in haist thair horsis ren3eit,
> Proclamand loude, 'Quhair is 3one Poid þat plen3eit,
> Quhilk deith deseruis committand sic dispite?'
> Fra tre to tre thay seirching but respite,
> Quhil ane me fand, quhilk said – and greit disden3eit –
> 'Auant, veillane, thow reclus Imperfite!'
>
> Al in ane Feuir out of my muskane bowre
> On kneis I crap and law for feir did lowre.   (639–47)

In this ignominious situation Douglas is abused, beaten, besmeared with filth, and tormented as if by hobgoblins. '"Pluk at the Craw," thay cryit, "deplome the Ruik!"' (651): it is tempting to compare the fate of '3one Poid' Gavin Douglas with that of the poet as Apollo's crow in *The Manciple's Tale*. He is tried before Venus, Cupid and Mars for blasphemy. The idea of a trial with Venus as judge had become something of a convention in fifteenth-century French courtly poetry; whether Douglas had read any is uncertain, but he had certainly read the Prologue to *The Legend of Good Women*, where Chaucer is arraigned before Cupid for having written against the religion of love, and he had probably read *The Testament of Cresseid*, Henryson's alternative ending to *Troilus and Criseyde*, in which Cresseid is put on trial before the planetary gods for a comparable blasphemy against Venus and Cupid. Douglas's grovelling plea for mercy is refused, so he makes what legal case he can. His response calls attention precisely to his anomalous position as a courtly poet who is also a priest: the courtly poet writes in the service of ladies and submits himself and his writings to their judgment, but Douglas claims that no lady is allowed to be a judge, and that, as a 'spirituall man' (697), he can only be tried by an ecclesiastical court. Since Venus is judge in her own case, it is not surprising that her *Interlocuture*, or interim judgment on the validity of his objections, is

far from *gratious* (701), and, blaming him and all clerks for their
blasphemies against her servants, she points out that by his very
presence he has submitted to her authority. Venus is surely right –
after all, what can a priest be doing eagerly spying on the goddess of
love and her company from a tree-stump? Douglas is indeed, as
Venus claims, a 'reclus Imperfite', imperfect in the double sense
that his concealment is inadequate and that he has not fully
detached himself from the worldly love he spies on. He vividly
describes his terror, writhing within his skin as he awaits sentence,
fearing to be transformed into some monstrous beast, and often
looking at his hand and feeling his face to see whether the metamorphosis has occurred. We remember the transformation of the
landscape from paradisal to hellish at the beginning of the dream,
and the fact that he crawled through it on all fours. Douglas recalls
mythological instances of such transformations, and it is surely not
by accident that the first of them is once again that of Actaeon
(745–6), punished not for blasphemy but for voyeurism. Book I of
The Palice of Honour ends with the poet in this fearful state of
suspense; and there I leave him to turn to William Dunbar's *Goldyn
Targe*.

Dunbar, like Douglas, had noble connections (though less close
ones) and a university education. Like Chaucer, he was a diplomat
as well as a poet, and in 1501 he visited England in connection with
negotiations for the marriage of James IV to Henry VII's daughter
Margaret Tudor; like Chaucer too, he was the recipient of a royal
pension. Like Lydgate and Douglas, he was a priest, ordained not
later than 1504. He was a court poet, the author of a large number of
mainly short, often occasional poems, many presumably written in
response to commissions, and revealing little individual personality.
He worked within a long-established and largely autonomous poetic
tradition, consciously literary in its interests and themes,
consciously looking back over a poetic history that, in English,
began with Chaucer, and that shared Chaucer's sense of having its
remoter origins in classical antiquity. The Chaucer Dunbar looked
back to, like the Chaucer Lydgate looked back to, was the author of
courtly poems in an elevated style: the first author of such poems in
English, but owing a large debt to an earlier French tradition
represented especially by the *Roman de la Rose*. I know of no evidence
that Dunbar had any direct acquaintance with Chaucer's Italian
reading, and apart from the *Roman de la Rose* itself he may have

possessed little knowledge of Chaucer's French sources. He did know some of the work of Chaucer's English successors, and especially of Lydgate, the most admired of them. The nine-line stanza in which *The Goldyn Targe* is written is also the staple of Douglas's *Palice of Honour*; both borrowed it from Chaucer's *Anelida and Arcite*, a work that displays at its highest the technical virtuosity that was one of the Chaucerian achievements most admired by his late-medieval followers. In both *The Goldyn Targe* and *The Palice of Honour*, the effect is appropriately processional and pageant-like, each stanza marking a new stage in the emblematic display of meaning. Meaning manifests itself as fixed, visible and labelled; since both poems are dream-allegories, meaning is observed and transmitted by the poet as dreamer; but in Dunbar's poem as in Douglas's the poet begins as a hidden voyeur, only to be dislodged from this privileged yet shameful position, to become part of a meaning that he no longer merely observes but suffers.[8]

I shall begin examining *The Goldyn Targe* not at the beginning but with the dream, which commences at line 49. Most of the dream forms an allegorical narrative that is manifestly dependent on the *Roman de la Rose*. It is much more compressed than the *Roman*, and it can afford to be, precisely because the *Roman* and its tradition were so well known: its doctrines and allegorical method had come to be constitutive assumptions of courtly poetry. So Guillaume's leisurely exposition can be reduced to shorthand, to give the effect of a production script for a court masque, in which the figures have only to be identified for their meaning to become plain. *The Goldyn Targe* was not intended for performance – it includes a strong emphasis on its own textuality – but it does offer a poetic equivalent to the kind of masque, mumming or disguising that might really have been performed at James IV's court.[9]

The dream opens with a ship appearing, as if it were a piece of masque machinery. (In England only a few years earlier, Skelton had set his dream-allegory *The Bowge of Court* on board a ship.) From the ship disembark a company of 'Ane hundreth ladyes' (58),[10] enticing creatures with white breasts and slender waists and their hair hanging loose. They include all imaginable female deities – classical goddesses, the muse Clio, Fortune, spring months – ruled over by two goddesses who play crucial parts in the *Roman*, 'Nature and Venus, quene and quene' (73). Nature presents May with a gown, and the birds greet Nature and Flora and sing 'ballettis in lufe' (103) to Venus; and meanwhile Dunbar secretly watches all this, 'Quhare that I lay, ouerhelit wyth levis ronk' (93). But now another company appears, consisting of male deities, led by another dominant figure from the *Roman*,

> Cupide the king wyth bow in hand ybent
> And dredefull arowis grundyn scharp and square.   (110–11)

They too play and sing, and then the male and female companies join in a dance. If the poem is envisaged as corresponding to an imagined courtly entertainment, this dance in which the sexes are first separate and then mingle together is a natural enough part of it; but, at the same time, given the way the figures are labelled as pagan gods and goddesses, and the leading ones are Nature, Venus and Cupid, it also resembles a fertility rite. At any rate, Dunbar finds it dangerously exciting, and desires a closer look:

> Than crap I throu the levis and drew nere,
> Quhare that I was rycht sudaynly affrayt,
> All throu a luke, quhilk I have boucht full dere.   (133–5)

The mere wish to look proves to be his downfall: he does not even sing a song that annoys Venus.

Behind the perilous look there lies, of course, the metaphor of 'falling in love' as a wound received by the heart through the eye. In the *Romaunt of the Rose* Swete-Loking carries Cupid's arrows for him, and once Amant has looked into the well of Narcissus and selected his rosebud Cupid fires them at him one after another. Amant does something to provoke this attack – he is at least eager to enter the garden – but Dunbar is completely passive: the mythological processions come to him, he seeks to do nothing *but* look, yet he immediately becomes the victim of terrifying female aggression. He is not completely innocent, however; this really is scopophilia in its Freudian sense, and it is precisely his voyeuristic longing that gets him into trouble. Luther himself could not have given a more exact diagnosis of how clerical celibacy is likely to lead to sexual obsession. Venus catches a glimpse of him as he crouches ignominiously in the foliage, and has him arrested by her archers:

> And schortly for to speke, be lufis quene
> I was aspyit. Scho bad hir archearis kene
> Go me arrest, and thay no tyme delayit.
> Than ladyes fair lete fall thair mantillis gren,
> With bowis big in tressit hairis schene
> All sudaynly thay had a felde arayit.   (136–41)

Whereas in the *Romaunt* the aggression attributed to female sexuality was allegorized as male, here it is presented much more directly. Venus's ladies are an Amazonian bodyguard in green livery, and, like so many female flashers, they let fall their mantles to reveal their terrifying weapons. They are phallicized females; and Dunbar finds their assault pleasant enough at first, 'A wonder lusty bikkir' (144). The archers personify female attractions, with Beauty (the first arrow with which Cupid attacked Guillaume in the *Romaunt*) at their head. Against them, Dunbar's only ally is Reason – again a key figure in the *Romaunt*, and an opponent of Cupid and Venus. But whereas Guillaume's Reason was a female teacher, here he is male and a 'nobil chevallere' (153), defending the poet with his golden shield. The opposition between male and female is much more rigid and explicit than in the *Romaunt*, in accordance with Dunbar's clerical status.

Venus launches a series of attacks on the helpless Dunbar with her *artilye*, a Scots word for artillery that may also suggest the feminine artfulness allegorized by Venus's weapons. The series has a specific meaning: it represents the increasing threat posed by female sexuality to male rationality as the female grows up, from a girl to a woman to a lady of high rank capable of exercising all her wiles. First comes 'Tender Youth' (154) with her virgin followers Innocence, Bashfulness, Timidity and Obedience, but they do little damage to the golden shield because 'Curage in thame was noucht begonne to spring' (158). (*Curage*, as courage and as sexual desire, again bridges the gap between the allegorical narrative and its sexual meaning.) Then 'Swete Womanhede' (160) attacks, with her more mature supporters such as Good Breeding (*Nurture*), Humility (*Lawlynes*), Self-Control (*Contenence*), and so on for four more lines; their arrows damage Dunbar a little, but still Reason's shield protects him. Next 'Hie Degree' enters the battle (172), assisted by the concomitants of the aristocratic lady such as *Estate* (social rank), Will, Wantonness, and Wealth – again no more than a list is needed to complete this part of the diagram. Their arrows rain down like hail, but they too are repulsed. Finally Venus decides that the only way to overcome Reason's shield is to appoint *Dissymilance* (dissimulation), 'of doubilnes the rute' (184), as leader of her next attack. Dissymilance chooses as her archers *Presence* (187, the attraction exerted by physical closeness), *Fair Callyng* (188, fair greeting, the Bialacoil of the *Romaunt*), *Cherising* (189), and *Hamelynes* (190, familiarity), and she brings Beauty once more into the field (192).

These enticing female qualities are the most dangerous of all, but still Reason maintains a skilful defence, until Presence manages to get close enough to throw a powder in his eyes that blinds him. Sight is the medium of erotic assault, but it is also, by contrast with the less noble senses of contact, the means of rational defence, and it has now been lost. This is the sixteenth-century equivalent of chemical warfare – against the Geneva Convention, perhaps, but in 'love' all's fair. The meaning of the allegory is obviously that even the most rational man cannot resist a woman's attraction once she gets near enough; and Reason is sent staggering off 'as drunkyn man' (204) to be made a fool of by these ruthless Amazons.

Dunbar, captured, becomes the prisoner of Beauty. The lover as prisoner is a time-honoured metaphor in courtly poetry, but here it is only one element in an extended allegory of love as warfare. To become beauty's prisoner means to be captivated by a beautiful woman; but love is hardly the word for the aggression to which Dunbar has fallen prey, or for his entirely passive response to it. At first, he thinks Beauty even lovelier once Reason has been blinded; but Dunbar intervenes, stepping outside the experience of the dream (as Guillaume does several times in the *Romaunt*) to indicate its true, retrospective meaning:

> Quhy was thou blyndit, Resoun, quhi allace?
> And gert ane hell my paradise appere,
> And mercy seme quhare that I fand no grace.   (214–16)

What seems a paradisal experience is really a hell, what seems like the lady's mercy is really its opposite.[11] These are the literal consequences of Reason's allegorical defeat. Dunbar rapidly becomes more deeply beguiled by the pretence of female favour, but as soon as 'New Acquyntance' (220) has embraced him for a moment (and how could a personification so named embrace him for longer?), she disappears for ever, and then with equal rapidity *Dangere* (223: disdain, as in the *Romaunt*) makes her appearance with hostile looks. Dangere gives way to Departing (226) – that is, presumably, the lady ceases to pay any attention to her lover at all – and Dunbar is left the prey to *Hevynesse* (227, depression) for ever. But at this moment, fortunately, Aeolus blows every sign of spring from the landscape, leaving it a mere wilderness; and this happens 'in the space of a luke' (232) – the single look embraces the entire experience of 'love'. The fierce wind, even in May, reminds us that this is a Scottish poem; unlike the hot-blooded Latins with whom the courtly tradition originated, Dunbar is protected against desire and its dangerous consequences by his native land's chilly climate. The dream-figures re-embark on the ship 'In twynklyng of ane eye' (235), and it sails away, like one of James IV's warships, firing its guns. The violent noise brings Dunbar to his feet, and, with great relief, he wakes from his nightmare.

So we can perhaps say that the celibate poet's doomed fascination with sex is revealed as a mere fantasy. If on one level *The Goldyn Targe* is a textualization of the kind of allegorical masque that was performed before James IV, it can be interpreted as a warning to the king, a notorious philanderer, not to let female attractions overcome his reason.[12] On a primary level, though, this is Dunbar's dream; no royal philandering occurs in it, but rather it is composed of the anxieties and fears that might haunt a celibate cleric's unconscious and find censored expression as allegory in his dreams. It might seem safer for Dunbar to stick to poetry; and *The Goldyn Targe* is as much about poetry as it is about love, for in the courtly tradition the two themes are inextricably linked. If we now return to the waking prologue, we find the poet rising from bed just as the evening star and the moon go to sleep, and settling himself down by a rosebush. The landscape is evidently that of the *Romaunt of the Rose*, but it is also, more obviously than there, a landscape of art, a garden of the flowers of rhetoric. Nature is described in terms of the artifices of human culture: the evening-star and moon have 'gone to bed' (2); the rising sun is 'the goldyn candill matutyne' (4) and Phoebus wearing a 'purpur cape' (7); the lark is 'hevyns menstrale' (8); the birds are singing matins (10); the leaves concealing them are 'courtyns grene into thair bouris' (11); the field is 'Anamalit ... wyth all colouris' (13); the dew is 'perly droppis' (14), the 'cristall teris' (17) shed by Aurora (the dawn) when Phoebus (the sun) rises and leaves her – tears which he then 'drank up wyth his hete' for love of her (18); and the birds singing matins reappear as 'Venus chapell clerkis' (21). This consciously artificial effect of painting and gilding, enamelling and bejewelling, is common enough in late-medieval poetry, but I know of no other passage where it is so concentrated and intense. Dunbar is not just following the poetic tradition inherited from Chaucer and Lydgate, he is pushing it to the utmost extreme, so that, in effect, it becomes its own subject: style is thematized. Also, as the natural landscape is humanized, it is sexualized too, with the repeated hints of beds and bedrooms, and especially perhaps in that disturbingly powerful image of the sun drying the dew as Apollo drinking Aurora's tears. It seems likely enough that a poet falling asleep in such an eroticized landscape should dream of a mating dance of pagan deities and then of irresistible and destructive sexual temptation.

The final touch in this humanization and sexualization of the landscape comes when Dunbar falls asleep on 'Florais mantill' (48), that is, among the spring flowers. Then he dreams; and in the dream-world the process is reversed, and instead of nature described in terms of culture we have cultural artifice described in natural terms. The ship's sail is 'als quhite as blossom upon spray' (51); its topcastle is 'brycht as the stern of day' (52); it approaches land 'As falcoun swift desyrouse of hir pray' (54). The ladies are 'Als fresch as flouris that in May up spredis' (59), their waists are as slender as young branches (63), and they themselves are 'lilies quhite' covering the fields (65). The reversal from one type of metaphor to its opposite is so systematic as to indicate intentionality; and indeed the distinction between the two closely resembles that drawn by Geoffroi de Vinsauf in the *Poetria nova* between two types of *translatio* (metaphor), one that speaks of the human in non-human terms (snowy teeth), and another that speaks of the non-human in human terms (spring paints the earth with flowers).[13] At this point, sure enough, Dunbar inserts a stanza using the latter example and explicitly referring to the powers and limits of the arts of poetry and rhetoric:

> Discrive I wald, bot quho coud wele endyte
> How all the feldis wyth thai lilies quhite
> Depaynt war brycht, quhilk to the heven did glete?
> Noucht thou, Omer, als fair as thou coud wryte,
> For all thine ornate stilis so perfyte,
> Nor yit thou, Tullius, quhois lippis swete
> Of rethorike did into termes flete.
> Your aureate tongis both bene all to lyte
> For to compile that paradise complete.   (64–72)

In this modesty-topos he claims to be unable to describe what he has just described; not even Homer or Cicero, representing classical poetry and rhetoric, would have had the skill to 'compile' the paradisal world of his dream.

Even during the dream's action, Dunbar's role as poet is never quite forgotten: the female deities include 'My lady Cleo, that help of makaris bene' (77) and the male deities include Mercury 'Of rethorike that fand the flouris faire' (117). The end of the dream reveals that the poet's erotic fantasy, however nightmarish, is as fragile as the literary conventions used to express it. The dream vanishes with a blast of wind which at once provides power for the ship to depart and strips the landscape of its rhetorical flowers, revealing that the paradise of love is really a wilderness. Yet when Dunbar wakes, it is to find himself in a 'real' landscape that fully restores the springtime convention – no wind or gunfire, but only singing birds, sunshine, and balmy air. And, needless to say, this reality is itself a form of rhetorical artifice, 'depaynt wyth flouris ying' (248) and made red and white with 'Naturis nobil fresch anamalyng' (251).

It is appropriate, then, that Dunbar should now reintroduce the literary tradition more explicitly, in its medieval English form of 'reverend Chaucere' (253), 'morall Gower' and 'Ludgate laureate' (262). In the two stanzas devoted to praising these writers, traditional representatives of the courtly and learned tradition of native poetry, the terms applied to poets and poetry correspond with an exactness that must surely be deliberate to those that described the garden where Dunbar originally fell asleep. Chaucer is now a 'flour imperiall', the 'rose of rethoris all' (253–4), corresponding to the 'rosis yong' (22) on the *rosere* (3) by which Dunbar rested in the garden. Chaucer's 'fresch anamalit termes celicall' (257) recall the field 'Anamalit ... wyth all colouris' (13); and those fresh, enamelled, celestial terms might have 'illumynit' (258) Dunbar's subject-matter as the leaves in the garden were 'enlumynit' with reflections (45). Chaucer surpasses all earthly poets 'Alls fer as Mayis morow dois mydnycht' (261), a reminder of the 'morow' in May on which the poem begins (9). Gower and Lydgate, speaking with 'angel mouthis' (265), correspond to the birds singing 'Full angellike' (10) in the garden; their eloquence has 'ourgilt' (267) the native tongue, just as the brilliant heaven 'Ourgilt' the garden foliage (27); and their 'goldyn pennis' (268) are analogous to the 'goldyn candill' of the sun (4). The rose-garden of love has now been fully redefined as a garden of poetic language; and one begins to suspect, looking back, that the *colouris* with which the field was enamelled (13) were, precisely, the colours of rhetoric. And indeed, in the final stanza, where Dunbar addresses his book, like Chaucer at the end of *Troilus and Criseyde* and Lydgate at the end of the *Complaynt of a Loveres Lyfe*, he says,

> I knaw quhat thou of rethorike hes spent;
> Off all hir lusty rosis redolent
> Is none into thy gerland sett on hicht.   (274–6)

I know how you have striven to show all the eloquence you have, but none of all her splendid fragrant roses is set on high in your garland.

The roses of love have now become definitively those of the rhetoric of love-poetry.

This is what makes Dunbar's role as voyeur less dangerous than it might seem. The erotic attraction with which he deals in *The Goldyn Targe* is imagined as no more than a fiction, a dream less real than the realm of verbal artifice which is his true home. In the dream, he is drawn out of his concealment by the female glance that intercepts his surreptitious male gaze; but in the waking world he modestly urges his poem to avoid the same danger of seeing and being seen:[14]

> Eschame tharof and draw the out of sicht.
> Rude is thy wede, disteynit, bare and rent,
> Wele aucht thou be aferit of the licht.   (277–9)

Yet if the poem has readers – and why else should it be written? – it will suffer the same fate of being seen while attempting concealment that it describes as being undergone by its poet. *The Goldyn Targe* is a hall of mirrors, in which art and nature watch each other in never-ending reflections – an idea that Dunbar himself suggests when he writes of the 'secund bemys' (32), the reflections of reflections that illuminate the branches overhanging the river. Who is to say which is the real wilderness, the one revealed when Aeolus blows the leaves from the dream-landscape –

> All was hyne went, thare was bot wildernes,
> Thare was no more bot birdis, bank and bruke   (233–4)

– the one that was the state of English poetry before Chaucer, Gower and Lydgate illuminated it –

> This ile before was bare and desolate
> Of rethorike or lusty fresch endyte   (269–70)

– or that of Dunbar's own poem, 'disteynit, bare and rent' (278) through his lack of rhetorical skill? In such a poem, the poet as voyeur is also no more than a fiction, and the humiliation he undergoes is ultimately only that of lacking the roses of rhetoric in his garland.

CHAPTER 13

The Tretis of the Twa Mariit Wemen and the Wedo

The Tretis of the Twa Mariit Wemen and the Wedo, 'Dunbar's longest and most ambitious poem',[1] is another first-person narrative in which a male observer secretly watches and listens to women. Unlike the speakers of *The Palice of Honour* and *The Goldyn Targe*, though, he is not dreaming and he is not dragged out of hiding to be looked at himself and to suffer female aggression. What happens is simple: out alone after midnight on Midsummer Eve, he comes upon three splendidly dressed ladies sitting drinking in a garden; he conceals himself to listen to their conversation, and finds himself hearing scurrilous accounts of their marriages. Two are wives and one a widow: the widow invites her companions to disclose their experiences and views of marriage, and they do so, each of their speeches being followed by laughter and more drinking; then the widow, at more than twice the length and scurrility, relates her dealings with her two husbands and her subsequent conduct. By the time they finish dawn is breaking, and Dunbar creeps away undiscovered, to ask his 'auditoris most honorable' (527) which lady they would choose to marry. Most of the poem's narrative material is doubly framed, 'autobiographical' stories told by the women and then retold by the man who overhears them; its meaning lies not in any allegorical action but in the rhetorical force of its language; and this means not only its force for us, but whatever we may imagine it to be for the listener in the poem, the voyeur-poet who discovers – or fantasizes that he discovers – what women say about men in men's absence. Because the poem's language makes so essential a contribution to its meaning, and also because it is unfamiliar and difficult, I shall read it somewhat closely. The question of the poet as voyeur will not always be in the foreground, but the relevance of the details to that question will, I hope, ultimately become clear.

The *Tretis* is composed in ornate unrhymed alliterative verse, an unusual form by the sixteenth century, especially for a work of over five hundred lines; it is Dunbar's only poem in that form. Poems in rhyming alliterative stanzas, like *A Pistel of Susan*, were not uncommon in northern England and lowland Scotland in the late Middle Ages; but poems in the unrhymed long line were so rare that the choice of that metre must have meant something for Dunbar and his public; yet our knowledge of the later history of alliterative verse is too insecure for us to be sure what its meaning was. The last surviving unrhymed alliterative poem of any length was written on the other side of the Anglo-Scottish border between 1513 and the death of Henry VIII in 1547 (probably soon after 1513): this is *Scottish Field*, a heroic account of the battle of Flodden from the English viewpoint, praising the Earl of Derby's part in it. This suggests at least that Dunbar had no reason to think of unrhymed alliterative verse as especially associated with satire or abuse, and that his original audience, first encountering the opening lines of the *Tretis*, would not have guessed from the metre that they prefaced an exposure of human animality.

Some elements in the *Tretis*'s opening suggest that it is to be a dream-poem. An unnamed 'I' wanders alone through a beautiful meadow, delighted by birdsong and sweet odours. The lines

> Quhat throw the sugarat sound of hir sang glaid
> And throw the savour sanative of the sweit flouris   (7–8)

sound likely to lead into sleep and a dream, but what follows, as if a natural consequence needing no explanation, is 'I drew in derne to the dyk to dirkin efter mirthis' (9) [I drew secretly to the wall, to lurk in search of entertainment]. Thus the poet identifies himself from the start as a Peeping Tom, whose pleasures come from watching and listening rather than doing. Like Guillaume at the beginning of the *Roman de la Rose*, he is outside an enclosed garden, 'ane gudlie grein garth, full of gay flouris' (3), surrounded by a natural wall of close-knit hawthorn. Through it he hears 'Ane hie speiche at my hand with hautand wourdis' (12), and this attracts his curiosity; but never does he think of trying to enter and take part. Instead, and before he knows the speakers' sex, he hides himself more completely, in hope of getting a glimpse of them:

> With that in haist to the hege so hard I inthrang
> That I was heildit with hawthorne and with heynd leveis.

Throw pykis of the plet thorne I presandlie luikit,
Gif ony persoun wald approche within that plesand garding.

(13–16)

The season is early summer, several weeks later than the usual
Maytime setting for a poetic dream or amorous encounter. That
makes it likelier to be pleasant outdoors in Scotland, and probably
light enough to see even in the small hours; but Midsummer Eve is
also the time for fertility rites, folk-customs going back to pre-
Christian times, when young people choose lovers for the coming
year – a human equivalent to the Saint Valentine's day of *The
Parliament of Fowls*. It is a licensed occasion, a moment for the
temporary return of what is repressed by civilization and more
specifically by medieval Christianity. It is presumably the hope of
getting a furtive glimpse of this that has led the poet out on his
night-time ramble; now he is to receive his reward.

This prologue's language has the Latinate, aureate dignity of
late-medieval verse in the Chaucerian tradition – 'sugarat sound',
'savour sanative', 'hautand wourdis', and especially, a little later,
'riche vardour / That Nature full nobillie *annamalit* with flouris'
(30–1). *Annamalit* is a recurrent marker of stylistic elevation,
implying 'a finely worked, jeweled quality' transforming the poem's
occasion 'into an event of permanence and value'.[2] The 'thre gay
ladeis' (17) are described in the idealizing style of courtly poetry,
and in a way that associates them with the season's fertility: they are
garlanded with 'fresche gudlie flouris' (18), their mantles are green
as May grass (24), their faces are 'full of flurist fairheid as flouris in
June' (27), they are compared to lilies and freshly-opened roses
(28–9), and it is hard to tell whether it is the greensward or the ladies
that are 'Fragrant, all full of fresche odour fynest of smell' (33). The
description is as idealizing as that of Emelye in *The Knight's Tale*,
though with the heightened concreteness normal in alliterative
verse. The ladies please all three of the senses that operate at a
distance (sight, hearing, smell), but especially sight; and here, as we
have found previously, the obsessive watcher implied by the rhetorical convention of *effictio* is recuperated in material form as a man
whose mastery depends on distance and concealment. He fixes the
scene, but at the same time, locked in position by desire extended
over a separating space, is fixed by it.

Dunbar, though, aims at no consistency in his representation of
the observer's viewpoint. At the beginning, the poet 'inconsistently'

anticipates for our benefit what he will learn later as listener to the ladies' conversation:

> And of thir fair wlonkes twa weddit war with lordis,
> Ane was ane wedow, iwis, wantoun of laitis. (36–7)

'Wantoun of laitis' [behaviour], far more direct than anything said about Criseyde's widowhood, places this widow in the context of fabliau or antifeminist satire rather than of courtly idealization; and the identification of the ladies as a widow and two wives makes us reconsider the way we have been told they wear their hair:

> Kemmit war thair cleir hair and curiouslie sched,
> Attour thair schulderis doun schyre schyning full bricht,
> With curches cassin thair abone of kirsp cleir and thin. (21–3)

Hair hanging loose about the shoulders is a style suitable for maidens, but not for women who are or have been married;[3] and the thinness of the kerchiefs suggests enticement rather than any wish to conceal those dazzlingly seductive locks. Again, the presence of 'ryalle cowpis apon rawis, full of ryche wynis' (35) on the table before them (not wine but rich wines, not goblets but rows of goblets), and the association of plentiful drink with conversation that 'sparit no matiris' (40), already begin to modify the idealization of the ladies before they speak.

Before passing to the *Tretis*'s main text, I want to add something about the poem's relation to Chaucer's development of voyeuristic narrative. It is widely held that Dunbar's *Tretis* owes much to Chaucer's *Wife of Bath's Prologue*; and in a general sense that is true. Dunbar's women resemble Chaucer's Wife in their combination of lasciviousness with self-assertion, and there are also verbal recollections. The first wife says that, if only she were free again,

> I suld at fairis be found new faceis to se,
> At playis and at preichingis and pilgrimages greit,
> To schaw my renone royaly quhair preis was of folk, (70–2)

thus recalling Alisoun of Bath's account of how, in order 'to be seye / Of lusty folk', she attended vigils, processions, sermons, and pilgrimages (III 552–7). But most of the similarities go little beyond what can be accounted for by a long tradition of clerical writing about women, especially widows, who challenge orthodox notions of feminine submissiveness and propriety. Gregory Kratzmann more subtly suggests that in the *Tretis* we can find 'an ironic tension created by the juxtaposition of two conventional ways of writing about sexual relationship, the modes of courtly romance and fabliau',[4] a tension paralleled less within the Wife's *Prologue* than in its relation with her *Tale*, the tale being a kind of courtly romance. That is more convincing, but, in my view, the *Tretis* has far closer links to Chaucer's *Merchant's Tale*, with its harsh inner conflict between romance and fabliau, between idealization and denigration of women and marriage – a conflict that ultimately leaves readers with no resting-place for their sympathies. That is a case I have argued elsewhere,[5] but what I hope will now emerge from the discussion of *The Merchant's Tale* in Chapter 7 is that the *Tretis* is also indebted to that poem's voyeurism. The poet as voyeur is submitted to harsher scrutiny in the *Tretis* than in the other late-medieval examples we have examined, and the contempt now includes a peculiarly masochistic self-contempt – in *The Merchant's Tale* conveniently displaceable on to the unhappily married Merchant, but in the first-person narrative of the *Tretis* directed simply at 'I'. The *Tretis* as I read it offers a unique diagnosis of some of the most damaging consequences of the contradictory attitudes towards women and sexuality built into the dominant structures of medieval thought and feeling and presumably internalized by Dunbar himself.[6]

After the prologue, the widow invites the wives to speak confessionally about the *mirth* (42) they have found in marriage, that 'rakles conditioun' (43) – *rakles* inviting us to choose between 'carefree' and 'carelessly undertaken'. Have they ever loved a man more than their husbands? if they could choose again, would they choose better? and do they not think marriage which lasts until death a blessed state? These are the three questions she puts, urging them to *Bewrie* [disclose] (41) and *Reveill* (43) the hidden truth.

The first wife begins by taking up the last question, repeating the words 'blist band that bindis so fast' (50) just used by the widow (47), and exploring further the notion of marriage as a form of constraint, binding so fast that only death may undo it. This recalls *The Merchant's Tale*'s harshly ironic praise (IV 1283–5) of the 'blisful and ordinaat' life led by the 'wedded man' 'Under this yok of mariage ybounde'; and the wife's assertion that this supposedly 'blist band' is actually 'bair of blis' (51) recalls Justinus's warning that he has found marriage 'of alle blisses bare' (1548). Would she choose better if she could choose again? Surely she would, because

'Chenyeis ay ar to eschew and changeis ar sweit' (53): the pun on *chenyeis* [fetters] and *changeis* [changes] underlines the contrast. She would prefer matrimony to be an annual contract, and she contrasts 'the law of luf, of kynd, and of nature' (58) with the ecclesiastical law that makes marriage a life sentence. To propose Nature as the rule for human beings in sexual matters is to wish that they lived like animals – a wish that goes back at least to Ovid's Myrrha in *Metamorphoses* x (who uses it as an argument for incest), and is also prominent in the speech of Jean de Meun's La Vieille in the *Roman de la Rose*. (Dunbar may have encountered it in both places.) The parallel between human beings and animals runs throughout the *Tretis*; it degrades humanity, but we should remember that orthodox ecclesiastical thought, likely to be familiar to the clerical observer, leaves an opening for this heretical misinterpretation by frequently attempting to use the natural as a norm for human sexual conduct.[7] The law governing human beings, the wife says, is inferior to that governing birds,

> That ilk yeir with new joy joyis ane maik
> And fangis thame ane fresche feyr, unfulyeit and constant,
> And lattis thair fulyeit feiris flie quhair thai pleis.   (61–3)

We may recall the parallel between avian mating and human courtship in *The Parliament of Fowls*, but in the *Tretis* the emphasis is on the wearying nature of sexual fidelity. The text reveals its own contradiction: the *constant* mate is *unfulyeit* [unwearied], yet constancy is evidently wearying.

The mates that are rejected because wearied may 'flie quhair thai pleis', a formulation implying that they too are being granted freedom, as when a dismissed employee is said to be 'let go'. Constancy is wearying for women because men get so easily wearied, in the sense of losing their potency; if marriage lasted only a year, women could 'gif all larbaris thair leveis quhen thai lak curage' (67) – *curage* meaning specifically sexual desire or potency. What underlies this complaint is doubtless the physiological difference between men and women in their capacity for orgasm – not a subject normally mentioned in courtly conversation or poetry, but one that Dunbar supposes women might freely discuss among themselves in men's absence. So the wife fantasizes about how she would seek far and wide to gain a potent mate 'That suld my womanheid weild the lang winter nicht' (77). (Scottish winter nights being very long,

Scottish husbands presumably get worn out faster.) But, having
'preveit his pith the first plesand moneth' (80), she would already
start searching again to ensure a suitable successor 'For to perfur-
neis furth the werk quhen failyeit the tother' (84). *The Merchant's Tale*
is full of images of male sexual activity as a form of hard labour. The
Tretis makes them more concrete by combining them with the image
of the 'yoke' of marriage: Dunbar imagines the yoke not as linking
husband and wife as a team, but as borne only on the husband's
neck. He needs to be 'A forky fure, ay furthwart and forsy in
draucht' (85), a powerful horse or ox harnessed to the plough.
Ploughing is a familiar image for male love-making, often carrying
the implication of fruitfulness to follow, as in Enobarbus's laconic
remark about Caesar and Cleopatra: 'He ploughed her, and she
cropp'd'.[8] Here, though, the image is degraded, with the husband
imagined only as the beast pulling the plough. And the fruitfulness
is evidently not procreation but the wife's sexual pleasure, 'For al
the fruit suld I fang, thocht he the flour burgeoun' (88). We may
wonder what interest all this could have for the clerical Dunbar;
what is striking is that the fantasies of aggressive female sexuality
recurrent in ecclesiastical thought should here seem to be confirmed
for the celibate listener.

The first wife turns from these polyandrous dreams to give a
scathing account of her actual husband, who is old, ugly, and
impotent. The focus on his bristly face unquestionably derives from
The Merchant's Tale. There a close-up view was given of Januarie
taking his bride to bed:

> With thikke brustles of his berd unsofte,
> Lyk to the skyn of houndfyssh, sharp as brere –
> For he was shave all newe in his manere –
> He rubbeth hire aboute hir tendre face.   (1824–7)

In the *Tretis* there is the same reference to shaving to evoke
bristliness, and a similar comparison with a prickly creature from
the animal world (hedgehog instead of dogfish):

> Quhen schaiffyn is that ald schaik with a scharp rasour
> He schowis on me his schewill mouth and schendis my lippis,
> And with his hard hurcheone scyn sa heklis he my chekis
> That as a glemand gleyd glowis my chaftis.   (105–8)

But Dunbar adds two further ingeniously repellent effects. Line 108,
taken alone, would surely evoke a lady's blush, arising from shame

but itself sexually attractive; here it refers to the irritation produced by the friction of the husband's bristles, and the whole confessional context indicates the wife's shamelessness – this is the only kind of blushing she is likely to do. Second, there is an earlier reference to his bristly skin:

> Quhen kissis me that carybald, than kyndillis all my sorow.
> As birs of ane brym bair his berd is als stif,
> Bot soft and soupill as the silk is his sary lume. (94–6)

By contrast with the bristles, line 96 caressingly evokes the rich texture of silk, only to end by applying it to the husband's flaccid penis. In *The Merchant's Tale*, we saw how Chaucer arouses disgust by forcing us to imagine Januarie's embraces in May's sensory perspective. Dunbar goes further, giving us everything from the viewpoint of the young wife married to an old husband who, like Januarie, has exhausted his sexual powers by an earlier life of debauchery. Chaucer writes,

> But God woot what that May thoughte in hir herte,
> Whan she hym saugh up sittynge in his sherte,
> In his nyght-cappe, and with his nekke lene;
> She preyseth nat his pleyyng worth a bene. (1851–4)

Dunbar follows up with

> For he is waistit and worne fra Venus werkis,
> And may nought beit worth a bene in bed of my mystirs,
>
> (127–8)

using the same 'not worth a bean' expression. It is proverbial, but the context indicates that Chaucer's use put it in Dunbar's mind.

As in *The Merchant's Tale*, what is voyeuristic about such passages is that the position in which they place us is one of intrusion into the privacy of marital relations: we watch and even feel what should be veiled from all but the couple concerned. The difference is that in this doubly inset narrative the teller is the wife herself, brazenly revealing her experience to other women, and that her words are then reported by a man who only overhears them, gaining secret female knowledge as much as if he were concealed in the temple of Diana. Still from the wife's viewpoint, we get a graphic account of the husband's inept yet persistent fumbling, which makes her define him as diabolic – *Mahowne* (101), *Sathane* (102), *Belzebub* (112) – despite his lack of power. We also learn of his jealousy (an inevitable attribute of old husbands in medieval narrative, and in this case well-founded), and of how she retaliates – and this is more like the Wife of Bath than like May – by making him pay for his feeble pleasures. She puts it especially sharply in stating that, though 'his pen purly me payis in bed, / His purse pays richely in recompense after' (135–6). Here *pen* stands for penis but also retains its literal significance, in the recurrent parallel between sex and writing. *Pay(i)s* means both 'pays' and 'pleases'; he pleases her poorly in bed, but pays her richly afterwards. And *purse* too probably has a double sense, for it can mean scrotum.[9] When the first wife in the *Tretis* finishes her speech, all three cackle with laughter and pass the wine round. In its appalling way, it *is* funny, and may well have appealed to the sense of humour at the Scottish court. Whether it is only funny is another matter.

Dunbar follows the stylistic habit of alliterative verse in using adjectives absolutely to stand for nouns. Such adjectives can be marvellously inappropriate to the women to whom they are formulaically applied – the first wife is 'the semely' (146), the second is 'the tothir wlonk' (150) and 'The plesand' (158) – and since this happens most frequently in the transitional passages where Dunbar's presence is most noticeable, it is easy to attribute to him the incomprehension implied by their inappropriateness. The effect, here and throughout, is of a listener who misses the point of what he hears. The widow urges the second wife to follow the first and 'confese us the treuth' (153) about her experience of marriage and whether she finds it blessed or cursed. In this part of the poem there is repeated stress on truth-telling: the widow instructs the second wife to speak 'but fenying' (151), and promises that she in turn will 'say furth the south, dissymyland no word' (157); the second wife answers that if she is to reveal 'the treuth' (158) the other two must promise to keep it secret, and when they agree she responds, 'To speik ... I sall nought spar, ther is no spy neir' (161). That of course reminds us, if we need reminding, that there *is* a spy, Dunbar himself, and that we share his position. One scholar has suggested the possibility of explaining the women's freedom of speech by supposing that they have noticed the concealed listener, and are deliberately exaggerating for his benefit;[10] but that would be to misunderstand the confessional convention in medieval literature and, I think, to deprive the poem of its main point for the sake of a trivial defence of its realism. If Dunbar had intended us to grasp that the women knew they were being spied on, he would have said so much more clearly. The paradox of the public revelation of secret behaviour and speech, which, as we have seen, many medieval poets approach, is here directly confronted; and it also raises questions about the nature of the concealed observer and the effect on him of what he sees and hears.

The second wife refers to what she has to reveal as *roust* (163, rancour), the contents of a *byle* (164, boil), *venome* (166): it is filthy, and she cannot wait to let it out. Her husband is young, yet his reality belies his outward appearance, 'For he is fadit full far and feblit of strenth' (171). He has been a *lychour* (174) and a user of whores; now impotent, he still likes to play the part of a swaggering dandy. She has splendidly dismissive phrases for him: he is a 'syphyr in bour' (184)[11] or 'a right lusty schadow' (191), and there is a comparison, adapted from Chaucer's *Parson's Tale*, with the dog that persistently raises its leg to no effect (186–7). The husband's penis is treated as a being separate from himself: it is exhausted and 'lyis into swoune' (175), but 'Wes never sugeorne wer set na on that snaill tyrit' (176) [never was rest more futilely prescribed than for that tired snail]. What happens, or rather fails to happen, in *chalmer* (183, 194) or in *bour* (184) is contrasted several times with what his public behaviour promises. So what the second wife reveals is the secret truth not just about herself but about her husband: and Dunbar secretly overhears her revelation of the secrets of the *chalmer*. Her 'Bot God wait quhat I think' (195), recalls 'But God woot what that May thoughte in hir herte' (*Merchant's Tale* 1851), but now it refers not to the husband's performance but to his outward show, given what she knows of his performance. She argues that her situation is worse than the first wife's; if you marry an old man, at least you know what to expect, but she has purchased jet for a gem, glass for gold (201–2).

Then she returns to the first wife's comparison with birds; if only she could make a fresh choice each Saint Valentine's day! Instead, she can only fantasize about it at night; and this is the fault of her kinsfolk, who married her off to 'a craudoune but curage' (215). Dunbar spares little pity for these women, but here we get a glimpse of the relationships of power and money that really deprived most medieval women of a choice of partner. In what follows, the reader's sense of intruding into what should be the most private part of life is at its strongest. She not only tells us what happens when she is in bed with a husband of 'tume person' (219) and 'yoldin yerd' (220) who cannot give her the one thing she wants, and what excuse she makes to discourage him from handling her (not the now conventional headache but 'A hache ... at my hert rut' [224]); she also tells what she secretly thinks in the *chalmer* of inner consciousness: 'Than think I on a semelyar, the suth for to tell ... ' (217). If only he could have been married to one of those timid girls who are afraid of being hurt by a man 'with hard geir' (232), and she could be in bed with a man who pleased her! Then both women would be happy, and the girl would not be in a position to make jokes about *her* happy state.

Once more, when 'this amyable' (239) has finished, the three women laugh and drink. Here an absolute adjectival phrase (almost a kenning) is used with particularly apt ineptness to refer to them: 'thai swanquit of hewis' (243) – as if their purity of complexion were the essential truth about them. Now it is the widow's turn, and she begins with a preacher's prayer, requesting divine inspiration to pierce the 'perverst hertis' of her listeners, to make them 'mekar to men in maneris and conditiounis' (249–50). This is the effect a real preacher might hope to have on female listeners; but in the widow's case the meekness she wishes to teach is to apply *only* to 'maneris and conditiounis' – a demure outward surface that will enable her congregation to deceive men more cunningly, while avoiding slander from 'losingeris untrew' (258). (Dunbar, in the *losinger*'s position of surveillance, evidently lacks the wit to report anything but the truth.) Like her they are to be 'dissymblit suttelly in a sanctis liknes' (254) and to 'counterfeit gud maneris' (259), angels in outward appearance but secretly 'stangand as edderis' (266). She explains that she has had two husbands. The first was an old man, crook-backed, crop-headed, forever coughing up phlegm; she kissed and fondled him openly, while behind his back she had 'a lufsummar leid my lust for to slokyn' (283). She got pregnant by her lover, convinced her old husband that the son she bore was his, even though he was impotent before the child was conceived, and even persuaded him to bequeath his chief manor house to her bastard. That story is a straightforward illustration of the principles she preaches – it is easy to imagine May doing the same – but her account of her dealings with her second husband is more disturbing.

He was a wealthy merchant, but, as she tells the story (and we have to reconstruct it, because she tells it allusively, not in chronological order), he was short and middle-aged (297) and below her in

social rank: 'we na fallowis wer in frendschip or blud' (298) [we were
not comparable in kin or descent]. The discrepancy in rank she was
able to use as a verbal weapon, for, she says, she was a promising
talker even when young – 'Sa sais the curat of our kirk, that knew me
full ying' (306). We are left to guess whether 'that fair worthy prelot'
(307) 'knew' her in the Biblical sense or more innocently. Her social
superiority, real or imagined, enables her to play out within
marriage a scathing parody of the game of courtship that is the
central theme and purpose of courtly poetry. Before she married her
merchant, she showed him good will (323–4), evidently for the sake
of his wealth; afterwards nothing but hostility. It was only once she
was a wife that she adopted the role of cruel mistress. She constantly
reminded him of his inferiority, claiming (314–17) that it was only
out of *peté*, *mercy*, *ruth* and *grace* that she had accepted him. Here
again Dunbar must be recalling *The Merchant's Tale*. One of the most
destructive of that tale's assaults on courtly values lies in its
adaptation of the courtly doctrine that *gentillesse* shows itself in ready
compassion to the situation in which May, through sheer appetite,
allows herself to be seduced by the fawning Damyan. The Merchant
applies to her ready surrender that favourite line of Chaucer's, 'Lo,
pitee renneth soone in gentil herte!' (1986). The widow makes
precisely the same application of the doctrine in a similar line: 'For
never bot in a gentill hert is generit ony ruth' (316).

She taunted her second husband with the ignoble means by which
he acquired the wealth she married him for, calling him *peddir* (302,
pedlar) and *buthman* (309, shopkeeper). The more she domineered,
the more he cringed, and yet, 'The mair he loutit for my luf, the les of
him I rakit' (322). It is like a reversal of *The Clerk's Tale*: there
Griselda's patient submission to her husband's cruelty only encourages him to redouble it; here the jackboot is on the other foot. He
gave her fine clothes, but she saved the best of them to make herself
attractive for his successor. While he was ruining himself financially
to make her splendid, she cuckolded him, so the result of his
generosity was to create 'a stalwart staff to strik him selfe doune'
(384).[12] She refused sexual relations with him for a year and, when
she finally let him have his way, took care to imagine that it was
someone else enjoying her:

> Alse lang as he wes on loft I lukit on him never,
> Na leit never enter in my thoght that he my thing persit,
> Bot ay in mynd ane othir man ymagynit that I haid.   (388–90)

Even more than with the second wife's story, the intimate detail is comic – the widow calls it a *bowrd* (385) – but shameful; and perhaps especially so for the male reader, overhearing with the concealed poet what a woman among women might secretly say about him.

The degrading of the widow's second husband goes even further. Bird imagery underlines the reversal of orthodox sexual roles: 'I crew abone that craudone as cok that were victour' (326). The rooster is the epitome of male sexual dominance, and *cok* had the same double sense in Middle as in Modern English: humiliating him, she gains the phallus herself. His submission made him despicable to her, and once more the image is of a beast, only now she remains human and it is the man who is bestialized:

> Qhuen I him saw subjeit and sett at myn byddyng,
> Than I him lichtlyit as a lowne and lathit his maneris.
> Than woxe I sa unmerciable, to martir him I thought.
> For as a best I broddit him to all boyis laubour.
> I wald haif ridden him to Rome with raip in his heid,
> Wer not ruffill of my renoune and rumour of pepill.   (327–32)

At first she usually managed to conceal her hatred with feigning; but once she had gained control of his property (337–8), as May did of Januarie's in *The Merchant's Tale*, further concealment was unnecessary. No longer did the husband control the wife, as the rider controls a steed; on the contrary, she feminized her husband, and urged her female friends to note how she had transformed a restive stallion into an obedient cart-horse. This lurid passage deserves detailed attention:

> Bot quhen my billis and my bauthles wes all braid selit,
> I wald na langar beir on bridill bot braid up my heid.
> Thair myght na molet mak me moy na hald my mouth in.
> I gert the renyeis rak and rif into sondir,
> I maid that wif carll to werk all womenis werkis,
> And laid all manly materis and mensk in this eird.
> Than said I to my cummaris in counsall about,
> 'Se how I cabeld yone cout with a kene brydill.
> The cappill that the crelis kest in the caf mydding
> Sa curtasly the cart drawis and kennis na plungeing.
> He is nought skeich na yit sker na scippis nought on syd.'
> And thus the scorne and the scaith scapit he nothir.   (347–58)

But when my letters and documents were sealed and witnessed, I would no longer endure a bridle; but tossed my head; there was no bit that could make me submissive or control my mouth; I put the reins under such a strain that they broke apart; I made that woman-man perform female tasks of all kinds and set aside completely all manly business and dignity. Then I said secretly to my women friends here and there, 'See how I brought that colt under control with a harsh bridle! The horse that threw its baskets into the dung-heap now pulls the cart so humbly without thought of leaping about. He isn't spirited or restive, and doesn't spring aside.' And thus he escaped neither scorn nor humiliation.

The themes of this section can be paralleled elsewhere in medieval literature and art; there is the widespread legend, for example, of Aristotle being bridled and saddled by the beautiful Campaspe.[13] But they are also found in some types of modern pornography, where female superiority is asserted by devices such as the enforced feminization of men and the harnessing of men as horses.[14] Sadism is apparently rare among women, and fictions of this kind are designed to appeal not to them but to men who enjoy masochistic fantasies; and this suggests that the story the widow tells is more an uncovering of male sexual fantasies than a revelation of any 'truth' about women hidden behind the façade of courtliness. The effect of the widow's treatment of her husband is to geld him of both goods and potency (392): in this analysis of orthodox ideas about marital relations, economic and sexual power are rightly seen as bound up together. Her final lines on this wretched man concern her triumph in the field of family politics: she favours her own children 'like baronis sonnis' (402), treats his sons by his first wife with contempt, banishes his brothers from the house, treats his relations as her enemies. Not surprisingly, the story ends with his death.

The rest of the widow's speech is rich in reflexive passages alluding to its fictional and textual contexts and thus to its voyeuristic setting. She has told her story in the secrecy of night, but with her second husband's death *her* night is over and her 'day is upsprungin' (412). She underlines the crucial truth that the wise woman is not what she outwardly appears by stating it repeatedly in a whole variety of different ways (415–21). This technique, called *expolitio* by the rhetoricians, is defined and illustrated as follows by Geoffroi de Vinsauf:

although the meaning is one, let it not come content with one set of apparel. Let it vary its robes and assume different raiment. Let it take up again in other words what has already been said. Let it reiterate, in a number of clauses, a single thought. Let one and the same thing be concealed under multiple forms – be varied and yet the same [*varius sis et tamen idem*].[15]

The image of clothing employed by Geoffroi to define *expolitio* (and by rhetoric generally to refer to verbal style) is used by the widow in a literal sense to express the truth her *expolitio* is designed to emphasize: her widow's weeds are one thing, but the 'courtly and ryght curyous' body beneath them (419) is quite another. She describes how in church she has open on her knee a 'bright buke ... With mony lusty letter ellummynit with gold' (424–5); pretending to concentrate on her devotions, she is always peering round secretly to identify the most attractive man. The book too has a reflexive function: the language of manuscript illumination (illuminated, gilded, aureate, ornamented ...) is also that of the stylistic elevation of late-medieval poetry, and the widow's book of hours thus becomes a figure of the style of courtly poetry, as found in the prologue of this very poem – a veil or veneer concealing animal lust. She employs that very style herself to convey its, and her, deceptiveness, using a romantic extended simile of the new moon glimpsed through clouds to describe herself peeping through her weeds to leer at men in church:

> And as the new mone all pale oppressit with change
> Kythis quhilis her cleir face throw cluddis of sable,
> So keik I throw my clokis and castis kynd lukis
> To knychtis and to cleirkis and cortly personis. (432–5)

Sight is at once a means of deception –

> According to my sable weid I mon haif sad maneris,
> Or thai will *se* all the suth; for certis we wemen
> We set us all *for the syght*, to syle men of treuth (447–9)

– the first stage on the road to bodily contact (as in the many 'kynd lukis' [434] and 'sweit blenkis' [494] she directs towards likely men), and, above all, the means of exercising secret mastery, 'That I may spy unaspyit' (427). To spy unaspied is precisely Dunbar's aim as poet.

In the final stage of the widow's autobiography she offers women a concise *ars amatoria*. She has 'ane secrete servand' (466) who is also different from what he appears to sight: 'Thoght he be sympill to the sicht he has a tong sickir' (468). Thanks to the ambiguity of 'servant', we cannot know whether he satisfies her sexual needs himself or procures other men to do so, or indeed both; but whichever it is,

> Thoght I haif cair under cloke the cleir day quhill nyght,
> Yit haif I solace under serk quhill the sone rise.　　　(470–1)

These lines play deceptive games with deception: now 'care' is attributed not to her 'cloak', her sombre outward appearance, as when she remarked earlier, 'My clokis thai ar caerfull' (418), but to what is 'under cloak' during daytime, her body with its unsatisfied appetite; while during the hours of darkness she has 'solace under serk', sexual satisfaction concealed only by her nightgown. What she enjoys most, she says, is the crowds of men who pursue her to her lodgings, all making amorous advances in their different ways, from distant *blenkis* (487) to less subtle approaches:

> Sum stalwardly steppis ben with a stout curage,
> And a stif standand thing staiffis in mi neiff.　　　(485–6)

As she details her various responses, distributing her favours in all directions, her statement that 'with my fair calling I comfort thaim all' (489) evokes the *Roman de la Rose*: her 'fair calling' reveals what the courtly Bialacoil means in reality – at least in the widow's reality. She possesses above all the supreme womanly virtue of compassion; and she breathtakingly asserts that her compassionate promiscuity will bring her a heavenly reward besides all its earthly rewards: 'My sely saull salbe saif quhen sabot all jugis' (502). She had claimed earlier no more than the outward appearance of a saint – 'I sane me as I war ane sanct and semys ane angell' (444) – but now she claims the reality of sainthood, and this claim is repeated in her final line: 'This is the legeand of my lif, thought Latyne it be nane' (504).

Her speech too is greeted with laughter and further drinking, and the wives promise to model their lives on the widow's *prudent* (508) teaching. They pass the night with conversation and dances, and now day begins to break. (This poem occupies a night, just as Lydgate's *Complaynt of a Loveres Lyfe* occupied a day; but even in southern Scotland there would be only a short period of darkness on Midsummer's Eve.) Despite all that has happened since nightfall, the courtly high style is wheeled back unchanged to describe the beauty of dawn, with birdsong and sweet smells just like the evening before:

The morow myld wes and meik the mavis did sing,
And all remuffit the myst and the meid smellit.
Silver schouris doune schuke as the schene cristall
And berdis schoutit in schaw with ther schill notis.
The goldin glitterand gleme so gladit ther hertis,
Thai maid a glorius gle amang the grene bewis.   (513–18)

As the mist rises, the veil of poetry descends. This is the moment at which we are explicitly reminded of Dunbar's role as voyeur, to which the reflexive elements in the latter part of the widow's speech have been repeatedly pointing; and I now want to reconsider the implications of that role. The widow's second husband is emasculated by her, but Dunbar has been emasculated from the beginning – no participant in the vigorous sexual life he has been hearing about, not even pulled from his hiding-place by the women he has been observing, but only a fascinated celibate spy. What he has seen and heard constitutes a demystification of the idealizing of women on which the courtly tradition is based. The three women have unmasked themselves, revealing at least in words the lustful bodies that lie beneath the decorous outward garments of courtly style, and they would not have done it if they had known that a man was secretly witnessing them. Yet the 'truth' they reveal is no more than an unusually graphic realization of orthodox clerical antifeminism; it is precisely what Dunbar as priest ought to have known all along, though it is what (in theory at least) Dunbar as courtly poet must not say. Moreover, what the women reveal is not just their own natures, it is what they really think about men. Sexual difference is a prominent feature of human experience, and it was probably still more prominent in the Middle Ages, when the roles and cultural formations of the two sexes were more sharply differentiated than they are in the modern West. The fantasy of discovering what the other sex says about one's own when one's own is absent is powerfully attractive; perhaps all the more so for men in a culture in which men are dominant, the male is regarded as the norm, and the female is defined as an inferior but mysterious and dangerous Other. It may have been particularly attractive for a man theoretically committed to celibacy. Yet in most circumstances, before the invention of electronic bugging devices, it could be only a fantasy. Fantasies are likely to reveal more about the people who have them than about their subject-matter. The questions raised by one recent scholar as to whether the women speak 'female language' and why they sometimes use 'unfeminine devices' such as four-letter words,[16] are surely beside the point, because they involve forgetting that this 'female language' was actually written by a male poet. Dunbar, consciously or unconsciously, has unmasked not the truth about women but the truth about the nature of male fantasy about women in a patriarchal society.[17] I suggested that that was so when noting similarities between the widow's treatment of her second husband and certain themes in modern pornography written for men, but it is equally true of the poem's whole content.

Courtly idealization of women and ecclesiastical denigration of women existed side by side, intricately interwoven in the high culture of the Middle Ages, yet neither could ultimately absorb or accommodate the other. In writing they were generally separated by the boundaries of genre, but the existence of explosive generic mixtures such as *The Merchant's Tale* and Dunbar's *Tretis* shows, what could in any case be guessed, that the conflict between them was a living and lived conflict; it could not be simply a matter of demonstration by either side of its authority over the other. A courtly poet who was also a celibate priest was in an especially favourable (because especially unfavourable) position to experience that unresolvable conflict and to diagnose its damaging con-sequences not only for women but for men – or at least for himself, that is, for the William Dunbar made of words who is inscribed in the poem as male voyeur and poet. (I do not presume to psycho-analyse the once living but now dead William Dunbar who did the inscribing.)

The first wife implied an analogy between writing and sex, when she said that her husband's 'pen' paid/pleased her poorly in bed (135). At the end of the poem, Dunbar, as he says, 'with my pen did report ther pastance most mery' (526). For him, appropriately for one whose profession is defined at once by celibacy and by the power to write, one kind of pen is a substitute for another. He writes what he has heard, and it is significant that the watcher of the prologue, whose penetrative secret gaze could make some claim to mastery, is so soon reduced to a listener, passive before women who actively 'put out ther vocis' (244). He remains in the listener's role through most of the poem; at the end he once more becomes a watcher, but, if he thinks what he has heard a 'pastance most mery', he must be quite unchanged by hearing it. Forgetting nothing, he has also learned nothing. The widow remarked wonderingly on how, despite all that men have said down the ages about women's deceptiveness, 'thir wismen, thai wait that all wiffis evill / Ar kend with ther conditiounis and knawin with the samin' (408–9) [those wise men believe that all evil wives are known and can be recognized by their outward dispositions]. Dunbar has had a unique opportunity to learn about women's deceptiveness from their own eloquent mouths, but it has made not the least impression on him: to him they are 'ryall rosis' (523) at the end just as they were at the beginning. If we may suppose him just a little disturbed by the more outrageous comments on his own sex made by the women, the disturbance is quickly forgotten now that morning has come:

> The soft sowch of the swyr and soune of the stremys,
> The sweit savour of the sward and singing of foulis
> Myght confort ony creatur of the kyn of Adam,
> And kindill agane his curage, thoght it wer cald sloknyt.

> (519–22)

This cheerful ending is one of the poem's funniest and most depressing features. The night may have brought an experience gruesome enough to quench any man's *curage*, but morning comes, the birds sing, and the kin of Adam are mechanically restored to their former state of aspiring rampancy. It is precisely that irrational, biologically implanted *curage* of men that makes them project falsely idealizing images on to women, and thus enables women to gain the mastery over men; and the *Tretis* holds out no hope that this will ever change. 'There is no sexual relation'; the poem has revealed a more deep-rooted barrier than the hawthorn hedge between the sexes. The conclusion with a *demande d'amour* only confirms this, by taking for granted that the really interesting question raised by Dunbar's experience is which of the three women would be preferable as a wife (rather than, say, what it is that makes women like this or what it is that makes men imagine women like this). It is as true of the Dunbar inscribed in the *Tretis* as it is of Januarie in *The Merchant's Tale*, that while outwardly his eyes (or rather ears) may have been opened, he remains as complacently blind and deaf within as he ever was.

CHAPTER 14

Phyllyp Sparowe

The career of John Skelton (*c.* 1460–1529) in England has something in common with that of William Dunbar in Scotland. Skelton spent parts of his life associated with the royal court: he entered the service of Henry VII in 1488, was tutor to Prince Henry (the future Henry VIII) from about 1496 to 1501, and returned to court with the title *orator regius* after his former pupil came to the throne in 1509. At the same time, Skelton was a priest, ordained in 1498 and rector of Diss in Norfolk from about 1503. He was of lower birth but a greater and more famous scholar than Dunbar, receiving the title of 'laureate' from Oxford, Cambridge and Louvain universities; he was also a more prominent and more riskily exposed figure in the intellectual and political controversies of his time. The clerkly predominates over the courtly in most of his work, but in some poems the poetic 'I' is coloured with a voyeurism that derives from the distance between the clerk's celibate profession and the erotic attraction of the courtly poet's subject-matter. I refer to 'the clerk's celibate profession', though, if the Skelton legend that originated in his own lifetime has any connection with reality, he certainly did not practise celibacy; but, if in turn a loucheness is detectable in his poetry, it only adds piquancy to the relation constructed there between the male watcher and the female object. One mask he adopts for poetic purposes is that of 'Parott', the caged pet fed with delicacies and kisses by 'greate ladyes of estate' (*Speke Parott* 6),[1] who repeats the fragments of language he overhears – a later and more complex development of Apollo's crow, not silenced by his master but urged by a muse-like lady called Galathea to 'speke now trew and playne' (448) about the state of England. The relation between a pet bird and its mistress is also the theme of *Phyllyp Sparowe*, an earlier poem, from the same decade as Dunbar's *Tretis*, where it is the poet, not the bird, who is the watcher. Now, however, voyeurism begins to dissolve into more freely ranging erotic fantasy, and shame gives way to shamelessness.

Like Dunbar's, most of Skelton's work is occasional; but whereas Dunbar wrote many short poems provoked by separate occasions, Skelton tended to put together longer poems from sections provoked by a sequence of occasions. *Speke Parott* is the most notorious of these, because it has a series of envoys that can be related to the arrival of successive reports of a peace conference in Calais presided over by Wolsey. *Phyllyp Sparowe*, too, is a poem of this kind, and in the Kele printed version of about 1545, on which Scattergood bases his text, it is headed 'Here after foloweth the boke of *Phyllyp Sparowe* compyled by Mayster Skelton, poete laureate'. 'Compyled' cannot be strictly interpreted as implying a poetic activity that consisted solely of bringing together previously separate materials, but we do know that the last of the poem's three main sections, headed 'Thus endeth the boke of Philip Sparow, and her foloweth an addicyon made by Maister Skelton', was added later and first appeared as part of another poem, *The Garland of Laurel*. In a typical Skelton poem, however, the separately composed sections form a combinatory structure that has its own internal dynamic, and, like *Speke Parott*, *Phyllyp Sparowe* is a poem of this kind. I shall first offer an exposition of *Phyllyp Sparowe*,[2] and then comment on the part played in it by voyeurism.

Part 1, lines 1–844, written some time between 1502 and 1505, consists of an elegy on the death of a pet sparrow belonging to Jane Scrope. Jane was a young woman who, after her stepfather's execution as a Yorkist rebel in 1502, was taken by her mother to live at Carrow Abbey, a small Benedictine convent near Norwich (thus also near Diss). It was 'at Carowe / Among the Nones Blake' (8–9), the Benedictine sisters, that Phyllyp (the usual name for a sparrow) was killed – by a wicked cat, as we later learn. Most of Part 1 is spoken as if by Jane herself, but the opening lines (1–16) seem to represent a whispered explanatory conversation in the church where a service is being performed for Phyllyp's soul, and the Latin closing lines are spoken by Skelton, in explanation of the fiction which is now complete:

> Per me laurigerum
> Britanum Skeltonida vatem
> Hec cecinisse licet
> Ficta sub imagine texta.

> Cuius eris volucris,
> Prestanti corpore virgo:
> Candida Nais erat,
> Formosior ista Joanna est:
> Docta Corinna fuit,
> Sed magis ista sapit.
> Bien men souvient. (836–44)

Through me, Skelton the laureate bard of Britain, it was possible for these compositions to be sung under a feigned likeness. She whose bird you were is a maiden of outstanding physical beauty: the Naiad was fair, but this Jane is more beautiful; Corinna was learned, but Jane knows more. I recall it well.

Here Skelton explains the concept of the poetic persona: he, the laureate bard, has adopted the feigned voice of Jane Scrope as the speaker of the poem's first section; this explains the apparent simplicity and naïveté of that section's thought and style, but it also explains how the eight lines immediately preceding, Jane's epitaph for Phyllyp, could be in Latin verse, a feat that would surely have been beyond Jane unless the laureate bard had acted as her ventriloquist. The name Corinna is a sufficient reminder, for those more learned than Jane, of Ovid's *Amores* II 6, the lament for Corinna's parrot, a poem which is itself a detailed pastiche of a Roman dirge. There it is the parrot that says *vale* (line 48), as Jane does in her epitaph for Phyllyp; and the epitaph with which Ovid's poem concludes defines not Corinna but the parrot as possessing *ora ... docta*, a learned mouth (line 62). The implication, I think, is that the 'Jane' of *Phyllyp Sparowe* is herself a parrot, in the sense that she speaks words taught her by Skelton. The final line, in French, evokes the courtly eroticism that, as we shall see, characterizes both Jane's relation to the sparrow and Skelton's to Jane. The interaction of languages – simple English, allusively clerkly Latin, courtly French – makes an important contribution to the poem's effect.

Part I is punctuated by quotations from a specific liturgical service, the Vespers of the Dead, known from its first word, which is also the poem's, as the *Placebo*. We may perhaps imagine that the service is being chanted by 'Dame Margery' (4) (the real name of the senior nun at Carrow at this time), and that Jane only fantasizes that it is for her sparrow. As F. W. Brownlow puts it,

Jane, in the priory church, following the service in her primer, transforms it into something quite different, but in doing so she is fulfilling, like Dame

Margery, a proper liturgical role. For it was customary for lay people to use their primers for private devotion during the recitation of either the Divine Office or the Mass.[3]

Primers included the Vespers of the Dead. So, while the service pursues its proper course, most of Part I consists of an interior monologue by Jane concerning herself and her sparrow. From 'Lauda, anima mea, Dominum!' (387) onwards she imagines the various species of birds singing a Mass for the Dead for Phyllyp; and from line 513 she imagines them performing the service called the *Absolutio super Tumulum* (Absolution over the Tomb), led by the phoenix 'In a blacke cope' (529), with the eagle as subdeacon in charge of the choir and various other noble birds of prey playing appropriate parts. At line 571 the Vespers of the Dead resume, but then something new occurs to Jane:

> Yet one thynge is behynde,
> That now commeth to mynde:
> An epytaphe I wold have
> For Phyllyppes grave. (603–6)

Yet, she reminds herself, she is only 'a mayde, / Tymerous, halfe afrayde' (607–8), and she has never drunk 'Of Elyconys well' (610), the source of poetic inspiration. This leads into a long survey, with her own commentary, of what she has read – many works in English, from *The Canterbury Tales* on, and some classical stories, presumably in translation – and what she has not read – 'Frauncys Petrarke' (758) and the 'poetes of auncyente' (767). The epitaph, 'In Latyne playne and lyght' (823), by contrast with Skelton's own more difficult Latin, forms the closing lines of Jane's meditation (826–33):

> Flos volucrum formose, vale!
> Philippe, sub isto
> Marmore iam recubas,
> Qui mihi carus eras.
> Semper erunt nitido
> Radiantia sydera celo;
> Impressusque meo
> Pectore semper eris. (826–33)

Beautiful flower of birds, farewell! Phyllyp, you now rest beneath that marble, you who were dear to me. There will always be shining stars in the clear sky; and you will always be imprinted in my breast.

Part II, headed 'The Commendacions', consists of lines 845–1267. Skelton, who had entered the poem by way of the Latin at the end of

Part I, remains the speaker. Part II also has a liturgical basis, in the
form of a private devotion found in English primers, called the
Commendation of All Souls. A large part of this devotion consists of
Vulgate Psalm 118, a long psalm made up of twenty-two eight-verse
sections, which in Hebrew were arranged alphabetically, with every
verse in each section beginning with a single letter of the Hebrew
alphabet. In books of hours and primers the twenty-two sections
were treated as eleven pairs, and Skelton uses the opening verse of
each pair to begin the successive segments of his 'Commendacions'.
Then he ends each section with the same refrain:

> For this most goodly floure,
> This blossome of fresshe coulour,
> So Jupiter me socour,
> She floryssheth new and new
> In bewte and vertew.
> *Hac claritate gemina,*
> *O gloriosa femina.*   (893–9, 989–95, etc.)

But whereas in the original the *gloriosa femina* is the Blessed Virgin,
Skelton addresses all this praise to Jane herself; so he is parodying
the Marian devotion of the late Middle Ages to form a secular
love-commendation – as indeed is indicated by the startling appearance of Jupiter rather than Christ in the refrains. Though Part II
seems to be separable from Part I, we are surely intended to notice
the parallels between them. In Part I Jane speaks of her relationship
with her sparrow, and in Part II Skelton speaks of his relationship
with Jane; each praises the beloved extravagantly and yet with
provocative intimacy, and each ends with a modesty-topos. Jane's is
humble and womanly:

> Wherfore hold me excused
> If I have not well perused
> Myne Englyssh halfe-abused;
> Though it be refused,
> In worth I shall it take,
> And fewer wordes make.
> But for my sparowes sake,
> Yet as a woman may,
> My wyt I shall assay
> An epytaphe to wryght
> In Latyne playne and lyght ...   (813–23)

Skelton's is more elevated in style, more obviously the enactment of a learned formula, more a defence than an apology (he mentions the possibility that he may have offended only to deny it), and its masculinity is underlined by the reference to 'my pen':

> And where my pen hath offendyd,
> I pray you it may be amendyd
> By discrete consyderacyon
> Of your wyse reformacyon;
> I have not offended, I trust,
> If it be sadly dyscust.
> It were no gentle gyse
> This treatyse to despyse
> Because I have wrytten and sayd
> Honour to this fayre mayd;
> Wherefore shulde I be blamed
> That I Jane have named,
> And famously proclamed? (1245–57)

Each of these modesty-topoi is followed by a Latin eulogy, Jane's of Phyllyp and Skelton's of Jane; and Skelton's eulogy also corresponds to the lines in which he introduces himself after Jane's eulogy of Phyllyp, both calling attention to his role as laureate national poet by beginning with the same hexameter line: 'per me laurigerum Britonum Skeltonida vatem' (1261, cf. 834–5).

Part III is the 'addicyon made by Maister Skelton', beginning at line 1268. This section of 115 lines was apparently added to the poem in response to criticism of *Phyllyp Sparowe*'s triviality made by Alexander Barclay in his *Shyp of Folys*, published in 1509. The additional lines were first published, as far as we know, not in *Phyllyp Sparowe*, but in Skelton's *Garland of Laurel* when it was printed in 1523, the year of its completion. They consist of a defence of the first two parts of *Phyllyp Sparowe*, referred to as 'His *Dirige*, her commendacyon' (1276) – that is, Jane's application of the Office of the Dead (known as the *Dirige*) to Phyllyp and Skelton's application of the Commendation of All Souls to Jane. Skelton defends his work not only against Barclay's attack but also against Jane's alleged annoyance at being shamed by the work:

> Alas, that goodly mayd,
> Why shuld she be afrayde?
> Why shuld she take shame ...? (1282–4)

Most of Part III consists of an elaborate conjuration of Phyllyp's soul, by a long series of figures from classical myth associated with

the other world, and also by King Saul (who made the Witch of
Endor raise Samuel from the grave), to rise from the dead and
explain something that Skelton professes not to understand: it was
Jane who originally requested him to write a poem about her
sparrow, so 'cur nostri carminis illam / Nunc pudet?' (1372–3) [why
is she now ashamed of our song?].

Many aspects of *Phyllyp Sparowe* deserve consideration: it is, for
example, as much concerned as Dunbar's *Goldyn Targe* with poetic
history and the role of the poet. Here, though, I shall focus on its
relation to voyeurism, to which Jane's alleged shame provides a
good entry. In *Phyllyp Sparowe* the poet's role does not immediately
appear to be that of a voyeur, as in the other late-medieval
first-person narratives discussed in Chapters 11–13. He does not
represent himself as a concealed spy embarrassingly exposed or as a
male secretly overhearing female discourse. Part I, as I noted,
appears to be an interior monologue of Jane's during the performance of the Vespers of the Dead in the chapel of Carrow Abbey, and
Skelton is not apparently hidden behind a pillar noting it down; he
seems completely absent from Part I. If present, he would learn
some interesting and exciting things about Jane's relationship with
Phyllyp. Her extreme grief at his death is modelled on Marian
laments at the death of Christ (she laments like Mary in Part I and
then is praised like Mary in Part II). Her

> Great sorowe than ye myght se,
> And lerne to wepe at me!   (56–7)

could easily be the refrain of a Marian lyric. But the motivation for
this grief, it soon emerges, is an affection which is erotic as much as
maternal. (Here Skelton is doubtless responding to classical sources
– the association of sparrows with Venus, and writings such as
Catullus's two poems on Lesbia's sparrow, which are more
explicitly erotic, and which are among the probable sources of
Amores II 6.) Phyllyp, Jane tells us, 'wold syt upon my lap' (121),

> And many tymes and ofte
> Betwene my brestes softe
> It wolde lye and rest –
> It was propre and prest.   (124–7)

> And whan I sayd, 'Phyp, Phyp,'
> Than he wold lepe and skyp,
> And take me by the lyp.   (138–40)

Shortly comes a more detailed account of the liberties the sparrow
took with its mistress's body:

> on me it wolde lepe
> Whan I was aslepe,
> And his fethers shake,
> Wherewith he wolde make
> Me often for to wake
> And for to take him in
> Upon my naked skyn.
> God wot, we thought no syn –
> What though he crept so lowe?
> It was no hurt, I trowe.
> He dyd nothynge, perde,
> But syt upon my kne.
> Phyllyp, though he were nyse,
> In him it was no vyse;
> Phyllyp had leve to go
> To pyke my lytell too,
> Phillip myght be bolde
> And do what he wolde;
> Phillip wolde seke and take
> All the flees blake
> That he coulde there espye
> With his wanton eye. (161–82)

In our age of bodily hygiene fleas may have an anaphrodisiac effect,
but Donne's 'Marke but this flea' and its many Renaissance
analogues, making explicit use of the flea's freedom to visit a
woman's most intimate parts, confirm that this was not Skelton's
intention. Here the emphasis on innocence through repeated denials
of guilt – 'God wot, we thought no syn . . . It was no hurt, I trowe. /
He *dyd* nothynge, perde . . . In him it was no vyse . . .' – surely has a
similar effect to that of Guillaume de Lorris's descriptions of the
dances and embraces of prepubertal children. It describes erotically
stimulating behaviour on the part of supposedly innocent creatures
(children, a bird); but in doing so it displays innocence as itself an
erotic spectacle, and thus makes it something other than innocence.
In *Phyllyp Sparowe*, moreover, only the bird could possibly be
thought innocent: the denials by Jane herself only serve, charmingly
enough, to convey her sexual awareness.

Jane, as we have seen, presents herself as childlike, as 'a mayde, /
Tymerous, halfe afrayde'. The real Jane Scrope was at least
nineteen when Part I was written; for her Skelton has substituted the

fictional Jane of the poem, but knowledge of the real Jane's age can help to confirm our interpretation of the fiction. The conscious naïveté that goes with the self-characterization attributed to her is important for the whole conception of the poem. It is what justifies the apparently innocent and breathless survey of her reading of English poetry in lines 612–818 and enables her to come up with devastatingly perceptive judgments about the relative worth of Chaucer and Lydgate. In Chaucer's writing, she says, 'There is no Englysh voyd' (795) and 'Ne worde he wrote in vayne' (803), whereas Lydgate

> Wryteth after an hyer rate;
> It is dyffuse to fynde
> The sentence of his mynde. (805–7)

Not many in the first decade of the sixteenth century could see so clearly what an obscure and pompous writer the much-admired Lydgate often was: it took a child to point out that the emperor was ludicrously overdressed. Some degree of childlikeness might be thought appropriate to a grown but unmarried and devout young woman in this period; and if it makes possible such penetrating literary criticism, so much the better. But it surely would not be expected that her innocence should lead her to reveal so much about the erotic aspects of her relationship with a pet bird.

　　Yet more detail of the relationship is given elsewhere. Jane remembers

> How my byrde so fayre,
> That was wont to repayre,
> And go in at my spayre,[4]
> And crepe in at my gore
> Of my gowne before,
> Flyckerynge with his wynges.
> Alas, myne hert it stynges,
> Remembrynge prety thynges!
> Alas, my hert it sleth
> My Phyllyppes dolefull deth!
> Whan I remembre it,
> How pretely it wolde syt
> Many tymes and ofte,
> Upon my fynger aloft!
> I played with him tytell-tattyll,
> And fed him with my spattyl,
> With his byll betwene my lippes,

> It was my prety Phyppes!
> Many a prety kusse
> Had I of his swete musse. (343–62)

Another glimpse of this intimacy is given later: after praying that Phyllyp might fly to heaven, Jane adds,

> For he was a prety cocke,
> And came of a gentyll stocke,
> And wrapt in a maidenes smocke,
> And cherysshed full dayntely, (588–91)

and she goes on to hope that when he reaches heaven he may 'treade the prety wren / That is our Ladyes hen' (600–1). A sparrow's heaven might be endless copulation; and one scholar, noting that 'Philip Sparrow' is a regular euphemism for the male sexual organ, proposes that Phyllyp should be interpreted as a phallic symbol.[5] Another has rightly objected that this is too limited a description of his role in Skelton's poems.[6] The eroticism of the Jane/Phyllyp relationship is more generally diffused, taking in many bodily parts, and it manifestly cannot be directed towards Freud's 'final sexual aim' of genital copulation. It can rather be seen either as corresponding to the 'polymorphous perversity' that Freud attributes to infantile sexuality before the development of the ego, or, perhaps more persuasively, as corresponding to the concept of female sexuality developed by Luce Irigaray. Here I take up again the argument offered in Chapter 7 in connection with *Partonope of Blois*. Irigaray claims that female sexuality is not 'unified', and this is because '*woman has sexual organs more or less everywhere*. She finds pleasure almost anywhere.'[7] She wishes to distinguish between this '*plurality of the erogenous zones* that are specifically feminine' and Freud's polymorphous perversity, based in her view on the assumption of the male as norm, 'in which the erogenous zones would lie waiting to be regrouped under the primacy of the phallus'.[8] Hence Jane's exhilarating indifference, in the passages quoted above, as to whether her contact with Phyllyp is via breasts, lip, naked skin, knee, toe, finger, or whatever is accessible through her *spayre* or *gore*. The effect is similar to the eroticism evoked in the darkened bed in *Partonope*, except that in *Phyllyp Sparowe* the question of mutuality simply fails to arise. Phyllyp evidently gains pleasure through his contact with Jane, but it is of a kind beyond our imagining.

It would be mistaken, though, to suppose that the Jane/Phyllyp relationship could be seen as an authentic imagining of a female sexuality not dominated by phallocentrism. This becomes apparent once we remember that all three parts of the poem were written by Skelton and ask, 'How does Skelton know about these revelations by Jane of her relationship with Phyllyp?' For the reader of the earliest printed text, as we have seen, Skelton's role as *compilator* is declared by the opening rubric, and the reference there and later to his laureateship implies that he is in fact *auctor* rather than *compilator*. And even if the manuscripts in which the poem may originally have circulated (none of them survive) had no such rubric, we can reasonably assume that most readers knew from the beginning that they were reading a work by Skelton rather than by Jane Scrope. (Jane as reader certainly knew this, supposing she commissioned the poem.) Skelton may not be hiding in a bush or behind a column in the nuns' chapel, but he is there somehow, hiding in Jane's mind – or rather, of course, inventing the mind of the fictional Jane who is part of the poem.[9] As with Dunbar's *Tretis of the Twa Mariit Wemen and the Wedo*, and even in the absence of a prologue such as Dunbar's, we surely have to bear in mind all along that this is female discourse imagined by a male poet: dialogue in the *Tretis*, soliloquy or stream of consciousness in *Phyllyp Sparowe*. The imagining of this unselfconscious and deliciously playful, mobile, decentred sexuality is that of Master Skelton, highly self-conscious poet laureate, and it is Master Skelton, priest and rector of Diss, who draws on the resources of Christian devotion as a means of evoking it. His assumptions are phallocentric, and he imagines female sexuality, I would argue, as the polymorphous perversity of the infant rather than in what Irigaray would see as more authentic terms; that is why Jane appears in the poem as a child, one much younger than the real Jane Scrope.

The eroticism of *Phyllyp Sparowe* is in this sense voyeuristic. Actaeon once more puts in his expected appearance, though only in the wish that the cat that killed Phyllyp might be killed by

> Melanchates, that hounde
> That plucked Acteon to the grounde,
> Gave hym his mortall wounde,
> Chaunged to a dere,
> The story doth appere ...   (296–300)

This time there is no explicit connection with a forbidden gaze at female nakedness, so perhaps Skelton did not really regard himself

(or Phyllyp) as an Actaeon peeping at Diana, even though in Part III
he conjures Phyllyp to explain why the poem should be discom-
mended

> Now by these names thre,
> Diana in the woodes grene,
> Luna that so bryght doth shyne,
> Procerpina in hell. (1363–6)

There is certainly little sign that Skelton feels shame, or feels that he
deserves punishment.

Phyllyp Sparowe has something in common with the eroticism of
that widespread kind of soft-porn movie that takes its viewers inside
an all-female institution such as a convent or a girls' boarding
school, and purports to reveal what surprisingly various forms are
assumed there by desire. There is much more to it than that, but
Part II surely confirms that there is an element of that voyeurism.
When he first openly intervenes in the poem, emerging from the
Latin curtain between Parts I and II, Skelton praises Jane not for her
moral qualities (except learning) but almost exclusively for her
physical attractiveness: she is 'Prestanti corpore virgo' (839), a
maiden surpassing in body. In the refrains in Part II she is celebrated
for the twin fame – *Hac claritate gemina* – of beauty and virtue; but
when, after elaborate preliminaries, Skelton finally begins his praise
of her in English, it is again physical beauty that is emphasized. He
divides and fetishizes her bodily parts, converting them into jewels
and food, as in the rhetoricians' recipes for *effictio*, and then moves
in, like Guillaume de Lorris, from the scopic to the oral:

> The Indy saphyre blew
> Her vaynes doth ennew;
> The orient perle so clere,
> The whytnesse of her lere;
> The lusty ruby ruddes
> Resemble the rose buddes;
> Her lyppes soft and mery
> Emblomed lyke the chery,
> It were an hevenly blysse
> Her sugred mouth to kysse. (1031–40)

He even includes those delightful imperfections, the 'warte upon her
cheke, ... Lyke to the radyant star' (1043–7) and the 'sker upon her
chyn' (1077) which

> wold make any man
> To forget deadly syn
> Her favour to wyn.   (1080–2)

The wish to forget deadly sin is a longing for innocence like that
attributed earlier to Jane in her dealings with the sparrow: 'God
wot, we thought no syn ...' (168). What most attracts him about
Jane is not a dazzling and detached vision of beauty as jewel-like or
star-like, but just the kind of physical contact that he imagines her
having with Phyllyp. He remembers a squeeze from her hand, given
perhaps to emphasize persuasively some point she was making in
conversation:

> And with her fyngers smale,
> And handes soft as sylke,
> Whyter than the mylke,
> That are so quyckely vayned,
> Wherwyth my hand she strayned,
> Lorde, how I was payned!
> Unneth I me refrayned,
> How she me had reclaymed,
> And me to her retayned,
> Enbrasynge therewithall
> Her goodly myddell small
> With sydes longe and streyte;
> To tell you what conceyte
> I had than in a tryce,
> The matter were to nyse,
> And yet there was no vyce,
> Nor yet no vyllany,
> But only fantasy ...   (1118–35)

The veins in her hands are now thought of not as like sapphires but
as full of living blood, not distant but close, not visual but tactile –
'soft as sylke' – with the tactility verging on orality in 'Whyter than
the mylke'. The syntactical vagueness in the middle of this passage
expresses the uncertainty of the relation between what really
happened when she squeezed his hand and what he only imagined.
(It is like a cinematic sequence designed so that one cannot be sure,
at least until it is complete, whether it is intended to represent a real
fictional event or 'only fantasy'.) Thus Skelton embarks on a fantasy
about physical intimacy with Jane comparable to what she allowed
to the sparrow, and he defends that fantasy against possible
criticism just as he had fantasized she defended Phyllyp's intimacy

with her. He asks a series of rhetorical questions, which pretend not to reveal precisely what they *are* revealing about his erotic imaginings:

> But whereto shulde I note
> How often dyd I tote
> Upon her prety fote?
> It raysed myne hert rote
> To se her treade the grounde
> With heles shorte and rounde. (1145–50)

> Wherto shuld I disclose
> The garterynge of her hose?
> It is for to suppose
> How that she can were
> Gorgiously her gere. (1175–9)

That second passage is particularly tricky in its effect, since it asks why he should 'disclose' what he presumably has not literally disclosed or uncovered, but only 'supposed'. We are very close to the kind of pin-up picture of a young woman in her underwear that is generally associated with the age of photography. This verbal picture, however, is more complex, since Skelton refers not to what is seen but to what he only imagines being able to see – and the reader can only imagine him imagining it. And in a third passage he goes on implicitly to invite the reader – doubtless always male in Skelton's mind – to construct the imaginings that he can 'Neyther wryte nor say':

> Her kyrtell so goodly lased
> And under that is brased
> Such pleasures that I may
> Neyther wryte nor say;
> Yet though I wryte not with ynke,
> No man can let me thynke,
> For thought hath lyberte,
> Thought is franke and fre;
> To thynke a mery thought
> It cost me lytell nor nought. (1194–203)

What cannot be written with the phallic clerical pen can always be fantasized. The disingenuous defence of 'mery thought' is reminiscent of the passage from *The Knight's Tale* discussed in Chapter 8, where the storyteller says he 'dar nat telle' (1 2284) in detail how Emelye performed the rites involving female nakedness in the temple of Diana, 'But it is good a man been at his large' (2288).

These passages confirm Skelton's role in *Phyllyp Sparowe* as an imaginative voyeur, and the role seems likely to be connected with his priestly status and the celibacy to which it theoretically committed him. After these suggestive passages, Skelton begins talking explicitly about his pen–

> My pen it is unable,
> My hand it is unstable ...   (1219–20)

> And where my pen hath offendyd,
> I pray you it may be amendyd ...   (1245–6)

– and the unconscious pun on 'pen', of the kind I suggested in Dunbar's *Tretis*, comes nearer to the surface. The pen intrudes as Skelton's representative where Skelton himself is forbidden; and this also confirms the phallocentrism implicit precisely in his imagining of female sexuality as polymorphous perversity. No wonder Jane felt shame (if that is not also part of the fiction) at this literary uncovering of what in reality she no doubt kept modestly covered. Skelton's 'I have not offended, I trust' (1249) is laughably disingenuous, and it already prepares the way for the *addicyon* that was evidently not made until some years later. Yet ultimately what is uncovered is not Jane's garters but Skelton's voyeuristic imagination. In Dunbar's case, I suggested that some Merchant-like self-contempt was involved in his self-presentation as voyeur; I do not see that in Skelton's case, only a much more cheerful self-knowledge and even self-exposure: the voyeur as exhibitionist, inviting us to watch him watching. But if (which may be doubted) Skelton was capable of shame, it was himself he had shamed in writing, and still more in publishing, *Phyllyp Sparowe*.

Notes

1 THEORIES OF LOOKING

1 For obvious reasons, I generally refer to medieval writers by masculine pronouns. In Chapter 5 I discuss the treatment of looking by a female poet.

2 Cf. Skinner, ed., *Return of Grand Theory*.

3 Lacan, *Four Fundamental Concepts*, p. 118. That the eye is actually aggressive as well as luring 'in nature' is made clear by Argyle and Cook, *Gaze and Mutual Gaze*; they note indeed that 'it is only in the primates and man that gaze functions as an affiliative signal: in all the other species gaze is primarily a signal for aggression' (p. 4).

4 See the English title of his 1925 paper, 'Einige psychische Folgen des anatomischen Geschlechtsunterschieds' (English version in *SE*, XIX, pp. 248–58). I find myself similarly sceptical about Freud's assertion in his 1927 paper 'Fetishism' that 'Probably no male human being is spared the fright of castration at the *sight* of a female genital' (XXI, p. 154) – recognizing, however, that Freud elsewhere describes such scepticism about the castration complex as 'a piece of virtuosity in the art of *overlooking*' ('Some Psychical Consequences', XIX, p. 253, n. 4).

5 Barthes suggested that 'we ought to be able to say *écouteur* as we say *voyeur*' (*S/Z*, p. 132). Except where otherwise indicated, I include listening within looking and 'écouteurism' within voyeurism; but occasionally (e.g. Chapter 7) I take up questions of differences between the two. I have little to say about oral delivery and aural reception in the Middle Ages, topics about which less is known than I once supposed.

6 References to *SE*, VII.

7 Here of course Freud uses the term 'voyeur' in a specialized sense. Cf. pp. 172–3.

8 Or as more perverse than any other form of desire; for within psychoanalytic thought the child's original union with the mother is always irrecoverably lost, and even genital sexuality is a 'perverse' substitute for that unattainable goal.

9 Bergstrom, 'Sexuality at a Loss', p. 258.

10 See Davidson, 'How to Do the History of Psychoanalysis'; also Marcus, 'Freud's *Three Essays*'.
11 Brundage, *Law, Sex, and Christian Society*, p. 5.
12 Payer, *Sex and the Penitentials*, p. 115.
13 Cf. Brundage, *Law, Sex and Christian Society*, pp. 197–8. An extreme though respected view was that of Saint Jerome: 'Nothing is filthier than to have sex with your wife as you might do with another woman' (*Adversus Jovinianum* 1 49, cited Brundage, pp. 90–1).
14 Lindberg, *Theories of Vision*, p. x.
15 *Commentary on Aristotle's De anima*, Lectio 13 on Book III, par. 792, cited Carruthers, *Book of Memory*, p. 54.
16 *On the Properties of Things*, I, p. 108.
17 *Homilies on the Statues* xv, cited by Bloch, 'Medieval Misogyny', p. 15.
18 Chaucer quoted from *Riverside Chaucer*.
19 English text of Scripture taken from the Douay translation of the Vulgate.
20 *Piers Plowman* quoted from Langland, *Vision of Piers Plowman*, ed. Schmidt. My remarks about 'lust of the eyes' are based on Howard, *Three Temptations*, ch. 1.
21 *Handlyng Synne* quoted from ed. Sullens.
22 This may mean mental handling, as in the title of *Handlyng Synne*.
23 Andreas quoted from *Andreas Capellanus on Love*, ed. Walsh.
24 *Cligés* quoted in French from ed. Wendelin Foerster, rev. Hilka. In English translation, all Chrétien's romances are quoted from *Arthurian Romances*, trans. Owen.
25 *Eneas*, ed. Salverda de Grave; trans. Yunck, p. 217.
26 This case is argued by Kline, 'Heart and Eyes', but not conclusively; see, e.g., the sixth-century passage from Musaeus Grammaticus cited by Grabes, *Mutable Glass*, p. 335: 'The renowned beauty of a superb example of womanhood affects a mortal more immediately and strongly than an arrow shot from a bow. It is the eye, however, that is the pathway; the missile flies through and beyond the eye and makes its way to the man's heart.'
27 Argyle and Cook, *Gaze and Mutual Gaze*, p. 1.
28 Sartre, *Being and Nothingness*, pp. 277, 288–9 (Sartre's italics). Sartre explains earlier that by 'the Other' he means that which transcends my own transcendence as a subject, and thus 'God here is only the concept of the Other pushed to the limit' (p. 266). For Lacan's critique of Sartre's analysis of the look, see *Four Fundamental Concepts*, pp. 84–5.
29 For a placing of *The City of God* within the complicated history of Augustine's views of marriage, see Clark, '"Adam's Only Companion"'.
30 For acute analysis of this connection in *King Lear*, see Cavell, 'The Avoidance of Love'.
31 *City of God* quoted in Latin from ed. Levine, IV, and in English from the

translation of Healey, ed. Tasker, II – less exact but more eloquent than more recent versions.

32 'On the Sexual Theories of Children', p. 220; see also *Three Essays*, p. 196.

33 Another source of information is court records, from which the lack of privacy available to most medieval people also obliquely emerges. Thus Brundage refers to an English case about 1200 in which a woman sought to prove her married status by witnesses who had seen her and her alleged husband 'in bed together on several occasions'; and to one of 1270 in which 'three witnesses asserted that while on their way to the tavern they had observed Richard Wood copulating with Matilda Goderhele in a neighbor's croft' (*Law, Sex, and Christian Society*, pp. 413, 460).

34 *Sir Gawain and the Green Knight* quoted from ed. Tolkien and Gordon, rev. Davis.

35 Cf. Ribard, 'Espace romanesque', p. 76, on the forest as 'espace romanesque privilégié' opposed to the restricted realm of daily life.

36 Given-Wilson, *Royal Household*, pp. 29, 32.

37 Beroul quoted in French and English from ed. and trans. Lacy. Danielle Régnier-Bohler's discussion of this passage, *Revelations of the Medieval World*, p. 318, misrepresents the situation, implying that Mark's knights know that his intended destination is the dangerous forest. See also lines 389–90, where Iseult expresses astonishment that Mark should even enter their chamber alone.

38 Noted by Wilson, *Gawain-Poet*, p. 123. In this Bertilak resembles the English kings of the poet's time, who rebuilt royal castles and palaces to provide more chambers, usually with fireplaces (see Given-Wilson, *Royal Household*, pp. 30–9). Cf. Foucault: 'beginning at a certain moment it was possible to build a chimney inside the house – a chimney with a hearth, not simply an open room or a chimney outside the house . . . at that moment all sorts of things changed and relations between individuals became possible' (*Foucault Reader*, ed. Rabinow, p. 253).

39 See e.g. Pearsall, 'Gardens as Symbol and Setting'.

40 See Bloch, *Medieval French Literature and Law*. Note especially Bloch's statement that 'Within a feudal accusatory system entrapment *in flagrante delicto* represents the chief method of verifying suspected criminal offense . . . Since the judge cannot accuse on his own and since the plaintiff must wait until an infraction has actually taken place before lodging an *apel*, the attempt to set the stage for and to lure the criminal into purposeful wrongdoing was an important prosecutory mechanism of the feudal court' (p. 59). This mechanism accounts for much of the narrative material of romances of adultery.

41 The general principle is stated by Ovid, *Amores* II 19.3, 'quod licet, ingratum est; quod non licet acrius urit' [What one may do freely has no harm; what one may not do pricks more keenly on], and III 4.17,

'nitimur in vetitum semper cupimusque negata' [We ever strive for what is forbid, and ever covet what is denied] (*Heroides and Amores*, ed. and trans. Showerman, rev. Goold). Freud makes the same point in 'On the Universal Tendency': 'the psychical value of erotic needs is reduced as soon as their satisfaction becomes easy. An obstacle is required in order to heighten libido; and where natural resistances to satisfaction have not been sufficient men have at all times erected conventional ones so as to be able to enjoy love' (*SE*, XI, p. 187). See also Lacan, quoted in Chapter 10, n. 10.

42 *Filostrato* IV 153 (*Chaucer's Boccaccio*, trans. Havely, p. 73): 'The reason why our love is such a delight to you is that you are able to attain this paradise only rarely and by means of stealth. But if you were able to possess me without difficulty, the torch of passion which now makes you burn would quickly be put out, and the same would happen with me. Thus if we want our love to last, we must always enjoy it secretly as we are doing now.'

43 Miller, *Novel and the Police*, pp. 195, 207. My train of thought about secrecy was first published in my *Chaucer: Troilus and Criseyde*, pp. 32–5.

44 Charles d'Orléans, *English Poems*, ed. Steele and Day, line 1609. Charles imagines his heart being wakened in this chamber when the light of his mistress's beauty shines 'In at the wyndowes of my derkid eyne' (1608).

45 *Ways of Seeing*, pp. 47 (Berger's italics), 49, 50, 54.

46 'Visual Pleasure and Narrative Cinema'; see also Kaplan, 'Is the Gaze Male?'. For a critique of the emphasis on male mastery in the experience of watching movies, see Williams, 'Power, Pleasure, and Perversion', pp. 48ff.

47 *English Poems*, lines 311–12, 294–7.

48 The ambiguity may be illustrated from an example in Doane's important article, 'Film and the Masquerade'. Doane reproduces a Robert Doisneau photograph in which the camera's eye, looking outward through a shop window, catches a middle-aged woman looking at a picture invisible to us, while an accompanying man (presumably her husband) surreptitiously gazes at another picture which we can see to be a crudely erotic painting of a young woman. Doane analyses the photograph in terms of the dominant male gaze, yet it could well be seen as conveying male powerlessness: the man wants what he cannot have, while his wife is evidently unaware and/or heedless of his desire and is content with the object of *her* gaze. The object of the man's look is not a woman but a picture from which he is separated by the window, and the picture is not even a photograph but a talentless painting; thus it is multiply removed from the possibility of possession. The man would be shamed to know he had been photographed; the woman would not.

49 See Hanning, *Individual in Twelfth-Century Romance*, pp. 54ff.

2 EXAMPLES OF LOOKING

1 A pre-courtly word with sexual connotations (cf. Middle English *lemman*).

2 *Gedichte Walthers von der Vogelweide*, ed. Kuhn, pp. 52–3.

3 Translation by Vickie Ziegler, to whom I am much indebted for calling the poem to my attention and annotating it for me.

4 'ir meisterinne . . . diu von der Vogelweide' (4800–1). Gottfried's *Tristan* quoted in German from Friedrich Ranke's text given in ed. Krohn, and in English from trans. Hatto (here p. 107).

5 Cf. the more literal analogy between cinema and voyeurism developed by Metz in *Psychoanalysis and Cinema*, especially pp. 58–78.

6 Text and translation from Goldin, *Mirror of Narcissus*, pp. 109–10; I am indebted to Goldin's discussion of the poem.

7 In early sixteenth-century England, John Skelton develops the second idea in *Speke Parott*, where he is himself the caged bird who conveys biting satire through multilingual allegorical chattering that he purports not to understand. See my *Medieval to Renaissance*, pp. 265–77; and, for a Skeltonian example of the bird as voyeur, Chapter 14 below.

8 *Mirror of Narcissus*, p. 112.

9 I quote *A Pistel of Susan* from *Alliterative Poetry*, ed. Turville-Petre, pp. 120–39.

10 Noted by Turville-Petre, *Alliterative Poetry*, p. 131.

11 *Alliterative Poetry*, p. 126.

12 For this distinction, see Clark, *The Nude*, p. 1: 'To be naked is to be deprived of our clothes and the word implies some of the embarrassment which most of us feel in that condition.' Berger uses the terms in an approximately opposite sense: 'To be naked is to be oneself. To be nude is to be seen naked by others and yet not recognized for oneself' (*Ways of Seeing*, p. 54).

13 *Metamorphoses* III quoted in Latin and English from ed. and trans. Miller, rev. Goold.

14 *Faerie Queene* quoted from ed. Hamilton; here III vi 17, line 6, and 18, lines 4 and 8. I am indebted to the discussion of this passage by Krier, *Gazing on Secret Sights*, pp. 118–21. Krier stresses the difference made by the athletic context of the bathing, which tends to de-eroticize the spectacle; her remarks seem to me, however, to be truer of Ovid's than of Spenser's version, even though Spenser's fictional spectator is a female deity.

15 *Gazing on Secret Sights*, p. 64.

16 Barkan, *Gods Made Flesh*, p. 45.

17 On connections among blushing, sexual arousal, and voyeurism see Ricks, *Keats and Embarrassment*, especially chs. III-IV.

18 Cf. Vickers, 'Diana Described', p. 273: 'such a transgression violates proscriptions placed upon powerless men (male children) in relation to

powerful women (mothers)'. If Lacan's view that 'all human desire is based on castration' were accepted, the underlying experience might be interpreted as the male gaze directed at the female body marked by the scandal of phallic absence, and punished by a sparagmos corresponding to castration.

19 Both poems are quoted from *Surrey: Poems*, ed. Jones, pp. 18–20, but with repunctuation of the final couplet of 'Wrapt in my careless cloke'.

20 Cf. note 14 above.

21 Lines 563ff., ed. Faral, *Arts poétiques*; trans. Nims, *Poetria nova*, p. 36.

22 Williams, *Hard Core*, pp. 42–3, describing the fetishizing of the female body in Hollywood films as discussed by Mulvey, 'Visual Pleasure and Narrative Cinema'.

23 Such is the implication of Stanbury's thought-provoking study, 'Feminist Film Theory'. One medieval rhetorician states that 'in praising a woman one should stress heavily her physical beauty. This is not the proper way to praise a man' (Matthieu de Vendôme, *Art of Versification*, trans. Galyon, p. 46), thus reflecting his age's assumption that 'Men look at women'. But even Matthieu acknowledges that poets may sometimes describe 'the splendor of a young man's beauty'.

24 Jean Frappier in *Arthurian Literature*, ed. Loomis, p. 295.

25 *Lancelot do Lac*, ed. Kennedy, I, p. 40; *Lancelot of the Lake*, trans. Corley, p. 29.

26 'Diana Described', p. 266. Developing Vickers's thought, Patricia Parker recognizes this technique's connection with Renaissance rhetoric (e.g. Erasmus, *De copia*), but she too seems unaware of its earlier history, and connects it with post-medieval commercialism and territorial exploration; see her *Literary Fat Ladies*, ch. 7.

27 Ed. Faral, line 558; trans. Nims, p. 36.

28 Williams, *Hard Core*, p. 207.

29 Page references to 1983 edn; extended quotation from ch. II:8.

30 *Novel and the Police*, p. 20 (Miller's italics).

3. THE TRISTAN STORY

1 De Rougemont, *Passion and Society*, p. 18.

2 Varvaro, *Beroul's 'Romance'*, p. 178.

3 Cf. Bloch, *Medieval French Literature and Law*, quoted Chapter 1, n. 40 above.

4 E.g. misericord carvings at Lincoln and Chester reproduced by Anderson, *Choir Stalls of Lincoln Minster*, plate 14, and *Misericords*, plate 31; and a French ivory casket in the Metropolitan Museum of Art.

5 *Passion and Society*, esp. Book 1.

6 Bédier, *Romance of Tristan and Iseult*, p. 13.

7 For listeners to an oral performance, the effect would differ in ways about which I can only speculate.

8 *Psychoanalysis and Cinema*, pp. 60, 64 (Metz's italics).

9 Bryson, *Vision and Painting*, p. 93.

10 As explained above, Thomas's version, not Beroul's, was Gottfried's actual source; but from the Norse translation it can be deduced that in this scene Thomas and Beroul were closely similar. (See *Saga of Tristram and Ísönd*, trans. Schach, p. 103.)

11 Cf. Quinn, 'Beyond Courtly Love', p. 193. For pictorial representations, see Baldwin, '"Gates Pure and Shining and Serene"', pp. 30ff.

12 *Tobler-Lommatzsch Altfranzösisches Wörterbuch*, under *escondit*.

13 Thus Tristan does not quite lie, contrary to the impression given by Fedrick's translation, p. 111: 'in their hearing I want you to allow me to clear myself and make my defence in your court. Never at any time did she or I love each other wickedly.'

14 I owe this point to David Hult.

15 Cf. Jackson, *Anatomy of Love*, pp. 164ff.

4. CHRÉTIEN DE TROYES

1 French text of Wendelin Foerster, as reprinted in ed. Reid.

2 An example of apparent improvisation occurs when Lunete offers as an argument for Laudine's marriage to Yvain the fact that Arthur is about to attack the magic spring and is due to arrive 'next week'. But, it seems suddenly to occur to Chrétien, how can Lunete and Laudine know of this? A makeshift explanation presents itself: 'You've already been informed of this in the letter sent you by the Dameisele Sauvage' (1617–21). Neither the letter nor the Dameisele Sauvage is mentioned elsewhere.

3 *Ywain and Gawain*, ed. Friedman and Harrington, line 806.

4 Metz, quoted p. 61.

5 For analysis of this description as an instance of rhetorical portraiture, see Colby, *Portrait in Twelfth-Century French Literature*, pp. 159–64.

6 *Ars amatoria*, ed. and trans. Mozley, III 431–2: 'Funere saepe viri vir quaeritur: ire solutis / Crinibus et fletus non tenuisse decet.' [Often a husband is sought for at a husband's funeral; it is becoming to go with dishevelled hair, and to mourn without restraint.]

7 Berger, *Ways of Seeing*, p. 47. Cf. the 'conception of womanliness as a mask, behind which man suspects some hidden danger', proposed by Joan Riviere in her 1929 paper, 'Womanliness as a Masquerade', p. 220. It seems likely that this conception would be all the more powerful, and all the more fully internalized by women, in a world generally more dominated than ours by male gazes, including that of the male deity.

8 It remains so to the end: when Lunete makes Laudine promise to obtain pardon for 'the Knight of the Lion', and then reveals that this is

Yvain himself, Laudine exclaims, 'God save me, you've got me well and truly in a trap!' (6760–1).

9 French text from ed. Foerster.

10 Cf. Meleagant's declaration to Bademagus: 'A vos tient la justise et monte, / Et je vos an requier et pri' (4872–3). [Justice is your business and responsibility, and I claim and beg it from you.]

11 Beroul 643–826; Gottfried 15117–266. Tristan's lack of scruple is partly justified by his being, unlike Lancelot, the victim of deliberate entrapment.

12 For a modern parallel (with pornographic film) cf. Williams, *Hard Core*, p. 49, citing Giles, 'Pornographic Space', and Lardeau, 'Le sexe froid'.

13 Zink, 'Chrétien et ses contemporains', p. 6.

14 Though not into that of the hero's parents on their wedding-night, where the narration dissolves into an impossibility-topos (lines 2353ff.). Perhaps this was felt to be a primal scene, and therefore taboo.

15 This indeed was one of the chief moral objections to Arthurian romances, that they were 'about the lies of this world and of the great Round Table', to quote an anonymous thirteenth-century life of Christ, cited by Kelly, 'Romance and the Vanity of Chrétien de Troyes', p. 76.

16 I discuss *King Horn* in these terms in my *Readings in Medieval Poetry*, ch. 2.

17 Freeman, '*Cligés*', p. 108. Freeman's essay includes a valuable sketch of the complex *Tristan–Cligés* relationships.

18 *Cligés* 548–61, echoed at 3100–3. In *Cligés* it is the hero's parents, not the hero and heroine, who fall in love on board ship.

19 *Cligés* 5772–8, referring to the drink taken by Fenice to give the appearance of death – a kind of narrative pun on the love-potion of *Tristan*.

20 See Fourrier, *Courant réaliste*, pp. 123–54.

21 *Three Essays*, quoted p. 3.

22 Hanning, *Individual in Twelfth-Century Romance*, *passim*, stresses the theme of *engin* in *Cligés* though, in my view, he draws mistaken conclusions.

23 Cf. Freeman, '*Cligés*', p. 116: 'in its metaphorical meaning the description [of Jehan's tower] shows the reader where Chrétien works, where he invents the artifices of romance narrative'.

5. THE LANVAL STORY

1 See Williams, '*Lanval* and *Sir Landevale*'. For fuller discussion of the two Middle English versions of *Lanval* and the one version of Marie's *Le Freine*, see Stemmler, 'Mittelenglischen Bearbeitungen', and my 'Marie de France'.

2 Marie de France quoted in French from her *Lais*, ed. Ewert (square brackets Ewert's); English translation from *Lais of Marie de France*, trans. Burgess and Busby.

3 This suggestion probably originated with Damon, 'Marie de France', p. 984; more recently, see Ramsey, *Chivalric Romances*, pp. 148–9. One scholar who rejects it as anachronistic is Clifford, *Marie de France: Lais*, p. 60. In fact the notion of wish-fulfilment is not anachronistic; the wish-fulfilling dream was recognized in the Middle Ages, e.g. in the widely used schoolbook known as the *Liber Catonianus* (see Pratt, 'Chaucer's Claudian', especially pp. 421–3 and n. 27). We do not of course have to suppose that wish-fulfilment was consciously intended by Marie.

4 Ménard, *Lais de Marie de France*, p. 182.

5 Ménard, p. 182.

6 'The fetish is a substitute for the woman's (the mother's) penis that the little boy once believed in and – for reasons familiar to us – does not want to give up' (Sigmund Freud, 'Fetishism', *SE*, xxi, pp. 152–3). The fetish, Freud adds, 'saves the fetishist from becoming a homosexual, by endowing women with the characteristic which makes them tolerable as sexual objects' (p. 154) – an insight it is tempting to connect with Guenevere's later accusation of homosexuality.

7 Berger, *Ways of Seeing*, p. 47. Marie de France tends to avoid voyeuristic moments in her *lais* (e.g. *Guigemar* 531–4); *Lanval* is a rare exception.

8 Cf. *Sir Gawain and the Green Knight* 1735–41.

9 For this general way of reading medieval romances, see Brewer, *Symbolic Stories*. Brewer's approach has been extended to Marie de France by Shippey, 'Breton *Lais* and Modern Fantasies', a paper which, however, treats *Lanval* only briefly.

10 *Symbolic Stories*, p. 11.

11 Critics have commented on the unknightly implications of Lanval's earlier abandonment of his horse by the stream, e.g. Koubichkine, 'A propos du *Lai de Lanval*', p. 474. Cf. Yvain's loss of horse and spurs when pursuing Esclados into his castle.

12 Cf. Hoepffner, *Lais de Marie de France*, p. 50, and Ménard, *Lais de Marie de France*, pp. 114, 116. Burgess, *Lais of Marie de France*, p. 20, sees the frequency of 'personal interventions' by Marie in this story (as in the following quotation above) as revealing her identification with her hero.

13 On Chestre's pretentious incompetence, see Mills, 'Composition and Style' and 'Note on *Sir Launfal* 733–44'.

14 *Sir Launfal* and *Sir Landevale* are quoted from *Sir Launfal*, ed. Bliss.

15 E.g., Bliss, ed. *Sir Launfal*, p. 28, and Lucas, 'Towards an Interpretation of *Sir Launfal*', p. 292.

16 Thus the formulaic phrase 'berde yn bour' (548) has a special, unformulaic appropriateness when applied to Tryamour.

17 Noted by Bliss, ed. *Sir Launfal*, p. 92.

18 There is a clear opposition in lines 496–501 between the *sale* where Launfal feasts 'Erles & barouns fale' and the *bour* where Tryamour

visits him; Chestre grasped this opposition but also felt impelled to dissolve it, hence the appropriateness of referring to 'resistance'.

19 *Must We Mean What We Say?*, p. 278.

20 Cf. Bradstock, ' "Honoure" in *Sir Launfal*'.

21 Whereas in *The Awntyrs off Arthure*, for example, King Arthur's hunt is interrupted by 'rydour of reyne' and 'snetterand snawe' (ed. Hanna, lines 81–2).

22 See John of Salisbury, *Frivolities of Courtiers*, trans. Pike, p. 18, and *Partonope of Blois*, ed. Bödtker, line 6356; references provided by Anne Rooney.

23 'Fetishism', pp. 153–4.

24 See Maraud, 'Lai de *Lanval* et *La Chastelaine de Vergi*', and Rychner, 'Présence et le point de vue'.

25 *La Chastelaine de Vergi* quoted in French from ed. Raynaud, rev. Foulet, and in English from *Aucassin and Nicolette*, trans. Matarasso, pp. 138–52.

26 See Reed, '*Chastelaine de Vergi*'. Her *seignor* (714) might mean her feudal lord, the Duke, rather than her husband.

27 Noted by Clifford, *Chastelaine de Vergi*, p. 15. The same words echo throughout the poem subsequently, with forms of *celer* at 319, 391, 499, 505, 603, 623, 638, 665, 679, 692, 947, 952, 955, and of *descouvrir* at 627, 634, 666, 771, 809, 814, 954. Another word frequently repeated, usually in combination with one or both of the others, is *conseil* [secret] (3, 10, 319, 499, 623, 626, 771, 809).

28 Cf. DuBruck, 'Rhetoric of Fin'Amors', pp. 77–8: 'It seems fitting ... that "her beautiful eyes" follow the Lover, since love begins with the sight of the beloved ... '.

6. TROILUS AND CRISEYDE AND THE MANCIPLE'S TALE

1 I do not imply that Chaucer had read any of the texts discussed in Chapters 3–5, though he was certainly generally familiar with the tradition of French courtly romances. One of the *romans d'antiquité*, Benoît de Sainte-Maure's *Roman de Troie*, is among the sources of *Troilus and Criseyde*.

2 Cf. Bloomfield, 'Distance and Predestination'.

3 E.g. Carton, 'Complicity and Responsibility' and, recently, Stanbury, 'Voyeur and the Private Life'. Also worth mention is Andrea Newman's novel, *An Evil Streak*: narrated by an academic who is producing a modern English version of Chaucer's poem, it retells Chaucer's story, with the narrator as pandar, as one of peculiarly perverse voyeurism. I am grateful to A. S. G. Edwards for calling it to my attention and giving me a copy.

4 'Voyeur and the Private Life', p. 144. This study of looking in

Chaucer's poem makes duplication unnecessary; I am grateful to the author for letting me see it before publication.

5 Smyser, 'Domestic Background', an article to which I am indebted throughout the present chapter.

6 Smyser, 'Domestic Background', p. 301, notes an apparent inconsistency as between *closet* and *chaumbre* in Book IV; I am not sure that it is real, but only because it is impossible, as it would surely never be in a novel, to be certain in whose house this episode takes place.

7 A more allusive instance of intertextuality occurs when Criseyde, having looked down from her window to see Troilus riding past, murmurs, 'Who yaf me drynke?' (II 651), thus recalling the magic potion of the Tristan story.

8 Cf. Fyler, 'Fabrications of Pandarus', p. 122: 'his action reminds us that we are doing exactly the same thing. We too are voyeurs, if only in the benign sense that all readers of literature are ...'.

9 See Mustanoja, *Middle English Syntax*, pp. 331ff.

10 Cf. Donaldson, 'Chaucer and the Elusion of Clarity'.

11 Windeatt, '"Love that oughte been secree"', p. 116.

12 E.g. II 76.

13 See Chapter 1, n. 42.

14 'Domestic Background', p. 311.

15 Green, 'Women in Chaucer's Audience', p. 149. Insofar as Chaucer's was a court audience, Given-Wilson's work confirms Green's argument, seeing the royal court as 'an almost exclusively male society' where women were likely to be present only as prostitutes (*Royal Household*, p. 60).

16 Windeatt, '*Troilus* and the Disenchantment of Romance', p. 141, notes parallels in the tailrhyme version of *Ipomadon*.

17 Cf. Stanbury, 'Voyeur and the Private Life', p. 153.

18 Fyler, 'Fabrications of Pandarus', pp. 115–16.

19 Not all readers agree that Pandarus stays all night: Ricks, *Keats and Embarrassment*, p. 62, writes that 'any sense of embarrassment within our contemplation, any voyeurism, is precluded: first by Pandarus's having espoused voyeurism and having left ...'.

20 For a statement of the opposing case, see apRoberts, 'Contribution to the Thirteenth Labour'.

21 To see Pandarus's motivation as involving sexual arousal is not merely a modern interpretation. In *The Garland of Laurel* 871–2 Skelton, one of Chaucer's most perceptive late-medieval readers, compliments Lady Elizabeth Howard on her beauty by addressing her as 'Goodly Creisseid, fayrer than Polexene, / For to envyve [i.e. revive] Pandarus appetite' (*Complete English Poems*, ed. Scattergood).

22 Cf. Carton, 'Complicity and Responsibility', pp. 56–8.

23 Subsequent references to *The Manciple's Tale* by line-numbers only.

24 For a recent listing of studies that thus read the tale as concerned with poetry, see Herman, 'Treason in the *Manciple's Tale*', p. 318, n. 4.
25 Cf. Delany, *Writing Woman*, p. 67.
26 For the view that *The Manciple's Tale* is a planned part of a pessimistic ending to the collection, see Howard, *Idea of the Canterbury Tales*, pp. 298–306, and Patterson, '*Parson's Tale* and the Quitting', pp. 377–8.

7 PARTONOPE OF BLOIS

1 Fourrier, *Courant réaliste*, 1, p. 315.
2 See Whiting, 'Fifteenth-Century English Chaucerian', and Windeatt, 'Chaucer and Fifteenth-century Romance'.
3 *Partonope*, ed. Bödtker (from British Museum MS), with my emendations in square brackets.
4 See Grigsby, 'Narrator in *Partonopeu de Blois*', and Krueger, 'Author's Voice', pp. 125–30.
5 French text quoted from *Partonopeu de Blois*, ed. Gildea.
6 See pp. 7–8.
7 Irigaray, *This Sex*, pp. 23–6. The essay quoted may be read in the context of Irigaray's extended critique of Freud, and especially of his lecture 'Femininity' (*New Introductory Lectures on Psychoanalysis*), in her *Speculum*, pp. 13–129.
8 Quotations from *SE*, XXI, p. 226.
9 Phrase used in English in *Question of Lay Analysis*, *SE*, XX, p. 212.
10 Krueger, 'Textuality and Performance', p. 60 and n. 10, notes the contrast between 'Partonopeu's visual discoveries in Melior's kingdom and his tactile experience of her bed' and the way this is expressed in the substitution of *sentir* for *veoir*.
11 Cited by Heath, 'Difference', p. 84.
12 III, 1247–53; see p. 132.
13 Ramsey, *Chivalric Romances*, pp. 139–40.
14 *This Sex*, pp. 139, 63, 31.
15 See Geoffroi de Vinsauf, *Poetria nova*, ed. Faral, *Arts poétiques*, lines 87ff., and, for application to Virgil and Lucan, Bernardus Silvestris, *Commentary on the First Six Books*, trans. Schreiber and Maresca, pp. 3–4.
16 Ed. Faral, lines 121–3; trans. Nims, p. 20.
17 On *engin* in *Partonopeus*, see Hanning, *Individual in Twelfth-Century Romance*, pp. 86–8; also Edwards, *Ratio and Invention*, ch. 6.
18 I 1564–66.
19 For this scene at least, Ihle's argument ('English *Partonope of Blois* as Exemplum', p. 305) that the English translator makes the poem 'an exemplum, providing good and bad examples of self-governance and other-governance', does not work.

8 THE KNIGHT'S TALE

1 Kolve, *Chaucer and the Imagery of Narrative*, p. 86.
2 Cf. my *Medieval to Renaissance*, chs. 1–2. See also Bloomfield, 'Chaucer's Sense of History', and Minnis, *Chaucer and Pagan Antiquity*.
3 Boitani, 'Style, Iconography and Narrative', p. 195.
4 The tale reflects the antifeminism of its Boccaccian source, but at the same time transmutes it into a vision of what we have learned to call a 'homosocial' culture (see Sedgwick, *Between Men*).
5 Subsequent references to *The Knight's Tale* will be by line-number only.
6 I refer indifferently to 'the Knight', 'the storyteller', 'the speaker', etc. *The Knight's Tale* existed as a separate work before becoming part of *The Canterbury Tales* (see Prologue to *The Legend of Good Women* F 420–1) and I see no evidence that its narrator is characterized in ways that distinguish him significantly from Chaucer, still less that he should be given credit 'for understanding and facing his own tale, for being fully capable of seeing what we see in it' (Leicester, *Disenchanted Self*, p. 222). The only significant 'characterization' of the tale's narratorial subject is as an adult heterosexual male.
7 For discussion, see Kolve, *Chaucer and the Imagery of Narrative*, pp. 86–105.
8 *Teseida* quoted in English from *Chaucer's Boccaccio*, ed. and trans. Havely, and, for parts omitted by Havely, from *Book of Theseus*, trans. McCoy; quoted in Italian from *Tutte le opere*, ed. Branca.
9 For opposing views, see Pratt, 'Conjectures regarding Chaucer's Manuscript', and Boitani, *Chaucer and Boccaccio*, especially ch. VI.
10 I 60 and gloss.
11 *Medieval to Renaissance*, p. 39.
12 Crane, 'Medieval Romance and Feminine Difference', p. 48.
13 E.g. Boitani, *Chaucer and Boccaccio*, and Salter, 'Chaucer and Boccaccio' in her *Fourteenth-Century English Poetry*, pp. 141–81.
14 'Repression', *SE*, XIV, p. 151.
15 E.g. 'Repression', p. 153; *Introductory Lectures on Psychoanalysis*, *SE*, XV, pp. 295–6.
16 *This Sex*, p. 123. Cf. Huchet, *Le Roman médiéval*, p. 218: 'La femme est l'Autre du récit qui en parle ...' (Huchet is discussing the *Eneas*).
17 For further emphasis on sight as wounding, see Arcite's account of how Cupid's fiery arrow has stabbed him through the heart (1563ff.).
18 I owe this point to Barbara Nolan.
19 It might be suggested that Fortune, a more slippery and unpredictable alternative to providence or destiny as an explanation of earthly events, is another form in which the repressed feminine returns.
20 'Medieval Romance and Feminine Difference', p. 48.
21 Crane refers to 'the masculine observer who edits out Emelye's body' (p. 55), but by mentioning it as a body he does not quite edit it out.

22 E.g. *Hali Meiðhad*, lines 518ff, in *Middle English Religious Prose*, ed. Blake, pp. 53ff.

23 Cf. Crane, p. 61: 'Diana is Emelye's celestial complement, feminine in romance's terms through her contradictory manifestations …'.

24 I owe this formulation to Lisa Samuels.

25 Suggested to me by Susan Crane.

26 E.g. Richard Neuse, 'The Knight: The First Mover'; Jones, *Chaucer's Knight*, pp. 192–211; Aers, *Chaucer*, pp. 24–32.

27 Subsequent references to *The Merchant's Tale* by line-number only.

28 *Tendre*, a recurrent word in this tale (see 1407, 1420, 1601, 1738, 1827), evokes the woman as a being made of flesh, delicious to devour, as in 'tendre veel' at 1420, and easily shaped or bruised. May proves to be tougher beef than Januarie imagines.

29 See p. 3.

30 Tatlock, 'Chaucer's *Merchant's Tale*', p. 370.

31 'On the Universal Tendency', *SE*, XI, p. 189.

32 The *Oxford English Dictionary* records no other fourteenth-century uses of *unsoft*, apart from Chaucer's own in *The House of Fame* 36.

9 THE SQUYR OF LOWE DEGRE

1 Pearsall, 'English Romance in the Fifteenth Century', p. 66, states that it 'should be dated not much earlier than the earliest [print] (c. 1520)'. 'Complete form' is misleading if A. S. G. Edwards's view is accepted that we have only 'variant versions of the poem that are late, corrupt, reflections of a design that was initially imperfect' ('Middle English Romance', p. 103).

2 References to ed. Mead; quotations, unless otherwise indicated, from Mead's text of the Copeland print (1555–60), but with modified punctuation.

3 See Kiernan, '*Undo Your Door*' (this being the romance's title in the fragmentary Wynkyn de Worde edition of c. 1520), and Rivers, 'Focus of Satire'. Kiernan's parodic interpretation is rejected by Pearsall, 'English Romance in the Fifteenth Century', p. 66, n. 1, as 'based upon an insensitive modern reading of the poem'; arguments against it are offered by Fewster, *Traditionality and Genre*, p. 130, n. 9. I am indebted to Fewster's chapter on the *Squyr*, and especially to her emphasis on storytelling: she describes it as 'a text concerned with narrativity' (p. 148), and notes how 'The emphasis … shifts from actions as actions, to action as narration, and even to narration without action' (p. 139). (See my review of Fewster, *Review of English Studies* ns 40 [1989], 546–7.)

4 'Anti-romance', a concept so dear to recent scholars that probably no major Middle English romance has not been so categorized, is here the suggestion of Kiernan, '*Undo Your Door*', p. 347.

5 Cf. Kane's praise of it as a product of 'the romantic imagination of a rare poet' (*Middle English Literature*, p. 99).

6 See Herman, 'Treason in the *Manciple's Tale*'.

7 Nearly all examples in the *Middle English Dictionary* are from Latin or French texts; in the *Oxford English Dictionary*, apart from the *Promptorium parvulorum* and the *Squyr* itself, the earliest instance in this sense is seventeenth-century. The only recorded use in a Middle English romance, the mid-fifteenth-century *Erle of Tolous*, ed. Rumble, line 310, refers to a place for secret observation that does not appear to be windowed.

8 Ed. Pearsall, lines 66–71. In Dunbar's *Tretis* (discussed in Chapter 13) the situation is reversed: Dunbar peers *in* through the hedge walling a garden.

9 The three florins are 'In tokenyng of the Trynyté' (246); the five are to be offered 'Whyles that ye are man on lyve' (244), possibly indicating that, like the first of the five fives of the pentangle in *Sir Gawain and the Green Knight* 640, they symbolize the five senses. Peck, 'Number as Cosmic Language' p. 77, notes that the five senses are 'the most common gloss for biblical 5s'.

10 'Digression to another part of the subject-matter', a rhetorical concept employed by Geoffroi de Vinsauf in his *Documentum de modo et arte dictandi et versificandi* (*Arts poétiques*, ed. Faral, p. 274).

11 Mead notes close parallels to this passage in four other Middle English romances (ed. *Squyr of Lowe Degre*, notes to lines 337 and 338); Fewster observes that three of them 'refer to the love of the hero and heroine' (*Traditionality and Genre*, p. 130). The human effect of the moment is strange, anticipating as it does the King's own plans for the story.

12 See p. 21.

13 This is followed by an explicit defence of male upward social mobility, whether by 'By fortune', 'By herytage' or 'by purchace' (379–80). Such passages are evidence for thinking of the *Squyr* as an early Tudor work: in the age of 'new men' the nature of nobility and the possibility of social advancement, discussed by Chaucer and other medieval writers as a largely theoretical ethical issue, had become of keen practical interest.

14 Rivers, 'Focus of Satire', p. 382.

15 In one line she addresses the intruder as 'squyer' (563); this may be inadvertence on the poet's part, or confusion on that of the half-asleep Princess, or possibly a generic term of address, to which the hero responds by saying 'I am your owne squyr' (567).

16 'I pray to God and Our Lady / Sende you the whele of vyctory' (257–8) reappears as lines 591–2, and 'And if we may not so come to, / Other wyse then must we do' (267–8) reappears in the form 'And yf ye may not do so, / Otherwyse ye shall come to' (587–8). The poem is

full of repeated and varied lines and phrases, creating an effect of
almost liturgical artifice, but repetition is especially noticeable here.

17 Rivers, 'Focus of Satire', p. 381.
18 Luke 11:17.
19 *The Winter's Tale* III 3.
20 Fewster, *Traditionality and Genre*, p. 138.
21 Cf. note 3 above.
22 'A gentylman borne' in the Wynkyn de Worde text (line 20).
23 Jones, *Origins of Shakespeare*, especially ch. 1.
24 Noted by Kiernan, '*Undo Your Door*', p. 348.
25 Ryan, *Shakespeare*, p. 103.
26 *King Lear* IV 6; *Measure for Measure* IV 3.

10. THE ROMAUNT OF THE ROSE

1 Vitz, 'The *I* of the *Roman*', pp. 52–5.
2 English text of *The Romaunt of the Rose* quoted from *Riverside Chaucer*.
3 For the relationship between the two, see Eckhardt, 'Art of Translation'.
4 Ed. Lecoy, from which I quote the *Roman* in French.
5 Lewis, *Allegory of Love*, p. 126.
6 Topsfield, '*Roman de la Rose*', p. 228.
7 Dahlberg, trans. *Romance of the Rose*, p. 3.
8 Robertson, *Preface to Chaucer*, p. 104. This view has been most fully
  developed by Fleming, *Roman de la Rose* and *Reason and the Lover*.
9 Cf. my *Medieval Dream-Poetry*, especially pp. 24ff.
10 See 'God and the *Jouissance* of The Woman', from Lacan's 1972–3
  Seminar XX, in *Feminine Sexuality*, ed. Mitchell and Rose, pp. 138, 143.
  The paper includes some discussion of 'courtly love' as being, for men,
  'an altogether refined way of making up for the absence of sexual
  relation by pretending that it is we who put an obstacle to it' (p. 141);
  but, except that he had read Denis de Rougemont, it is rather unclear
  what medieval phenomena Lacan was referring to as 'courtly love'.
11 Cf. McCash, 'Mutual Love as a Medieval Ideal'.
12 Hult, *Self-Fulfilling Prophecies*, Part III.
13 Cf. Köhler, 'Narcisse, la Fontaine d'Amour et Guillaume de Lorris',
  p. 150: 'Oiseuse ... est la personnification d'un temps dont on peut
  librement disposer.' 'Oiseuse' is most commonly, though not always,
  used in an unfavourable sense in Old French, but this reflects the
  predominance of a clerical value-system that Guillaume may reject.
14 Topsfield, '*Roman de la Rose*', p. 224.
15 *Douz Regart* is masculine in gender; but, as we shall see in Dunbar's
  Goldyn Targe (Chapter 12 below), the sex of Middle English and Scots
  personifications is not necessarily determined by the grammatical
  gender of their French or Latin originals.

16 Matthieu de Vendôme, *Ars versificatoria* 74, ed. Faral, *Arts poétiques*, p. 135, trans. Galyon, *Art of Versification*, p. 49. The terms *effictio* and *notatio* are used by Geoffroi de Vinsauf, *Poetria nova*, lines 1262–4.

17 In the *Roman* Jalousie is first mentioned earlier, at line 2844.

18 The reading of Guillaume by Chaucer and other medieval English poets was inevitably influenced by Jean's continuation, and this influence is recognizable in relatively small ways in the Middle English *Romaunt*. Thus what appears as a covert warning in the account of the fruit trees in Myrthe's garden – 'But it were any hidous tree, / Of which ther were two or three' (1353–4) – has an opposite sense in the French, which denies that there are any such trees (*Roman* 1324–7), while Amant's rejection of Resoun's advice is categorized as folly (3334–6) although no such condemnation appears in Guillaume's original.

19 Line 1284 has no equivalent in the French.

20 Of these features, only the passive verb is not present in the French (*Roman* 1481–6).

21 Wollheim, *Freud*, p. 118 (italics Wollheim's).

22 Cf. Chrétien's account of how Narcissus 'Vit an la fontainne sa *forme*' [saw his form in the spring] and died 'Por tant qu'il ne la pot avoir' [because he could not have it] (*Cligés* 2768–71).

23 See 'The mirror stage as formative of the function of the I', in Lacan, *Écrits*, pp. 1–7.

24 *Metamorphoses* III 420.

11. THE PARLIAMENT OF FOWLS AND A COMPLAYNT OF A LOVERES LYFE

1 *Fasti* I 415–40.

2 For other accounts, to both of which I am indebted, see Bennett, *Parlement of Foules*, pp. 91–106, and Salter, *Fourteenth-Century English Poetry*, pp. 132–40.

3 For fuller accounts, see my *Medieval Dream-Poetry*, pp. 89–101, and '"Al This Mene I Be Love"'.

4 See, e.g., Benson, 'The Occasion of *The Parliament of Fowls*'.

5 *Complaynt of a Loveres Lyfe* quoted from *John Lydgate: Poems*, ed. Norton-Smith; square brackets Norton-Smith's.

6 Like Chaucer in the *Book* Lydgate appears as a poet only at the end of his poem; Ebin, *John Lydgate*, p. 23, is mistaken in stating that 'the narrator's ... inability to write' is mentioned in the *Complaynt*'s prologue.

7 For this observation I am indebted to Kelly Sundberg Seaman.

8 *Fonteinne Amoureuse* quoted in French from *Œuvres de Guillaume de Machaut*, ed. Hoepffner; in English from *Chaucer's Dream Poetry*, ed. and trans. Windeatt, pp. 26–40.

9 Brownlee, *Poetic Identity*, p. 188, notes that Machaut begins by describing

his *Dit* as 'Faite de sentement' (11), but that the phrase is ambiguous as to *whose* feeling is the poem's inspiration.

10 See Pearsall, *John Lydgate*, pp. 84ff.
11 *Celured* 'canopied'; *cure* 'cover'.
12 Also Kelly Sundberg Seaman's suggestion.
13 Ed. *John Lydgate: Poems*, p. 174. Lydgate must be recollecting Arcite's reference to the same incident in his prayer to Mars (*Knight's Tale* 2388–90), where, however, there is no mention of laughter.
14 *Medieval Literary Theory and Criticism*, ed. Minnis and Scott, p. 229. For discussion see Minnis, *Medieval Theory of Authorship*, pp. 94–5.
15 See my *Medieval to Renaissance*, pp. 68, 108–9.
16 Reproduced in Minnis, *Medieval Theory of Authorship*, p. 195.

12. THE PALICE OF HONOUR AND THE GOLDYN TARGE

1 Douglas says that he completed his *Eneados* in July 1513, and that it fulfilled his promise to Venus (in the *Palice*) twelve years before.
2 For fuller accounts see Bawcutt, *Gavin Douglas*, ch. 3, and my *Medieval Dream-Poetry*, pp. 202–11.
3 *The Palice of Honour* quoted with occasional small modifications from the Charteris print of 1579, as represented in *Shorter Poems of Gavin Douglas*, ed. Bawcutt.
4 Bawcutt is rightly sceptical about R. D. S. Jack's claim that Petrarch's *Trionfi* influenced the *Palice*.
5 E.g. the *Kingis Quair* manuscript, the Bannatyne manuscript, and a Chepman and Myllar print. See Kratzmann, *Anglo-Scottish Literary Relations*, pp. 14–15.
6 *The Bestiary*, trans. White, p. 24.
7 *Being and Nothingness*, p. 263.
8 The date of *The Goldyn Targe* being uncertain, we do not know whether it or *The Palice of Honour* is earlier. The similarities make influence in one direction or the other seem likely.
9 Cf. King, 'Dunbar's *Goldyn Targe*'.
10 *The Goldyn Targe* quoted from *Longer Scottish Poems*, ed. Bawcutt and Riddy.
11 Ramson, 'Aureate Paradox', p. 102, notes the riddling quality of these lines, in which 'The courtly and religious meanings of "mercy" and "grace" are interchangeable, as "hell" and "Paradyce" are syntactically.' Similarly, towards the end of *The Palice of Honour*, Douglas comes to see the paradisal garden in which the poem began as 'maist like to Hell' (2094).
12 Cf. King, 'Dunbar's *Goldyn Targe*', p. 127.
13 *Poetria nova* 766ff.: 'Dentes nivei' (773), 'Tempora veris / "pingere" flore solum' (791–2).

14 Laura Brodie suggested this parallel.

13. THE TRETIS OF THE TWA MARIIT WEMEN AND THE WEDO

1 *Longer Scottish Poems*, ed. Bawcutt and Riddy, p. 195; *Tretis* quoted from this edition.
2 Ebin, *Illuminator, Makar, Vates*, p. 80.
3 Edwina Burness, 'Female Language', p. 362, observes that their loose hair 'can be seen as the physical counterpart of their free behaviour', rather than, as Hope proposes (*Midsummer Eve's Dream*, pp. 11–12), as indicating otherworld origins.
4 *Anglo-Scottish Literary Relations*, p. 132.
5 See *Medieval to Renaissance*, pp. 216–19.
6 Cf. Moore, 'Setting of the *Tua Mariit Wemen and the Wedo*', p. 62; 'Perhaps only the mind of a celibate, warped by repeated fits of hysterical longing for forbidden expression, could impugn the motives of women with such obvious pleasure and artful malice ... '; and, on the other hand, Lewis, *English Literature in the Sixteenth Century*, p. 94: 'If you cannot relish a romp, you had best leave this extravaganza alone ... '.
7 See Boswell, *Christianity, Social Tolerance, and Homosexuality*, pp. 146ff.
8 *Antony and Cleopatra* II 2.
9 Cf. *Wife of Bath's Prologue* 44b, a line that may not be genuinely Chaucerian but probably appeared in the text Dunbar read.
10 Pearcy, 'Genre of William Dunbar's *Tretis*', p. 72; for a contrary view, see Burness, 'Female Language', p. 362.
11 In courtly poetry the unhappy lover is compared to zero, as when Charles d'Orléans, after his lady's death, laments, 'Me thynkith right as a syphir now y serue, / That nombre makith and is him silf noon' (*English Poems*, lines 2042–3). The effect of 'syphyr *in bour*' is to reduce romantic melancholy to physical incapacity.
12 For this line's phallic connotation, cf. 485–6, quoted below.
13 Or Phyllis. Cf. Ross, *William Dunbar*, p. 229 and n. 21, and Bitterling, 'Tretis of the Tua Mariit Wemen and the Wedo', especially pp. 349–50.
14 See Freeman, *Undergrowth of Literature*, chs. 7–8.
15 *Poetria nova*, ed. Faral, lines 220–5; trans. Nims, p. 24.
16 Burness, 'Female Language', *passim*.
17 Cf. Ross, *William Dunbar*, p. 218: 'the satire of the poem ... is as much directed against men's obsession with sexuality in the love relation as that of women'.

14. PHYLLYP SPAROWE

1 Skelton quoted from ed. Scattergood; I have retranslated Skelton's Latin, though often borrowing phrases from Scattergood's versions.

2 For the liturgical sources I rely on Gordon, 'Skelton's *Philip Sparrow*', Brownlow, '*Boke of Phyllyp Sparowe*', and Wilson, '"Phillip Sparrow"'.

3 Brownlow, '*Boke of Phyllyp Sparowe*', p. 10.

4 *spayre*, opening in gown.

5 McConchie, '"Phillip Sparrow"'.

6 Halpern, 'John Skelton and Poetics', p. 240.

7 *Speculum*, p. 233; *This Sex*, p. 28 (Irigaray's italics).

8 *This Sex*, pp. 63 (Irigaray's italics) and 31; see also pp. 139–40.

9 Cf. Schibanoff, 'Taking Jane's Cue', p. 841: 'just as men of Skelton's era might claim ownership of female bodies, so this author claims proprietorship of Jane's text and arrogates to himself the exclusive control of her body'. Schibanoff, however, pursuing her argument that the poem's value lies in its being, 'quite simply, about reading and about readers' (p. 832), and thus in its having the good fortune to anticipate perfectly the theoretical assumptions of the 1980s, seems to forget that Skelton really is the author of 'Jane's text' and thus of her (textual) body.

Bibliography

A: TEXTS

Alliterative Poetry of the Later Middle Ages: An Anthology, ed. Thorlac Turville-Petre (London: Routledge, 1989)

Aquinas, Thomas, *Commentary on Aristotle's De anima*, trans. Kenelm Foster and Sylvester Humphries (London: Routledge, 1951)

Les Arts poétiques du XIIe et du XIIe siècle, ed. Edmond Faral (Paris: Champion, 1924)

Aucassin and Nicolette and Other Tales, trans. Pauline Matarasso (Harmondsworth: Penguin, 1971)

Augustine, *The City of God Against the Pagans*, ed. and trans. Philip Levine, 7 vols. (London: Heinemann, 1966)

    The City of God, trans. John Healey, ed. R. V. G. Tasker, 2 vols. (London: Dent, 1945)

The Awntyrs off Arthure, ed. Ralph Hanna (Manchester: Manchester University Press, 1974)

Bernardus Silvestris, *Commentary on the First Six Books of Virgil's Aeneid*, trans. Earl G. Schreiber and Thomas E. Maresca (Lincoln NE: University of Nebraska Press, 1979)

Beroul, *The Romance of Tristan by Beroul*, trans. Alan S. Fedrick (Harmondsworth: Penguin, 1970)

    The Romance of Tristran, ed. and trans. Norris J. Lacy (New York: Garland, 1989)

The Bestiary: A Book of Beasts, trans. T. H. White (New York: Putnam, 1954)

Boccaccio, Giovanni, *The Book of Theseus*, trans. Bernadette Marie McCoy (New York: Medieval Text Association, 1974)

    Chaucer's Boccaccio: Sources of Troilus and the Knight's and Franklin's Tales, trans. N. R. Havely (Cambridge: D. S. Brewer, 1980)

    Tutte le opere di Giovanni Boccaccio, ed. Vittore Branca (Verona: Mondadori, 1967)

Bradbury, Malcolm, *Rates of Exchange* (London: Secker and Warburg, 1983)

Capellanus, Andreas, *Andreas Capellanus on Love*, ed. and trans. P. G. Walsh (London: Duckworth, 1982)

Charles d'Orléans, *The English Poems of Charles of Orleans*, ed. Robert Steele and Mabel Day, Early English Text Society os 215, 220, rptd (London: Oxford University Press, 1970)

La Chastelaine de Vergi, ed. Gaston Raynaud, 3rd edn rev. Lucien Foulet (Paris: Champion, 1921)

Chaucer, Geoffrey, *Chaucer's Dream Poetry: Sources and Analogues*, ed. and trans. B. A. Windeatt (Cambridge: D. S. Brewer, 1982)

The Riverside Chaucer, ed. Larry D. Benson (Boston: Houghton Mifflin, 1987)

Chrétien de Troyes, *Arthurian Romances*, trans. D. D. R. Owen (London: Dent, 1987)

(Kristian von Troyes) *Cligés*, ed. Wendelin Foerster, 4th edn rev. Alfons Hilka (Halle: Max Niemeyer, 1921)

(Christian von Troyes) *Der Karrenritter (Lancelot)*, ed. Wendelin Foerster (Halle: Max Niemeyer, 1899)

(Chrestien de Troyes) *Yvain (Le Chevalier au Lion)*, ed. T. B. W. Reid (Manchester: Manchester University Press, 1942)

Chrysostom, John, *Homilies on the Statues*, in *A Select Library of Nicene and Post-Nicene Fathers*, ed. Philip Schaff, vol. ix (New York: Scribners, 1908)

Douglas, Gavin, *The Shorter Poems of Gavin Douglas*, ed. Priscilla J. Bawcutt, Scottish Text Society (Edinburgh: Blackwood, 1967)

Eneas: A Twelfth-Century French Romance, trans. John A. Yunck (New York: Columbia University Press, 1974)

Eneas: Roman du XIIe siècle, ed. J.-J. Salverda de Grave, 2 vols (Paris: Champion, 1925–9)

The Erle of Tolous, ed. Thomas C. Rumble, *The Breton Lays in Middle English* (Detroit: Wayne State University Press, 1965)

The Floure and the Leafe and The Assembly of Ladies, ed. D. A. Pearsall (London: Nelson, 1962)

Geoffroi de Vinsauf, *Poetria nova of Geoffrey of Vinsauf*, trans. Margaret F. Nims (Toronto: Pontifical Institute, 1967)

Gottfried von Strassburg, *Tristan*, ed. Rüdiger Krohn (Stuttgart: Reclam, 1980)

Tristan, trans. A. T. Hatto (Harmondsworth: Penguin, 1960)

Howard, Henry, Earl of Surrey, *Surrey: Poems*, ed. Emrys Jones (Oxford: Clarendon Press, 1964)

John of Salisbury, *Frivolities of Courtiers and Footprints of Philosophers*, trans. J. B. Pike (London: Oxford University Press, 1938)

Lancelot do Lac, ed. Elspeth Kennedy, 2 vols. (Oxford: Clarendon Press, 1980)

Lancelot of the Lake, trans. Corin Corley (Oxford: Oxford University Press, 1989)

Langland, William, *The Vision of Piers Plowman: A Complete Edition of the B-Text*, ed. A. V. C. Schmidt (London: Dent, 1978)

Longer Scottish Poems: Volume One, 1375–1650, ed. Priscilla Bawcutt and Felicity Riddy (Edinburgh: Scottish Academic Press, 1987)

Lydgate, John, *John Lydgate: Poems*, ed. John Norton-Smith (Oxford: Clarendon Press, 1966)

Machaut, Guillaume de, *Œuvres de Guillaume de Machaut*, ed. Ernest Hoepffner, vol. III (Paris: Champion, 1921)

Mannyng, Robert, *Handlyng Synne*, ed. Idelle Sullens (Binghamton NY: CEMERS, 1983)

Marie de France, *Lais*, ed. A. Ewert (Oxford: Blackwell, 1944)
  The Lais of Marie de France, trans. Glyn S. Burgess and Keith Busby (Harmondsworth: Penguin, 1986)

Matthew of Vendôme, *The Art of Versification*, trans. Aubrey E. Galyon (Ames: Iowa State University Press, 1980)

Medieval Literary Theory and Criticism c. 1100–c. 1375: The Commentary Tradition, ed. A. J. Minnis and A. B. Scott (Oxford: Clarendon Press, 1988)

Middle English Religious Prose, ed. N. F. Blake (London: Edward Arnold, 1972)

The Middle English Versions of Partonope of Blois, ed. A. Trampe Bödtker, Early English Text Society ES 109 (London: Kegan Paul, 1912)

Newman, Andrea, *An Evil Streak* (London: Michael Joseph, 1977)

Ovid, *Ars amatoria*, ed. and trans. J. H. Mozley, *The Art of Love, and Other Poems* (London: Heinemann, 1939)
  Fasti, ed. and trans. J. G. Frazer (Cambridge MA: Harvard University Press, 1967)
  Heroides and Amores, ed. and trans. Grant Showerman, 2nd edn rev. G. P. Goold (Cambridge MA: Harvard University Press, 1977)
  Metamorphoses, 2 vols., ed. and trans. Frank Justus Miller, 3rd edn rev. G. P. Goold (Cambridge MA: Harvard University Press, 1977)

Partonopeu de Blois, ed. Joseph Gildea, 2 vols. (Villanova PA: Villanova University Press, 1967–70)

Le Roman de la Rose, ed. Félix Lecoy, 3 vols. (Paris: Champion, 1965–70)

The Romance of the Rose, trans. Charles Dahlberg, 2nd edn (Hanover: University Press of New England, 1983)

The Saga of Tristram and Ísönd, trans. Paul Schach (Lincoln NE: University of Nebraska Press, 1973)

Sir Gawain and the Green Knight, ed. J. R. R. Tolkien and E. V. Gordon, rev. Norman Davis (Oxford: Clarendon Press, 1967)

Sir Launfal, ed. A. J. Bliss (London: Nelson, 1960)

Skelton, John, *John Skelton: The Complete English Poems*, ed. John Scattergood (Harmondsworth: Penguin, 1983)

Spenser, Edmund, *The Faerie Queene*, ed. A. C. Hamilton, corrected edn (London: Longman, 1980)

The Squyr of Lowe Degre, ed. William E. Mead (Boston: Ginn, 1904)

Trevisa, John, *On the Properties of Things: John Trevisa's translation of*

Bartholomæus Anglicus De proprietatibus rerum, ed. M. C. Seymour, 2 vols. (Oxford: Clarendon Press, 1975)

Walther von der Vogelweide, *Die Gedichte Walthers von der Vogelweide*, ed. Hugo Kuhn (Berlin: De Gruyter, 1965)

Ywain and Gawain, ed. Albert B. Friedman and Norman T. Harrington, Early English Text Society os 254 (London: Oxford University Press, 1964)

B: STUDIES

Anderson, M. D., *The Choir Stalls of Lincoln Minster* (Lincoln: Friends of Lincoln Cathedral, 1951)

Misericords: Medieval Life in English Woodcarving (Harmondsworth: Penguin, 1954)

Aers, David, *Chaucer* (Brighton: Harvester, 1980)

apRoberts, Robert P., 'A Contribution to the Thirteenth Labour: Purging the *Troilus* of Incest', in *Essays on English and American Literature and a Sheaf of Poems*, ed. J. Bakker, J. A. Verleun and J. v.d. Vriesenaerde, *Costerus* ns 63 (Amsterdam: Rodopi, 1987), pp. 11–25

Argyle, Michael, and Cook, Mark, *Gaze and Mutual Gaze* (Cambridge: Cambridge University Press, 1976)

Baldwin, Robert, '"Gates Pure and Shining and Serene": Mutual Gazing as an Amatory Motif in Western Literature and Art', *Renaissance and Reformation* ns 10 (1986), 23–48

Barkan, Leonard, *The Gods Made Flesh: Metamorphosis and the Pursuit of Paganism* (New Haven: Yale University Press, 1986)

Barthes, Roland, *S/Z*, trans. Richard Miller (New York: Hill and Wang, 1974)

Batts, Michael S., *Gottfried von Strassburg* (New York: Twayne, 1971)

Bawcutt, Priscilla, *Gavin Douglas: A Critical Study* (Edinburgh: Edinburgh University Press, 1976)

Bédier, Joseph, *The Romance of Tristan and Iseult*, trans. Hilaire Belloc and Paul Rosenfeld (Garden City NY: Doubleday Anchor, 1953)

Bennett, J. A. W., *The Parlement of Foules: An Interpretation* (Oxford: Clarendon Press, 1957)

Benson, Larry D., 'The Occasion of *The Parliament of Fowls*', in *The Wisdom of Poetry: Essays in Early English Literature in Honor of Morton W. Bloomfield*, ed. Larry D. Benson and Siegfried Wenzel (Kalamazoo: Medieval Institute, 1982), pp. 123–44

Berger, John, *Ways of Seeing* (London: BBC/Penguin, 1972)

Bergstrom, Janet, 'Sexuality at a Loss: The Films of F. W. Murnau', in *The Female Body in Western Culture: Contemporary Perspectives*, ed. Susan Rubin Suleiman (Cambridge MA: Harvard University Press, 1985), pp. 243–61

Bitterling, Klaus, '*The Tretis of the Tua Mariit Wemen and the Wedo*: Some

Comments on Words, Imagery, and Genre', in *Scottish Language and Literature, Medieval and Renaissance: Fourth International Conference 1984 – Proceedings*, ed. Dietrich Strauss and Horst W. Drescher (Frankfurt: P. Lang, 1986), pp. 337–58

Bloch, R. Howard, *Medieval French Literature and Law* (Berkeley: University of California Press, 1977)

'Medieval Misogyny' in *Misogyny, Misandry, and Misanthropy*, ed. R. Howard Bloch and Frances Ferguson (Berkeley: University of California Press, 1989), pp. 1–24

Bloomfield, Morton W., 'Chaucer's Sense of History', in his *Essays and Explorations: Studies in Ideas, Language, and Literature* (Cambridge MA: Harvard University Press, 1970), pp. 12–26

'Distance and Predestination in *Troilus and Criseyde*', in ibid., pp. 200–16

Boitani, Piero, *Chaucer and Boccaccio*, Medium Ævum Monographs ns 8 (Oxford: Society for the Study of Mediæval Languages and Literature, 1977)

'Style, Iconography and Narrative: the Lesson of the *Teseida*', in *Chaucer and the Italian Trecento*, ed. Piero Boitani (Cambridge: Cambridge University Press, 1983)

Boswell, John, *Christianity, Social Tolerance, and Homosexuality* (Chicago: University of Chicago Press, 1980)

Bradstock, E. M., '"Honoure" in *Sir Launfal*', *Parergon* #24 (1979), 9–17

Brewer, Derek, *Symbolic Stories* (Cambridge: D. S. Brewer, 1980)

Brownlee, Kevin, *Poetic Identity in Guillaume de Machaut* (Madison: University of Wisconsin Press, 1984)

Brownlow, F. W., '*The Boke of Phyllyp Sparowe* and the Liturgy', *English Literary Renaissance* 9 (1979), 5–20

Brundage, James A., *Law, Sex, and Christian Society in Medieval Europe* (Chicago: University of Chicago Press, 1987)

Bryson, Norman, *Vision and Painting: The Logic of the Gaze* (New Haven: Yale University Press, 1983)

Burgess, Glyn S., *The Lais of Marie de France: Text and Context* (Manchester: Manchester University Press, 1987)

Burness, Edwina, 'Female Language in *The Tretis of the Tua Mariit Wemen and the Wedow*', in *Scottish Language and Literature, Medieval and Renaissance: Fourth International Conference 1984 – Proceedings*, ed. Dietrich Strauss and Horst W. Drescher (Frankfurt: P. Lang, 1986), pp. 359–68

Carruthers, Mary J., *The Book of Memory: A Study of Memory in Medieval Culture* (Cambridge: Cambridge University Press, 1990)

Carton, Evan, 'Complicity and Responsibility in Pandarus's Bed and Chaucer's Art', *Publications of the Modern Language Association of America* 94 (1979), 47–61

Cavell, Stanley, 'The Avoidance of Love', in his *Must We Mean What We Say?* (Cambridge: Cambridge University Press, 1976), pp. 267–353

Clark, Elizabeth A., '"Adam's Only Companion": Augustine and the Early Christian Debate on Marriage', in *The Olde Daunce: Love, Friendship, Sex, and Marriage in the Medieval World.*, ed. Robert R. Edwards and Stephen Spector (Albany: SUNY Press, 1991), pp. 15–31

Clark, Kenneth, *The Nude: A Study of Ideal Art* (Harmondsworth: Penguin, 1960)

Clifford, Paula, *La Chastelaine de Vergi and Jean Renart: Le Lai de l'Ombre* (London: Grant and Cutler, 1986)

Marie de France: Lais (London: Grant and Cutler, 1982)

Colby, Alice M. *The Portrait in Twelfth-Century French Literature: An Example of the Stylistic Originality of Chrétien de Troyes* (Geneva: Droz, 1965)

Crane, Susan, 'Medieval Romance and Feminine Difference in *The Knight's Tale*', *Studies in the Age of Chaucer* 12 (1990), 47–63

Damon, S. Foster, 'Marie de France: Psychologist of Courtly Love,' *Publications of the Modern Language Association of America* 44 (1929), 968–96

Davidson, Arnold I., 'How to Do the History of Psychoanalysis: A Reading of Freud's *Three Essays on the Theory of Sexuality*', in *The Trial(s) of Psychoanalysis*, ed. Françoise Meltzer (Chicago: University of Chicago Press, 1988), pp. 39–64

Delany, Sheila, *Writing Woman* (New York: Schocken Books, 1983)

Doane, Mary Ann, 'Film and the Masquerade: Theorising the Female Spectator', *Screen* 23:3/4 (1982), 74–87

Donaldson, E. Talbot, 'Chaucer and the Elusion of Clarity', *Essays and Studies* ns 25 (1972), 23–44

DuBruck, Edelgard E., 'The Rhetoric of Fin'Amors in the *Châtelaine de Vergi*: Inexpressibility and Hyperbole', in *Courtly Romance: A Collection of Essays*, ed. Guy Mermier (Detroit: Michigan Consortium for Medieval and Early Modern Studies, 1984), pp. 73–88

Duby, Georges, ed. *Revelations of the Medieval World*, trans. Arthur Goldhammer (vol. II of *A History of Private Life*, ed. Philippe Ariès and Georges Duby) (Cambridge MA: Belknap Press, 1988)

Ebin, Lois A., *Illuminator, Makar, Vates: Visions of Poetry in the Fifteenth Century* (Lincoln NE: University of Nebraska Press, 1988)

John Lydgate (Boston: Twayne, 1985)

Eckhardt, Caroline D., 'The Art of Translation in *The Romaunt of the Rose*', *Studies in the Age of Chaucer* 6 (1984), 41–63

Edwards, A. S. G., 'Middle English Romance: The Limits of Editing, the Limits of Criticism', in *Medieval Literature: Texts and Interpretation*, ed. Tim William Machan (Binghamton: MRTS, 1991), pp. 91–104

Edwards, Robert R., *Ratio and Invention: A Study of Medieval Lyric and Narrative* (Nashville: Vanderbilt University Press, 1989)

Fewster, Carol, *Traditionality and Genre in Middle English Romance* (Cambridge: D. S. Brewer, 1987)

Fleming, John V., *Reason and the Lover* (Princeton: Princeton University Press, 1984)

The Roman de la Rose: A Study in Allegory and Iconography (Princeton: Princeton University Press, 1969)

Foucault, Michel, *The Foucault Reader*, ed. Paul Rabinow (New York: Pantheon, 1984)

Fourrier, Anthime, *Le Courant réaliste dans le roman courtois en France au moyen âge*, vol. I (Paris: Nizet, 1960)

Freeman, Gillian, *The Undergrowth of Literature* (London: Nelson, 1967)

Freeman, Michelle A., '*Cligés*', in *The Romances of Chrétien de Troyes: A Symposium*, ed. Douglas Kelly (Lexington KY: French Forum, 1985), pp. 89–131

Freud, Sigmund, 'Family Romances' (*SE*, IX, pp. 237–41)
  'Female Sexuality' (*SE*, XXI, pp. 225–43)
  'Femininity' (*SE*, XXII, pp. 112–35)
  'Fetishism' (*SE*, XXI, pp. 152–7)
  Introductory Lectures on Psychoanalysis (*SE*, XV–XVI)
  'On Narcissism: An Introduction' (*SE*, XIV, pp. 73–102)
  'On the Sexual Theories of Children' (*SE*, IX, pp. 209–26)
  'On the Universal Tendency to Debasement in the Sphere of Love' (*SE*, XI, pp. 177–90)
  The Question of Lay Analysis (*SE*, XX, pp. 18–258)
  'Repression' (*SE*, XIV, pp. 146–58)
  'Some Character-Types Met with in Psychoanalytic Work' (*SE*, XIV, pp. 311–33)
  'Some Psychical Consequences of the Anatomical Distinction between the Sexes' (*SE*, XIX, pp. 248–58)
  The Standard Edition of the Complete Psychological Works of Sigmund Freud, trans. James Strachey et al., 24 vols (London: Hogarth Press, 1953–74)
  Three Essays on the Theory of Sexuality (*SE*, VII, pp. 135–243)
  'The "Uncanny"' (*SE*, XVII, pp. 217–52)

Fyler, John M., 'The Fabrications of Pandarus', *Modern Language Quarterly* 41 (1980), 115–30

Gamman, Lorraine, and Marshment, Margaret, eds., *The Female Gaze: Women as Viewers of Popular Culture* (Seattle: Real Comet Press, 1989)

Giles, Dennis, 'Pornographic Space: The Other Place', in *The 1977 Film Studies Annual: Part 2*, pp. 52–65

Given-Wilson, Chris, *The Royal Household and the King's Affinity: Service, Politics and Finance in England 1360–1413* (New Haven: Yale University Press, 1986)

Goldin, Frederick, *The Mirror of Narcissus in the Courtly Love Lyric* (Ithaca: Cornell University Press, 1967)

Gordon, Ian A., 'Skelton's *Philip Sparrow* and the Roman Service Book', *Modern Language Review* 29 (1934), 389–96

Grabes, Herbert, *The Mutable Glass: Mirror-Imagery in Titles and Texts of the Middle Ages and English Renaissance*, trans. Gordon Collier (Cambridge: Cambridge University Press, 1982)

Green, Richard Firth, 'Women in Chaucer's Audience', *Chaucer Review* 18 (1983–4), 146–54

Grigsby, John L., 'The Narrator in *Partonopeu de Blois, Le Bel Inconnu,* and *Joufroi de Poitiers', Romance Philology* 21 (1968), 536–43

Halpern, Richard, 'John Skelton and the Poetics of Primitive Accumulation', in *Literary Theory/Renaissance Texts,* ed. Patricia Parker and David Quint (Baltimore: Johns Hopkins University Press, 1986), pp. 225–56

Hanning, Robert W., *The Individual in Twelfth-Century Romance* (New Haven: Yale University Press, 1977)

Heath, Stephen, 'Difference', *Screen* 19:3 (1978–9), 51–112

Herman, Peter C., 'Treason in the *Manciple's Tale', Chaucer Review* 25 (1990–1), 318–28

Hoepffner, Ernest, *Les Lais de Marie de France* (Paris: Boivin, 1935)

Hope, A. D., *A Midsummer Eve's Dream: Variations on a Theme by William Dunbar* (New York: Viking, 1970)

Howard, Donald R., 'Experience, Language and Consciousness: *Troilus and Criseyde,* II, 596–931', in *Medieval Literature and Folklore Studies,* ed. Jerome Mandel and B. A. Rosenberg (New Brunswick: Rutgers University Press, 1970), pp. 173–92

 The Idea of the Canterbury Tales (Berkeley: University of California Press, 1976)

 The Three Temptations (Princeton; Princeton University Press, 1966)

Huchet, Jean-Charles, *Le Roman médiéval* (Paris: Presses Universitaires de France, 1984)

Hult, David F., *Self-Fulfilling Prophecies: Readership and Authority in the First Roman de la Rose* (Cambridge: Cambridge University Press, 1986)

Ihle, Sandra, 'The English *Partonope of Blois* as Exemplum', in *Courtly Literature: Culture and Context,* ed. Keith Busby and Erik Kooper (Amsterdam: John Benjamins, 1990), pp. 301–11

Irigaray, Luce, *This Sex Which Is Not One,* trans. Catherine Porter (Ithaca: Cornell University Press, 1985)

 Speculum of the Other Woman, trans. Gillian C. Gill (Ithaca: Cornell University Press, 1985)

Jackson, W. T. H., *The Anatomy of Love: The Tristan of Gottfried von Strassburg* (New York: Columbia University Press, 1971)

Jones, Emrys, *The Origins of Shakespeare* (Oxford: Clarendon Press, 1977)

Jones, Terry, *Chaucer's Knight: The Portrait of a Medieval Mercenary* (London: Eyre Methuen, 1980)

Kane, George, *Middle English Literature* (London: Methuen, 1951)

Kaplan, E. Ann, 'Is the Gaze Male?', in *Desire: the Politics of Sexuality,* ed. Ann Snitow, Christine Stansell and Sharon Thompson (New York: Monthly Review Press, 1984), pp. 321–38

Kappeler, Susanne, *The Pornography of Representation* (Minneapolis: University of Minnesota Press, 1986)

Kelly, Douglas, 'Romance and the Vanity of Chrétien de Troyes', in *Romance: Generic Transformations from Chrétien de Troyes to Cervantes*, ed. Kevin Brownlee and Marina Scordilis Brownlee (Hanover: University Press of New England, 1985), pp. 74–90

Kiernan, K. S., '*Undo Your Door* and the Order of Chivalry', *Studies in Philology* 70 (1973), 345–66

Kinney, Arthur F., *John Skelton, Priest as Poet: Seasons of Discovery* (Chapel Hill: University of North Carolina Press, 1987)

King, Pamela M., 'Dunbar's *Goldyn Targe*: A Chaucerian Masque', *Studies in Scottish Literature* 19 (1984), 115–31

Kline, Ruth H., 'Heart and Eyes', *Romance Philology* 25 (1971–2), 263–97

Köhler, Erich, 'Narcisse, la Fontaine d'Amour et Guillaume de Lorris', in *L'Humanisme médiéval dans les littératures romanes du XIIe au XIVe siècle*, ed. Anthime Fourrier (Paris: Klincksieck, 1964), pp. 147–64

Kolve, V. A., *Chaucer and the Imagery of Narrative: The First Five Canterbury Tales* (London: Edward Arnold, 1984)

Koubichkine, Michèle, 'A propos du *Lai de Lanval*', *Le Moyen Age* 78 (1972), 467–88

Kratzmann, Gregory, *Anglo-Scottish Literary Relations 1430–1550* (Cambridge: Cambridge University Press, 1980)

Krier, Theresa M., *Gazing on Secret Sights: Spenser, Classical Imitation, and the Decorums of Vision* (Ithaca: Cornell University Press, 1990)

Krueger, Roberta L., 'The Author's Voice: Narrators, Audiences, and the Problem of Interpretation', in *The Legacy of Chrétien de Troyes*, ed. Norris J. Lacy, Douglas Kelly and Keith Busby, 2 vols. (Amsterdam: Rodopi, 1987), I, pp. 115–40

'Textuality and Performance in *Partonopeu de Blois*', *Assays* 3 (1985), 57–72

Lacan, Jacques, *Écrits: A Selection*, trans. Alan Sheridan (London: Tavistock, 1977)

Feminine Sexuality: Jacques Lacan and the 'école freudienne', ed. Juliet Mitchell and Jacqueline Rose (London: Macmillan, 1982)

The Four Fundamental Concepts of Psycho-Analysis, ed. Jacques-Alain Miller, trans. Alan Sheridan (New York: Norton, 1978)

Lapsley, Robert, and Westlake, Michael, *Film Theory: An Introduction* (Manchester: Manchester University Press, 1988)

Lardeau, Yanne, 'Le sexe froid (du porno au delà)', *Cahiers du Cinéma* 289 (June 1978), 49–61

Leicester, H. Marshall, *The Disenchanted Self: Representing the Subject in the Canterbury Tales* (Berkeley: University of California Press, 1990)

Lewis, C. S., *The Allegory of Love: A Study in Medieval Tradition* (London: Oxford University Press, 1936)

English Literature in the Sixteenth Century, Excluding Drama (Oxford: Clarendon Press, 1954)

Lindberg, David C., *Theories of Vision from Al-Kindi to Kepler* (Chicago: University of Chicago Press, 1976)

Loomis, R. S., ed. *Arthurian Literature in the Middle Ages* (Oxford: Clarendon Press, 1959)

Lucas, Peter J., 'Towards an Interpretation of *Sir Launfal* with Particular Reference to Line 683', *Medium Ævum* 39 (1970), 291–300

Maraud, A., 'Le Lai de *Lanval* et *La Chastelaine de Vergi*: la structure narrative', *Romania* 93 (1972), 433–59

Marcus, Steven, 'Freud's *Three Essays on the Theory of Sexuality*', in his *Freud and the Culture of Psychoanalysis* (New York: Norton, 1984), pp. 22–41

McCash, June Hall, 'Mutual Love as a Medieval Ideal', in *Courtly Literature: Culture and Context*, ed. Keith Busby and Erik Kooper (Amsterdam: John Benjamins, 1990), pp. 429–38

McConchie, R. W., 'Phillip Sparrow', *Parergon* #24 (August 1979), 31–5

Ménard, Philippe, *Les Lais de Marie de France: Contes d'amour et d'aventure du Moyen Age* (Paris: Presses Universitaires de France, 1979)

Metz, Christian, *Psychoanalysis and Cinema: The Imaginary Signifier*, trans. Celia Britton et al. (London: Macmillan, 1982)

Miller, D. A., *The Novel and the Police* (Berkeley: University of California Press, 1988)

Mills, M. 'The Composition and Style of the "Southern" *Octavian*, *Sir Launfal* and *Libeaus Desconus*', *Medium Ævum* 31 (1962), 88–109

'A Note on *Sir Launfal* 733–44', *Medium Ævum* 35 (1966), 122–4

Minnis, A. J., *Chaucer and Pagan Antiquity* (Cambridge: D. S. Brewer, 1982)

Medieval Theory of Authorship, 2nd edn (Philadelphia: University of Pennsylvania Press, 1988)

Moi, Toril, *Sexual/Textual Politics: Feminist Literary Theory* (London: Routledge, 1988)

Moore, Arthur K., 'The Setting of the *Tua Mariit Wemen and the Wedo*', *English Studies* 32 (1951), 56–62

Mulvey, Laura, 'Visual Pleasure and Narrative Cinema', *Screen* 16:3 (1975), 6–18

Mustanoja, Tauno F., *A Middle English Syntax*, Part 1 (Helsinki: Société Néophilologique, 1960)

Neuse, Richard, 'The Knight: The First Mover in Chaucer's Human Comedy', *University of Toronto Quarterly* 31 (1962), 299–315

Parker, Patricia, *Literary Fat Ladies: Rhetoric, Gender, Property* (London: Methuen, 1987)

Patterson, Lee W., 'The *Parson's Tale* and the Quitting of the *Canterbury Tales*', *Traditio* 34 (1978), 331–80

Payen, Jean-Charles, 'A Semiological Study of Guillaume de Lorris', *Yale French Studies*, 51 (1974), 170–84

Payer, Pierre J., *Sex and the Penitentials: The Development of a Sexual Code, 550–1150* (Toronto: University of Toronto Press, 1984)

Pearcy, Roy J., 'The Genre of William Dunbar's *Tretis of the Tua Mariit Wemen and the Wedo*', *Speculum* 55 (1980), 58–74

Pearsall, Derek, 'The English Romance in the Fifteenth Century', *Essays and Studies* ns 29 (1976), 56–83
'Gardens as Symbol and Setting in Late Medieval Poetry', in *Medieval Gardens*, ed. Elisabeth B. MacDougall (Washington DC: Dumbarton Oaks, 1986), pp. 237–51
John Lydgate (London: Routledge and Kegan Paul, 1970)
Peck, Russell A., 'Number as Cosmic Language', in *By Things Seen: Reference and Recognition in Medieval Thought*, ed. David L. Jeffrey (Ottawa: University of Ottawa Press, 1979), pp. 47–80
Polak, Lucie, *Chrétien de Troyes: Cligés* (London: Grant and Cutler, 1982)
Pratt, Robert A., 'Chaucer's Claudian', *Speculum* 22 (1947), 419–29
'Conjectures regarding Chaucer's Manuscript of the *Teseida*', *Studies in Philology* 42 (1945), 745–63
Quinn, Esther C., 'Beyond Courtly Love: Religious Elements in *Tristan* and *La Queste del Saint Graal*', in *In Pursuit of Perfection: Courtly Love in Medieval Literature*, ed. Joan M. Ferrante and George D. Economou (Port Washington NY: Kennikat Press, 1975), pp. 179–219
Ramsey, Lee C., *Chivalric Romances* (Bloomington: Indiana University Press, 1983)
Ramson, W. S., 'The Aureate Paradox', *Parergon* ns #1 (1983), 93–104
Reed, J., '*La Chastelaine de Vergi*: was the heroine married?', *Romance Notes* 16 (1974), 197–204
Ribard, Jacques, 'Espace romanesque et symbolisme dans la littérature arthurienne du XIIe siècle', in *Espaces romanesques*, ed. Michel Crouzet (Paris: Presses Universitaires de France, 1982), pp. 73–82
Ricks, Christopher, *Keats and Embarrassment* (Oxford: Clarendon Press, 1974)
Rivers, Bryan, 'The Focus of Satire in *The Squire of Low Degree*', *English Studies in Canada* 7 (1981), 379–87
Riviere, Joan, 'Womanliness as a Masquerade', in *Psychoanalysis and Female Sexuality*, ed. Hendrik M. Ruitenbeek (New Haven: College & University Press, 1966), pp. 208–20
Robertson, D. W., *A Preface to Chaucer* (Princeton: Princeton University Press, 1962)
Rose, Jacqueline, *Sexuality in the Field of Vision* (London: Verso, 1986)
Ross, Ian Simpson, *William Dunbar* (Leiden: E. J. Brill, 1981)
Rougemont, Denis de, *Passion and Society*, trans. Montgomery Belgion, 2nd edn (London: Faber, 1956)
Ryan, Kiernan, *Shakespeare* (New York: Harvester Wheatsheaf, 1989)
Rychner, Jean, 'La présence et le point de vue du narrateur dans deux récits courts: *Le Lai de Lanval* et *La Chastelaine de Vergi*', *Vox Romanica* 39 (1980), 86–103
Salter, Elizabeth, *Fourteenth-Century English Poetry: Contexts and Readings* (Oxford: Clarendon Press, 1983)
Sartre, Jean-Paul, *Being and Nothingness*, trans. Hazel E. Barnes (New York: Philosophical Library, 1956)

Schibanoff, Susan, 'Taking Jane's Cue: *Phyllyp Sparowe* as a Primer for Women Readers', *Publications of the Modern Language Association of America* 101 (1986), 832–47

Sedgwick, Eve Kosofsky, *Between Men: English Literature and Male Homosocial Desire* (New York: Columbia University Press, 1985)

Shippey, T. A., 'Breton *Lais* and Modern Fantasies', in *Studies in Medieval English Romances*, ed. Derek Brewer (Woodbridge: D. S. Brewer, 1988), pp. 69–91

Skinner, Quentin, ed. *The Return of Grand Theory in the Human Sciences* (Cambridge: Cambridge University Press, 1985)

Smyser, H. M., 'The Domestic Background in *Troilus and Criseyde*', *Speculum* 31 (1956), 297–315

Spearing, A. C., '"Al This Mene I Be Love"', *Studies in the Age of Chaucer, Proceedings, No. 2, 1986* (1987), 169–78

Chaucer: Troilus and Criseyde (London: Edward Arnold, 1976)

'Marie de France and her Middle English Adapters', *Studies in the Age of Chaucer* 12 (1990), 117–56

Medieval Dream-Poetry (Cambridge: Cambridge University Press, 1976)

Medieval to Renaissance in English Poetry (Cambridge: Cambridge University Press, 1985)

Readings in Medieval Poetry (Cambridge: Cambridge University Press, 1987)

Stanbury, Sarah, 'Feminist Film Theory: Seeing Chrétien's Enide', *Literature and Psychology* 36 (1990), 47–66

'The Voyeur and the Private Life in *Troilus and Criseyde*', *Studies in the Age of Chaucer* 13 (1991), 141–58

Stemmler, Theo, 'Die mittelenglischen Bearbeitungen zweier Lais der Marie de France', *Anglia* 80 (1962), 243–63

Strohm, Paul, 'Guillaume as Narrator and Lover in the *Roman de la Rose*', *Romanic Review* 59 (1968), 3–9

Tatlock, J. S. P., 'Chaucer's *Merchant's Tale*', *Modern Philology* 33 (1935–6), 371–81

Topsfield, L. T., '*The Roman de la Rose*', in *Medieval Literature: the European Inheritance*, ed. Boris Ford (Harmondsworth: Penguin, 1983), pp. 223–35

Varvaro, Alberto, *Beroul's Romance of Tristran*, trans. John C. Barnes (Manchester: Manchester University Press, 1972)

Vickers, Nancy J., 'Diana Described: Scattered Woman and Scattered Rhyme', *Critical Inquiry* 8 (1981–2), 265–79

Vitz, E. B., 'The *I* of the *Roman de la Rose*', *Genre* 6 (1973), 49–75

Waswo, Richard, 'The Narrator of *Troilus and Criseyde*', *English Literary History* 50 (1983), 1–25

Whiting, B. J., 'A Fifteenth-Century English Chaucerian: The Translator of *Partonope of Blois*', *Mediaeval Studies* 7 (1945), 40–54

Williams, Elizabeth, '*Lanval* and *Sir Landevale*: a Middle English Translator and his Methods', *Leeds Studies in English* ns 3 (1969), 85–99

Williams, Linda, *Hard Core: Power, Pleasure, and the "Frenzy of the Visible"* (Berkeley: University of California Press, 1989)

'Power, Pleasure, and Perversion: Sadomasochistic Film Pornography', *Representations* 27 (Summer 1989), 37–65

Wilson, Edward, *The Gawain-Poet* (Leiden: E. J. Brill, 1976)

Wilson, Janet, '"Philip Sparrow": Skelton and the Sarum Primer', *Parergon* #32 (1982), 19–29

Windeatt, Barry, 'Chaucer and fifteenth-century romance: *Partonope of Blois*', in *Chaucer Traditions: Studies in Honour of Derek Brewer*, ed. Ruth Morse and Barry Windeatt (Cambridge: Cambridge University Press, 1990), pp. 62–80

'"Love that oughte been secree" in Chaucer's *Troilus*', *Chaucer Review* 14 (1979–80), 116–31

'*Troilus* and the Disenchantment of Romance', in *Studies in Medieval English Romances*, ed. Derek Brewer (Woodbridge: D. S. Brewer, 1988), pp. 129–47

Wollheim, Richard, *Freud* (London: Fontana/Collins, 1971)

Zink, Michel, 'Chrétien et ses contemporains', in *The Legacy of Chrétien de Troyes*, ed. Norris J. Lacy, Douglas Kelly and Keith Busby, 2 vols. (Amsterdam: Rodopi, 1987), I, pp. 5–32

Index